Occult Traditions
Edited by Damon Zacharias Lycourinos © 2012

The copyright of each article is retained by their respective authors.

Published by Numen Books 2012
ISBN 978-09871581-3-0

Thee I invoke alone, thou who alone in all the world imposes order upon gods and men, who dost transform thyself in holy forms, making to be from things that are not, and from the things that are making the not to be.

O holy Thoth, the true sight of whose face none of the gods endures!

Make me to be every creature's name — wolf, dog, lion, fire, tree, vulture, wall, water, or what thou will'st, for thou art able so to do.

Even as Horus, if e'er he called on thee, O greatest of all gods, in every trial, in every space, 'gainst gods, men, and daimones, and things that live in water and on Earth — had grace and riches with gods, and men, and every living thing beneath the Earth; so let me, too, who call on thee! So give me grace, form, beauty!

For I know thy name that shineth forth in Heaven; I know thy forms as well. I know thy names in the Egyptian tongue, and thy true name as it is written on the holy tablet in the holy place, where thou dost have thy birth.

I know thee, Thoth, for I am thou, and thou art I!

CONTENTS

Author biographies

Damon Zacharias Lycourinos has an academic background in the fields of anthropology and religious studies from the University of Wales, Lampeter, the University of Oxford, and the University of Cambridge. He is currently engaged in a Doctor of Philosophy at the University of Edinburgh exploring the meanings and weavings of ritual and magic in the West, both from a diachronic and synchronic perspective. Other current academic areas of research include paradigms of sex, gnosis, and liberation, the embodiment of states of consciousness, the notion of ritual body and performance, and the history, philosophy, and practice of magic in Western contexts and beyond. When not engaged within the arena of academia, he can be found embodying the *Greek Magical Papyri* through intense study and performance, wandering the wilderness, fighting, and indulging in rural wine. He currently resides in Britain, but when not he can be found in Athens or on the volcanic island of Thira overlooking the Aegean.

Aaron Cheak's personal and professional interests centre on the dynamics of apotheosis conceived as a process of ontological mutation. His early academic work focused on the intellectual history of magic, with an emphasis on the faculty of imagination as a magical instrument (*phantasia, mundus imaginalis*, and *vis imaginative*). Over the past seven years, his research has focused on theories of ontological mutation and qualitative exaltation in the works of German *Kulturphilosoph* Jean Gebser, 1905-1973, and Alsatian Egyptosophist, René-Adolphe Schwaller de Lubicz, 1887-1961. Part of this research has recently been submitted as a doctoral dissertation, *Light Broken through the Prism of Life: René Schwaller de Lubicz and the Hermetic Problem of Salt*, University of Queensland, 2011, which focuses on alchemy as a non-dual process. His current writing projects are devoted to articulating the deep connections between integral and hermetic philosophy. Aaron Cheak is currently the editor of *Alchemical Traditions*, which will be published by Numen Books in 2012.

Christopher A. Plaisance is a graduate student at the University of Exeter's Centre for the Study of Esotericism. He holds a Bachelor of Arts in Philosophy from the American Military University and an associate degree in Mandarin Chinese from the Defense Language Institute. He is presently the editor in chief of *The Journal of Contemporary Heathen Thought*. His current research interests include Neoplatonic theories of sacrifice viewed through the lens of emergent process theology, and the cosmogenic functions of the sublunary and hylic archons in the hierology of Iamblichus.

David Rankine is an author, esoteric researcher, and magician who has been making major contributions to the modern occult revival since the 1980s. His published works include *The Grimoire of Arthur Gauntlet, The Book of Gold, The Veritable Key of Solomon,* and *Climbing the Tree of Life*. Also see www.ritualmagick.co.uk.

Ioannis Marathakis studied Theology at the University of Athens. His main interest is the history of the Western esoteric tradition, and especially the history of magic. In 2007 he published the book *Anazetontas ten Kleida tou Solomonta*, which is English is translated as *Searching for the Key of Solomon*, a history of the Solomonic literature. In 2011 he published the book *The Magical Treatise of Solomon or Hygromanteia* through Golden Hoard Press, which includes a commentary and a translation of the Greek prototype of the *Key of Solomon*. Among his articles there is a survey of invisibility spells, *From the Ring of Gyges to the Black Cat Bone*.

Christopher A. Smith was born in 1954 and is still very much alive. He gained an honours degree in Political Theory and Institutions at Sheffield University. Life being what it is, this led circuitously to a chequered but very interesting series of careers in transport management, reflexology, chiropody, and freelance translation. In short, anything but politics. Christopher became interested in the Germanic runes and their magical applications in the early 1980's and is currently a Fellow of the Rune Gild. In recent years he has spent much time in Iceland in order to learn the Icelandic language and study Icelandic magic and folk beliefs. His other interests include foreign travel and military history. He now lives in North Yorkshire and is self-employed as a freelance translator.

A qadish for over thirteen years, **Tess Dawson** established the largest Canaanite groups and she is a leader in the Near Eastern and Middle Eastern polytheist communities. Her work, *Whisper of Stone: Natib Qadish, Modern Canaanite Religion* provides the foundation of Natib Qadish religion. Ms. Dawson edited *Anointed: A Devotional Anthology for the Deities of the Near and Middle East*; and she awaits the 2013 release of her new book *The Horned Altar: Rediscovering and Rekindling Canaanite Magic*. She earned her Bachelor of Arts in Anthropology and received ordination through the ULC. Visit her on Facebook or through her website, http://canaanitepath.com.

Gwendolyn Toynton was the recipient of the Ashton Wylie Award for Literary Excellence in 2009 for her first book, *Primordial Traditions Compendium 2009*, which featured a collection of articles from the periodical *Primordial Traditions*, which ran from 2005 to 2010. *Northern Traditions* is her second book. Her poetry is also featured in the New Zealand Collection of Poetry and Prose, 2002. She has written for numerous periodicals, including *New Dawn*. Gwendolyn also has articles published in *The Radical Tradition* and has recently returned to fictional work with her latest short story published by Numen Books in *Mythos: The Myths and Tales of H. P. Lovecraft & Robert E. Howard*. Gwendolyn's first major work, *The Tantrik Tradition*, is also scheduled for publication in 2012.

Sorita d'Este is an esoteric researcher and author who manifests her knowledge and passion for the Mysteries through her work. Her published work includes *Hekate*

Liminal Rites, *The Cosmic Shekinah*, and *Visions of the Cailleach*. Also see www.sorita.co.uk.

Melissa Harrington's religiosity and psychism, combined with her love of folklore, mythology, and magic, would lead her into Wicca in her mid-twenties. Curiosity, fate, and a religious calling then led her in and out of the Ordo Templi Orientis, through Enochian, and on to work with many of the great magicians of modern times. Twenty five years later she teaches Wicca and the Western Mystery Tradition, but sees all spiritual paths that lead to peace, compassion, and enlightenment as equally valid expressions of the human search for communion with the divine. She is a psychologist with a Doctor of Philosophy in Religious Studies, and lectures at her local college. She uses an academic perspective to inform her writing on magic and spirituality for academic, esoteric, and popular publishers.

Matthew Levi Stevens was born shortly before midnight on 31 October, 1966. Matthew Levi Stevens is a writer and researcher, and rare book-dealer. He is also a former musician, performance artist, and poet. He has been exploring the avant garde, magic and the occult, matters sacred and profane, and other outer limits of the human experience for the past three decades. He has spoken and written on the occult influences behind the art, film, music, and writings of such figures as Kenneth Anger, William S. Burroughs, Coil, Brion Gysin, Derek Jarman, Austin Osman Spare, the Surrealists, and Throbbing Gristle. Other works include 'Aleister Crowley & the Yi-King', 'The Bull of Ombos: Ongoing Study of Set-Typhon', and 'Remembering Frater Aossic, the late Kenneth Grant'. 'The Sun At Midnight' and 'Memento Mori' were written with Emma Doeve, with whom he has also begun work with on a graphic novel, *The White Darkness*, in part inspired by the works of Maya Deren. Current projects include a study of David Curwen, 'Operation Rewrite: The Third Mind & The Other Method', about his experience and study of *The Magical Universe of William S Burroughs & Others*, and there is talk of *A Book of Dark Things…* For further information and contact, please see http://whollybooks.wordpress.com.

Rey De Lupos, also known as Companion Abraxas and Frater AOM, is the head of the Queen of Heaven Clerk-House, an active New Aeonic, Thelemic magickal order in the tradition of Aleister Crowley's A∴A∴, stemming from the lineage of Grady Louis McMurtry, also known as Frater Hymenaeus Alpha 777. Rey has been active in the study of shamanic, pagan, magical, and mysical traditions of the East and West since 1982. In 1996 Rey first aligned with the Ordo Templi Orientis, taking the Minerval and I degree initiations in Santa Fe, New Mexico, under the Soul of the Desert Camp, and then later joining Mons Abiegnus Oasis in 1996. During the coming years between 1996 and 2003, Rey would enter into the Blue Lodge Degrees of Freemasonry and the Work of the Ordo Aurum Solis. This eventually would lead to his current association with the Ordo Astrum Sophia, an adjunct of this Ogdoadic tradition. As noted, Rey is not limited to the engagement of one fixed tradition but actively seeks the eclectic immersion into a broader alignment of the World Magical Tradition. He currently resides in Santa Fe, New Mexico, the place of his birth and the heritage of his family history for the last two hundred years. He continues in the practices and academic studies associated with these traditions working with students and always taking the next step into deeper knowledge and greater wisdom.

FOREWORD

In my professional capacity as an author and editor, I have come across many writers and talented individuals. It was during my time as the editor of *Primordial Traditions* that I first met Damon. Since Numen Books begun as the periodical *Primordial Traditions*, Damon has played a vital role both as a writer and in an editorial capacity. Being strongly impressed with the calibre of his work, the articles contributed to *Primordial Traditions* ('*The Yezidis: Angel or devil worshippers of the Near East*' and '*Communing with the dead in Ancient Greece*') were included in my first book[1] which won the Ashton Wylie Award for Literary Excellence in 2009). Due to Damon's tenacity and prodigious writing talents, he quickly ascended the ranks to become the assistant editor. This process has culminated in Damon's own literary achievement, *Occult Traditions* which you are presently about to read.

The range and depth of material collected and assembled here is truly awe-inspiring, and is a reflection of the editor's knowledge and expertise in the occult. By assembling a team of expert writers in their individual fields from all across the globe, Damon has been able to ensure that the content of the book is of an extremely high level, which places his work light years ahead of its competitors. Drawing on his academic studies and practical knowledge, Damon has been able to identify highly qualified individuals with ease in many different specialist niches, ranging from the rites of the ancient world through to contemporary movements. Procuring this team of expert writers in the area of esoteric studies has not been an easy job, for this field is notoriously barren of serious academics and this in itself has been an arduous task which Damon has fulfilled superbly in his role of the editor. The amount of effort he has put into this book stands as a testament to his personal fortitude and inevitable triumph as a prominent author on occult lore.

As a book, *Occult Traditions* plays an important part in bridging the world of the esoteric with that of the spiritual world, and reminds us of a time when both magic and religion worked together to contact the divine and no rift or schism existed between the two schools of thinking. This is markedly different from the modern world, where occult practices are no longer viewed with the same esteem that is placed on religion, though, in fact, history shows that they have always been entwined. *Occult Traditions* plays an important role in illustrating that magic is connected to these older, authentic traditions in a way which is notably absent from some of the New Age movements in of the modern era which drift rootless through time and space, bereft of a solid anchor to base their ideas upon. *Occult Traditions* therefore serves as an intermediary link between the world of the past and the present, and as a powerful catalyst to once more

---

[1] *Primordial Traditions Compendium*, Twin Serpents, 2009

unite magic with spiritualty and tradition.

We have watched *Occult Traditions* develop from an idea to flourish as a publication in its own right, featuring a broad spectrum of talented authors from across the Occult world, without conforming to the set notions that fetter other publications to a single central concept. Like a mighty oak, it has grown from a tiny acorn into the tree of knowledge itself, to finally blossom and bear its own fruits of esoteric wisdom. Now that the fruit has ripened, we hope that you enjoy the taste and absorb the knowledge therein.

Gwendolyn Toynton

INTRODUCTION

BY

DAMON ZACHARIAS LYCOURINOS

According to its true, living meaning, Tradition is neither servile conformity to what has been, nor a sluggish perpetuation of the past into the present. Tradition, in its essence, is something simultaneously meta-historical and dynamic: it is an overall ordering force, in service of principles that have the chrism of a superior legitimacy.

Julius Evola, *Men Among the Ruins: Post-War Reflections of a Radical Traditionalist.*

The term 'occult' derives from the Latin *occultus*, meaning 'hidden' or 'secret', and from the root *occulere*, which means 'to hide' or 'to conceal'. Beyond the etymological sense of the word, the ontological quality of the appellation 'occult' stems from its attachment throughout history to various religious and cultural perspectives manifesting into a *mélange* of beliefs, practices, traditions, and organisations. More recently, it has been attached to what some identify as the Western Occult Tradition, embracing currents of antiquity that have both espoused a magical worldview and employed religious symbolism at times, such as Gnosticism, Neoplatonism, and Hermetism; alchemy, astrology, and divination; Neopythagoreanism, Hermeticism and Renaissance *magia naturalis*; the grimoire texts; the Kabbalah, Rosicrucianism, and Paracelsianism; *naturphilosophie* of German Romanticism; mechanisms of causality stemming from the post-Enlightenment era; occultism of the nineteenth century and its offshoots; and more recently the ritual magic of Neopaganism.[1] However, the roots of the contemporary understanding of the term 'occult' can most likely be traced back to Heinrich Cornelius Agrippa's *De Occulta Philosophia*, 1533, and the ideas of Giordano Bruno, 1548-1600, where the occult and *magia*, presented within the context of *occulta philosophia* and *magia naturalis*, were almost equivalent terms and provided the historical conditions for the emergence of nineteenth century occultism.[2] This connection between the Renaissance sense of the word *magia* and the character of magic espoused by some of

---

[1] For a more in depth presentation of this see Hanegraaff, Wouter J., *New Age Religion and Western Culture: Esotericism in the Mirror of Secular Thought*. Leiden: Brill, 1998, p. 392-395.
[2] Hanegraaff, Wouter J., *New Age Religion and Western Culture: Esotericism in the Mirror of Secular Thought*. Leiden: Brill, 1998, p. 394.

the most influential nineteenth century occultists attached to or extending from the lineage of the Hermetic Order of the Golden Dawn is conveyed by Faivre,

> To *Magia* belongs white magic or theurgy, which uses names, rites, and incantations with the aim of establishing a personal link with entities that are not part of the world of physical creation. These two aspects of *magia naturalis*… sometimes mingle, as in "celestial" or "astronomical" magic, where the stars can in fact be considered simultaneously from the point of view of the influence they are supposed to exert physically and of the influence exerted by their will.[3]

Since the nineteenth century, where the broad label 'occult' actually developed into a concrete historical movement referred to as 'occultism', the term has been used by some scholars and practioners alike to describe,

> A subculture of various secret societies and 'enlightened' teachers involved in disciplines concerned with the acquisition of arcane, salvific knowledge (*gnosis* and *theosophia*), the experience of 'illumination', the understanding of esoteric symbolism (often related to occult interpretations of the Kabbalah), the practice of secret rituals and initiatory rites, and particularly the quest for a *prisca theologia*, *philosophia occulta* or *philosophia perennis*.[4]

Despite some attempts to do justice in some form or fashion, or to objectively convey the descriptive essence of the term 'occult', many expressions have been employed to label, define, and categorise this essence, such as 'magic', 'sorcery', 'witchcraft', 'shamanism', 'theurgy', 'the black arts', 'paranormal', and 'psychic, which in the following have also been attached to broader scholarly fields of categorisation, such as 'the occult', 'esotericism', and even 'mysticism'. The indiscriminate method in which these expressions have been employed in relation to specific historical developments reflects that these expressions indeed can refer to a multitude of things. An insightful observation into the fallacious and confusing manner in which these terms are indiscriminately used, presented by Galbreath in his paper 'Explaining Modern Occultism', clearly examines the confusion that arises when one endeavours to place the terms 'magic', 'mystical', 'supernatural', 'paranormal', and 'esoteric' under the umbrella term of the 'occult',

> "Magic" seems to have once served as an inclusive term… but since the end of the seventeenth century it has become increasingly identified with a particular occult discipline… "Mystical" is properly limited to experiences, teachings, and consciousness of the state of oneness with ultimate reality; "psychic"

---

[3] Faivre, Antoine, *Access to Western Esotericism*. New York: Suny, 1994, p. 66.
[4] Partridge, Christopher, *The Re-enchantment of the West: Understanding Popular Occulture*, Vol. 1. London: T & T Clark International, 2005.

is used broadly, but it still retains its primary referent of psi phenomena…
"Supernatural" is rejected by modern occultists of all types for whom the point
of the occult is its ability to provide empirical, experiential, natural proofs of
matters heretofore accepted on faith. "Paranormal" avoids the suggestions of
irrationality and nonsense that taint "occult"… "Esoteric" still retains perfectly
good non-occult meanings of "abstruse" and "recondite".[5]

However, ignoring for a moment the scholarly arena of understanding and
representation, and instead seeking a path to dwell deeper into the occult dialectics
of the arcane matrimony of the macrocosm and microcosm, it becomes apparent, and
not always in a logical and pleasant fashion, that more is to be whispered, unveiled,
and conjured in regards to worldviews and conditions of experience pertaining to the
occult as a general designation. These can refer to correspondences and phenomena
that remain elusive to mundane states of consciousness, an ignorance of the potential
of the unseen forces of the cosmos, and positivistic passivity. Hence, the designation of
the occult, within the context of this book, is employed as a fluid, yet decisive, category,
indicating both the theory and practice of specific fields of discourse involving a
particular human awareness, and performance within a worldview characterised by a
resistance to the dominance of either sterile logic or doctrinal faith. Despite the occult
referring to vast array of grammars, what establishes occult paradigms with a unique
character are the emic recognitions of degrees of established or willed relationships
between seen and unseen realities, and the experience of them linked through a matrix
of sympathetic and antipathetic correspondences, which in itself is clearly echoed in
the Hermetic axiom, "That which is Below corresponds to that which is Above, and
that which is Above, corresponds to that which is Below, to accomplish the miracles of
the One Thing".[6] These correspondences, charged and vibrating with the pure forces of
the cosmos, resonate and naturally manifest within nature as an ensouled state of being
reflecting the idea of *psychê kosmou* of Platonic thought and the *anima mundi* within the
awareness of *magia naturalis* during the Renaissance period. In the following, These are
recognised and mediated through an active imagination corresponding to the *mundis
imaginalis*, which is, at times, the initial point of departure and fundamental impetus
for all esoteric workings collaborating with exoteric gestures. The final revelations can
be experienced as a *metamorphôsis* of inner and outer experiential dimensions. The
experience of these elements of occult theory and practice manifests when an embodied,
altered state of consciousness[7] is initiated, either temporarily or in a state of a fluctuating
continuum, and has "an intrinsically subjective and sensory quality that is embodied

---

[5]Galbreath, Robert, 'Explaining Modern Occultism'. In *The Occult in America*, edited by Howard Kerr and
Charles L. Crow. Chicago: University of Illinois Press, 1983, p. 16.
[6]Quoted in Scully, Nicki, *Alchemical Healing: A Guide to Spiritual, Physical, and Transformational Medicine*.
Rochester: Bear & Company, 2003, p. 321. quoted from where?
[7]This can be understood as a shift in perception from a mundane state of consciousness, yet not ignoring the
effects of unmediated occult participation within the mundane sphere of awareness and activity.

1 - define page 16.

and intuitive rather than purely reflective and intellectual, although the reflective and intellectual may be engaged *with* the intuitive and the embodied as there is no radical opposition."[8] This can also be translated as *gnôsis*, indicating 'true knowledge of what is' in contrast to mere sense perception, implying the act of knowing instead of just acquiring knowledge. Hence, *gnôsis* can be understood as a specific modality of consciousness, a breaking down of the barriers of the rational mind. Through *gnôsis*, the 'knower' therefore becomes immersed in the *mundus imaginalis*, and in terms of occult theory and practice, the individual or individuals actively engaged become the focal point of the unification of the corresponding relationships between the finite and the infinite.[9]

The arena in which what is whispered, unveiled, and conjured in regards to worldviews and conditions of experience pertaining to the occult ~~as a general designation~~ can be located within the *sui generis* category of 'magic' as a participatory worldview, manipulated as an instrument by the active person through the execution of the art and science of ritual, ~~as an extension~~ grounded in the belief in magical powers within the self and other. The purpose of this is to impose the human will on the self and the other, activating the embodiment of an altered state of consciousness in an endeavour to align the self with the corresponding ritual intent of understanding, connecting, and influencing the other.

The final question that might arise would be why use and advocate the term 'tradition'. I have already indicated that the designation of the occult relates both in theory and practice to fields of discourse. However, it is my responsibility to present to the reader that from my interpretative stance a 'discourse' should not be understood as being synonymous with a 'tradition' in the modern hermeneutic sense, which has evolved in the European context in the last two hundred years or more as philosophers and thinkers counterposed the concept of modernity with the concept of tradition within the context of progress. Instead, a discourse represents the organisation of tradition, opinion, and knowledge. Fields of discourse should not always be restricted to specific traditions, as they develop rather from common challenges and contemporary interests, yet this does not imply that they do not have origins in the past. Indeed, fields of discourse alter identities and develop at times astonishing alliances and parallels between supposedly separate traditions and epochs. Hence, discourse can only be equated with tradition if tradition is equated, in essence, with something simultaneously meta-historical and dynamic, serving as an overall ordering force in service of principles that have the chrism of a superior legitimacy from an emic perspective and conveyed as such from

---

[8] Greenwood, Susan, *The Nature of Magic: An Anthropology of Consciousness*. Oxford: Berg, 2005, p. 5.
[9] Although I am aware that the way in which I have expressed and structured these terms, concepts, and paradigms might not reflect etymologically or cosmologically some cultures and historical periods which do display in essence some of these elements of occult theory and practice, I have chosen to do so for purposes of self-clarification employing conceptual and linguistic expressions and equations which are more akin, both in diachronic and synchronic terms, with the nature of the majority of the papers presented in this book.

an etic perspective, which should take into explicit consideration, while yet not implying that one should always remain neutral, a personalised stylistic interpretation.

Having said all of this, I now invite you to journey with myself and the authors and conjurors who have been kind enough to share their visions and gestures in this book through various traditions relating to distinct historical developments, unique occult philosophies, and potent ritual practice, such as summoning magical assistants and the presence of the mystery traditions in the *Greek Magical Papyri*; deification through the arcane process of drowning in the *Greek Magical Papyri*; an exploration of occult theology as a continuation of Neoplatonism; a historical analysis of the grimoire traditions and a search for the original source of the *Key of Solomon*; the Icelandic tradition of magic as presented in an eighteenth century grimoire; a comparative analysis of medieval and Renaissance angel magic; Canaanite views of death and necromancy; an exploration of the use and attributes of incenses throughout history; a consideration of the science of divining the will of the gods; a representation of Seth as god of chaos and equilibrium; an in depth view of Julius Evola's ideas concerning the formula of sex, magic, and power; Buddhist 'wizards' at war in Thailand; a critical examination of the role of sex, magic, and initiation in the Wiccan Great Rite; the dynamics of altering consciousness within the spiral maze of Wiccan ritual; a restoration of the Rite of the Headless One from the *Greek Magical Papyri*; the elements of being and becoming in Conversation with one's Holy Guardian Angel; the Eucharistic Feast of Agathodaimon; the Rite of the Solar and Lunar Mysteries of the Altar of Eros for the Consecration of the Talismans of Helios and Selene; the Calling and Adoration of Aion, and the Spell of the Mystic Flame; and finally the Hymnic Adoration and Invocation of Thoth, to whom this book belongs, as He is lord of magic and scribe of the gods.

This book is an awakening to the occult reality that since the dawn of ages men and women have sought a glimpse of *gnôsis* within the awesome natural performance of ritual, the slithering flow of the elements, the sensational sounds of the spheres, the iconic form of dreams undreamt and now awoken, the irrational whispering of mystical verses, the silence of contemplation, and the passion drenched erotic thirst for life, death, and rebirth. Unlike the priesthood of sterile logic and doctrinal faith, these men and women have been a visible representation of spiritual virility, of the human condition, and many times the romantic ethos, (which many have convicted as an antinomian ethos), refusing, adapting, and also enchanting the dictates of conventional society, morality, and metaphysical culture, whilst aligning themselves purely with the laws of the pure forces of the cosmos. They have employed a multitude of arcane symbols reflecting other dimensions of spiritual and bodily rapture; they have howled barbarous names of holy and unholy power in the wilderness; they have communed with gods and goddesses deep within their own heavenly and earthly abodes; they have conjured the spirits of the netherworld within and outside geometrical patterns of arcane authority; they have glimpsed into the present reflecting itself through the future and echoing from the past; they have been hunted, praised, deified, and condemned to the abyss. Yet they are still amongst us, ~~essentially~~ attempting to adapt enchantment and its cosmic principles to a disenchanted world, where mystery, based upon an experience of the sacred as present in the mundane, remains hidden and patiently awaiting to be seductively conjured and then embraced.

CONJURING MAGICAL ASSISTANTS IN THE GREEK MAGICAL PAPYRI

BY

DAMON ZACHARIAS LYCOURINOS

Mistress, send forth your daimon from among those who assist you, one who is leader of night, because I adjure you by your great names, because of which no aerial or infernal daimon can ignore you.

PGM VII. 891-893[1]

B efore I endeavour to unveil the obscured tradition of conjuring magical assistants in the *Greek Magical Papyri*, I believe it is necessary to examine briefly and present to the reader what these mysterious, arcane, and neglected papyri actually are. In the nineteenth century, when the fervour of various amateur archaeologists and orientalists was at its peak, and diplomats and military men were passionate about collecting all kinds of objects from antiquity, there was among the diplomatic representatives at the court of Alexandria a man who went by the name of Jean d'Anastasi, 1780-1857,[1] who managed to acquire a vast collection of papyri from Egypt. Among these were the infamous and sizable magical books of Greco-Egyptian magicians, which he claimed to have obtained in Thebes. These collections were shipped to various places in Europe, such as the British Museum in London, the Louvre in Paris, the Staatliche in Berlin, and the Rijksmuseum in Leiden. However, it was not for a century afterwards before scholars began to explore and appreciate the value of the *Greek Magical Papyri*. Betz accurately describes the *Greek Magical Papyri* as,

A name given by scholars to a body of papyri from Greco-Roman Egypt containing a variety of magical spells and formulae, hymns and rituals. The extant texts are mainly from the second generation B.C. to the fifth century A.D. To be sure, this body of material represents only a small number of all the

---

[1]Some believe that he was actually a Greek named Giovanni d'Athanasi, from the island of Lesbos, the son of a merchant in Cairo. In his book, *A Brief Account of the Researches and Discoveries in Upper Egypt, made under the direction of Henry Salt, Esq., to which is added a detailed catalogue of Mr Salt's collection of Egyptian Antiquities; illustrated with twelve engravings of some of the most interesting objects, and an enumeration of those articles purchased for the British Museum*, London: John Hearne, 1836, he refers to his residence in Thebes where he entirely devoted himself to the study and collection of antiquities for eighteen years.

1- presumably Papyrus Graeci Magicae, and presumably Egyptian See p. 33
2- was there such a court? Egypt was Ottoman to 1799, then French, then British.

magical spells that once existed. Beyond these papyri we possess many other kinds of material: artifacts, symbols, and inscriptions on gemstones, on ostraka and clay bowls, and on tablets of gold, silver, lead, tin and so forth.[2]

The literature presented in the *Greek Magical Papyri* is a collection of texts originating from diverse sources. Hymns, spells, priestly invocations, conjurations, magical assistants, ritual instructions, remedies, curses, and a unique theology are all part of the fascinating and arcane world of the *Greek Magical Papyri*. Dating from the early Hellenistic era to Late Antiquity, the *Greek Magical Papyri* present a unique merging of Egyptian, Hellenic, Hebrew, Persian, Babylonian, Chaldean, Gnostic, and Coptic magic and religion. However, the Egyptian and Hellenic traditions, being the most dominant, display a Hellenisation of Egyptian religious and magical thought and an Egyptisation of Hellenic religion and magic, with the magician as the focal point, conjuring forth pure forces of the magical cosmos and also performing the duties of a religious functionary. On the whole, one could possibly argue in effect that the *Greek Magical Papyri* present an alternative attempt to initiate a new tradition altogether with unified religious beliefs, practices,[3] and a magical worldview. According to Mowinckel,

> Magical thinking and its practical application, called 'magic', is not a kind of religion, but a worldview, that is, a particular way to understand things and their mutual connectedness. Magic is the *Weltanschauung* which in a certain way is analogous to the view of the universe as we today attempt to formulate it on the basis of the laws of causality and the interaction between cause and effect, demonstrated by physics, chemistry, biology and psychology.[4]

This might indeed be a very bold statement, but it is my personal conviction that, although the aims of many of the rites and spells vary, there is a uniform foundation in regards to formal aspects of the *Greek Magical Papyri*. However, before unravelling this conviction, one must not ignore that the *Greek Magical Papyri* are primarily a collection of personal rites and spells belonging to different magicians, with instructions for single rites like the ones preserved in the formularies and assembled over time according to the taste of a single collector. Most likely this single collector was a priest-magician from Thebes, who managed to gather them so that this forbidden literature[5] would

---

[2]Betz, 'Introduction to the Greek Magical Papyri', in *The Greek Magical Papyri in Translation including the Demotic Spells,* Betz (ed.), p. xliii.
[3]There is much debate surrounding the relationship of magic and religion in the *Greek Magical Papyri*. For further reading I suggest Betz, Hans Dieter, 'Magic and Mystery in the Greek Magical Papyri'. In *Magika Hiera: Ancient Greek Magic and Religion,* edited by Christopher A. Faraone and Dirk Obbink. New York: Oxford University Press, 1991.
[4]Mowinckel, *Religion and Kultus,* p. 15.
[5]Sections in the *Greek Magical Papyri* which state that all rites must remain secret indicate the need for secrecy and the subsequent 'going underground'.

1. Did this collector transcribe or just collect? What language are they in? Must be in Greek, but the sentence structure is clearly Egyptian. See p.48 - also Demotic and old Coptic. Must have been c.e. 400AD

survive the flames of zealous funeral pyres that sought to burn at that time all magical literature.[6] Hence, priorities, formulae, and aims differ just as one magician did to another. However, if one can ignore the technicalities and focus on the essence, it becomes apparent that various features indicate a sense of uniformity in regards to a religious worldview, magical correspondences, and ritual gestures. The verses of the *Greek Magical Papyri* exemplify an attitude that demonstrates how humanity is directly dependant on the forces of the universe. The gods of the Greco-Egyptian pantheon now represent these forces, and in particular forces of nature. For example, the omnipresence of Helios in various amalgamated manifestations complies with the prominence of solar worship in that era. Selene's prominence in many rites is evident and abstract forces of nature have become personified deities, such as Aion, Tyche, Chronos, the Moirai and Physis. Even the relationship between the living and the dead has now been transformed into a set of magical negotiations, so that various human aims on earth may be achieved. Tyche appears to be a cosmic reality. Regardless of the deities invoked, one becomes aware that the average mortal fails to escape their dependency on the universe surrounding them, and as Betz sufficiently states,

> Religion is regarded as nothing but the awareness of and reaction against our dependency on the unfathomable scramble of energies coming out of the universe. In this energy jungle, human life can only be experienced as a jungle too. People's successes and failures appear to be only the result of Chance (Tyche). Individuals seem to be nothing but marionettes at the end of power lines, pulled here and there without their knowledge by invisible forces.[7]

So far I have presented in brief the cosmological outlook of the *Greek Magical Papyri*, but the question remains as to whether there is a soteriological dimension seeking liberation from this dependency on the forces of the universe by coercing or binding them. The answer to this question is 'yes', and these attempts manifest in the role of the magician operating as a religious functionary between the world of mortals and the world of the gods, angels, daimons, spirits, and the dead. The magician was most likely attached to either temples of Greco-Egyptian gods, and according to Egyptian practice, the magician might also have been a resident member of the temple priesthood. The magician sought personal soteriology through his own initiations, knowledge of magical ritual, and communion with the divine so he could employ his occult knowledge and skills for the salvation of the average man and woman in the transitional culture of Greco-Roman Egypt. He could identify, regulate, and manipulate the unseen, defining forces of the universe providing solutions to a myriad of troubles plaguing humanity.[8]

---

[6] The burning of magical literature in Ephesus in Acts 19: 19 is a characteristic example. But not until after Christianication aS. 800AD.

[7] Betz, 'Introduction to the Greek Magical Papyri', in *The Greek Magical Papyri in Translation including the Demotic Spells*, Betz (ed.), p. xlvii.

[8] The nature of this paper is not to examine the validity of these claims or the epistemology of the Roman aphorism, *Mundus vult decipi, ergo decipiatur*, 'the world wishes to be deceived, and so it may be deceived', which so many scholars refer to regarding the magician as a deceiver and a fraud. My intent is purely

1 - I don't believe salvation is the correct term. Egyptians didn't need salvation before Christ.

21

The objective of all magical gestures performed by the magician of the *Greek Magical Papyri* was to identify with divinity, which exemplifies a similarity with forms of applied magic in other parts of the ancient world. The primary foundation upon which the magician functioned was the religious knowledge and ritual experience he acquired through his own magical initiations.[9] From this, he knew how to influence invisible forces of the universe with the use of visible forces, such as ritual movements, magical objects, incenses, 'barbarous' words of power, hymns, prayers, and, above all, an understanding of the superstitions, myths, and, theologies that were prevalent at the time, which he would then re-introduce into a complex framework demonstrating the natural receptiveness of magic. Although it does appear that the main intention of the magical rites in the *Greek Magical Papyri* was to coerce divinity, reverence and piety featured a lot. This is obvious from the fact that 'magic' is referred to as *mystêrion*, 'mystery', *hiera mystêria*, 'holy mysteries', and the magician as *mystês*, 'initiate'. In *PGM* I. 42-195, the rite, which is referred to as *The Spell of Pnouthis, the sacred scribe, for acquiring an assistant*, is to be treated as "the great mystery" and must be kept secret.[10] The ritual instruction also refer to the magician as "O blessed initiate of the sacred magic."[11]

Most of the rites within the *Greek Magical Papyri* underline the magician's desire to accede to a non-material dimension that would put him into direct contact with a spiritual entity or current to bring forth into an earthly sphere of operation. The rites that allow the magician to participate in the realm of the divine are two fundamental but differing types. The first consists of rites of *systasis*, which 'present the magician to the divinity'. The second are ritual procedures that enable the magician to conjure a *parhedros*, 'a magical assistant'.

The idea of someone who has secret knowledge of magical expression and the ability to conjure an assistant, familiar or some other spiritual being from the netherworld, has always haunted popular imagination and fascinated the occult mind. In a generic sense, a familiar is a spiritual being that acts as an assistant for the magical practitioner. In the ancient Middle East, these familiars were normally the spirits of the dead. In Western Europe, during the Middle Ages, these magical entities were reinterpreted according to folklore traditions which speaking of magical animal guides who accompanied folk magicians. This reinterpretation inspired the whole concept of the witch's familiar, a demonic being in the form of an animal who acted as a magical assistant. However,

---

to explore one of the most prominent ritual gestures that the magician employed to coerce and bind the invisible forces of the universe, without judging whether or not the magician was truly manipulating magical forces or merely deceiving his 'customers'.

[9]There is an ongoing debate as to whether the magicians of the *Greek Magical Papyri* were either temple priests who had undergone a series of initiations in the mystery cults that prevailed in Greco-Roman Egypt, or if they had self-initiated themselves into magical theory and practice.

[10]*PGM* I. 130.

[11]*PGM* I. 127.

despite popular imagination and folk tales, there are some fundamental rites in the *Greek Magical Papyri* that provide the magician with arcane means to conjure a magical assistant.

There are ten texts in the *Greek Magical Papyri* that use the term *parhedros*, or one of its related forms.[12] Before I begin to analyse the ontological being of the *parhedros*, I believe it is necessary to demonstrate how the very presence of rites aiming to conjure a *parhedros* correspond to the cosmological outlook of the *Greek Magical Papyri* and the essence of soteriology. It is evident from historical sources on magic in the ancient world that the *parhedros* was only introduced into magical practice and theory around the second century C.E. Magicians before would perform rites without the need to call upon a magical assistant. From the perspective of the cosmology of the *Greek Magical Papyri*, the emergence of the *parhedros* can be interpreted as an increasing need for divine assistance ~~aiming~~ to coerce the unseen forces of the cosmos that controlled the lives of the inhabitants of Greco-Roman Egypt, which consequently corresponded with the need for the magician to have a more direct and personal relationship with the realm of the divine.

The word *parhedros* in Greek is an adjective[2] which means 'sitting near or beside' and derives from the verb *parhedreuô*, 'to attend upon'. Although the word itself did designate other things in the ancient world, such as a governmental official, in the *Greek Magical Papyri* it specifically refers to a magical assistant who serves and obeys the magician. Unlike other specifically designated spiritual beings, such as gods, angels, daimons, and spirits, the *parehdroi*[3] have more than one nature or title attached to their ritual identity. However, for the majority of instances the *parehdros* is mostly considered a being of divine origin.

In the *Greek Magical Papyri* there is a rite called the *Sword*[13] *of Dardanos*,[14] [15] where the *parehdros* is explicitly identified with a recognised deity and called upon with the deity's name. In this specific rite the *parehdros* is addressed as *Erôs*, 'Eros'.[4] When the *parehdros* is identified with a god or goddess, the name of the deity is used without hesitation, as it is not endowed with the same power as a less familiar name. When conjuring a *parehdros*, the most potent tool for the magician is to refer to it by its individual magical name. This is evident in *PGM* I. 36 where the magician states, "This is your authoritative name: ARBATH ABAÔTH BAKCHABR Ê." In some cases where the name is not already revealed the magician requests that the *parehdros* reveals its true magical name. Such an interchange of requests and revelations can be seen from a

---

[12]*PGM* I. 1-42; I. 42-195; IV. 1331-1389; IV. 1716-1870; IV. 1928-2005; IV. 2006-2125; IV. 2145-2240; VII. 862-918; XI. a. 1-40; XII. 14-95.

[13]This probably refers to a title of a certain type of formula.

[14]Dardanos was believed to have been the founder of the Samothracian Mysteries. After which the Dardanelle are named.

[15]*PGM* IV. 1716-1870.

1- What about parallels in the Ikea ☩ or shabti? ﹖ ﹖

2- But is used here as a ~~noun~~ one word is declined as 2nd declension in the plural, next paragraph.

3- Unclear which spelling is correct.

4- Eros can be a more fundamental generative force in Greek myth; unlikely a lot Eros is being summoned!

passage taken from *PGM* I. 42-195, where the magician speaks, "What is your divine name? Reveal it to me ungrudgingly, so that I may call upon it. It consists of 15 letters: SOUESOLYR PHTHÊ MÔTH."[16] Being able to call upon the *parehdros* by its real magical name was a source of authority and power for the magician, as it provided him with direct access to the *parehdros* by exemplifying ritual gnosis[17] and the ability to control and command it. Ciraolo correctly observes that,

> These individualized magical names may be divided into two categories for the sake of convenience: names which are relatively short and memorable such as *Αβαώθ βακχαβρή* and *σουεσολυρ φθη μωθ,* and the more longer, more conventionalized names which are commonly termed *voces magicae.*[18]

In some passages of the *Greek Magical Papyri*, the *parehdros* is not referred to by a specific name but instead is recognised by a descriptive title. In *PGM* I. 26, the magician is instructed to chant the seven Greek vowels and then say, "Come to me, Good Husbandman,[19] Good Daimon, HARPON KNOUPHI BRINTANT Ê N SIPHRI BRISKYLMA AROUAZAR BAMESEN KRIPHI NIPOUMICHMOUAÔPH." In a similar fashion, the *parehdros* in *PGM* I. 64-65 is called upon as "Aion," which as a title refers to an abstraction of eternity but may also refer to the deified force of eternity that was venerated in Hellenistic Egypt, who regulated the revolutions of the stars, and in consequence was the absolute master of all things. There is one rite, which is called *Apollonius of Tyana's old serving woman,*[20] where the magician conjures a *parehdros* in a human form. In this rite, a goddess[21] is summoned who is called "the goddess the mistress of the house."[22] It states in regards to this rite,

> After you say this, you will behold sitting on an ass a woman of extraordinary loveliness, possessing a heavenly beauty, indescribably fair and youthful. As soon as you see her, make obeisance and say, "I thank you, lady for appearing to me. Judge me worthy of you. May your Majesty be well disposed to me. And accomplish whatever task I impose on you."
> The goddess will reply to you, "What do you have in mind?"
> You say, "I have need of you for domestic service."
> At that, she will get off the ass, shed her beauty, and will be an old woman. And

---

[16]*PGM* I. 160-63.
[17]When using the Greek term *gnôsis* I am not referring to knowledge of the finite or material world but a spiritual knowledge that provides insight into the infinite and divine world.
[18]Ciraolo, 'Supernatural Assistants in the Greek Magical Papyri', in *Ancient Magic and Ritual Power,* Meyer and Mirecki (eds.), p. 279-296.
[19]Like the 'Good Oxherd', this is another title for Anubis.
[20]*PGM* XIa. 1-40.
[21]It is likely that the goddess referred to here is Nephthys, as in the opening formula names are chanted, "EILEITHNIA AND MEROPE," which are names associated with Nephthys.
[22]*PGM* XIa. 11.

the old woman will say to you, "I will serve and attend you."

After she tells you this, the goddess will again put on her beauty, which she had just taken off, and she will ask to be released.

But you say to the goddess, "No, lady! I will use you until I get her."

As soon as the goddess hears this, she will go up to the old lady, and will take her molar tooth and a tooth from the ass and give both to you; and after that it will be impossible for the old woman to leave you, unless perhaps you want to release her. From that time forth, you will receive a bounty of great benefits, for everything that your soul desires will be accomplished by her. She will guard all your possessions and in particular will find out for you whatever anyone is thinking about you.[23]

At the end of the rite it states that the magician should release the goddess only when he is sure that the old woman will serve him. After chanting a formula of *voces magicae*, which the old woman will hear, the goddess will mount the ass and depart. The interesting feature about this rite is how the goddess, who is reluctant to servitude, transforms herself into an old woman by shedding the decrepit body. At this point the goddess and the woman assume different identities with the goddess reconstituting herself and leaving the old woman in existence to act as the magician's *parehdros*. Although the old woman is not a goddess, she is a product of divine artifice.

Apart from the gods, *parehdroi* are also identified with angels and daimons, whose presence is frequent in the *Greek Magical Papyri*. In a generic sense, angels and daimons[24] are a class of beings who are intermediate, ~~apparently,~~ between gods and humans. These spiritual beings, in the sense that they do not have a human physical location and limitations, are subordinate to the gods. They are found in the air, on the earth, in the waters, and in the sea. Daimons can also be the spirits of the dead.[1] However, some passages in the *Greek Magical Papyri* refer to the gods as 'daimons'. For example, in *PGM* IV. 460 Helios Horus is referred to as "daimon of restless fire."[2] There are two rites which present the nature and purpose of angels and daimons assuming the form of a *parehdros*. The first rite, which is called *The spell of Pnouthis, the sacred scribe, for acquiring an assistant*,[25] the *parehdros* is characterised as an *angelos*, which means 'angel',[3] and at times this characterisation is interchangeable with *theos*, a 'god', without having any special connotations. This is clearly evident from the following passage of the rite,

And this is spoken next, "Hither to me, king, I call you, god of gods, mighty, boundless, undefiled, indescribable, firmly established Aion. Be inseparable

---

[23] *PGM* XIa. 12-26.

[24] For a referenced historical and theological investigation into the nature of angels and daimons in antiquity I recommend Hanegraaff, 'Intermediary Beings I: Antiquity', in *Dictionary of Gnosis and Western Esotericism*, Hanegraaff, Brach, van den Broeck, and Faivre, 2006.

[25] *PGM* I. 42-195.

1 - The δαίμων is the essential thething, of which the individual is constituted. The ba 𓅰 is the Egyptian equivalent. Here, the author seems to equate δαίμων and Christian demon.

2 - The author does not understand the term δαίμων.

3 - This must be a Christian influence.

from me this day forth through all the time of my life." Then question him by the same oaths. If he tells you his name, take him by the hand, descend and have him recline as I have said above, setting before him part of the foods and drinks which you partake of. And when you release him, sacrifice to him after his departure what is prescribed and pour a wine offering, and in this way you will be a friend of the mighty angel. When you go abroad, he will go abroad with you; when you are destitute, he will give you money. He will tell you what things will happen both when and at what time of the night or day. And if anyone asks you, "What do I have in mind? Or what has happened to me? Or even what is going to happen?" Question the angel, and he will tell you in silence. But you speak to the one who questions you as if from yourself. When you are dead, he will wrap up your body as befits a god, but he will take your spirit and carry it up into the air with him. For no aerial spirit which is joined with a mighty assistant will go into Hades, for to him all things are subject. Whenever you wish to do something, speak his name alone into the air and say, "Come!" And you will see him actually standing near you. And say to him, "Perform this task" and he does it at once, and after doing it he will say to you, "What else do you want? For I am eager for heaven." If you do not have immediate orders, say to him, "Go lord", and he will depart. In this fashion, then, the god will be seen by you alone, nor will anyone ever hear the sound of his speaking, just you yourself alone. And he will tell you about the illness of a man, whether he will live or die, even on what day and at what hour of the night. And he will also give you both wild herbs and the powers to cure and you will be worshipped as a god since you have a god as a friend. These things the mighty assistant will perform competently. Therefore share these things with no one except your legitimate son alone when he asks you for the magic powers imparted by us. Farewell.[26]

This angel and *parehdros*, whose magical name provided in the rite is "Souesolyr phthê moth,"[27] is revered as a "mighty angel,"[28] "a mighty assistant,"[29] and "god of gods."[30] The sovereignty of this mighty angel and *parehdros* is reinforced in lines 130-131, "And the gods will agree with him on all matters, for apart from him there is nothing." At one point the magician addresses a spell to Helios and Selene as an adjuration of the assistant but no words or phrases actually imply that the *parehdros* is subordinate to Helios and Selene. In the second rite, the *Lunar Spell of Claudianus and ritual of heaven and the north star over lunar offerings,*[31] the angel has a subordinate status who obeys the commanding spell of Selene. This radical difference in status is also emphasised by the

---

[26] *PGM* I. 164-194.
[27] *PGM* I. 161.
[28] *PGM* I. 173.
[29] *PGM* I. 181.
[30] *PGM* I. 164.
[31] *PGM* VII. 862-918.

fact that the angel or daimon acting as the *parehdros* is never referred to as a 'god'. The spell begins with instructions for the magician to create a pleonasm from which he is to mould an image of Selene, make a shrine of olive wood that should not face the Sun, dedicate it with lunar ointments and preparatory rites, and finally to proceed with the spell. The spell consists of the magician asking Selene to send forth one of her angels or daimons to act as a *parehdros* for the magician by reciting,

> I call upon you, mistress of the entire world, ruler of the entire cosmic system, greatly powerful goddess, gracious daimon, lady of night, who travel through the air, PHEROPHORÊ ANATHRA... OUTHRA. Heed your sacred symbols and give a whirring sound, and give a sacred angel or a holy assistant who serves this very night, in this very hour, PROKYNÊ BAUBÔ PHOBEIOUS MÊE, and order the angel to go off to her.[32]

The magician at this point is to continue the spell by reciting,

> Mistress, send forth your daimon from among those who assist you, one who is leader of night, because I adjure you by your great names, because of which no aerial or infernal daimon can ignore you, MESOURPHABABOR BRAL IÊÔ ISI Ê. Come to me just as I have summoned you, ORTHÔ BAUBÔ NOÊRE KODÊRE SOIRE SOIRE ERESCHIGAL SANKISTÊ DÔDEKAKISTÊ AKROUROBORE KODÊRE SAMPSEI; hear my words and send forth your daimon who is appointed over the 1st hour, MENEBAIN; and the one over the 2nd hour, NEBOUN; and the one over the 3rd hour, LÊMNEI; and the one over the 4th hour, MORMOTH; and the one over the 5th hour, NOUPHIÊR; and the one over the 6th hour, CHORBORBATH; and the one over the 7th hour, ORBEÊTH; and the one over the 8th hour, PANMÔTH; and the one over the 9th hour, THYMENPHRI; and the one over the 10th hour, SARNOCHOIBAL; and the one over the 11th hour, BATHIABÊL; and the one over the 12th hour, ARBRATHIABRI, so that you may do this for me.[33]

The interesting feature of this spell is the uncertainty regarding which angel or daimon will execute the magician's request. Although it is likely that the magician will expect the angel or daimon ruling over the hour the spell is executed to attend to his biding, this remains unclear. The ritual uncertainty as to which entity will become the *parehdros* appears in the rite called the *Powerful spell of the Bear*[34] *which accomplishes everything*,[35] where the *parehdros* is referred to as a daimon but is not identified with a daimon of a dead person. In many cases, *parehdroi* are identified with the daimons of the dead

---

[32] *PGM* VII. 880-886.
[33] *PGM* VII. 891-907.
[34] This spell, like many in the *Greek Magical Papyri*, invokes the astral constellation of *Arktos*.
[35] *PGM* IV. 1331-1389.

but I must stress that they are not acknowledged as merely being normal spirits of the dead, but instead a being of different and interchangeable status.[36] In this spell the daimons are referred to as "assistants of the great god, the mighty chief-daimons,"[37] but as in the case of the rite of the *Lunar Spell of Claudianus and ritual of heaven and the north star over lunar offerings*, the magician is unaware of which of these faceless and subordinate spirits will do his bidding. However, the daimon invoked to perform the ritual duty of a *parehdros* in *PGM* I. 1-42 is none other than the mighty *Agathos Daimôn*, the 'Good Daimon'. This *Agathos Daimôn* is Agathodaimon, who was the beneficent spirit, protector god, and guard of the city Alexandria. Agathodaimon was a Hellenistic merging of a popular serpent god with the Egyptian god Shai.¹ Although the magical name of the *parehdros* is "Arbath Abaôth Bakchabrê,"[38] it is not clear whether the magician is immediately equating the *parehdros* with the *Agathos Daimôn* or if it is merely a title, as the *parehdros* is also equated with Orion and Anubis, confusing the applied identity. However, it is truly a powerful entity and not subordinate like the daimons of the *Powerful spell of the Bear*[39] *which accomplishes everything*. As the text states,

> Come to me... who cause the currents of the Nile to roll down and mingle with the sea, transforming them with life as it does man's seed in sexual intercourse, you who have established the world on an indestructible foundation, who are young in the morning and old in the evening, who journey through the subterranean sphere and rise, breathing fire, you who have parted the seas in the first month, who ejaculated seeds into the sacred fig tree of Heliopolis continually.[40]

In four sections of the *Greek Magical Papyri* presenting ritual gestures attached to rites for summoning a *parehdros*, the *parehdroi* appear to be incorporeal entities. In three of these rites, the *parehdroi* are identified with the daimons of the dead. In *PGM* IV. 1928-2005 and *PGM* IV. 2145-2240 the *parehdros* is the daimon of a deceased person who fell victim to a violent death. In *PGM* IV. 2006-2125 the *parehdros* is the daimon of dead person whose manner of death is unspecified. However, in *PGM* I. 42-195 the magician addresses the *parehdros* as "friend of aerial spirits."[41] In the same rite the *parehdros* is identified as a star and he only manifests into an angel and a god when he reveals his magical name. This entity is also associated with a star emphasising his heavenly origin along with the air being his permanent dwelling where he will carry off the magician upon his death.

---

[36] This is apparent in *PGM* IV. 1367 where the *parehdros* is mentioned as *tartaroforos*, which means 'guarding Tartaros'.
[37] *PGM* IV. 1349-1350.
[38] *PGM* I. 36.
[39] This spell, like many in the *Greek Magical Papyri*, invokes the astral constellation of *Arktos*.
[40] *PGM* I. 31-36.
[41] *PGM* I. 50.

1 - That's a big statement to make without context or explanation. I am not familiar with Shai. The link to Alexandria suggests Serapis.

Although there is a tendency amongst scholars to recognise the *parehdros* as a type of spiritual being with specific functions, there are six ritual passages in the *Greek Magical Papyri* that identify the *parehdros* as a physical object. In *PGM* IV. 1928-2005 and *PGM* IV. 2006-2125 the *parehdroi* are skulls, in *PGM* I. 1-42 the *parehdros* is a mummified falcon, in *PGM* IV. 1716-1870 and *PGM* XII. 14-95 the *parehdroi* appear as statuettes of the god Eros, who also appears in conjunction with an engraved magical stone in *PGM* IV. 1716-1870. Finally, the *parehdros* is an inscribed metal lamella in *PGM* IV. 2145-2240.

The interesting feature that indicates how these *parehdroi* as physical objects differ can be found in the initial ritual procedures employed for the magical activation of the object.[42] In *PGM* IV. 1928-2995 and *PGM* IV. 2006-2125, the magician is instructed to chant a series of magical formulae, write magical words, sacrifice aromas, and then wreathe the skull. In *PGM* I. 1-42, the magician is to repeat a very similar series of ritual gestures as the ones used in the skull rites. In *PGM* IV. 2145-2240, the *parehdros* is a lamella, which is a thin metal sheet, inscribed with Homeric verses. The required preliminary ritual gestures are immersing the lamella as a form of baptism and then magically activating it. The *parehdros* in *PGM* IV. 1716-1870 is an inscribed gold leaf and in *PGM* IV. 2145-2240 the gold leaf appears again but alongside an inscribed magnetic stone and a statuette of Eros. Some preliminary ritual instructions are provided where the magician must write some magical words, making a partridge swallow the leaf, and then sacrificing the bird so that the leaf can be used alongside the engraved stone and the statuette of Eros. In the other rite, which contains the statuette of Eros, the magician again must chant a series of magical words and phrases, perform an animal sacrifice before the statuette of Eros, and present a burnt offering.

In the all the rites that identify the *parehdros* as a physical object, the chanting and writing of magical formulae is a common feature along with non-animal offerings and the presentation of the physical object. However, the difference in the initial ritual procedure is the fact that the two skulls and the mummified falcon do not require an animal sacrifice. This surely indicates that depending on whether the physical object used as the *parehdros* was a human-made object or the remains of a living creature, designated the necessary initial ritual procedures. According to Ciraolo,

> When a magical object has its own origin in what was once a human being or animal, it is regarded as intrinsically possessing magical power. The purpose of preliminary rituals and spells in such a case is to harness this supernatural power, rather than to endow the object with a power it did not previously possess. Man-made objects such as the metal lamella, the two statuettes of the god Eros,

[42]Three different nouns employed to describe these initial ritual procedures indicate how important their differentiation is. The first noun is *aphierôsis*, which means 'to dedicate'. The second is *kathierôsis*, which means 'to introduce', and the third is *teletê*, which refers to act of performing ritually.

and the engraved magnetic stone and gold leaf which act in conjunction with the image of the god, lack this inherent connection to a source of supernatural power. The function of the ritual is to establish a bind between the object and a source of magical power.[43]

Although just by examining these rites it appears that different aspects of the *parehdroi* can be distinguished as a god, angel and daimon, celestial phenomenon, and a physical object, these aspects occur in places as related. For example, in *PGM* IV. 1716-1870 and XII. 14-95, the *parehdros* is both the god Eros and a statuette, whilst in *PGM* IV. 1928-2005 and IV. 2006-2125 the *parehdros* is a skull and a daimon of a person who met a violent death. Likewise, in *PGM* IV. 2145-2240 the *parehdros* is the daimon of a deceased person and a physical object. However, in *PGM* I. 1-42 and *PGM* I. 42-195 matters become a bit more complicated as the *parehdros* is identified with a god, a celestial phenomenon, the Good Daimon, an angel, and an aerial spirit, and in *PGM* I. 1-42 as a mummified falcon. It is obvious that there different types of *parehdroi* and that each type possesses certain parts and functions, but as Ciraolo indicates, "We might think of different types of πάρεδροι as the various declensions of nouns in a language. We can figure out the case endings, in this case the broader categories which encompass the various aspects of each πάρεδρος, for some of the declensions."[44] However, with the possession of more *parehdros* material other types of *parehdroi* would become available, which in one sense would enable the identification of other types of *parehdroi* that could shed light on what appears at first sight to be a series of anomalous correspondences between different types of magical assistants.

Despite this, the *parehdros* rites in the *Greek Magical Papyri* do display an element of consistency and the variations appear as different versions of an over-arching ritual structure. The aims of the individual rites in the *Greek Magical Papyri* might differ, but there is a sense of uniformity in regards to ritual mechanisms. It is obvious that all the *parehdros* texts seek to establish a relationship between the magician and the divine sphere by aligning the magician with the correspondences of the spiritual beings and the ritual intent. Hymns are sung, prayers are recited, long series of words or collection of vowels that are apparently incomprehensible are chanted, and the name of the divinity is revealed, which is instrumental in obtaining the desired effects. These spoken parts of magical action are individually referred to as *logos*, which means 'formula', and consist of a tripartite functional structure. The invocation of the magician begins by inviting the god or spiritual being to participate in the rite and is addressed by listing epithets, cult-places, and myths to assure that the divinity is addressed in all its relevant aspects, obliging it to attend the rite. Following this, the magician presents himself

[43]Ciraolo, 'Supernatural Assistants in the Greek Magical Papyri', in *Ancient Magic and Ritual Power,* Meyer and Mirecki (eds.), p. 289-290.
[44]Ciraolo, 'Supernatural Assistants in the Greek Magical Papyri', in *Ancient Magic and Ritual Power,* Meyer and Mirecki (eds.), p. 292.

establishing his right to ask the god or spiritual being for assistance. After they have caught its attention they state their ritual desire. The ritual statement "I know your signs, symbols and forms, who you are each hour and what is your name"[45] is a very common statement in the *Greek Magical Papyri* displaying the intention of the formulae as an ample display of arcane knowledge. This identification with the deity through the display of names, signs, symbols, and forms will guarantee the magician access to a form of magical operation in an inner-worldly context. The formulae are nearly always accompanied by the offering of *thymiamata*, 'fumigations', or *thysies*, 'sacrifices', both of which correspond to various aspects of the spiritual being or the ritual intent.

All the *parehdros* rites display magical formulae enriched by contributions from a variety of mythologies and pantheons. I personally do not like to refer to this as a form of mindless syncretism but as an aspect of magic's natural receptiveness and fluidity. However, the underlying uniform feature is the attempt to dominate through power and knowledge that the *parehdros* provides the magician with. Magic in the *Greek Magical Papyri* is characterised by power, the power to attract and manipulate through ritual formulae and spells, operating through coercion. Coercion itself can be considered a fundamental unifying element and is justified by the needs of the magician and represent the magicians' endeavour to seek communion with the transcendent, Apuleius' *Communio loquendi cum deis*, and manifest the purpose for communion in the mundane through magical assistance. To end I shall to quote from Butler's *Ritual Magic* a paragraph which so eloquently grasps the appearance and essence of magic in the *Greek Magical Papyri*, and especially the *parehdros* rites,

> Some of the rites are radiant and serene; others are lurid and even sinister; others again vibrate with spiritual power; and the boons demanded are not so disproportionate to the pressure brought to bear upon the gods as is too often the case. Although they include immunity from such commonplace ills as headaches and fevers and requests for beauty, victory and misfortunes on one's foes, the most important processes were undertaken for loftier reasons: for divine visions or communion with gods, for immortality or regeneration, for dreams, for prophecies and oracles. And when the aim was a lower one: the procuring of a familiar spirit, or the constraint of another's love, the language in its intensity and fecundity rises above the normal ritual level.[46]

---

[45] *PGM* III. 500.
[46] Butler, *Ritual Magic*, p. 8-9.

Bibliography

Betz, Hans Dieter (ed.), T*he Greek Magical Papyri in Translation including the Demotic Spells*. Chicago: University of Chicago Press, 1992.

Betz, Hans Dieter, 'Magic and Mystery in the Greek Magical Papyri'. In *Magika Hiera: Ancient Greek Magic and Religion*, edited by Christopher A. Faraone and Dirk Obbink. New York: Oxford University Press, 1991.

Butler, Elizabeth M., *Ritual Magic*. Pennsylvania: Pennsylvania State University Press, 2002.

Ciraolo, Leda Jean, 'Supernatural Assistants in the Greek Magical Papyri'. In *Ancient Magic and Ritual Power*, edited by Marvin Meyer and Paul Mirecki. Leiden: Brill, 1995.

Faraone, Christopher A. and Obbink, Dirk (eds.), *Magika Hiera: Ancient Greek Magic and Religion*. New York: Oxford University Press, 1991.

Hanegraaff, Wouter J., Brach, Jean-Pierre, Broeck, Roelof van den and Faivre (eds.), Antoine, *Dictionary of Gnosis and Western Esotericism*. Leiden: Brill, 2006.

Luck, Georg, *Arcana Mundi: Magic and the Occult in the Greek and Roman Worlds*. Baltimore: John Hopkins University Press, 2006.

Meyer, Marvin and Mirecki, Paul, (eds.), *Ancient Magic and Ritual Power*. Leiden: Brill, 1995.

Mowinckel, Sigmund, *Religion and Kultus*. Gottingen: Vandenhoeck And Ruprecht, 1953.

THE SPELL OF PNOUTHIS AS A MYSTERY RITE IN THE GREEK MAGICAL PAPYRI

BY

DAMON ZACHARIAS LYCOURINOS

It is acknowledged that he is a god; he is an aerial spirit which you have seen. If you give him a command, straightaway he performs the task.

PGM I. 96-98

The *Greek Magical Papyri*, also referred to as the *PGM*,[1] are a collection of original documents and primary sources consisting of hymns, spells, priestly invocations, conjurations, magical assistants, ritual instructions, remedies, curses, and a unique theology presenting a merging of Egyptian, Hellenic, Hebrew, Persian, Babylonian, Chaldean, Gnostic, and Coptic magic and religion.[1] The ritual gestures and verses of the *Greek Magical Papyri* exemplify a worldview that demonstrates how humanity is directly dependant on the forces of the universe. The gods of the Greco-Egyptian pantheon now represent these forces, and in particular forces of nature. Regardless of the gods, it is obvious that the average mortal fails to escape their dependency on the universe surrounding them, and as Betz sufficiently states,

> Religion is regarded as nothing but the awareness of and reaction against our dependency on the unfathomable scramble of energies coming out of the universe. In this energy jungle, human life can only be experienced as a jungle too. People's successes and failures appear to be only the result of Chance (Tyche). Individuals seem to be nothing but marionettes at the end of power lines, pulled here and there without their knowledge by invisible forces.[2]

However, it was believed that these unseen powers of the cosmos that controlled the lives of mortals could be coerced, bound, and manipulated by a religious specialist. In the case of the *Greek Magical Papyri*, it was the *magos*, 'magician', who was called upon to fulfil this task of identifying the occult correspondences and employing them for terrestrial and cosmic pursuits. A vast collection of the rites and spells in the *Greek Magical Papyri* demonstrate the necessity for achieving aims of human

---

[1]*PGM* is the abbreviation for the Latin *Papyri Graecae Magicae*.
[2]Betz, 'Introduction to the Greek Magical Papyri', in *The Greek Magical Papyri in Translation*, Betz (ed.), p. xlvii.

[1 - There is Egyptian origin and Hellenic transliteration. Possibly, they may they are Gnostic or Coptic. The rest however certainly not been demonstrated.]

life on earth, such as the acquisition of love, wealth, health, fame, knowledge of the future, revenge, manipulation of others, and so on. Despite the presence of rites and spells seeking immunity from the misfortunes of life, some of the most beautiful and eloquent passages in the *Greek Magical Papyri* present ritual procedures undertaken for loftier reasons, such as divine visions, communion with the gods, immortality, oracles, exorcisms, and even at times control over nature without even the conjuration of a magical assistant.[3] These ritual procedures are usually accompanied by prayers, hymns, and invocations, along with practical instructions that betray at times "a primitive origin and eloquent at times of the dark subsoil from which the arresting flowers of Greek magical poetry have sprung."[4] Although on the whole the ritual instructions in the *Greek Magical Papyri* are not difficult to comprehend, they are by no means an easy matter, and would frequently demand considerable mental and physical effort. Along with these ritual gestures and verses, ritual preparations are also insisted upon in many of the rites. These consist of comprising various periods of purity, chastity, sobriety, and austerity, ceremonial ablution and the donning of garments of clean linen underlining the priestly attributes of the magician's function.

Although the *Greek Magical Papyri* amongst contemporary scholars are a valuable resource for the study of magic and religion in Greco-Roman Egypt, as they are primary sources of investigation, many still consider them as merely being a collection of magical recipes executed by *goêtes*, 'charmers',[5] which in the Hellenistic world was a derogatory title referring to a practitioner of low, specious or fraudulent magic, instead of the *hiera mystêria*, 'holy mysteries', performed by a *theourgos*, 'theurgist'. Dodds, in regards to the essence and purpose of theurgy, wrote,

> It may be described more simply as magic applied to a religious purpose and resting on a supposed revelation of a religious character. Whereas vulgar magic used names and formula of religious origin to profane ends, theurgy used the procedures of vulgar magic primarily to a religious end.[6]

Despite the popular opinion that the *Greek Magical Papyri* are merely a collection of malefic folk superstitions devoid of all genuine spiritual endeavours, and purely a fallacious attempt to bind spiritual beings and invisible forces of the cosmos for

---

[3] "… and if I command the moon, it will come down; and if I wish to withhold the day, night will tarry over my head; and again, if I wish to embark on the sea, I need no ship; and if I wish to fly through the air, I am freed from my weight." Quoted in Butler, *Ritual Magic*, p. 17.

[4] Butler, *Ritual Magic*, p. 9.

[5] However, in regards to the operational distinction of the *goêtes*, Stratton-Kent argues in his book *Geosophia: The Argo of Magic*, Volume II, p ii, that the "word *goes* relates to terms describing the act of lamenting at funeral rites; the mournful howling considered as a magical voice. These magical tones can guide the deceased to the underworld, and raise the dead. This is the root of the long connection of goetia with necromancy, which has come to be termed black magic."

[6] Dodds, *The Greeks and the Irrational*, p.291.

selfish material gain, there is enough evidence suggesting that many of these rites were essentially thaumaturgical renditions of theurgical operations. One must not neglect the fact that the *Greek Magical Papyri* are a collection of personal rites and spells that belonged to different magicians for a vast array of purposes.[1] Although many of the rites and spells seek to achieve aims that purely fulfil terrestrial needs, such as the acquisition of a lover, many of them present *symbola*, 'symbols', and *synthêmata*, 'formulas', that can be traced back to more hieratic forms of magical practice, and even the *mystêria*, 'mysteries'.[2] Many of the individual rites and spells also consist of a series of formulae, chants, ritual gestures, and hymns that appear frequently in the ritual structure of theurgical practice, initiation ceremonies, and even at times express soteriological objectives.

To explore the concept of magic in the *Greek Magical Papyri* I believe it is necessary to allow the *Greek Magical Papyri* to speak for themselves. Within them, magic is identified as *hiera mageia*, 'holy magic', and the one who is initiated into this 'holy magic' is referred to as *ô makarie mysta*, 'blessed initiate', with no explicit distinction being established between higher and lower forms of magic.[7] According to Betz,

> There are, however, different levels of cultural sophistication in the papyri, and it is in sections representing a higher cultural level that we find descriptive terms such as *μαγεία* (magic), *μαγικός* (magical), and *μάγος* (magician). These terms are used always with positive connotations so that for *Papyri Graecae Magicae* magic and religion are a single entity. This does not mean, however, that for the magicians whose writings are included in the *Papyri Graecae Magicae* all magic is simply legitimate and acceptable. The magical handbooks that make up most of the material represent collections, that is, selections of those texts that were deemed by the collectors to constitute an authoritative tradition. By implication, other materials not judged worthy of tradition were discarded.[8]

Although at times the magician does admit that his rites may be illegitimate and hazardous, he assures the gods that what he is performing has merely been revealed to him by the gods themselves or some other spiritual being under their authority. In the same fashion, the magicians of the *Greek Magical Papyri* did not distinguish between magic and mystery cults. Magic is referred to as *mystêrion* or *mystêria*, 'mystery' or 'mysteries', *mega mystêrion*, 'great mystery', and *theion mystêrion*, 'divine mystery'. The magician also refers to himself as *mystês*, 'initiate', and *mystagôgos*, 'mystagogue'. In various passages the outsider is called *amystêriastos*, 'uninitiated'. This clearly shows that for the magicians of the *Greek Magical Papyri*, in various parts of the body of texts,

---

[7] However there is one passage, *PGM* IV. 2081-2087, where an inferior style of magic that employs ritual tools is distinguished from a higher form that uses only magical words.

[8] Betz, 'Magic and Mystery in the Greek Magical Papyri', in *Magika Hiera: Ancient Greek Magic and Religion*, Faraone and Obbink (eds.), p. 248.

1 – but collected by a single person? See p. 20.
2 – particularly of Middle and Old Egypt.

magic and the mysteries belonged to the same sphere of ideas and operations.

Sections of the *Greek Magical Papyri* that clearly express mystery cult symbolism and gestures are normally associated with Greek gods, hymns, rituals, and fragments of myths. Although some would argue that magic was never an intrinsic part of the ancient Greek mystery cults, evidence such as the purifications, oaths of secrecy, the symbols, the formulas, the quotations on the Orphic Gold Tablets, and even the fire ritual of Eleusis,[9] all indicate that magic was an integral part of the mysteries. However, the mystery cult element in the *Greek Magical Papyri* appears to be an imposition of the Greek mystery cults, along with their magical constituencies, upon older systems of Egyptian magic. In the Hellenistic period this appears to not have been an uncommon phenomenon. There are countless examples of merging different systems of magic, which is an aspect of magic's natural receptiveness and fluidity, and the transformation of aspects of 'foreign' religions into mystery cults. Reinhold Merkelbach, in his book *Mithras*,[10] argued that this mechanism of transformation was responsible for turning the older Persian Mithra religion into the Hellenistic Mysteries of Mithras.

One rite in particular from the *Greek Magical Papyri* displays a severe reverence for the divine. Although it is an initiatory rite seeking to procure a *parehdros*, a 'magical assistant', it is also an initiatory rite of *systasis*, which means 'to present the magician to divinity' through ritual procedures of reverence and identification. This rite, the *Spell of Pnouthis, the sacred scribe, for acquiring an assistant*,[11] is a ritual manual in the form of a magical letter from the famous scribe Pnouthis to a man named Keryx. The letter, which is pseudepigraphical, contains instructions for acquiring a *parehdros daimôn*, an 'assistant daimon'. This *parehdros* is also characterised as an *angelos*, 'angel', and at times this characterisation is interchangeable with *theos*, a 'god', without having any special connotations. Keryx is instructed to treat the spell as "the great mystery,"[12] and he is addressed as "O blessed initiate of the sacred magic."[13] The opening section of the spell instructs the magician to perform a series of purifications, such as abstaining from all uncleanliness. He must then go unto a lofty roof at night clothed in ritual garments, the black Isis band on his eyes, and a falcon's head in his right hand, which he must shake at the rising sun whilst sacrificing frankincense and rose oil. With the rising sun, the magician is to recite a spell to Helios seven times. The spell consists of a long series of words and vowels, which most appear to be incomprehensible, and are known as *barbarika melê*, 'barbarian words'.[14] [15] As the magician recites the spell a falcon will fly

a rite also associated with Isis at Byblos.

---

[9] I am referring to the fire ritual at Eleusis by which Demeter made Demophon or Triptolemos immortal.
[10] Merkelbach, Reinhold, *Mithras. Königstein im Taunus*: Hain, 1984.
[11] *PGM* I. 42-195.
[12] *PGM* I. 130.
[13] *PGM* I. 127.
[14] Euripides stressed this curious phenomenon in his *Iphigeneia in Tauris*, lines 1337-1338.
[15] The reason why these collections of words and vowels were referred to as barbarous is due to the fact that appeared incomprehensible to the Greeks and henceforth associated with a foreign origin. However, as

fire, the human tendency to syncretize.

down and drop and oblong stone, on which he is to engrave Helioros as a lion-faced figure holding a celestial globe in the left hand and a whip in the right hand. Around the figure a serpent biting its tail is to be carved and on the exergue of the stone the name ACHA ACHACHA CHACH CHARCHARA CHACH. After this, he is to pass an Anubian string through it and wear it around his neck. The magician is then instructed to return to his housetop in the evening and to face the Moon, recite the hymnic spell to Selene whilst sacrificing myrrh and salute the goddess by lighting a fire and shaking a branch of myrtle.

The magician after this will witness a blazing star descending from heaven and becoming the messenger and assistant, who is referred to as being an angel and in some parts of the spell a god. The magician is specifically told not to fear this angel but instead take him by the hand, kiss him, and recite a spell. At this point, an oath is made that the angel will serve the magician when called upon and if the divine messenger decides to reveal his name the magician must take him into his house and offer him food and wine. Before allowing the messenger to depart, the magician reminds the angel of the oath and then offers a sacrifice and pours wine of offering to the angel as he departs. The magician is informed in the ritual letter that the angel will always appear when called upon to assist in various affairs, but it is fundamental that the magician does not reveal the messenger's identity or presence. Although some aspects of the magical assistant are revealed by the angel himself, the divine character, attributes, and abilities of the assistant are revealed in the letter where it states,

> It is acknowledged that he is a god; he is an aerial spirit which you have seen. If you give him a command, straightaway he performs the task: he sends daimons, he brings women, men without the use of magical material, he kills, he destroys, he stirs up winds from the earth, he carries gold, silver, bronze, and he gives then to you whenever the need arises. And he frees from bonds a person chained in prison, he opens doors, he causes invisibility so that no one can see you at all, he is a bringer of fire, he brings water, wine, bread and whatever you wish in the way of foods: olive oil, vinegar – with the single exception of fish – and he will bring plenty of vegetables, whatever kind you wish, but as for pork, you must not ever tell him to bring this at all! And when you want to give a dinner, tell him so. Conjure up in your mind any suitable room and order him to prepare it for a banquet quickly and without delay. At once he will bestow chambers with golden ceilings, and you will see their walls covered with marble – and you consider these things partly real and partly just illusionary – and costly wine, as is meet to cap a dinner splendidly. He will quickly bring daimons, and for

---

Iamblichus stressed, "But the foreign priests are steadfast in their customs, and continue firmly with the same words; for which reason, making use of the words grateful to them, they are themselves beloved by the gods. Nevertheless, to change them in any way is not lawful for any human being." Iamblichus, Wilder (trans.), *Theurgia or the Egyptian Mysteries*, p. 247.

Probably an ancient translation of a foreign tongue.

you he will adorn these servants with sashes. These things he does quickly. And as soon as you order him to perform a service, he will do so, and you will see him excelling in other things: he stops ships and again releases them, he stops very many evil daimons, he checks wild beasts and will quickly break the teeth of fierce reptiles, he puts dogs to sleep and renders them voiceless. He changes into whatever form of beast you want: one that flies, swims, a quadruped, a reptile. He will carry you into the air, and gain hurl you into the billows of the sea's current and into the waves of the sea; he will quickly freeze rivers and seas in such a way that you can run over them firmly, as you want. And especially will he stop, if ever you wish it, the sea-running foam, and whenever you wish to bring down stars and whenever you wish to make warm things cold and cold things warm, he will light lamps and extinguish them again. And he will shake walls and cause them to blaze with fire; he will serve you suitably for whatever you have in mind, O blessed initiate of sacred magic, and will accomplish it for you, this most powerful assistant, who is also the only lord of the air.[16]

Apart from considering the function and nature of the *parehdros*, the *Spell of Pnouthis, the sacred scribe, for acquiring an assistant* presents the essence of the relationship that might occur between the realm of divinity and the magician being a "blessed initiate of the sacred magic."[17] Despite some elements of coercion and constraint when addressing Helios, who is also identified as Aion, to obtain the *parehdros* the magician seeks a personal relationship with the magical assistant. This attitude, along with the fact that the magician has to purify himself before the spell, includes in the magical operation elements typical of religious practice and devotion. The divine assistant is qualified as good and holy and is invoked as the Agathos Daimon, holy Orion, a god, and aerial spirit. Following this, the magician is called "a friend of aerial spirits"[18] and that he "will be worshipped as a god for he has a god as a friend."[19] These epithets and characterisations echo the claim of Porphyry in the *Life of Plotinus*, "Blessed are you who has a god as a friend and not a spirit of an inferior class."[20] This surely indicates a presence and awareness of theurgical practices along with the fact that the element of *systasis* included in the dynamic of a magical operation distinguishes it from adherents to non-theurgical traditions. In the following verses this term is not employed for the magical assistant, but for the magician himself after death, signifying an eschatological variation. However, the aerial spirit himself also changes in status as he is now referred to as "the only lord of the air."[21]

---

[16] *PGM* I. 96-132. Sounds like an Arabian Djinn.
[17] *PGM* I. 127.
[18] *PGM* I. 50.
[19] *PGM* I. 191.
[20] Quoted in Luck, *Arcana Mundi: Magic and the Occult in the Greek and Roman Worlds: A Collection of Ancient Texts*, p. 22.
[21] *PGM* I. 129-130.

The letter itself containing the ritual instructions was sent to Keryx by a man called Pnouthis, whose piety is confirmed and who most likely belonged to a temple priesthood. The ritual prescriptions concerning preliminary attainment of purity, the proper execution of the spell, and how Pnouthis attests that the spell itself as a rite, stands in a long tradition attaches a mystical and religious element to the nature of the spell reminiscent of the mystery cults. The need for preliminary purity and the ritual abstention from impure food, such as pork,[22] evoke a sense of mystical piety adhering to an ancient tradition of religious observance. In the spell there is a passage that commands an oath of silence,

> But you adjure him with this oath that he meet you and remain inseparable and that he not keep silent or disobey in any way. But when he has with certainty accepted this oath of yours, take the god by the hand and leap down, and after bringing him into the narrow room where you reside, sit him down.[23]

It is this oath that forms a pact with the divine assistant for his permanent presence and attachment to the magician. The permanency of the magical assistant is also firmly established when he is instructed to recite, "Hither to me King... firmly established Aion. Be inseparable from me from this day forth through all the time of my life."[24] In addition, the emphasis on the magical operation taking place in a liminal space, which in this case is the elevated space of the housetop, invokes the impression of crossing the threshold from the realm of mortals into a more sacred realm of the divine.

Pnouthis' letter also informs towards the end the spheres of influence that belong to the magical assistant. This *parehdros* can provide material wealth, dream divinations, spells of attraction to bind lovers, the cause of death, protection from malevolent daimons and fierce beasts, power over storms, and the cause of destruction. According to Pnouthis, "It is acknowledged that he is a god; he is an aerial spirit which you have seen. If you give him a command, straightaway he performs the task."[25] Finally, after having provided a detailed description of the nature and spheres of influence of the *parehdros*, the ritual instructions conclude,

> He will serve you suitably for whatever you have in mind, O blessed initiate of the sacred magic, and will accomplish it for you, this most powerful assistant... Share this mystery with no one else, but conceal it, by Helios, since you have been deemed worthy by the lord god.[26]

---

[22] The pig was considered unclean as it was associated with Seth/Typhon. As of what date?
[23] *PGM* I. 80-83
[24] *PGM* I. 164-167.
[25] *PGM* I. 96-98.
[26] *PGM* I. 125-133.

The magician, who is referred to as an "initiate of the sacred magic," is fully aware that in the spell itself he has become the focal point of all ritual gestures that are both magical and sacred.

Unlike many of the spells in the *Greek Magical Papyri*, the *Spell of Pnouthis, the sacred scribe, for acquiring an assistant*, in addition to providing the magician with magical means to acquire material gains, presents an eschatological perspective and a soteriological dimension. This is evident from the verses of the spell that explicitly states,

> When you are dead, he will wrap up your body as befits a god, but he will take your spirit and carry it into the air with him. For no aerial spirit which is joined with a mighty assistant will go into Hades, for to him all things are subject.[27]

The magician, unlike all other mortals, undergoes an initiation through the *Spell of Pnouthis, the sacred scribe, for acquiring an assistant*, and instead of venturing into Hades in the afterlife he passes through a ritual process of osirification that enables him to acquire a celestial and otherworldly essence in the afterlife. The power of this spell allows the magician not only to participate in the divine in life but also in death. The ulterior soteriological benefit provided by the divine messenger, along with all the material benefits, is the effect of *apothanatismos*, where one 'achieves immortality in the heavenly realms'. As the spell itself claims, "You will be worshipped as a god since you have a god as a friend."[28] However, the magician can only acquire this ulterior eschatological effect by ~~applying~~ the powers of the spell provided to him to coerce divinity to act through a series of spells of coercion combined with sacred magic and acts of piety, where the magician can achieve a sense of *henôsis*, 'union', with the divine.

This concept of soteriology, combined with the otherworldly ascent through the heavens in the afterlife, echoes one of the most sacred mysteries of various Gnostic traditions that spoke of the salvation of the individual through a process of ascent returning to the heavenly realms of pure spirit. To achieve this, the individual must acquire through personal divine *gnôsis*, 'gnosis', which is the spiritual knowledge of a mystically enlightened individual who has received ~~such~~ insight into the infinite and the realm of spirit through divine revelation. The ultimate object of this spiritualised sense of knowledge is for the soul to transform the knower by assimilating him or her into the divine realm, and serve as an instrument of salvation. This idea can be identified in the *Spell of Pnouthis, the sacred scribe, for acquiring an assistant*, with the divine messenger being the revelation providing the magician with the practical gnosis for salvation upon death, where he will be carried away into the heavenly realms becoming one with the

---

[27] *PGM* I. 173-181. The function of the basic traditional Egyptian religion.
[28] *PGM* I. 190-191.

1 - Greek writing one would presume.

spirit of the divine. According to Rudolph,

> All Gnostic teachings are in some form part of the redeeming knowledge which gathers together the object of knowledge (the divine nature), the means of knowledge (the redeeming gnosis) and the knower himself. The intellectual knowledge of the teaching which is offered as revealed wisdom has here a direct religious significance since it is at the same time understood as otherworldly and is the basis for the process of redemption. A man who possesses 'gnosis' is for that reason a redeemed man.[29]

This threefold pattern of revelation can be acknowledged in the spell with the *parehdros* acting as the divine messenger being the object of knowledge of the divine nature, the ritual instructions being the means of knowledge on how to acquire the revelation of the divine messenger, and the magician becoming the knower himself through the initiation provided by the spell.

The apparent objective of the *Spell of Pnouthis, the sacred scribe, for acquiring an assistant* is to acquire a *parehdros*, as the title of the spell clearly expresses, for personal empowerment of the magician on the terrestrial plane. This may lead one to understand the purpose of the spell as merely yet another attempt to coerce and bind forces of the universe for personal material needs without displaying any form of a sacred objective. However, what one might fail to recognise is the emphasis on genuine divine revelation through a series of ritual gestures that are similar to theurgical workings, and seek not only material gain but a sense of gnosis, union, and salvation. Iamblichus presents this elaborately by clarifying that,

> It is not thought that links the theurgist to the gods; else what should hinder the theoretical philosopher from enjoying theurgic union with them? The case is not so. Theurgic union is attained only by the perfective operation of unspeakable acts correctly performed, acts which are beyond all understanding, and by power of the unutterable symbols intelligible only to the gods.[30]

In theory and practice this spell does contain elements of theurgy, as it is a set of ritual techniques seeking communion with the realm of the gods and subsequently a manifestation of it. Pnouthis, in his letter to Keryx, clearly states that all ritual procedures in the letter are to be followed to avoid failure and acquire a revelation of the divine along with power attached to it in the form of a divine messenger acting as a *parehdros*. One of the main purposes of learned ritual techniques of the theurgists, according to Cumont,[31] was to have an experience of the manifestation of the divine and a sense of

---

[29]Rudolph, *Gnosis: The Nature and History of Gnosticism*, p. 55-56.
[30]Proclus, Dodds (ed.), *Elements of Theology*, p. xx.
[31]Cumont, *Lux Perpetua*, p. 363, 367.

1 - This is more likely a development of the Middle Egyptian idea of the ba.

union with it in this life here on earth, but which also promised salvation in the life to come. Again we see this in the *Spell of Pnouthis, the sacred scribe, for acquiring an assistant* with the magician experiencing divine revelation with the manifestation of the angel and his divine attributes. As theurgists aimed to unite with the heavens through salvation acquired through their sacred ritual operations and achieve union with the gods, so the magician also through the performance of the ritual dynamics of the spell "will be worshipped as a god since he has a god for a friend."[32]

The spell consists of a long series of barbarous words of power and mystic hymns to Helios and Selene, along with the offering of fumigations, such as uncut frankincense, rose oil and myrrh troglitis, and specific ritual gestures and tools, such as the shaking of a branch of myrtle to Selene and the black Isis band. Theurgists themselves also ritually employed the use of gestures, symbols, and correspondences. Some of these were words recited and written down, whilst others were material things pertaining to the principle of cosmic sympathy. Barbarous names' and mystical hymns were of prime significance as they served to establish a contact between the theurgist and the gods, where the gods would recognise the human practitioner as a legitimate theurgist who had come to know the names and epithets of the gods and the magical formula to which they would respond, and the theurgist would recognise the gods as being a genuine manifestation of the divine. Material things, such as herbs, stones, and specific magical tools, were essential to all theurgical operations and abided to the principle of cosmic sympathy. Theurgical instructions were a guardedly kept secret handed down through certain families, initiatory traditions, and philosophical schools. This attitude is also inherently attached to the instructions set down by Pnouthis, who presents himself as following in a long-lived sacred tradition[33] and explicitly instructs the magician that he is not to speak of the *parehdros* to any one.

Despite the opinion of early Christian authors, such as Gregory of Nazianzus, theurgy was a sacred form of worship and higher form of magic, but not resembling what the Greeks labelled as *goêtia*, for in the eyes of theurgists, such as Iamblichus, these *goêtes* were merely 'makers of images' who produced only false apparitions of gods for a monetary price. Many theurgists actually saw themselves as belonging to a priestly caste and for this reason they labelled theurgy as *hieratikê technê*, 'priestly art'. Judging from other terms that were applied to theurgy, such as *orgia*, 'ecstatic form of worship', *mystêria*, 'mysteries', *teletai*, 'rite of initiation', and *mystagôgia*, 'education in the mysteries', indicates that theurgy of the Late Antiquity had acquired the status of the old mystery religions in a similar fashion to the way in which the magicians of the *Greek Magical Papyri* viewed themselves.

Ignoring the misconception that still prevails in regards to the *Greek Magical Papyri* as

---

[32]*PGM* I. 190-191.
[33]*PGM* I. 46-47.

I - When known correctly, I'm sure.

being a syncretic attempt to collect and display a variety of malefic and low magical spells, the very fact that magic in the *Greek Magical Papyri* is referred to as *mystêrion* or *mystêria*, 'mystery' or 'mysteries', and the magician referring to himself as *mystês*, 'initiate', indicates that the rites themselves might indeed have been continuous parts of sacred practices stemming from the mysteries. The mysteries, like many of the rites in the *Greek Magical Papyri*, were considered to be secret rites of initiation. The individual who was attached to a mystery school was referred to as a *mystês*. Secrecy was a fundamental element within the mysteries and only initiates were allowed to participate in the rites. Like in the *Greek Magical Papyri*, an uninitiated was referred to as *amystêriastos*. The rites, along with symbols and meanings expressed in the mysteries, were always to be kept secret from the uninitiated and any divulging of the secrets kept within the mysteries was punishable even by death. This emphasis on secrecy features in the *Spell of Pnouthis, the sacred scribe, for acquiring an assistant*, where the magician is instructed to not share his knowledge of the divine messenger to anyone,[34] as the angel himself is a sacred revelation of the divine that is to be kept secret from the uninitiated.

The main purpose of the mysteries was to unite the initiated with an aspect of divinity through revelation, and the eschatology of the mysteries was to provide personal salvation in the afterlife, along with promises of divine powers and rewards in life after death. Again we witness these key elements of the mysteries having a direct effect on the soteriological aspect of the *Spell of Pnouthis, the sacred scribe, for acquiring an assistant* with the magician undergoing the initiation of the spell in order to receive a revelation of the divine, the *parehdros*, who will offer him salvation upon death by wrapping up his body as if he was a god and taking him with him to the heavens.

A significant feature of the mysteries was the repetition of features of the cultic aspects of public religion, such as sacrifice, ritual meals, and ritual purity. These ritual requirements also appear in the *Spell of Pnouthis, the sacred scribe, for acquiring an assistant*, where the magician is instructed to perform a sacrifice of a falcon, to abstain from animal food, uncleanliness, and sexual intercourse.[35] The importance of ritual meals is also emphasised, with the magician being told to take the angel by the hand and lead him back into the house to partake in the foods and drinks that have been ritually prepared with the angel.[36] As I have already demonstrated, in the *Spell of Pnouthis, the sacred scribe, for acquiring an assistant* there are many elements which echo loudly practices and beliefs pertaining to the mystery cults of antiquity. The whole rite is to be treated

---

[34]*PGM* I. 192-193.
[35]Although these requirements are not explicitly stated in *PGM* I. 42-195 but in *PGM* I. 1-42, it is my personal conviction that *PGM* I. 1-42 acts as a set of instructions for the ritual preliminaries for the *Spell of Pnouthis, the sacred scribe, for acquiring an assistant*. Based on what?
[36]*PGM* I. 168-170.

as "the great mystery"[37] and its recipient is addressed as "O blessed initiate of the sacred magic."[38] However, juxtaposing magic and the religious elements of the mystery cults may be at times incomprehensible if one is to merely treat religion as defined in the narrower sense as merely worship of a deity and not pertaining to an attitude towards a reality and application of a worldview. Mowinckel, in his book *Religion und Kultus*, rightly emphasised that,

> Magical thinking and its practical application, called 'magic', is not a kind of religion, but a worldview, that is, a particular way to understand things and their mutual connectedness. Magic is the *Weltanschauung* which in a certain way is analogous to the view of the universe as we today attempt to formulate it on the basis of the laws of causality and the interaction between cause and effect, demonstrated by physics, chemistry, biology and psychology.[39]

But in order to understand the distinction between magic and religion, one must explore and refer to theological concepts that were recognised in pre-Christian antiquity, and also have a high degree of understanding of the life and thought of the cults in question.

Sections of the *Greek Magical Papyri* that exemplify attitudes, practices, and symbols pertaining to elements of the mystery cults come along with Greek deities, fragments of hymns and invocations, rituals, and myths. According to Betz, "Obviously, in the eyes of the magicians who wrote and transmitted these texts, the mystery cult language and ritual provided religious legitimacy and cultural approval for all the other magical materials."[40] This phenomenon of the imposition of mystery cult ideas, rituals, and tradition indicates and testifies how the Greek mysteries expanded their influence, along with the expansion of other religious fields of discourse into mystical cults enriched with magical rites and spells. Apart from the *Spell of Pnouthis, the sacred scribe, for acquiring an assistant*, the *Mithras Liturgy*[41] also attests to this with verses such as "mysteries handed down not for gain but for instruction"[42] and "O lord, while being born again, I am passing away; while grown and having grown, I am dying; while being born from a life-generating birth, I am passing on, released to death – as you have founded, as you have decreed, and have established the mystery."[43] Other rites that reveal mystery cult terminology with some Hebrew influences are the *Stele of Jeu the hieroglyphist in his letter*, which includes a verse summoning the Headless One by declaring, "I am Moses,

---

[37] *PGM* I. 42-195.
[38] *PGM* I. 127.
[39] Mowinckel, *Religion and Kultus*, p. 15.
[40] Betz, 'Magic and Mystery in the Greek Magical Papyri', in *Magika Hiera: Ancient Greek Magic and Religion*, Faraone and Obbink (eds.), p. 250.
[41] *PGM* IV. 479-829.
[42] *PGM* IV. 476.
[43] *PGM* IV. 718-724.

your prophet to whom you have transmitted your mysteries,"[44] and the *Eighth Book of Moses* which states "Now begin to recite the stele and the mystery of the god."[45] These verses testify to the influence that mystery cult terminologies and practices had on the *Greek Magical Papyri*. According to Betz, under this impact,

> Earlier Egyptian magic was transformed, enriched, brought up to date, and thus legitimated. By presenting themselves as mystagogues, the magicians doubtless added to their prestige... The mystagogue-magician of the Greek mystery cults transformed the older magic into a new and higher "religion." For the mystagogue-magician, the syncretistic amalgam was indeed "religion."[46]

However, one must not discredit the fact that there were differences between magic and religion in the *Greek Magical Papyri*, which were determined by theological issues inherent within the structures of the mystery cults and the fashion in which they were adopted within the realm of magic. To an extent, it appears logical that most of magicians were not fully aware of the entirety of the inner dimensions of the mystery cults whose material they appropriated. For they believed that their 'art' was indeed a fully operational religion, which they referred to as 'magic', and themselves as the operators of it as 'magicians', reflecting yet again the natural receptiveness, fluidity, and impressive power of the magician's worldview. To conclude, I shall quote a passage from Butler's exceptional tome, *Ritual Magic*, which so eloquently invokes and encaptures the diachronic fascination we have up until this day with ritual conjuring the natural receptiveness, fluidity, and impressive power of the magical worldview,

> For the inventors and practioners of the rites, however deeply versed in the lore of their subject and however obedient to its rules, often gave proof of the artistic temperament, to the advantage of the literature which has survived. The aim, like that of astrology, alchemy and applied science as a whole, was strictly practical; the means show evidence of creative instincts, poetical imagination and feeling for beauty and drama... this is what makes the study of ritual magic still interesting to-day.[47]

---

[44] *PGM* V. 108-111.
[45] *PGM* XIII. 685.
[46] Betz, 'Magic and Mystery in the Greek Magical Papyri', in *Magika Hiera: Ancient Greek Magic and Religion,* Faraone and Obbink (eds.), p. 254.
[47] Butler, *Ritual Magic*, p. 4.

BIBLIOGRAPHY

Betz, Hans Dieter (ed.), *The Greek Magical Papyri in Translation including the Demotic Spells*. Chicago: University of Chicago Press, 1992.

Betz, Hans Dieter, 'Magic and Mystery in the Greek Magical Papyri'. In *Magika Hiera: Ancient Greek Magic and Religion*, edited by Christopher A. Faraone and Dirk Obbink. New York: Oxford University Press, 1991.

Butler, Elizabeth M., *Ritual Magic*. Pennsylvania: Pennsylvania State University Press, 2002.

Ciraolo, Leda Jean, 'Supernatural Assistants in the Greek Magical Papyri'. In *Ancient Magic and Ritual Power*, edited by Marvin Meyer and Paul Mirecki. Leiden: Brill, 1995.

Cumont, Franz V. M., *Lux Perpetua*. Paris: Paul Geuthner, 1949.

Dodds, E. R. *The Greeks and the Irrational*. Berkley: University of California Press, 2004.

Faraone, Christopher A. and Obbink, Dirk (eds.), *Magika Hiera: Ancient Greek Magic and Religion*. New York: Oxford University Press, 1991.

Iamblichus, Wilder, Alexander (trans.), *Theurgia or the Egyptian Mysteries*. London: Metaphysical Publishing Co., 1911.

Luck, G. *Arcana Mundi: Magic and the Occult in the Greek and Roman Worlds: A Collection of Ancient Texts*. Baltimore: John Hopkins University Press, 2006.

Merkelbach, Reinhold, *Mithras*. Königstein im Taunus: Hain, 1984.

Meyer, Marvin and Mirecki, Paul, (eds.), *Ancient Magic and Ritual Power*. Leiden: Brill, 1995.

Mowinckel, Sigmund *Religion and Kultus*. Gottingen: Vandenhoeck And Ruprecht 1953.

Proclus, Dodds, E. R. (ed.), *Elements of Theology*. Oxford: Clarendon Press, 1933.

Rudolph, Kurt, *Gnosis: The Nature and History of Gnosticism*. Edinburgh: T&T Clark Ltd, 1983.

Stratton-Kent, Jake, *Geosophia: The Argo of Magic*, Volume II. UK: Scarlet Imprint, 2010.

WATERS ANIMATING AND ANNIHILATING APOTHEOSIS BY DROWNING IN THE GREEK MAGICAL PAPYRI

BY

AARON CHEAK

Death is the inverse, the undescribed side of life: we must attempt to achieve the greatest awareness of our existence which resides in both unlimited regions and nourished by both [...] This true form of life penetrates both regions, the blood of the greatest circulation courses through both: there is neither a here nor a thereafter, but rather the greater unity.

Rainer Maria Rilke, *Briefe aus Muzot*

The terminology of initiatory apotheosis emerges right at the beginning of the *Greek Magical Papyri*, also referred to as *Papyri Graecae Magicae* and abbreviated as *PGM*, an anthology of ritual manuals chiefly composed in Greek, but also in Demotic Egyptian and Old Coptic, and most probably produced by a milieu of Theban lector-priests in Ptolemaic and Roman Egypt.[1] In *PGM* I. 1-42 the verb *apotheóō* is used to describe a rite of drowning. Here, deification by drowning follows the model of the eternally rejuvenated Osiris and is further assimilated to the Egyptian solar cosmology where to descend into the primordial waters[2] is necessary to rejuvenation.[3] As among early Pythagoreans and southern Italian mystery cults, continual renewal through death and revivification is mediated by a descent, *katabasis*, into the underworld, and in Egyptian cosmology the *duat*. Apotheosis and drowning therefore cohere in the praxis of initiatory death, the *conditio sine qua non* of rebirth into immortal life. This paper will examine some of the finer details of the drowning motif in the *PGM*, and in particular the *materia magica* of milk, honey, and oil of lilies, along with their connections to divine rebirth, and upon this basis trace the symbolic resonance of these motifs in classical and late antique

---

[1]Brashear, 'The Greek Magical Papyri: An Introduction and Survey; Annotated Bibliography (1928-1994)', in *ANRW*, vol. 2, 18.5, p. 3380-3684; Fowden, *The Egyptian Hermes: A Historical Approach to the Late Pagan Mind*, p. 168-76; Frankfurter, 'Ritual Expertise in Roman Egypt and the Problem of the Category 'Magician'', in *Envisioning Magic: A Princeton Seminar and Symposium*, Schäfer and Kippenberg (eds.), p. 116.
[2]West, decline, and death.
[3]East, incline, and life.

texts. Ultimately, the overarching logic at the heart of these symbolic registers will be emphasised in terms of a Heraclitean 'harmony of contraries' seen to exist between the chthonic and the ouranian; like the lightning bolt, drowning deifies because the primordial forces that kill are deeply bound to those that animate and enliven.

I. Magic, *Apotheosis*, and the Underworld
Papyri Graecae Magicae I. 1-42

Let us begin with the full ritual. The text of *PGM* I. 1-42 proceeds as follows,[4]

Praxis. To get a daimon as an assistant (*paredros*) who will reveal everything to you clearly, will be your [companion, and] will eat and sleep with you. Take two of your fingernails and all the hairs from your head; then take a Circaean falcon (*hieraka kirkaion*) / and deify it (*apoth[e]ōson*) in the [milk] of a black [cow] mixed with Attic honey. Wrap [the deified falcon] with an undyed piece of cloth and place your fingernails and hairs upon it; taking [a piece of royal papyrus], inscribe the following formula in myrrh ink and place it together with your hairs and nails. Then smother/ it [or: anoint it?] with [uncut] frankincense [and] old wine. / Then write the following: "a ee ēēē iiii ooooo yyyyyy ōōōōōō," but make two columns (*klimata*):

			a					ō	ō	ō	ō	ō	ō ō
		e		e				y	y	y	y	y	y
	ē		ē		ē			o	o	o	o	o	
	i	i	i	i				i	i	i	i		
o	o	o	o	o				ē	ē	ē			
y	y	y	y	y	y			e	e				
ō	ō	ō	ō	ō	ō	ō		a					

Then take the honeyed milk and drink it before the rising of the sun, and there will be something divine (*entheon*) in your heart. Take the falcon and set it up as a statue in a shrine (*naōs*) made of juniper wood. And after you have crowned the shrine itself, make an offering of non-animal foods and have on hand some old wine. Before you recline, speak directly to the bird itself after you have made / sacrifice to it, as you usually do, and say the prescribed spell (*logos*):

---

[4]We have adapted and modified O'Neil's translation in Betz, H. D. (ed.), *The Greek Magical Papyri in Translation, Including the Demotic Spells*, 2nd ed. Chicago: University of Chicago Press, 1992, p. 3-4, and cross-referenced it with the Greek text and German translation provided in Preisendanz, Karl Lebrecht and Henrichs, Albert (eds.), *Papyri Graecae Magicae: Die griechischen Zauberpapyri*, 2. verb. Aufl., 2 vols., Sammlung wissenschaftlicher Commentare. Stuttgart: Teubner, 1973, vol. I, p. 2-5.

"a ee ēēē iiii ooooo yyyyyy ōōōōōō, come to me, good husbandman[1] (*Agathē George*), good daimon (*Agathos Daimon*): *harpon knouphi brintantēn siphri briskylma arouazar [bamesen] kriphi niptoumichmoumaōph.*[5] Come to me, O holy Orion, [you who lie] in the north, / who cause [the] currents of [the] Nile to roll down and mingle with the sea, [transforming them with life] as it does man's seed in sexual intercourse, you who have established the world on an indestructible ... [foundation], who are young in the morning and [old in the evening], who journey through the subterranean sphere and [rise], breathing fire, you who have parted the seas in the first / month, who [ejaculate] seeds into the [sacred fig] tree of Heliopolis continually. [This] is your authoritative name: *arbath abaōth bakchabrē.*"

[But] when you are dismissed, [go without shoes] and walk backwards and set yourself to the enjoyment of the food [and] dinner and the prescribed food offering, [coming] face to face as companion [to the god]. / [This] rite [requires complete purity]. Conceal, conceal the [procedure and] for [seven] days [refrain] from having intercourse with a woman.

Katabasis and *Anabasis*

What we are presented with here is a rite in which the magician identifies himself with the drowned and deified falcon, an animal sympathetic to the solar-regal principle, in order that he may be immortalized, thus gaining a divine assistant or *paredros*. This identification is clearly indicated by the use of the magician's own hair and fingernails as extensions of the body, which are repeatedly prescribed throughout the *Greek Magical Papyri*. The hair and fingernails were used to connect an effigy to a specific individual. This is especially pronounced in erotic spells of the *Greek Magical Papyri*, in which the hair and nails of the beloved are required in order to effectively perform the spell, for example to effectively link the magic to its intended object. The use of hair and fingernails in this manner allowed a sympathetic connection to be effected in which the person who the effigy represents could be magically manipulated or subjected to symbolic processes. In the case of the erotic spell, the love-object was bound by the lover, with control through binding being a traditional modality of Egyptian ritual

---

[5]Correcting O'Neil's "*nipoumichmoumaōph*" in Betz (ed.) *The Greek Magical Papyri in Translation, Including the Demotic Spells*, 2nd ed., p. 3. These are the precise names that figure in the ancient Egyptian sun hymns as preserved elsewhere throughout the magical corpus, for instance, *harpon knouphi*, being perhaps the most recognisable element, is based on the Egyptian phoneme *hr* = Hor. We can note further that the specific connection to Horus, already explicit in the use of the falcon and the name Har/Hor, also coheres more implicitly in the divine names. The phrase *mesen kriphi*, although some versions of the hymn have *besen kriphi*, but in any event, the *m* and *b* assimilate phonetically, refers to one of the major cult site of Horus, Mesen, the ancient name for Edfu, where the remains of the temple of Horus still preserve a colossal statue of Horus in hawk form.

1 - shepherd
2 - or is the falcon just the best way to embody Horus?

praxis.[6] In the apotheosis spell, however, the magician is clearly identifying himself with the living effigy to be magically manipulated. Specifically, the magician is symbolically and sympathetically subjecting himself to the same process of death and deification that is undergone by the falcon. The process is mirrored in the use of *voces magicae*,

Here we may refer to the distinct tradition that associates the seven vowels used in Greek magical rites with not only the seven planetary divinities, but also the seven harmonies of the diatonic scale.[7] This cosmological and harmonic schema suggests not only that the vowels were associated with specific notes or harmonics, but that these tones were used to effect a conscious resonance with the corresponding planetary spheres. In *PGM* I. 1-42, there is good reason to take the seven vowels as representative of descending and ascending vocalisations. As they are displayed here, the progression from alpha, *a*, to omega, *ō*, and back again indicates the upper and lower limits of an octave or harmonic register. The vowels in the left column thus proceed from the highest limit to the lowest limit, alpha to omega. In the right column, the vowels proceed in reverse, from the lowest to the highest, from omega back to alpha. Clearly these descending and ascending vocalisations are intended to evoke the process of *katabasis/descensus* and *anabasis/ascensus*, mirroring, and thus overdetermining, the key ritual act of drowning and deification. As Heraclitus remarks in his famous *dictum*, "the path up and the path down are one and the same."[8]

Beyond these general pointers, the crux of the rite may be seen to reside in the establishment of "something divine", *entheon*, in the magician's "heart", *kardia*. In order to attain this, the magician is requested to "drown", *apotheōson*, a "Circaean" falcon in the milk of a black cow mixed with Attic honey. After the liquid is imbibed, the falcon is subsequently wrapped, mummified, and enshrined as a statue as the

---

[6]One famous spell from the *Greek Magical Papyri*, *PGM* IV. 296-466, prescribes the creation of two effigies from wax or clay, with one in the form of Ares brandishing a sword and the other in the form of a woman, bound, and kneeling. The 'magical material', for example hair or nails of the beloved, is attached to the female figure, who represents the object of desire subjected to the control of the magician/gods. On this theme, see especially Ritner, Robert, K., *The Mechanics of Ancient Egyptian Magical Practice*. Studies in Ancient Oriental Civilization no. 54. Chicago: Oriental Institute, 1993.
[7]See Godwin, *The Mystery of the Seven Vowels in Theory and Practice*, p. 27.
[8]Diels and Kranz, 'Fragment 60', in *Die Fragmente der Vorsokratiker: Griechisch und Deutsch*, Kranz (trans.); Kirk, G. S., Raven, J. E., and Shofield, M., *The Presocratic Philosophers*. Second edition. Cambridge: Cambridge University Press, 1983.

"living image", which is then given offerings and approached by the magician for oracular communication and the execution of his "spell", *logos*. Much can be gained from unravelling these details. What we propose to do in the balance of this paper is to unravel some of the key elements of this specific rite. By doing this, we hope to gain insight into not only the cosmological contexts that underpin Graeco-Egyptian apotheosis, but also their deeper initiatic dynamics. Before we examine the details of this text, however, a few remarks are necessary on the word 'apotheosis' itself and how it came to be used in this double manner of drowning and deification.

The Word *Apotheosis*

The word 'apotheosis' originally emerges in the context of Alexander the Great and points ultimately to the ideology of divine filiation, with Alexander as son of Zeus-Amun.[9] Although the political appropriation of the word 'apotheosis' generally leads

---

[9]The word *apothéōsis* derives from the Greek verb *apotheóō* or *apotheióō*, which emerges in the second century B.C.E. in the literature surrounding Alexander the Great. The Liddell-Scott-Jones Lexicon translates the word after the Latin *deificatio*, 'deification' (*deus* + *ficare*, 'to make god' = *consecratio*, 'consecrate, make sacred'). The common Greek preposition *apó* means 'away from'. When used in constructions with a similar morphology to the word apotheosis (words formed from the *apo-* prefix, a verbal or nominal root, and the *-is* or *-ōsis* suffix) a dual signification emerges. Here *apo-* takes on either a prepositional function or an intensifying function. A few examples serve to illustrate, (i) *apokalypsis*, 'revelation' = *apo* (preposition: 'away from') + *kalyps-* (root verb: *kalypsein*, 'to conceal, hide' + *-is* (feminine declension (3e), denoting 'action') = *apo-kalyps-is*, 'away from concealment', that is 'revelation'. Here the function of *apo-* takes its common meaning, but in this particular construction it serves to signify the opposite activity of the process-noun to which it is attached. *Kalypsis*, 'concealment' thus becomes 'revelation', *apokalypsis*. Similar transformations are observed in words such as *apostasis*; (ii) *apolysis*, 'liberation' = *apo-* (intensifier: 'complete, full, extreme') + *lys-* (root verb: *lysein*, 'to loose, free, liberate') + *-is* (feminine declension (3e), denoting 'action') = *apo-lys-is* 'complete liberation.' Here *apo-* takes on an intensifying function. *Apo-*, instead of turning the noun *lysis* into its opposite, as in the previous example, turns it into its extreme expression, 'complete release, complete liberation.' Clearly, *apothéōsis* belongs to this second category. We can thus define *apotheōsis* as the intensification, the complete or extreme expression, of *theōsis* (deification). There is one further connotation, however, which must not be overlooked. The model here is, (iii) *aposiōpesis*, 'to become silent' = *apo-* (preposition: 'to break away from' + *siōpaein* (root verb: *siōpaein*, 'to become silent') = *apo-siōpes-is*, 'to break off speech and become completely silent.' The word *aposiōpesis* is derived from the verb *siōpaein*, 'to become silent.' *Aposiōpesis* thus means 'to become completely silent,' but it holds the distinct connotation of 'breaking off speech.' Here *apo-* indicates an intensification, to be sure, but its prepositional function also pertains. The difference here is that the preposition does not oppose the root noun, 'silence', as in the first example; rather, it opposes its hidden polar compliment, 'speech'. This sense of 'breaking away from' or 'breaking off' that pertains here to *apo-* becomes all the more prevalent when bearing in mind the cognates of the preposition in Indo-European languages (Sanskrit *apa-*, Latin *ab-*, Germanic *af-*, and so on), all of which evince the same dynamic as we have seen in the Greek, helping us to see the dual signification at play here all the more clearly. Now, if we apply this analysis to apotheosis, we arrive at the following meaning of 'breaking away from mortality to become completely deified.' This sense holds with it the same mutually exclusive quality we saw in *aposiōpesis*, but in relation to mortality, the hidden pole of *theōsis*. Thus, whereas *theōsis* indicates a process of becoming god, where textual contexts invariably describe it as a participation of the soul in the divine, *apo-theōsis* suggests the full breaking away from the mortal condition by becoming completely and utterly divinised. Here the words of Empedocles come distinctly to mind, "I come before you an immortal god, no longer mortal,"

us away from the essence of the matter with which we are concerned, a few important keys are nevertheless concealed in this material, and it will be expedient to dip, albeit briefly, into the ocean of scholarship on Graeco-Roman ruler cult.[10] The enormous influence of Alexander the Great clearly set the mould for all who followed him, but it is important to recognise that he himself was merely following the mythological models set by divinities and heroes, such Dionysus and Heracles. Here the motif of divine filiation becomes pronounced and must be deemed central. Alexander went to extraordinary lengths to confirm his divine lineage as son of Zeus-Amun. Unlike his late Roman imitators, for whom *deificatio* was little more than an extension of their political persona, Alexander took his divine filiation seriously.

In Roman times, apotheosis, *deificatio/consecratio*, became the standard fate of a dead emperor. Following in the footsteps of Alexander and the Hellenistic ruler cult, the emperors Caesar and Augustus clearly established the model that would be subsequently followed. In particular, the emperor's *genius*-bearing image would be promoted as a cult object. On 1 January 42 B.C.E., the Senate decreed Caesar a *divus*, 'god', and the comet that appeared when he died was seen as confirmation of this; symbolically, it was seen as his divine *genius* or soul ascending to heaven. Caesar's son, Octavius, was thus regarded as a *divi filius*, 'son of a god', later receiving the title Augustus. When he died in 14 C.E., the Senate voted and declared him a *divus*, as they had done with his father. With no comet to mark the occasion, an eagle, *aquila*, was released from Augustus' funeral pyre to represent his soul soaring to the Empyrean and henceforth the eagle became a distinct symbol of apotheosis.[11] More and more, the determination of divine status was increasingly secularised by the all-too-human procedures of the Roman Senate. Eventually, the death of the emperor became so synonymous with apotheosis that Vespasian, on his death-bed, famously joked: "O dear, I fear I am becoming a god."[12]

---

quoted in Diels and Kranz, 'fragment 112', in *Fragmente der Vorsokratiker: Griechisch und Deutsch*, Kranz (trans.). Thus, apotheosis may be most accurately, or at least literally, defined as an act by which one 'breaks away from mortality to become completely divine.'

[10]Our discussion relies on the following sources, such as Badian, 'The Deification of Alexander the Great', in *Ancient Macedonian Studies in Honor of Charles F. Edson*, Dell (ed.), p. 27-71; Bosworth, 'Alexander and Ammon', in *Greece and the Mediterranean in Ancient History and Prehistory*, Kinzl (ed.), p. 51-75; Bosworth, 'Alexander, Euripides and Dionysus: The Motivation for Apotheosis', in *Transitions to Empire: Essays in Greco-Roman History 360-146 B.C., in Honor of E. Badian*, Wallace and Harris (eds.), p. 140-166 ; Edmunds, 'The Religiosity of Alexander the Great', *Greek, Roman and Byzantine Studies* 12.3, p. 363-391; Fredricksmeyer, 'On the Background of the Ruler Cult', in *Ancient Macedonian Studies in Honor of Charles F. Edson*, Dell (ed.), p. 145-156; von Gaertringen, 'Apotheosis', in *Paulys Realencyclopadie der classischen Altertumswissenschaft (Second Series)*, von Pauly and Wissowa (eds.) vol. 1, cols. 184-8; Langer, 'Alexander the Great at Siwah', in *Ancient World* 4, p. 109-127; Lehmann-Haupt, 'Alexanders Zug in die Oase Siwah', in *Klio* 24, p. 169-190; Nock, 'Notes on Ruler-Cult, I-IV', in *Journal of Hellenic Studies* 48.1, p. 21-43.
[11]Russell, *The Doctrine of Deification in the Greek Patristic Tradition*, p. 22.
[12]*Vae, puto deus fio*, quoted in Cassius Dio, Cary and Foster (trans.) *Roman History, Vol. VIII: Books 61-70*, 66.17.

At the roots of this lies the ancient belief that a human could not become a god whilst alive. Mortality and immortality were mutually exclusive, as per Heraclitus' chiasmus, "a man is a mortal god; god is an immortal man."[13] In a similar vein, Empedocles could proclaim: "I come before you an immortal god, no longer mortal."[14] Here, however, the initiatic undertones of such a statement imply that mortality is overcome by the philosophical death,[15] as in Orphic and Buddhist praxis; initiation is undertaken as a preparation for death, of learning to "die before you die."

The cult of the deified ruler traditionally took effect after his death. To become a god, you had to die. Alexander was one of the first to seriously challenge this ontological barrier in a political context, seeking to instantiate the rites of his divine cult during his life, a point that proved enormously controversial. From an initiatory perspective, these basic beliefs persisted, but we gain a deeper insight into their fundamental metaphysics. Death represented the barrier between mortality and immortality because the mortal, by nature and definition, was subject to birth and death; only the immortal could transcend such contingencies. To become immortal one had to go beyond death and to do this one had to confront it, something which only the *hērōs*, the very prototype of the *deus filius* whom Alexander sought to imitate, instinctively engaged through the path of virile action. In the esoteric world, the core praxis was no less direct, as it sought to give up mortal life in order to attain the immortal by learning to "die before you die." Initiatory death, and by extension ritual rebirth as an immortal, thus formed the *conditio sine qua non* of apotheosis.

In order to understand the deeper meaning of apotheosis, rather than the political vicissitudes to which the term succumbed, one must look not to the late antique conventions of imperial apotheosis, which are largely propagandistic, but to the contemporary initiatic traditions, which used the term in a very different and much more revealing manner. In the magical and theurgical milieux of Hellenistic antiquity, a rich heritage of esoteric meanings had accrued around the term 'apotheosis'. One of the most revealing of these is the use of the term to signify not just initiatic death, but initiatic death by drowning, and thus an Egyptian mythological context. It is to this that we now turn.

Apotheosis by Drowning

In the fifth century B.C.E., Herodotus records the Egyptian practice of deifying the

---

[13]Diels and Kranz, 'Fragment 62', in *Die Fragmente der Vorsokratiker: Griechisch und Deutsch*, Kranz (trans.).

[14]Diels and Kranz, 'Fragment 112', in *Die Fragmente der Vorsokratiker: Griechisch und Deutsch*, Kranz (trans.).

[15]See Kingsley, Peter, *In the Dark Places of Wisdom*. Inverness: Golden Sufi Centre, 1999.

drowned through mummification,

> When anyone, be he Egyptian or stranger, is known to have been carried off
> by a crocodile or drowned by the river itself, such an one must by all means be
> embalmed and tended as fairly as may be and buried in a sacred coffin by the
> townsmen of the place where he is cast up; nor may any of his kinsfolk or his
> friends touch him, but his body is deemed something more than human, and is
> handled and buried by the priests of the Nile themselves.[16]

From Diodorus of Sicily we learn that the crocodiles themselves were regarded as
equally sacred.[17] F. L. Griffiths saw this as necessarily following from the Egyptian
reality by which those who were drowned in the Nile were often, ultimately, drowned
by crocodiles.[18] However one happened to drown, they were invariably eaten by
crocodiles, which were consequently regarded and feared as a Typhonian force.

In Egypt, 'drowning', *mḥj, ḥrp, 'g3*, appears originally to have signified absolute
extinction, a form of corporeal destruction which rendered afterlife impossible.[19] This
follows from the fact that an intact body was a prerequisite to continued existence in
the afterlife.[20] Along with death by fire, death by water was regarded among the most
feared of Typhonian forces.[21] Only later, from the New Kingdom through to the late
period, were the drowned increasingly regarded as sacred. This is due chiefly to the
increasing significance of the role of Osiris, for whom drowning becomes instrumental
to his revivification and deification. As Hopfner observes, "only after death by drowning
could he [Osiris] become a god."[22] It is thus the myth of Osiris, and more significantly
his death and resurrection at the hands of his enemy, Seth-Typhon, which underpins
the motif of apotheosis by drowning that we meet in the *Greek Magical Papyri*.

---

[16]Herodotus, *Histories*, II.90.

[17]Diodorus Siculus, Oldfather (trans.), *Library of History*. 12 vols., I. 89, 1-3.

[18]Griffith, 'Herodotus II. 90: Apotheosis by Drowning', in *ZÄS* 46, p. 134.

[19]Early references to drowning include *Pyramid Texts* §692 (utt. 396) and §1925 (utt. 666A) with notable
mention of adzes and imperishable stars following, that is the symbolic instruments/powers of the Opening
of the Mouth ritual.

[20]For example, *Books of Breathing* (Book 1); Erik Hornung, *The Ancient Egyptian Books of the Afterlife*.
New York: Cornell University Press, 1999 = *Altägyptische Jenseitsbücher*. Darmstadt: Wissenschaftliche
Buchgesellschaft, 1977; Horrack, P. J., *Le Livre des Respirations d'après les manuscrits du Musée du Louvre*.
Paris: C. Klincksieck, 1877; Goyon, Jean-Claude, *Rituels funéraires de l'ancienne Égypte*. Paris: Editions du
CERF, 1972.

[21]Strauss, C., 'Ertrinken/Ertränken', in *Lexikon der Ägyptologie*, Helck and Eberhard (eds.), col. 17; Leahy,
'Death by Fire in Ancient Egypt', in *Journal of the Economic and Social History of the Orient* 27, p. 2.

[22]Hopfner, Theodor, *Griechisch-Ägyptischer Offenbarungszauber: Mit einer eingehenden Darstellung des
griechisch-synkretistischen Daemonenglaubens und der Voraussetzungen und Mittel des Zaubers überhaupt und
der magischen Divination im besonderen*, p. 130, "erst nach dem Ertrinkungstode konnte er zu einem Gott
werden."

1- Then how could you buy then? What about Sobek? When did this view originate?
2- Would it be better to have the quotes here.

According to the *Interpretatio Graeca*, Typhon corresponds to the Egyptian god Seth, Egyptian *swtk, stš*, Greek *Sēth-Typhōn*, who, as murderer and drowner of Osiris, must be regarded as instrumental to the process of apotheosis by drowning. As Herman te Velde notes, Seth is not only the murderer but also the reviver of Osiris.[23] Upon closer inspection, the mythology of Seth-Typhon reveals a complex divinity presiding over all dangerous thresholds and ontological transitions. As such he is pivotal not only to the death, but also to the rebirth of Osiris; and as Ann Macy Roth has shown, this is implicit in the deeply Sethian symbolism of the Opening of the Mouth ceremony, *wp.t r'*, a rite of rebirth, in which ritual *synthemata*, such as the adze, the bull's thigh, and ritual blades made from meteoric iron, regulate the Sethian threshold between existence and non-existence so crucial to the triumph of the solar procession, *prohodos/processio*, over the inimical forces of chaos, the serpent Apep/*Apōphis*.[24]

This brings us to one of the main points of the present paper, the deeper significance of drowning, as well as the overarching symbolism of all the drowning rites in the *PGM*, as being best understood in the context of the Egyptian solar cosmogony, particularly as expressed in the underworld books. As Erik Hornung points out, "in the late period the Egyptians formally recognised the process of "divinisation by drowning"; monuments were even erected for people who had drowned in the Nile. The Egyptians could thus rest assured that an elaborate, official burial was not the crucial prerequisite for a blessed afterlife."[25] It must be emphasised, however, that with the *Greek Magical Papyri* we are dealing with a rite that is intended not for the common purposes of securing a blessed afterlife *per se*, but with the initiatic purpose of encountering death as a means to apotheosis. As shall be seen, the deeper Egyptian context of this rite only becomes explicit when one examines the nature of the Sun's nocturnal journey. Before we turn to this, however, a few remarks are necessary on the general structure of Egyptian cosmogony.

The Roots of Egyptian Cosmology
Nun and his Hypostases

The theologies of Egypt, of Hermopolis, Memphis, and Heliopolis, are to be seen less as competing ideologies and more as specialised foci within the purview of one integral cosmological perception. From this integral perspective, it may be said that the three chief centres of cosmological doctrine represent the phases of pre-creation; emergence of the creative forces themselves; and creation proper. Accordingly, the theologies elaborate

---

[23]Velde, *Seth, God of Confusion: A Study of his Role in Egyptian Mythology*, p. 84-91.

[24]Roth, 'The Pss-Kf and the 'Opening of the Mouth' Ceremony: A Ritual of Birth and Rebirth', in *JEA* 78, p. 113-47; 'Fingers, Stars and the 'Opening of the Mouth': The Nature and Function of the Ntrwj-Blades', in *JEA* 79, p. 57-79.

[25]Hornung, *Idea into Image*, p. 105 = *Geist der Pharaonenzeit*. Zurich: Artemis, 1990.

the divinities personifying the potential of pre-creation; the divinities personifying creative power; and the *neteru* proper, who constitute the natural cosmos.[26]

The Hermopolitan theology is essentially an elaboration of the Ogdoad, the eight-fold personification of the primordial waters, which is the inert potential which precedes and underpins creation and out of which creation rises. The word 'Ogdoad' comes from the Greek *ogdoas*, but is a direct translation of the Egyptian expression *ḥmnyw*, *ḥmnjw*, 'group of eight.'[27] The primordial waters were conceived as a limitless ocean known as *nw(j)*, 'the watery one,' personified as the male god Nu, and later as Nun. The characteristic qualities of the 'watery one' were further developed as four pairs of gods and goddesses,

(i) wateriness (*nwj*), inertness (*njnj*)	Nun and Naunet
(ii) infinity (*ḥḥw*)	Huh and Hauhet
(iii) darkness (*kkw*)	Kuk and Kauket
(iv) hiddenness (*tnm*)	Amun and Amaunet

As the personification of the primeval waters, Nun was seen as that element which gives rise to and therefore sustains, generates, and animates all things; it came to be signified not only in all life-giving water, such as the Nile and other source-waters, but in all vital life-fluids, such as sap and blood.[28] Thus, because of his status as the ground of all being, Nun was comprehended as the father of the gods, that is, of the first beings.[29] Origin, the ground of being, is not only existentiating, it is also de-existentiating. That which arises out of origin must also sink back into it. This accounts for the simultaneously creative yet destructive potency, or *dynamos*, that origin holds. The primordial waters of life are also the waters of dissolution, the alpha and omega. As such, they delimit the threshold between non-being and being, that which is subject to birth and death, and that which is immortal. For this reason they form the vital crux of apotheosis.

---

[26]The Hermopolitan theology, embodied in Nun, represents the primordial forces of pre-creation in which the divinity and cosmos lie latent. The Memphite theology, headed by Ptah, represents the emergence of the creative potencies, the demiurgic or hypercosmic forces which shape the cosmos, but which are not a part of it. The Heliopolitan theology is represented by Atum, 'the finisher', head of the Ennead, the nine encosmic gods who embody the created cosmos itself. [1]

[27]Hermopolis, Egyptian *ḥmnu*, 'eight-town', is named in honour of the eight divinities of pre-creation; via its Coptic form, *Shmoun*, it survives down to its modern Arabic name, al-Ashmunein.

[28]On water as the primordial element or *archē*, see Thales, who is generally considered the first of the Greek philosophers, who returned from Egypt to teach that the living and causal/animating substance comprising the unity of all things was water, or moisture, which included blood, plant-sap, and the like.

[29]Hornung, Erik, *Conceptions of God in Ancient Egypt: The One and the Many*. New York: Cornell University Press, 1982.

1 - This may be a later or even middle syncretism of the three doctrines. However, they emerged at different times and appear to be distinct, foreign forms of worship introduced into Egypt.

2 - I believe the one-ness of the eight axes considered separately from its components. There is also a dialectic of water-dry, infinite-finite, dark-light, hidden-seen in the Ogdoad.

The Sun's Nocturnal Journey

As Christine Strauss has pointed out, drowning as the means to deification is ultimately bound to the cyclical rebirth of the sun god, who descends nightly into the watery depths of Nun to be reborn again with the morning sunrise.[30] The nocturnal journey of the Sun finds its most distinctive representation in the New Kingdom underworld books, the *Amduat*, which literally means 'what is in the underworld', and the *Book of Gates*.[31] Depicted in royal tombs and on sarcophagi, these so-called *Unterweltsbücher* begin with the Sun's setting in the western horizon and conclude with it rising on the eastern horizon. During the interim, the solar barque moves through the depths of the earth, traversing the twelve hours of the night, which form the structure of the text. The underworld, *dwȝt* or *duat*, is essentially a place of regeneration. It is also a place of ultimate destruction. Despite or perhaps because of such dangers, however, the nightly descent of the Sun into the depths of the netherworld allows the solar divinity to be revitalised. This takes place in the primordial waters of Nun. It occurs precisely at sixth hour, the nadir of the journey, corresponding to midnight.

The fact that this is a soul journey as well as a cosmogonic *processio* is emphasised by the fact that, throughout the *duat*, the sun god takes his nocturnal, ram-headed form. Here the ram represents the *ba*, or *psychē*, of Ra; this is an onomatopoeic rebus, and in addition to *psychē*, 'soul', the word *ba* means 'ram.'[32] The essential concern of the sixth hour of the *duat* is the unification of the divine *ba*-soul with its body, *ḥ.t*. Whereas the *ba* of Ra is represented as a ram-headed divinity, the *body* of Ra is represented as Osiris, the corpse of the sun god, who lies waiting in the waters of Nun to be reanimated by his *ba*.[ ] Interestingly, Osiris, the corpse of Ra, takes the form of a scarab, the beetle that raises the disc of the rising sun, and whose hieroglyph is *ḫpr*, 'to evolve, come into existence, be', prefiguring even in death the form of the rejuvenated, rising sun.[33] The resurrection of the Sun thus proceeds from the moment of unification of what in alchemical terms would be called the 'volatile' and the 'fixed'.[34] [35] After the soul of

---

[30]Strauss, 'Ertrinken/Ertränken', in *Lexikon der Ägyptologie*, Helck and Eberhard (eds.) col. 18; Derchain, 'Kosmogonie', in *Lexikon der Ägyptologie*, Helck and Eberhard (eds.), cols. 749-750.

[31]See Hornung, Erik, *Texte zum Amduat*. Genève: Editions de belles-lettres, 1987-1994. Other notable underworld books from this period include the *Book of Caverns* and the *Book of the Earth*, while in the Armana period, the *Book of Nut*, and the *Book of the Night* recapitulate the same essential themes. For a useful survey, see Hornung, *The Ancient Egyptian Books of the Afterlife*, p. 26-135.

[32]Erman and Grapow, (eds.), *Wörterbuch der ägyptischer Sprache*, p. 410-14.¹

[33]As will be noted later, the scarab also figures in other apotheosis/drowning rites in the *PGM*.

[34]Ra and Osiris; soul and body.

[35]On *ka* and *ba* as volatile and fixed, see Schwaller de Lubicz, *Le Temple de l'homme: Apet du sud à Louqsor* I, p. 65, "Any body, vegetable or animal, is reduced by putrefaction into two separable states, one volatile and the other constituting a fixed residue. This fixed part, when desiccated, contains an alkaline salt. Similarly, but more violently, combustion divides all vegetal or organic bodies into volatile parts, leaving behind an ash containing a fixed, alkaline salt. "Man thou art ash and unto ash thou shalt return". Thus every thing is essentially composed of a volatile part and a fixed part, a generating principle that pharaonic theology, for example, summarises in its teachings on the *ba* and *ka*."

1 - I am presuming these are homonyms with different determinatives.
2 - This interpretation would have been difficult in the Middle Kingdom. It could be Newer Old Kingdom in origin. This raises questions about the nature of Re-Osiris throughout.

the sun god has reunited with its corpse, it proceeds to provide the denizens of the underworld with cloth, clothing, as if to suggest the vital, bodily textures that begin to envelope the solar embryo as it moves from its conception, midnight, to its birth, dawn. As Stricker observes, "ontogeny," for the Egyptians, "recapitulates cosmogony";[36] the development of the being is a mirror of the process of cosmogenesis; both, moreover, are theophanies, a point made explicit in the hermetic maxim, "god has two forms: cosmos and man."[37]

The regeneration of the drowned is one of the many parallel motifs which accompany the central motif of solar regeneration. Here, the waters in which the drowned die are assimilated to the waters by which the drowned are regenerated. In the tenth hour of the *Amduat*, the ninth hour in the *Book of Gates*, the waters of Nun are represented by a large, blue rectangle in which the naked bodies of the improperly buried dead float. By being assimilated to the primordial waters of Nun, however, the annihilating waters that cause death also enable the drowned access to the regenerating capacities of the underworld. Through their assimilation to the rejuvenating underworldly waters, the dead are offered the chance to escape ultimate destruction, represented by the chaos serpent Apophis, the inimical force which Seth conquers, evincing his positive, cosmogonic function through the facilitation of *ḫpr/genesis.* By partaking of the regenerating nature of the primordial waters, the drowned escape destruction and, like Osiris, become sacred, whereupon the Osirian epithet, *ḥsy*, 'sacred drowned, blessed dead,' is applied to them.[38]

The drowned are regenerated by the same power that regenerates the sun god and are thereby immortalised. This is most emblematically represented in the twelfth and final hour of the *Amduat*, where the Sun is depicted, along with the gods and the sacred dead, *ḥsy*, being drawn backwards through the body of a giant serpent symbolising eternity. Entering the serpents tail aged, the gods and the dead emerge from its mouth rejuvenated.[39] However, whereas the Sun and his divine entourage emerge from the underworld reborn, Osiris, and by extension the sacred drowned, must remain in the underworld. It is pre-eminently the power of the Sun, in particular the rising sun represented in Egyptian iconography by the falcon-formed Horus that emerges

---

[36] See Renggli, Franz, 'Der Sonnenaufgang als Geburt eines Babys: Der pränatale Schlüssel zur ägyptischen Mythologie. Eine Hommage an den holländischen Religionshistoriker Bruno Hugo Stricker', in *International Journal of Prenatal and Perinatal Psychology and Medicine* 12.2, p. 365-382.

[37] Scott and Ferguson (trans.), 'Asclepius 1. 10', in *Hermetica: The Ancient Greek and Latin Writings Which Contain Religious or Philosophic Teachings Ascribed to Hermes Trismegistus*, p. 304-305, "Aeternitatis dominus deus primus est, secundus est mundus, homo est tertius [...] cuis sunt imagines duae mundus et homo."

[38] As Griffith has shown, the Egyptian term *ḥsy*, the 'sacred drowned, blessed dead', gives rise to the Osirian epithet *Hēsies*. This is one of the many ways in which Egyptian theology permeates the Greek magical corpus, for the name *Hēsies* occurs in numerous spells of the *Greek Magical Papyri*, precisely in reference to a sacred, blessed or divine entity.

[39] Hornung, *Idea into Image*, p. 105-106.

1- This is a late Old Kingdom interpretation. Is the author saying this appears in ... ? If so, please see note.
2- The trouble with this is that Re doesn't die to the Duat, but travels through it, conquering death.
3- I would like to see this.

victoriously from the underworld as a fully-fledged *renatus*.[40] The character of Horus as *sol invictus/hēlios anikētos* goes a long way to explaining why the magician of *PGM* I. 1–42, although undergoing the general Osirian drama of death and revivification, ultimately identifies himself with the drowned and deified falcon, thus signifying the ability of the invincible Sun to overcome death and emerge as an immortal god.[2] The finer details of the falcon *symbolique* point directly to the divine presence of *phōs*, 'spiritual light', *nikē*, 'victory', and *doxa*, 'glory', which the falcon and eagle, as victorial birds *par excellence*, eminently symbolise.[3] In order to understand this, it is first necessary to examine Horus in his role as divine son, *deus filius*, and here we must place our emphasis less on his divine paternity and more on the divine maternal principle. Only by examining the significance of what it means to be nourished by the deifying power of a goddess will we come to comprehend the deeper meaning of milk as an instrument of apotheosis.[1]

II. Milk, Goddess, Galaxy

The Philosophers thus speak clearly when they teach that the mercury, following the effectuated dissolution, carries the child, the Son of the Sun, the Little King (Kinglet), like a true mother, since in effect the gold is reborn in its womb.

Fulcanelli, *Le Mystère des Cathédrales*

Phenomenologically, milk and honey are both natural foodstuffs produced for the specific purpose of nourishing the young of the given species;[41] they are also the only foods produced for this purpose that are cultivated and consumed by humans. Generally speaking, milk and honey reinforce the motif of nourishment necessary to the newly born, rebirth, and allude to the topography of paradise, lands flowing with milk and honey.[4] Not insignificantly, milk and honey were traditionally given to initiates of the Coptic and Ethiopian Church after baptism, and the symbolism is closely connected. More specifically, however, milk and honey have some very distinct mythological connotations that deeply illuminate the significance of the rite from the *Greek Magical Papyri*. This section will examine the nature of milk as intimately connected with the role of the goddess in initiatory rebirth, as well as the nature of honey as the divine solar principle borne by the goddess' milk. Through this we will

---

[40]Spiegelberg, 'Zu dem Ausdruck *hsj* Hesiēs für die durch Ertrinken im Nil bewirkte Apotheose', in *ZÄS* 53, p. 124, suggests the dead were also identified with the Sun, "Gewiß hängt diese bildliche Darstellung damit zusammen, daß der Tote nicht nur mit Osiris, sondern auch mit dem Sonnengott Rê identifiziert wurde, in dessem Barke er über den Himmel fuhr." (These representations are known to go together; the dead would not only be identified with Osiris, but also with the Sun-god Ra, in whose bark they travel over the heavens.)

[41]Darby, Ghalioungui, and Grivetti, *Food: The Gift of Osiris*, p. 430-440; honey is a royal privilege in Egypt, a "highly expensive commodity" based upon an "industry of luxury."

1 - Sounds like the author is headed off track.
2 - how about, instead, the drowning of the falcon traps its ba in the fluid, which the magician consumes in an archotic identity.
3 - I don't know the falcon of Egypt and the eagle of Rome can be made equivalent here.
4 - Is there a pre-Biblical source for this?

come to a deeper understanding of the power to which the initiate must wed himself, whence the significance of the *paredros*, the magical partner which becomes attached to the magician.[42]

Milk from a Black Cow

In an Egyptian context, 'milk from a black cow' indicates fertility, birth, and nourishment, for the black colour, as is well-known, evoked the fertile nilotic soil that gave Egypt its very name, *km.t*, 'black earth, the black land', as contrasted with *dšrt*, 'the desert, the arid red land'. A black cow is a fertile cow and thus a potential mother.[43] In regards to the symbolism of black, Mathieu has drawn attention to a passage from the *Pyramid Texts* that confirms the more specific connection to maternity, milk, and suckling, "N. has drunk the milk from the two black cows, the two wet-nurses of the *ba*-souls of Heliopolis."[44] From the black cow comes the white milk, and the ancient association of blackness with fertility thus gives rise to the complementary association of whiteness with nourishment, "here," comments Mathieu, "the meeting of the fertile black and the nourishing white, for us paradoxical, finds its full coherence."[45]

More specifically still, we would suggest that the symbolism of white emerging from black may be more deeply understood in terms of contemporary Hellenistic alchemical processes.[46] Here, black and white represent the first two phases of the alchemical

---

[42]The paredros or 'assistant' is in fact the raison d'être of this particular logos. Preisendanz's Beisitzer is truer to the Greek and suggests a comparison with the concept of *systasis*, is in fact the *raison d'être* of this particular *logos*.

[43]"The cow is the perfect mother," writes Svoboda, *Aghora: At the Left Hand of God*, p. 74-75, remarking on the meaning of the sacred cow from the perspective of Aghori Tantra, "and the cow is passionately devoted to her calf, just as a real mother must be to her child. Sometimes the mere sight of the calf makes milk flow from the cow's udders; not drip—flow. I have seen this more than once when I owned a dairy. And if the calf dies the cow refuses to give milk—not like our water buffaloes who can be tricked with the head of a calf on a stick. [...] And not just buffaloes, even your Western cows will give milk whether or not the calf is still alive. When I always say that this is the fundamental difference between East and West I am not just talking through my hat. What is so great about giving milk? All animals do it. The greatness in our Indian cows is that they give milk only out of an outpouring of love. That is the value of cow's milk. Won't at least a little of that love come through into the milk? It must. That emotion separates cows from other animals. So how are we wrong to worship cows? We are not worshipping the hide, hooves, and tail; we worship the essence."[1]

[44]*PT* §531c: *snq-n N. pn m jrṭ.t Jd.tj km.t(j) mn'.tj bꜣ.w Jwnw.*[2]

[45]Mathieu, 'Les couleurs dans les Textes des Pyramides: approche des systèmes chromatiques', in *ENIM* 2, p. 26, "C'est probablement cette association du noir et de la fertilité qui justifie dans les *TP* : « car tu es le Bélier noir, fils de la Brebis noire » (*n ṭwt js Sj km sꜣ Sj.t km.t*); et surtout « N. a tété le lait des Deux Vaches noires, les deux nourrices des Baou d'Héliopolis » (*snq-n N. pn m jrṭ.t Jd.tj km.t(j) mn'.tj bꜣ.w Jwnw*), où la rencontre du noir de la fertilité et du blanc nourricier, pour nous paradoxale, trouve toute sa cohérence."

[46]This is not as much of a stretch as it might first appear, as on one hand, the Graeco-Egyptian alchemical corpus is intimately linked to the *Greek Magical Papyri*; 'protochemical recipes' of the *Leiden Papyrus*, for instance, come from the *Demotic Magical Papyri*, abbreviated as *PDM*, which forms a unified corpus with the *PGM*. On the other hand, alchemy itself has its roots deep in the 'black' earth of Egyptian temple cult.

1-Netthebetreudoue,
2-Muckbetter

transmutation, *melanōsis*, 'blackening', and *leucōsis*, 'whitening', in which the dark, fertile *prima materia*, 'virgin earth', secretly contains and gives rise to an occult white or silver, the virgin milk. Just as the black contains the white, so too does the white culminate in the emergence of the tincture, the chromatic principle proper, firstly with *xanthōsis*, 'yellowing', in which occult gold emerges from the white matrix, and finally *iōsis*, 'reddening' or 'purpling', in which the immortalising alchemical tincture is made present in its most virulent form.[47]

The black cow and its virginal milk thus represent the first chromatic shift in the Hermetic opus, *melanōsis* to *leucōsis*, 'perfect black' to the 'pristine white'. The honey, the solar falcon, on the other hand, represents the presence of the masculine tincture that enters or develops within the purified feminine body, inducing the transition from white to gold/red, the *citrinitas* and *rubedo* that imbues the goddess' milky body with the Sun's radiant lustre. Taken as a whole, we are dealing with a feminine, black-lunar matrix and a masculine, golden-solar embryo that comes to fruition within this matrix. Theologically, we are dealing with Isis as the 'black virgin' who nourishes the golden *divus filius*, Horus, on her divine 'virgin's milk'. Such a motif could delay us indefinitely if we were to trace its resonances throughout alchemy and Christianity. But the Egyptian funerary texts are explicit enough, as we are presented with the image of a cow suckling her young, the cow numen as divine wet-nurse, the goddess that feeds initiates and divinities alike on her immortalising milk. For this reason, when the dead king of the *Pyramid Texts* becomes a *renatus*, he is identified with a calf, suckled by a black cow to signify his nourishment by the fertile divine mother.

Isis and Hathor

In pharaonic iconography, both Isis and Hathor are represented as cows. They are not only mothers, but transmitters of divine sovereignty, effectuating thereby the link between divinity and royalty. In the *Pyramid Texts*, the pharaoh drinks the divine milk from the breasts of his mother Isis, an image replicated by a wealth of statuettes of Isis seated on a throne suckling the young Horus.[48] In the Hathor chapel in Queen Hatshepsut's XVIII Dynasty temple at Deir el-Bahari, the pharaoh is depicted suckling on the udders of Hathor in her cow form.[49] In both cases, the suckling of the king by his divine wet-nurse is merely a recapitulation of the suckling of Horus by Hathor. Here in the papyrus marshes, in the form of a wild cow, Hathor suckles and nourishes

---

A reappraisal of evidence for the Egyptian origins of alchemy is given in our forthcoming essay, 'The Perfect Black: Egypt and Alchemy', in *Alchemical Traditions*, Aaron Cheak (ed.). Melbourne: Numen Books, 2012.
[47] See Hopkins, 'A Study of the Kerotakis Process as Given by Zosimos and Later Alchemical Writers', p. 328.
[48] Hart, *The Routlege Dictionary of Egyptian Gods and Goddesses*, p. 80-81.
[49] Hart, *Egyptian Gods and Goddesses*, p. 63.

1. Neither example is of the suckling of Horus by Hathor. Hatshepsut was a female pharaoh who declared herself a man.

the young god on his rightful divine power. That Horus is gaining more than mere milk is corroborated by a complementary image in which the king receives from Hathor the *mn'.t* necklace, a symbol of divine *charisma* or grace'.[1] In such images we are to recognise that the pharaoh is not merely imbibing common milk, but rather the very power of divine sovereignty itself, the force that makes him the living symbol of Ra-Horus on earth. This power is nothing less than the royal *ka* and is identical with the Avestan concept of the *xvarnah*, 'light, glory, victory', which took the form of a falcon.[50][2]

Hathor has a specific relation to Horus, the falcon, and by extension the pharaoh, the king as incarnation of Horus, that consolidates the deeper symbolism at play in the *Greek Magical Papyri*. While many goddesses, including Isis, took cow forms, Hathor was the perhaps most preeminent in this role. According to the *Interpretatio Graeca*, Hathor was regarded as the Egyptian Aphrodite.[3] She was depicted as a cow, or as a goddess with the ears and horns of a cow; significantly, between her horns she bore the solar disc, *aten*. Although Hathor wasn't the only Egyptian goddess depicted as a cow, she was the only one who uniformly took these characteristics in her anthropomorphic form. Moreover, because her horns bore the disk of the Sun, she was a quintessentially solar goddess. It is here that her close connection to Horus becomes explicable. This relationship is confirmed all the more by the fact that the name Hathor itself, *ḥt-ḥr*, 'Hat-Hor', literally means the 'house or mansion of Horus'; in hieroglyphic, her name is depicted by a falcon within a rectangular enclosure.

Hathor (ḥt-ḥr), the 'Mansion of Horus'

The same deep connection between Hathor, the cow, and the Sun also persists in Hellenistic astrology, and here it may be noted that the zodiacal sign of Taurus, the bovine, is ruled by Venus-Aphrodite, the planetary divinity associated with the 'warm', solar lineage as opposed to the 'cool', lunar lineage. Astrologically, and theologically, the difference between Venus and the Moon corresponds to that between Venus/Aphrodite/Hathor, and Artemis/Diana/Isis;[4] metallurgically, and alchemically, it is the difference between copper, which bears a golden or solar tincture, and silver, which is pure.[51] Just

---

[50]Stricker, 'Varegna the Falcon', in *Indo-Iranian Journal* 7.4, p. 310-317.

[51]These are the traditional associations between the planetary divinities and their planetary metals; the theological basis of such connections is evident in the fact that our word for copper actually comes from an ancient name for Venus-Aphrodite, Kypri, which in turn gave the name to her ancient cult site, Kypris, an

1 – cp. w/ Freyja's necklace, Brisingamen, and her daughter – Menglad u. Egyptian 𓂝𓈖𓈖𓈖𓏏𓎡, Menaht.

2 – "identical" is too strong. Perhaps distant cognate. I don't know that the power is the ka. The ka may possess the power.

3 – very significant. Thank you for the reference.

4 – Both correct and incorrect – Isis as Sekhmet not as Isis perse.

as these two metals are the best conductors of electricity, next to gold, so too are their respective feminine divinities to be regarded as either sensuous, resplendent bearers, or pure, virginal reflectors of the Sun's divine light.

The idea that Hathor bears something of the Sun's tincture or energy goes a long way to explaining the presence of honey, a pre-eminently royal and solar symbol, in the divinising milk of the *Greek Magical Papyri*. If milk is feminine and lunar and honey golden and solar, then Hathor, who bears the epithet 'the golden one', is thus the divine feminine bearer of this royal tincture, the alchemical *xanthōsis* or *iōsis*. That Isis and Hathor are both nourishers and, in effect, mothers of Horus, brings us to an important point that requires clarification. Horus, Isis, and Hathor, as well as Osiris, are presented in shifting roles that blatantly contradict the ordinary standards of familial logic. In looking at the relationships, we find,

    (i) Isis as mother of Horus; Isis as wife of Horus
    (ii) Hathor as mother of Horus; Hathor as wife of Horus
    (iii) Horus as brother of Osiris; Horus as son of Osiris.

Horus thus has the role of both the child-god and sky-god[1]. Hart gives a good summary of the usual, historical explanation for this,

> The king of Egypt is called "son of Hathor." This of course leads to a complication since the king as Horus is the son of Isis. It seems most probable that Hathor is the original mother of the hawk-god in the cycle of myth where Horus and Seth are brothers. She gave way to Isis when the legend was absorbed into the myth of Osiris, necessitating Horus to become the son of that goddess in order to gain the throne of Egypt. There is a further realignment in the relationship when Hathor becomes regarded as the wife of the sky-god Horus of Edfu.[52][2]

At the root of these shifting roles, however, lies a deeper theological paradox whose metaphysical implications thoroughly eclipse the historical explanation. It is summarised in the phenomenon by which the son is also the father of his mother. This morphology occurs in numerous theological traditions, but in Egyptian texts we find it in the expression *ka-mut-tef*, the 'bull of his mother', which is applied to the pharaoh as incarnation of Horus.[3]

Essentially we are dealing with the phenomenon of a tri-unity in which the *ka*, which means both 'bull' and 'spirit', indicates the active masculine force in the triad; *mut*, the mother, represents the feminine receptive force; while the child or son represents the product. However, the paradox that binds the three aspects of this lineage into a

---

ancient source of copper.
[52]Hart, *Egyptian Gods and Goddesses*, p. 80-81.

1- Here, distinct roles of different periods are being imposed on each other. Ultimately, the confusion comes from syncretisms of Horus with other cults being reintroduced into the cycle interpretation.
2- Horus is older in Egyptian myth than Osiris. Hathor is quite young. It is difficult to place Hathor before Isis unless there is an old living demon reference I am unaware of.
3- I don't know ka was bull. But "bull" does not imply father.

triangular unity lies in the fact that the son, by recapitulating, and indeed reincarnating his father, becomes thereby the bull, the spirit and inseminator of his mother. In short, he is the father of himself. Rather than being a simple product, he exists both in a primary state, before the separation or differentiation into gendered polarity, and in an ultimate state, after the two poles have been differentiated and then recombined, per the alchemical *conjunctio* or *cohabation*. The motif has a number of important resonances in Platonic and alchemical metaphysics that cannot be detailed here, suffice to say that the tri-unity equates to the *eidos*, 'form/father', *hypodochē*, 'receptacle/mother', and *mimēma*, 'copy/offspring', of Plato's *Timaeus*, while in alchemy it equates to the *tria prima* of sulphur, mercury, and salt, that is cinnabar, or mercuric sulphide, being the salt of mercury and sulphur.[53]

Among other things, this phenomenon explains why Horus is both son and brother of Osiris, and by extension, brother and nephew of Seth. In terms of the goddess, it explains how the unity of *divus filius* to the *diva matrix* is not only a maternal bond but a conjugal bond. These two relationships thus explain the presence of Isis, as virgin mother, and Hathor, as venusian lover, in the initiatic process, in which Horus is, at varying stages, both son and lover of the goddess.

Oil of Lilies

Our suggestion that the milk of the drowning rite refers to the divine nourishment that enables the initiate to partake of divinity is closely corroborated by specific details from other drowning rites from the *Greek Magical Papyri*. PGM VII.628-42, in particular, instructs the initiate to drown/deify a field-lizard not in milk but in "oil of lilies." This detail of the substance in which the entity is drowned confirms the overarching

---

[53]This theme is discussed at length in our doctoral dissertation, *Light Broken through the Prism of Life: René Schwaller de Lubicz and the Hermetic Problem of Salt*. University of Queensland, 2011. We may note that the distinction here may be compared to the relationship between the simultaneously paternal and maternal aspects of the alchemical process in which one substance or entity is both agent, sulphur; patient, mercury; but also instrument, salt, of one single act. In the tomb of Ramses IX, the pharaoh as *ka-mut-tef* is depicted as the hypotenuse of a right-angled triangle and just as the hypotenuse both separates and reconnects the two lines of the right-angle, effecting thereby the juncture of abstract and concrete, the vertical and the horizontal, so too is the alchemical sulphur-mercury dyad reconciled, as *initium* and *telos*, in the integrating salt. To understand this is to understand that linear causality, being time-bound, and therefore only able to comprehend reality within temporal sequence does not grasp how the hypercosmic creative principle is at once *archē* to the material substratum, which in turn is the material matrix, womb, of the physical prime substance, a material recapitulation of the hypercosmic 'father', born through the material 'mother' as the incarnate 'son'. Here, as in Trinitarian theology, the *logos*, or *spermatikos logos*, is in fact eternal and pre-exists its manifestation; it incarnates in matter through the material mother in order to give visible form to the invisible father. It is at once seed, womb, and fruit. It may also be noted that the presence of the bull, *ka*, as both spirit and masculine/inseminating principle points to the deeper reason behind the thigh of the bull in the Egyptian Opening of the Mouth ritual and thus the associated role of Seth-Typhon in the Osirian dramaturgy.

1 - Needs illustration.
2 - I don't believe this is a correct interpretation.

presence of the goddess as *diva matrix*.[54]

The *Geōponica*, a seventh century Byzantine agricultural manual, informs us that lilies first came into being when the goddess Hera spilt her breast milk upon the earth. Lilies are thus the earthly signatures of the goddess' milk. Although expressed in different symbolic language, we are presented with nothing less than the exact same mythologeme that we meet in Egyptian sources, nourishment of the initiate on the immortalising milk of a goddess. The *Greek Magical Papyri*, by alluding to both Egyptian and Greek reflexes of the same theological reality, thus demonstrate a remarkably subtle cultural dexterity in its choice of *materia magica*, a hermeneutic sensitivity that cannot be dismissed as mere syncretism. The context of this detail is equally revealing. Hera, the ever-jealous wife of Zeus, spilt her divine milk precisely when she realised that the son of Zeus to a mortal woman was suckling on her breast. This *divus filius* was none other than Heracles, the very model that Alexander emulated in his historical quest for apotheosis.[55] Although Heracles' status as a semi-divine entity, *hērō*, followed from the fact that his father was a god, he was still half mortal. Zeus schemed to make him a complete god by tricking Hera into suckling him on her deifying milk, thereby fulfilling his divine ontogeny. According to other sources, Hera soon realised the ruse and pulled the child off her breast, spilling her divinising milk upon the earth in the process. According to the *Geōponica*, Heracles simply turned away from the breast when sated. In any event, before the milk fell upon the earth, it flowed through the sky. And so, what we have here is not only the genesis of lilies from divine breast milk, but also the origin of the Milky Way,

> When Jupiter had Hercules by Alcmena, who was mortal, he wished to make him partaker of immortality; and he laid him to Juno's breast, when she was asleep, while he was in the state of infancy; and the infant being satisfied with milk, turned away from the breast, but the milk still flowed copiously when the infant was removed; and what was diffused in the sky made what is called the milky-way; and what flowed on the earth and tinged its surface, produced the lily, which is like milk in respect of colour.[56]

---

[54] There are other spells in the *Greek Magical Papyri*, which prescibe drowning; different creatures are drowned and in different substances. *PDM* xiv. 636-69, for instance, prescribes the drowning not of a falcon but of a scarab in the milk of black cow. Other spells, such as *PGM* III. 1-64, prescribe the drowning of a cat in water to make it an *Esiēs*, or a falcon in wine to cause evil sleep, as seen in *PDM* xiv. 743-49. The nature of the materials has very specific connotations. As such, not all should be expected to reflect the exact chain of mythological references that we are detailing in the present paper.

[55] Heracles and Dionysus, both sons of Zeus to mortal women, formed the heroic and divine role models for Alexander, who tradition also considered as a son of Zeus.

[56] Owen (trans.), *Geōponica* 11.19, p. 81-82. See also, Manilius, Goold (trans.), *Astronomica*, Book 1; the divine suckling of Heracles by Hera is mentioned in more traditional sources, but without reference to either the Milky Way or to lilies.

Thus, the substances in which the falcon, lizard, or scarab are drowned, and deified, all point to the motif of divine suckling and rebirth. On one hand, 'milk from a black cow' indicates the milk of the goddesses Isis and Hathor, the bovinomorphic wet-nurses of the sun god Horus, while on the other hand, 'oil of lilies' points to the myth of Heracles being suckled on the immortalising milk of Hera. But this same milk is also the source of the Milky Way and as such, this last example provides the final key that we need in order to open up the deeper cosmological layers of the drowning motif in the *Greek Magical Papyri*. It takes us not only into the depths of Orphic-Bacchic mythology, but also invites us to return to some overlooked aspects of the Egyptian cosmograph with which we began.

Fallen into Milk

As Burkert has rightly suggested, Pythagorean, Orphic, and Bacchic Mysteries might best be understood as distinctly overlapping religious domains. While minimalist scholars have tended to play down any suggested connection between Pythagoreanism, Orphism, and Bacchic cultus, the discovery of new evidence, notably the gold plate uncovered at Valentia in southern Italy in 1969, provides a positive and incontrovertible link between Orphic and Dionysian ritual, and an initiation to immortality through death and revivification.[57] The process, mirroring on an individual level the cosmic journey undergone by the Egyptian solar divinity is clear. It is inaugurated by a *katabasis* or *descensus* into the underworld. The full implications of this have been drawn out most adeptly by Peter Kingsley, who situates the gold lamellae, and the related Bacchic and Pythagorean Mysteries, precisely in the context of initiatory rebirth symbolism.[58]

Among the bewildering complex of overlapping evidence for underworldly initiation, one textual fragment strikes a note of resonance that enables us to tie together a number of important threads. In an Orphic lamella discovered in a tumulus at Thurii, southern Italy, the Bacchic initiate is identified as a kid, *eriphos*, 'a young goat', signifying the *renatus* regenerated from initiatory death and nourished by the milk that flows from the breasts of the goddess, Persephone. Inscribed upon a thin sheet of gold, the inscription runs,

> *theos egenou ex anthrōpo.*
> *eriphos es gala epetes*

You have become a god instead of a mortal.

---

[57] Burkert, *Orphism and Bacchic Mysteries: New Evidence and Old Problems of Interpretation; Protocol of the Twenty-Eighth Colloquy*, 13 March 1977, p. 7.
[58] See Kingsley, *Ancient Philosophy, Mystery, Magic: Empedocles and Pythagorean Tradition*, p. 256-272.

1. This interpretation is tootenuous, given the evidence thus presented to base an argument on - even a good -sounding one.
2. Orphic and Dionysios is not so much the issue as the Pythagorean.
3. Description

A kid you fell into milk.[59]

Here, falling *es gala*, "into milk"[60] suggests a deeper cosmological coherence. The Greek word for milk, *gala*, gives us our word for 'galaxy' because it was originally applied to the Milky Way, with *gala* meaning 'milk', and *galaktos* meaning 'galaxy'; the *via lactea*.[61] To fall "into milk" takes on the additional meaning of 'diving into the stars' and thus of joining one's primordial, divine lineage. In effect, the milk of the goddess and the stars of the Milky Way are identical realities, and the initiate's descent into the underworld is simultaneously an ascent into the nocturnal heavens.

This motif of falling into milk to become a god, along with milk as an *Urelement* that provides the newborn divinity with its essential nourishment, brings us directly into contact with the deification motif of the *Greek Magical Papyri* of drowning, literally, apotheosis, in the milk of a black cow. Through these connections, deification in milk, rebirth, being suckled by a goddess, we begin to discern the significance that ingesting a divine substance, an *entheon*, holds for the process of apotheosis; at the same time, we realise that it is explicity bound to the process of initiatic death. All of this points to a very particular paradox lying at the heart of initiation, where just as one must die to be reborn, so, too, is it apparent that the means by which one is killed is also a deifying source of nourishment.[62] This explains why, in the Pythagorean, Orphic, and Bacchic *katabasis*, it is Persephone, the queen of the underworld, who plays the role of divine wet-nurse and initiatrix.

Heimarmenē

One further point needs to be made to properly understand the meaning of falling into the goddess' galactic milk. The galaxy specifically represents the domain of fixed stars that lie beyond the seven wandering stars, the *planetēs* or planets, which in traditional cosmology were seen to govern fate in the sublunary realm. The integration of the initiate into the primordial, celestial lineage is thus tantamount to overcoming the phenomenon of astral fatality, *heimarmenē*, transcending thereby the seven ontological

---

[59]Graf and Johnston (eds.), *Ritual Texts for the Afterlife: Orpheus and the Bacchic Gold Tablets*, p. 8-9; Burkert, *Orphism and Bacchic Mysteries: New Evidence and Old Problems of Interpretation; Protocol of the Twenty-Eighth Colloquy*, 13 March 1977, p. 44·

[60]See also *eriphos es gal epeton*, "a kid I fell into milk," quoted in Graf and Johnston (eds.), *Ritual Texts for the Afterlife: Orpheus and the Bacchic Gold Tablets*, p. 12-13; Kern, *Orphicorum Fragmenta*, 32c.

[61]*Galakt-*, 'milk', Mann, *An Indo-European Comparative Dictionary*, p. 389.

[62]Compare the Latin motto found on a 1585 portrait of what is believed to be Christopher Marlowe: *quod me nutrit, me destruit*, translated as "what nourishes me destroys me." For parallels to this motif in the writings of Marlowe and Shakespeare, see the discussion in Wraight, A. D. and Stern, Virginia, F., *In Search of Christopher Marlowe: A Pictorial Biography*. London: MacDonald, 1965; N.B. also in this regard the motif of the pelican nourishing its young with its own blood, which becomes significant in the imagery of European alchemy.

levels of the Hermetic cosmos. This is the deeper meaning of the *voces magicae*. The magician demonstrates his mastery over astral fatality by singing the seven descending and ascending vowels, sinking into fatality from above and rising above it from below. In effect, the initiate willingly drowns to be deified because, at the root of the septenary, but also beyond it lies its transcending culmination, its alpha and omega. Beyond the seven lies the eight, the octave or *ogdoad*, the eight hypostases of the god Nun that form the roots of Egyptian cosmogony and into which both the dead and the divine sink in order to be regenerated.

This distinction between astral fatality, the seven planets, and astral immortality, the fixed stars, is symbolically replicated in the choice of waters offered to the Orphic initiate. Repeated references in the gold lamellae to the Lake of Memory allude to the topography of the Greek underworld. The soul arrives "parched with thirst and dying" and a choice between two rivers confronts the deceased. On the left is the river Lethe, the Waters of Forgetfulness, which wipes one's memory clean and casts one back into the cycle of incarnations to live out another embodied life in the "heavy, difficult circle," *kyklo barypentheos argaleoio*. On the right is another river, which enables memory, for its waters are those of *anamnesis*. The memory afforded by this water, however, is of a specific kind, as it is not the memory of common, accumulated, human knowledge, but of the soul's knowledge, a knowledge of one's true, eternal, and divine nature, which is not earthly but sidereal.

In several of the gold lamellae, the Orphic initiate is admonished to "drink from the water of the river on the right,"[63] and it is evident that this remembrance, this gnosis of one's divine origin, is tantamount to apotheosis.[64] As such, gnosis equates to victory over the forces of forgetfulness induced by the process of incarnation. For the descent into matter corresponds to amnesia, *amnēsis*, of one's divine nature, just as ascent corresponds to its remembrance. Plato, writing after the Orphics but before the Gnostics, affirms the same essential motif as a philosophical doctrine, where knowledge is memory. Moreover, with Plato the fact is found encoded in the Greek word for 'truth', *alētheia*, literally meaning 'freedom from forgetfulness,' where the *alpha privativum* signifies 'absence of' or 'freedom from' the condition of *lētheia*, for example Lethe, the River of Forgetfulness.[65]

---

[63] Here "right" is to be understood in accordance with the Pythagorean correspondences of the *monad* versus the *dyad*.

[64] We are justified in using the word *gnōsis* insofar as we meet an identical soteriological paradigm in the 'Gnostic' texts discovered at Nag Hammadi in 1945. Herein, gnosis is precisely equated with a liberating knowledge of one's divine origin, which is located in the *plerōma*, the 'fullness' that precedes all created existence.

[65] It is not irrelevant to add that the *leth-* lexeme is cognate with English 'lethargy,' such that the word *a-lētheia* continues to possess the secondary connotations of waking and vigour versus lethargy and torpor. If sleep and forgetfulness are the companions of death, then waking and remembering are the companions of eternal life.

The astral or sidereal dimension is emphasised throughout the Orphic *Totenpässe*. Indeed, identification with one's sidereal lineage forms the key to the process of immortalisation; the Orphic texts specifically and repeatedly admonish the initiate to proclaim their astral geniture in order to be able to drink of the immortalising waters of *Mnemosyne*, the Well of Memory. To the guards who protect the well, the initiate is specifically admonished to proclaim,

> I am a child of Earth and starry Sky,
> but my race is heavenly. You yourselves know this.
> I am parched with thirst and am dying; but quickly grant me
> cold water flowing from the Lake of Memory.[66]

A lengthier lamella runs as follows,

> This is the work of Memory, when you are about to die
> down to the well-built house of Hades. There is a spring at the right side,
> and standing by it a white cypress.
> Descending to it, the souls of the dead refresh themselves.
> Do not even go near this spring!
> Ahead you will find the Lake of Memory,
> cold water pouring forth; there are guards before it.
> They will ask you, with astute wisdom,
> what you are seeking in the darkness of murky Hades.
> Say, "I am a son of Earth and starry Sky,
> I am parched with thirst and dying; but quickly grant me
> cold water from the Lake of Memory to drink."
> And they will announce you to the Chthonian King,
> and they will grant you to drink from the Lake of Memory.
> And you, too, having drunk, will go along the sacred road on which other
> glorious initiates and *bacchoi* travel.[67]

Such remarks draw out the duality of human nature, described here as part mortal, *Gē pais eimi*, "I am a son of earth," and part divine, *Ouranou asteroentos*, "of starry heaven."[68] Clearly, to realize, to have gnosis, that one's true race, or *genē*, is "of heaven

---

[66] Graf and Johnston (eds.), *Ritual Texts for the Afterlife: Orpheus and the Bacchic Gold Tablets*, p. 8-9; Burkert, *Orphism and Bacchic Mysteries: New Evidence and Old Problems of Interpretation; Protocol of the Twenty-Eighth Colloquy, 13 March 1977*, p. 6-7.

[67] Graf and Johnston (eds.), *Ritual Texts for the Afterlife: Orpheus and the Bacchic Gold Tablets*, p. 8-9; Burkert, *Orphism and Bacchic Mysteries: New Evidence and Old Problems of Interpretation; Protocol of the Twenty-Eighth Colloquy, 13 March 1977*, p. 5.

[68] See Graf and Johnston (eds.), *Ritual Texts for the Afterlife: Orpheus and the Bacchic Gold Tablets*, p. 8-9; Burkert, *Orphism and Bacchic Mysteries: New Evidence and Old Problems of Interpretation; Protocol of the Twenty-Eighth Colloquy, 13 March 1977*, p. 6-7.

— there is a later, Medieval Grail myth of the white tree.

alone" is to re-orient oneself toward one's sidereal and ouranian *genus* rather than one's human and earthly genesis. Falling "into milk" thus bears not only a linguistic but a symbolic coherence with the concept of celestial immortality.

To conclude our discussion of the goddess as galactic matrix of apotheosis and to tie it into the evidence adduced for the Sun's journey through underworld, it should be noted that the essential identity of the Pythagorean, Orphic, and Bacchic *Totenpässe* on one hand, and the Egyptian *Unterweltsbücher* on the other, becomes all the more clear when we recognise that the solar journey passed through the body of the goddess Nut. Whether it progressed through the celestial world or the underworld, the Sun's procession was always conceived as proceeding through water, and the divine entourage was depicted traversing the depths and heights of cosmos on barques.

III. Conclusion

In the rite from the *Greek Magical Papyri* with which we began, the galactic river of the Milky Way, the celestial mirror of the Nile, is specifically evoked through the power of Orion, "who causes the currents of the Nile to roll down and mingle with the sea." For just as the Nile was the source of all fertility on earth, so too was the galaxy of milky stars a deeper, cosmic reflection of the same nourishing life-force. In this way, the Egyptians and Orphics alike affirmed an essential, fluid continuity between the heavens, the earth, and the underworld. Here, the fertile character of the Nile and the immortal character of the heavens themselves proceeded precisely from their still deeper connection to the primordial regenerating source of all being, the cosmogonic waters of Nun. Given the foregoing, the essence of the *PGM* rite may be seen to reside precisely in the role of the feminine numen as a matrix for apotheosis. As Evola emphasises, "a very widespread symbolism has seen in woman a vivifying and transfiguring power, through which it is possible to overcome the human condition."[69] The divine *via lactea*, moreover, also represents the galaxy, the river of fixed stars, the white which is born from the midst of the perfect black. Just as the primordial darkness, the ocean of Nun, bears the river of eternal stars, so too are the waters of final dissolution also those of primordial deification. *Initium* is *telos*. Just as Dante's ascent to heaven required a descent into the *inferno* and only proceeded upwards once he had reached the cosmic nadir, the centre of the earth, the core of hell, so too, at the root of Orphic, Egyptian, and alchemical cosmology lies the perception that the underworldly journey is the gate to a celestial journey.[70] Both seek to dive into the river of rejuvenating milk by descending into the de-existentiating darkness of the underworld. And yet it is clear that the underworld is only the realm of death for mortals; for those of celestial origin, it is a path home, a

---

[69] Evola, Stucco (trans.), *The Mystery of the Grail: Initiation and Magic in the Quest for the Spirit*, p. 21.
[70] Dante, *Inferno*, XXXIV., p. 91-139.

1 – Not supported in the text.
2 – I would disagree that the waters of the N. [Nile] and of chaos are of the same source.

gate to the eternal.[71]

---

[71] It may be noted that the ancient imagery of death as a sidereal journey continues to this day in modern Europe. Several years ago we chanced upon a roadside grave in Füssen, Bavaria. Not only did it restate the very essence of the Orphic underworld texts, it also alluded to the descent of the sun in the West, *Abendland*, literally 'evening-land', *Es kam der Abend und ich tauchte in die Sterne*, which is translated as "Evening came and I dove into the stars."

BIBLIOGRAPHY

Badian, E., 'The Deification of Alexander the Great'. In *Ancient Macedonian Studies in Honor of Charles F. Edson*, edited by Harry J. Dell. Thessaloniki: Institute for Balkan Studies, 1981.

Betz, Hans Dieter (ed.), *The Greek Magical Papyri in Translation, Including the Demotic Spells*. 2nd ed. Chicago: University of Chicago Press, 1992.

Bosworth, A. B., 'Alexander and Ammon'. In *Greece and the Mediterranean in Ancient History and Prehistory*, edited by K. H. Kinzl. Berlin: Walter de Gruyter, 1977.

Bosworth, A. B., 'Alexander, Euripides and Dionysus: The Motivation for Apotheosis'. In *Transitions to Empire: Essays in Greco-Roman History 360-146 B.C., in Honor of E. Badian*, edited by R. W. Wallace and E. M. Harris. Oklahoma: Norman, 1996.

Brashear, William M., 'The Greek Magical Papyri: An Introduction and Survey; Annotated Bibliography (1928-1994)'. In *ANRW*, vol. 2, 18.5: 3380-684. Berlin: Walter de Gruyter, 1995.

Burkert, Walter, *Orphism and Bacchic Mysteries: New Evidence and Old Problems of Interpretation; Protocol of the Twenty-Eighth Colloquy, 13 March 1977*. Berkeley: The Centre for Hermeneutical Studies in Hellenistic and Modern Culture, 1977.

Cassius Dio, *Roman History, Vol. VIII: Books 61-70*. Translated by Earnest Cary and Herbert B. Foster. Loeb Classical Library 176. Cambridge: Harvard University Press, 1925.

Cheak, Aaron, *Light Broken through the Prism of Life: René Schwaller de Lubicz and the Hermetic Problem of Salt*. PhD diss., University of Queensland, 2011.

Cheak, Aaron, 'The Perfect Black: Egypt and Alchemy.' In *Alchemical Traditions*, edited by Aaron Cheak, forthcoming. Melbourne: Numen Books, 2012.

Darby, William, Ghalioungui, Paul, and Grivetti, Louis, *Food: The Gift of Osiris*. London: Academic Press, 1977.

Derchain, Philippe, 'Kosmogonie'. In *Lexikon der Ägyptologie*, III, cols. 747-756. Wiesbaden: O. Harrassowitz, 1972.

Diels, Hermann, and Kranz, Walther, *Fragmente der Vorsokratiker: Griechisch und Deutsch*. Translated by Walther Kranz. 6. verb. Aufl. Berlin: Weidmannsche Verlagsbuchhandlung, 1951.

Diodorus Siculus, *Library of History*. 12 vols. Translated by C. H. Oldfather. Loeb Classical Library. Cambridge: Harvard University Press, 1933-1967.

Edmunds, Lowell, 'The Religiosity of Alexander the Great'. In *Greek, Roman and Byzantine Studies* 12, no. 3, 1971: 363-91.

Erman, Adolf and Grapow, Hermann (eds.), *Wörterbuch der ägyptischer Sprache*. Berlin: Akademie Verlag, 1971.

Evola, Julius, *Il mistero del graal e la idea imperiale ghibellina*. 2. ed. Milano: Ceschina, 1962.

Evola, Julius, *The Mystery of the Grail: Initiation and Magic in the Quest for the Spirit*. Translated by Guido Stucco. Rochester: Inner Traditions, 1994.

Fowden, Garth, *The Egyptian Hermes: A Historical Approach to the Late Pagan Mind*. Princeton: Princeton University Press, 1993.

Frankfurter, David, 'Ritual Expertise in Roman Egypt and the Problem of the Category 'Magician''. In *Envisioning Magic: A Princeton Seminar and Symposium*, edited by Peter Schäfer and Hans G. Kippenberg. Leiden: Brill, 1997.

Faulkner, Raymond Oliver (trans.), *The Ancient Egyptian Pyramid Texts*. Oxford: Clarendon Press, 1969.

Fredricksmeyer, E. A., 'On the Background of the Ruler Cult'. In *Ancient Macedonian Studies in Honor of Charles F. Edson*, edited by Harry J. Dell. Thessaloniki: Institute for Balkan Studies, 1981.

Fulcanelli, *Le Mystère des Cathédrales*. Paris: Société Nouvelle des Éditions Pauvert, 1964.

Gaertringen, Hiller von, 'Apotheosis'. In *Paulys Realencyclopadie der classischen Altertumswissenschaft* (Second Series), edited by August Friedrich Von Pauly and Georg Wissowa, vol. 1, cols. 184-8. Stuttgart: Druckenmuller, 1914.

Godwin, Joscelyn, *The Mystery of the Seven Vowels in Theory and Practice*. Michigan: Phanes, 1991.

Goyon, Jean-Claude, *Rituels funéraires de l'ancienne Égypte*. Paris: Editions du CERF, 1972.

Graf, Fritz and Johnston, Sarah Iles (eds.), *Ritual Texts for the Afterlife: Orpheus and the Bacchic Gold Tablets*. New York: Routledge, 2007.

Griffith, F. L., 'Herodotus II. 90: Apotheosis by Drowning'. In *ZÄS* 46 1909: 132-4.

Guthrie, W. K. C., *A History of Greek Philosophy. Vol. I: The Earlier Presocratics and the Pythagoreans*. Cambridge: Cambridge University Press, 1962.

Hart, George, T*he Routlege Dictionary of Egyptian Gods and Goddesses*. London: Routledge, 2005.

Helck, Wolfgang and Otto, Eberhard, (eds.), *Lexikon der Ägyptologie*. Wiesbaden: O.Harrassowitz, 1972

Herodotus. *The Persian Wars I: Books 1-2*. Translated by A. D. Godley. Loeb Classical Library Volume 117. Cambridge: Harvard University Press, 1920.

Hopfner, Theodor, *Griechisch-Ägyptischer Offenbarungszauber: Mit einer eingehenden Darstellung des griechisch-synkretistischen Daemonenglaubens und der Voraussetzungen und Mittel des Zaubers überhaupt und der magischen Divination im besonderen*. Amsterdam: Adolf M. Hakkert, 1974.

Hopkins, Arthur John, 'A Study of the Kerotakis Process as Given by Zosimos and Later Alchemical Writers'. In *Isis* 29, 1938: 326-54.

Hornung, Erik, *Altägyptische Jenseitsbücher*. Darmstadt: Wissenschaftliche Buchgesellschaft, 1977.

Hornung, Erik, *Conceptions of God in Ancient Egypt: The One and the Many*. Ithaca: Cornell University Press, 1982.

Hornung, Erik, *Texte zum Amduat*. Genève: Editions de belles-lettres, 1987-1994.

Hornung, Erik, *Geist der Pharaonenzeit*. Zurich: Artemis, 1990.

Hornung, Erik, *Idea into Image: Essays on Ancient Egyptian Thought*. New York: Timken, 1992.

Hornung, Erik, *The Ancient Egyptian Books of the Afterlife*. Translated by David Lorton. Ithaca: Cornell University Press, 1999.

Horrack, P. J., *Le Livre des Respirations d'après les manuscrits du Musée du Louvre*. Paris: C. Klincksieck, 1877.

Kern, O., *Orphicorum Fragmenta*. Berlin: Weidmann, 1922.

Kingsley, Peter, *Ancient Philosophy, Mystery, and Magic: Empedocles and Pythagorean Tradition*. Oxford: Clarendon Press, 1995.

Kingsley, Peter, *In the Dark Places of Wisdom*. Inverness: Golden Sufi Centre, 1999.

Kirk, G. S., Raven, John Earle, and Schofield, Malcolm, *The Presocratic Philosophers: A Critical History with a Selection of Texts*. 2nd ed. Cambridge: Cambridge University Press, 1983.

Langer, Patricia, 'Alexander the Great at Siwah'. In *Ancient World* 4, 1981: 109-127.

Leahy, Anthony, 'Death by Fire in Ancient Egypt'. In *Journal of the Economic and Social History of the Orient* 27.2, 1984: 199-206.

Lehmann-Haupt, C. F., 'Alexanders Zug in die Oase Siwah'. *Klio* 24, 1931: 169-190.

Liddell, Henry George, Scott, Roberts, Jones, Henry Stuart, McKenzie, Roderick, and Barber, Eric Arthur, *A Greek-English Lexicon*. Rev. and augm. ed. Oxford: Clarendon Press, 1968.

Manilius, *Astronomica*. Translated by G. P. Goold. Loeb Classical Library. Cambridge: Harvard University Press, 1977.

Mann, Stuart E., *An Indo-European Comparative Dictionary*. Hamburg: H. Buske, 1984.

Mathieu, B., 'Les couleurs dans les Textes des Pyramides: approche des systèmes Chromatiques'. In *ENIM* 2, 2009: 25-52.

Nock, Arthur Darby, 'Notes on Ruler-Cult, I-IV'. In *Journal of Hellenic Studies* 48.1, 1928: 21-43.

Nock, Arthur Darby, and A. J. Festugière (eds.), *Corpus Hermeticum*. Paris: Société d'édition "Les Belles lettres", 1945.

Otto, Eberhard, *Das ägyptische Mundöffnungsritual.* 2 vols. Ägyptologische Abhandlungen, Bd. 3. Wiesbaden: Harrassowitz, 1960.

Owen, Thomas (trans.), *Geōponica: Agricultural Pursuits.* London: J. White, 1805-1806.

Pausanias, *Description of Greece, Volume IV: Books 8.22-10 (Arcadia, Boeotia, Phocis and Ozolian Locri).* Translated by W. H. S. Jones. Loeb Classical Library 297. Cambridge: Harvard University Press, 1935.

Preisendanz, Karl Lebrecht and Henrichs, Albert, *Papyri Graecae Magicae: Die griechischen Zauberpapyri.* 2., verb. Aufl. 2 Bänder. Sammlung wissenschaftlicher Commentare. Stuttgart: Teubner, 1973.

Renggli, Franz, 'Der Sonnenaufgang als Geburt eines Babys: Der pränatale Schlüssel zur ägyptischen Mythologie. Eine Hommage an den holländischen Religionshistoriker Bruno Hugo Stricker'. In *International Journal of Prenatal and Perinatal Psychology and Medicine* 12.2, 2000: 365-382.

Rilke, Rainer Maria, *Briefe aus Muzot.* Leipzig: Insel, 1935.

Ritner, Robert Kriech, *The Mechanics of Ancient Egyptian Magical Practice.* Studies in Ancient Oriental Civilization no. 54. Chicago: Oriental Institute of University of Chicago, 1993.

Roth, Ann Macy, 'The Pss-Kf and the 'Opening of the Mouth' Ceremony: A Ritual of Birth and Rebirth'. In *JEA* 78, 1992: 113-47.

Roth, Ann Macy, 'Fingers, Stars, and the 'Opening of the Mouth': The Nature and Function of the Ntrwj-Blades'. In *JEA* 79, 1993: 57-79.

Russell, Norman, *The Doctrine of Deification in the Greek Patristic Tradition.* Oxford: Oxford University Press, 2005.

Schäfer, Peter and Kippenberg, Hans G. (eds.), *Envisioning Magic: A Princeton Seminar and Symposium.* Leiden: Brill, 1997.

Schwaller de Lubicz, R. A., *Le Temple de l'homme: Apet du sud à Louqsor.* Paris: Dervy, 1993.

Scott, Walter, and Ferguson, Alexander Stewart (trans.), *Hermetica: The Ancient Greek and Latin Writings Which Contain Religious or Philosophic Teachings Ascribed to Hermes Trismegistus*. Oxford: Clarendon Press, 1924.

Spiegelberg, W., 'Zu dem Ausdruck hsj Hesiês für die durch Ertrinken im Nil bewirkte Apotheose'. In *ZÄS* 53,1917: 124-5.

Strauss, Christine, 'Ertrinken/Ertränken'. In *Lexikon der Ägyptologie*, edited by Wolfgang Helck and Otto Eberhard, cols. 17-9. Wiesbaden: O. Harrassowitz, 1972.

Stricker, B. H., 'Varegna the Falcon'. In *Indo-Iranian Journal* 7.4, 1964: 310-17.

Svoboda, Robert E., *Aghora: At the Left Hand of God. Brotherhood of Life*, 1986; New Delhi: Rupa, 1994.

Velde, Herman te, *Seth, God of Confusion: A Study of His Role in Egyptian Mythology and Religion*. Leiden: Brill, 1967.

Wraight, A. D., and Stern,Virginia F., *In Search of Christopher Marlowe: A Pictorial Biography*. London: MacDonald, 1965.

THE HIERARCHICAL COSMOS OCCULT THEOLOGY AS A DIRECT CONTINUATION OF NEOPLATONISM

BY

CHRISTOPHER A. PLAISANCE

From this One there has autonomously shone forth the self-sufficient god, for which reason he is termed "father of himself" and "principle of himself"; for he is first principle and god of gods, a monad springing from the One, preessential or principle of essence.

Iamblichus, *On the Mysteries of the Egyptians*

This is a paper in the history of philosophy. Its goal is to explore the thesis that Neoplatonism acted as the source for both the emanation cosmology and the rigidly hierarchical angelologies and demonologies that pervaded late Medieval and early Renaissance works on theurgy and goetia. As such, the paper begins by examining the Platonic roots of Neoplatonism, paying special attention to the theory of Forms espoused in the *Republic* and that of the demiurge found in *Critas* and *Timaeus*. Following this, the paper delves into Neoplatonism proper, beginning with an analysis of Plotinus' four-tiered emanative cosmos, and then heading forward in time to Iamblichus' *praxês* that developed in response to Plotinus' metaphysics, particularly the practice of theurgy and the end goal of *henôsis*, 'union'. The paper then makes a brief foray into the Judaic infusions that Neoplatonic metaphysics were met with in their transmission from the Mediterranean coasts to Western Europe, the primary form of influence in this case being one of nomenclature, with the hierarchical cosmos conceived by the Neoplatonists being given Hebrew names stemming from the Bible and the myths surrounding King Solomon. Following this, the paper looks at the theologies presented in medieval occult philosophies as exemplified by two texts, *The Book of the Sacred Magic of Abramelin the Mage* and *The Lesser Key of Solomon*, and correlates this with the previously examined Neoplatonic belief and praxis.

The Definitions

To begin, let us define our principal terms. The first, 'Neoplatonism', can be defined as the post-Platonic stream of philosophy that primarily flourished between the third and sixth centuries A.D., and whose hallmark ideas concentrated upon uncovering the

~ 79 ~

1~ are these necessarily Judaic?

second, on the ideas

implicit order of the cosmos as being hierarchical in nature, and that the orientation of the hierarchy is emanative.[1] The second, *theourgia*, 'theurgy', which means 'divine rite',[2] was conceived by the Neoplatonists as a path distinct from both theoretical work and rational theology. Theurgy was thought of as the 'practical' wing of Neoplatonic praxis, and specifically the practices, rituals, and prayers used to invoke, or 'call down', the influence and presence of the gods that were believed to occupy a higher place than man in the metaphysical chain of emanation.[3] The emphasis in theurgical practice on the divine being called down from 'above' is important to note here because it sets up the Medieval view of theurgy as being the divine counterpart to the infernal arts of evocation. *Goêteia*, 'goetia' which also means 'sorcery', 'juggling' or 'cheatery', was "more or less synonymous with magic, but with negative connotations, as distinguished from the more elevated theurgy."[4] As one contemporary theurgist writes, "to invoke is to call in, just as to evoke is to call forth or out."[5] It is for this reason that medieval treatises which dealt with both theurgy and goetia invariably segregated the two, treating the former as the higher and more noble art, and the latter as the lower and more base practice.

Platonic Origins

No treatment of Neoplatonic thought can begin without at least a brief exploration of Platonism as the foundational system upon which it is largely a hermeneutic. While a full examination of Plato's philosophy would stretch far beyond the boundaries imposed by this paper's size and scope, there are two key ideas found in his late thought that are imperative for us to detail for the Neoplatonic modifications to be fully grasped. First and foremost, Plato's theory of Forms looms in the background, being a necessary point of reference to any discussion of multi-tiered hierarchical cosmologies. The English word 'Form', which is generally capitalized in connection with Plato, is used to translate two terms which Plato used for the same concept, *eidos*, 'that which is seen', 'form', 'shape', or 'figure', and *idea*, 'the look of a thing, as opposed to its reality'.[6] The theory of Forms is outlined most clearly in the *Republic*, where Plato demonstrates his theory as a solution to the problem of universals.[7] To do so, he takes the example

---

[1] Remes, *Neoplatonism*, p. vii-viii.
[2] All Greek orthographic and etymological notes are derived from Liddell, H. G. and Scott, Robert (eds.), *An Intermediate Greek-English Lexicon: Founded upon the Seventh Edition of Liddell and Scott's Greek-English Lexicon*. Oxford: Oxford University Press, 2000.
[3] Remes, *Neoplatonism*, p. 170-171.
[4] Peterson, *The Lesser Key of Solomon: Lemegeton Clavicula Salomonis*, p. xiii.
[5] Crowley, Hymenaeus Beta (ed.), *Magick: Liber ABA, Book 4*, Parts I-IV, p. 147.
[6] Copleston, *Greece and Rome*, vol. 1 of *A History of Philosophy*, p.164.
[7] Roughly speaking, the problem of universals concerns the relationship between universals, for example the idea of redness, and particulars, for example concrete instances of red. The Platonic position described above derives particulars from universals. Aristotle reversed this flow, positing that universals were built up from particulars. Both positions fall into the modern taxonomic groping of realism, in that they both treat

1 - Hence Soros' "juggles".

of a bed. The bed made by a carpenter, Plato argues, is "only a bed;"[8] it is a particular instance of something that we recognize as belonging to the overarching type of phenomenon called 'Bed'. The particular bed of the carpenter is however "a somewhat dark affair in comparison to the true Form of the Bed."[9] What he means by this is that the Form of an object is the perfect universal of which instantiated particulars are but an imperfect reflection. That is to say that reality is emanative in nature, with the sensory world of phenomena being the lower tier of a dyadic cosmos, a level of existence in which plurality of instantiation radiates forth from a unity of conception. Each Form is a monadic unity. All plurality that exists in the world of perception is due to the reflective emanation of the Form when it shines from the upper level down into the lower. It is as if each Form is a star. That star casts light that is reflected in a myriad of imperfect ways as it penetrates the atmosphere. Yet these disparate reflections are all manifestations of one perfect source, the Form. This top to down orientation of Platonic metaphysics is the source of the Neoplatonic postulations that reality is both layered and that there is a unidirectional vector of contingency leading from the upper to the lower.[10]

The second element of Platonic thought that we must examine is that of the *demiourgos*, 'demiurge' which can mean 'one who works for the people', 'framer', or 'maker'. This term was, in Plato's day, commonly used to refer to common craftsmen and artisans. In the *Timaeus* dialogue, the demiurge is described as the animating motive behind creation, as the "reason becoming and this universe were framed," and as he "who framed them."[11] If the motion of all bodies is caused by the motion of an antecedent body acting upon it, it is natural to suppose that all motion leads back to a primal source, a being which Plato's student Aristotle described so famously as the "unmoved mover."[12] The demiurge then acts as the prime rational cause that initiates the ordering of the chaos that Hesiod described as existing prior to the shaping of things by the gods.[13] This notion of there being a 'singular' source that all resultant order was contingent upon is the source of the One around which all Neoplatonic thinkers center their metaphysical hierarchies. The demiurge is distinct from the God of classical theism in a very important respect as he is not a creator *per se*, but is a shaper as the very word 'demiurge' implies, for the Greeks had no conception of *ex nihilo* creation.[2] Something must always come from something else, there is no nothingness that exists apart from God and there is only the fluxating chaos that was ordered into actuality by

---

universals as being real in a metaphysical sense. In contrast to realism is nominalism, which treats universals as mere names for artificial groupings of phenomena. See Loux, Michael J., *Metaphysics: A Contemporary Introduction*. New York: Routledge, 2010, p. 17-18, 41.

[8]Plato, Grube and Reeve (trans.), *Republic*, p. 266.
[9]Plato, Grube and Reeve (trans.), *Republic*, p. 267.
[10]Remes, *Neoplatonism*, p. ix.
[11]Plato, 'Timaeus', in *Greek Philosophy: Thales to Aristotle*, Allen (ed.), p. 270.
[12]Aristotle, 'Metaphysics', in *Introduction to Aristotle*, McKeon (ed.), p. 285.
[13]Hesiod, 'The Theogony of Hesiod', in *Hesiod, Homeric Hymns, Homerica*, Evelyn-White (trans.), p. 87.

1 – Why not multiple unmoved movers? Why just one shaper? If one cannot be explained, why not many?
2 – In Gnostic theory he is also inferior to God and evil

the demiurge. Although in Plato's metaphysical system there is but one ordered layer of reality for the demiurge to shape, the Neoplatonists had no trouble transforming this to suit the increasing complexity of their cosmic manifold.

Neoplatonic Emanation

Plotinus, 204–270 A.D., was an Egyptian thinker whose "teaching and writings… form the backbone of Neoplatonic philosophy."[14] His writings, collected by his student Porphry as the *Enneads*, detail the foundational doctrines of Neoplatonism. As principally a commentator on Plato, there was much in his thought that was shared in common with his antecedent, yet there was equally much innovation and development of root ideas found in Plotinus as well. The commonalities include,

"A commitment to a first principle."[15]
"A proliferation of metaphysical layers and entities."[16]
The idea that "the metaphysically prior is always more powerful, better and more simple or unified than the metaphysically lower."[17]
That reality is "essentially mined or intelligible."[18]
That the perfection of the top of the hierarchy leads to an upwardly directed striving for those beneath.[19]

There are, however, numerous ways in which these common ideas were modified by the Neoplatonists. For the purposes of this paper, the most important distinction are the ways in which Plato and Plotinus differently conceived of reality's layering. Plotinus, and the Neoplatonists such as Porphry, Iamblichus, and Proclus who followed him, adhered to a cosmology composed of four emanations of,

The One, *To Hen*, literally meaning 'the one'.
The Intellect, *Nous*, meaning 'mind' or 'perception'.
The Soul, *Psychê*, meaning 'breath', 'life' or 'spirit'.
The Physical, *Physis*, meaning 'the nature' or 'natural qualities of a thing'.

The One[20] is also identified by Plotinus as *theos*, 'god', and sits at the very top of the series of *hypostasis*, 'that which settles at the bottom' or 'emanations that proceed downwards from it'. In contrast to the classical theists who would follow him, Plotinus

14 Remes, *Neoplatonism*, p. 19-21.
15 Remes, *Neoplatonism*, p. 7.
16 Remes, *Neoplatonism*, p. 7.
17 Remes, *Neoplatonism*, p. 7.
18 Remes, *Neoplatonism*, p. 8
19 Remes, *Neoplatonism*, p. 8.
20 For clarity's sake, I will capitalize the emanations as proper nouns.

did not identify the One with being. Indeed, Plotinus saw the One as transcendent to being for, "being is varied and many, whereas the One is absolute simplicity, and hence is not among beings but beyond being."[21] The One is uncaused, like Plato and Aristotle's demiurge. For, as Plotinus tells us, if it were itself caused by anything then it would not be the ultimate metaphysical category, and thus must self-caused.[22] While Neoplatonic metaphysics are monistic in that the One is both the highest category and is the source of all emanations secondary, tertiary, and quaternary to it, it is important to note that this is not the kind of illusory vision of plurality and temporality we find in the ontologies of the Eleatics, such as Parmenides or Zeno. Rather, the descending levels of reality are real, generated by and contingent upon the levels immediately higher. Thus, the One does not immediately generate all levels beneath it, but births the layer directly under it, which in turn does the same and so on.[23]

Immediately emanating from the One is the Intellect, which is identified by Plotinus as the Platonic world of Forms.[24] This secondary level of *hypostasis* is that of being. For, as mentioned earlier, in Neoplatonic metaphysics being emanates from the One, which is henologically prior to it.[25] The ideal world of the Intellect is characterized by a plurality of Forms, which are the "true or real beings"[26] from which all material beings emanate. In this regard, we may consider Neoplatonism to be in line with contemporary realism in that universals and ideas are real metaphysical entities that exist independent from particular and instantiated conceptions of them in a mind.[27]

However, just as the Neoplatonic schema differs in that it does not place the world of Forms as the ultimate metaphysical layer. It also differs in that it does not place the perceptible world directly beneath the Forms. In the Neoplatonic system there is a further intermediary realm that affects the emanative transition from ideal to actual. In classical Platonism there is, it seems, an abyss that yawns between the ideal Forms and the actual instantiations. Plotinus, however, sought to naturalize this by positing a transitional layer betwixt the two. This third level is that of the Soul.[28] As each *hypostasis* brings us closer to the human experience, it is unsurprising that the Soul level "even more emphatically than the Intellect sounds like something human."[29] The Soul functions as an intermediary step between the atemporal realm of the Intellect and the wholly temporal Physical. Thus, while the Soul itself is not strictly temporal,

---

[21] Remes, *Neoplatonism*, p. 49.
[22] Plotinus, 'Enneads', in *Neoplatonic Philosophy: Introductory Readings*, Dillon and Gerson (eds.), p. 176.
[23] Remes, *Neoplatonism*, p. 53.
[24] Plotinus, 'Enneads', in *Neoplatonic Philosophy: Introductory Readings*, Dillon and Gerson (eds.), p. 74.
[25] Here we must use henology in place of ontology, as *ontos*, 'being', is not the ultimate category involved, with that honor going to *hen*, 'one'.
[26] Remes, *Neoplatonism*, p. 54.
[27] Remes, *Neoplatonism*, p. 54.
[28] Remes, *Neoplatonism*, p. 55.
[29] Remes, *Neoplatonism*, p. 55.

it is the agent through which flux comes to be. The actions of the Soul create temporal succession and give this succession a directional vector that is responsible for producing the perception of time as a continuum in the fourth and final emanation.[30] As in so much of Greek thought, we find that ensoulment is not a particular feature that is limited to humanity. Rather than the kind of bifurcation between man and the world that humanism espouses, the Neoplatonists naturalized the *Psychê* and espoused a panpsychist[31] position in which Soul was participated in by all.[32] Furthermore, for Plotinus the Soul was the animating principle that brought life to the inanimate forms. He saw life and change as being fundamentally entwined, which is why they both have their genesis in the same emanatory layer.

The fourth tier of the cosmic ladder is the Physical world of materiality and sense perception.[33] This world is the culmination of the emanative process. As such it demonstrates both the greatest unfolding of the potentiality of the One into actuality and at the same time is the furthest from the perfection of the One. While we are all too familiar with our experience of this level of reality, it will do much good at this point to step back and examine just how this emanative schema explains the experience of sensory phenomena in the final layer. Let us take as an example a brown horse that we witness running across a field.[34] The horse appears as a unified being that is able to be identified as such due to its participation in the principle of unity that is at the top of the metaphysical ladder, the One. Its 'whatness', that aspect of its intelligible structure that identifies it as participating in 'horseness', is a reflection of the ideal Form of the Horse and is owed to the second emanation, the Intellect. The horse is also alive and is driven by an internal impetus to strive onwards and persist in time as a being whose goal is to actualize its potentiality. This animating core is caused by the third layer, the Soul. Finally, we come back to our immediate experience of the 'thatness' of this particular horse as an imperfect representative of the ideal Form that we hold in our minds of what a Horse really is. This horse before us has myriad imperfections as it limps slightly, its color is not as pure as it could be, and so on. This is the product of the culmination of the emanative process. The imperfect and temporal multiplicity that shines down from the perfected One.

Theurgy

Arising as a consequence of the experience of the imperfection of the final emanative

---

[30]Remes, *Neoplatonism*, p. 56.
[31]Panpsychism, deriving from the Greek roots *pan*, 'all' or 'everything', and *psychê*, 'mind' or 'spirit', is the position that all things have a mind or mind-like quality. While for some schools of thought this quality is more specifically mental in nature, in the case of Neoplatonism, it is Soul.
[32]Skrbina, *Panpsychism in the West*, p. 61.
[33]Remes, *Neoplatonism*, p. 58.
[34] This example is taken from Remes, *Neoplatonism*, p. 58-59.

layer was the practice of theurgy. Theurgical rites emerged from the innate orectic
impulse to rectify the imperfect state of multiplicity, and to return to the henologically
prior state of unity and perfection.[35] The end result, the *magnum opus* of the theurgic
process, was termed *henôsis*, 'oneness' or 'union'.[36] *Henôsis* was thought of as the
culmination of the climbing of the emanative ladder, the final state resulting from the
reversal of the hypostatic transformation. The means by which this result was obtained
was through the invocation of the various gods who inhabited the realms above the
fourth emanation. The purported ability of the theurgist to call down the divine into
the material sphere at first, however, appears pregnant with a problem, because if the
vector of causation is unidirection and strictly proceeds from the upper levels to the
lower, how is it that beings in the lowest sphere could exert any influence over those in
the higher layers, for in Neoplatonic theology the divine is clearly "not a self-evident
part of human nature, but a thing over and above it."[37]

That being the case, how does the theurgist accomplish his task? In his *On the Mysteries
of the Egyptians*, Iamblichus, 245-325 A.D., an Assyrian Neoplatonist who was a
contemporary of Plotinus' protege and biographer Porphry, was quick to resolve this
problem. What he proposed was that rather than attempting to command or control
the gods, theurgic praxes managed to shape the soul of the seeker so that the higher
beings would deign to descend.[38] The difference, then, is that the gods are invited into
the receptacle that the theurgist, through the correct practice of meditation, prayers,
and rituals, has transformed himself into the receptacle. He is like a lightening rod
which, by virtue of his very constitution, naturally calls down the fire from the heavens.
Through theurgy, man is able to bridge the gap between all the emanations, elevating
his soul into the form of a hollow tube, a tube through which the divine influence is
free to flow. This interfusion of the gods of the upper emanations into the lower has, in
its initial phases, the effect of raising the theurgist's soul to the level of the gods, in other
words, *theôsis*, meaning 'divinization' or 'deification'. It is only with the completion of
the theurgic process that the *theôsis* of the medial levels reaches the final state of *henôsis*,
perfect union with God.[1]

Divine Hierarchies

It is also in the writings of Iamblichus that we find the beginnings of the explicit
hierarchical ordering of the varying classes of holy beings which the Neoplatonists
believed populated the cosmos. Just as Thales before him,[39] Iamblichus' world was one

[35]Shaw, *Theurgy and the Soul: The Neoplatonism of Iamblichus*, p. 5.
[36]Dillon and Gerson (eds.), *Neoplatonic Philosophy: Introductory Readings*, p. 367.
[37] Remes, *Neoplatonism*, p. 171.
[38]Iamblichus, 'On the Mysteries of the Egyptians', in *Neoplatonic Philosophy: Introductory Readings*, Dillon
and Gerson (eds.), p. 229-230.
[39]"There are some, too, who say that soul is interfused throughout the universe: which is perhaps why Thales

1- This is the essential idea behind Indo-European magical practice, and is part of the idea of ritual purification and a purified and ascetic lifestyle.

that teemed with gods. Following the fourfold emanative cosmological scheme detailed above, Iamblichus presents us with a four-tiered theology to match,[40]

The Gods, *Theos*, meaning 'god', both in the general and particular sense.
The Daemons, *Daimôns*, meaning 'a god' or 'the link between gods and men'.
The Heroes, *Êrôs*, meaning 'inferior local deities' or 'patrons of tribes, cities, and so on'.
The Pure Souls, *Psychai Achratoi*, meaning 'undefiled' or 'immaculate person'.

Far from this being the only division, Iamblichus delineates a myriad of interwoven subdivisions within these four hierarchies, just as post-Plotinian Neoplatonists did with Plotinus' cosmological schema. The first and henologically highest class of beings, the gods, were divided into several sub-classes differently by different Neoplatonic thinkers. Sallustius, a fourth century Latin, presented a dichotomy in the first tier between *egkosmioi*, 'the cosmic' and *hyperkosmioi*, 'hypercosmic' gods, and within the latter he further sub-divided that into a threefold structure that mirrors the anthropic division of one's *ousia*, 'being', *nous*, and *psychê*.[41] Both Iamblichus and his successor Proclus proposed similar sub-hierarchies within the top tier as well.

The intermediary classes, the daemons and heroes, "bind together in a continuous link from highest to lowest and make indivisible the community of the universe"[42] that exists between the gods and the pure souls. The daemons "serve the will of the gods, make manifest their hidden goodness, and give form to their superior formlessness."[43] If a god is the being of whatever sphere of the cosmos is being considered, then the corresponding daemons would be the Forms and ideas that that being takes as it gathers shape in its emanative descent into the material world. Further down the chain are the heroes, beings who are "more akin to the gods, but still far inferior to them."[44] The heroes are thus the active agents who directly interface between the aethereal realms above and the material spheres below. If we say that the daemons "represent the lowest extension of the gods, one could say that the heroes represent the highest degree of the soul"[45] making the plenum between the highest and lowest emanations a fluid

---

supposed all things to be full of gods." Aristotle, Hicks (trans.) *De Anima*, p. 33.
[40]Dillon (ed.) (trans.), 'Introduction to Iamblichus', in *Iamblichi Chalcidensis in Platonis Diologos Commentariorum Fragmenta*, p. 49.
[41]Dillon (ed.) (trans.), 'Introduction to Iamblichus', in *Iamblichi Chalcidensis in Platonis Diologos Commentariorum Fragmenta*, p. 48.
[42]Dillon (ed.) (trans.), 'Introduction to Iamblichus', in *Iamblichi Chalcidensis in Platonis Diologos Commentariorum Fragmenta*, p. 49.
[43]Dillon (ed.) (trans.), 'Introduction to Iamblichus', in *Iamblichi Chalcidensis in Platonis Diologos Commentariorum Fragmenta*, p. 49.
[44]Dillon (ed.) (trans.), 'Introduction to Iamblichus', in *Iamblichi Chalcidensis in Platonis Diologos Commentariorum Fragmenta*, p. 49.
[45]Kazlev, *Iamblichus' Hierarchy of Spiritual Entities*, http://www.kheper.net/topics/Neoplatonism/Iamblich-beings.htm.

continuum. Below the heroes are the pure souls, which are a "somewhat free-ranging class of beings... endowed with very partial powers."[46] These are the lowest category of praeterhuman entities who, although are able to travel freely about the spiritual world, they "seem to retain about themselves something of the universal potentialities of the human soul."[47]

Christianization

In the intervening years between the peak of the Mediterranean Neoplatonism of Plotinus, Porphry, Iamblichus, Proclus, and so on, and the thoroughly Catholic theologies of Augustine of Hippo' and Thomas Aquinas, there were a handful of transitional thinkers who were responsible for Christianizing Neoplatonic philosophy and theology. Foremost among these thinkers was a man now known as the Pseudo-Dionysius, a late fifth century theologian and philosopher about whose personal life little is known.[48] Within the confines of our current discussion on divine hierarchies, his most important work was the tract *De Coelesti Hierarchia*, a highly influential work which adapted the Neoplatonic emanative schema to Christianity. It was through this work of the Pseudo-Dionysius that the gods, daemons, heroes, and pure souls of Iamblichus were translated into the Christian experience turning the Neoplatonic entities into varying types of angels.[49] What he presented us with is a nine-fold order with three classes, each with three sub-classes, that emanates forth from God,

The Godhead.

The First Triad.[50]
Seraphim, *śərāfîm*, which in Hebrew means 'burning ones'.
Cherubim, *kərūvîm*, which in Hebrew means 'winged angels'.
Thrones, from the Greek *thronos*, meaning 'seat' or 'throne'.

The Second Triad.[51]
Lordships, from the Latin *dominatio*, meaning 'dominions'.

---

[46]Dillon (ed.) (trans.), 'Introduction to Iamblichus', in *Iamblichi Chalcidensis in Platonis Diologos Commentariorum Fragmenta*, p. 51.
[47]Dillon (ed.) (trans.), 'Introduction to Iamblichus', in *Iamblichi Chalcidensis in Platonis Diologos Commentariorum Fragmenta*, p. 51.
[48]Copleston, *Medieval Philosophy: From Augustine to Duns Scotus*, vol. 2 of *A History of Philosophy*, p. 91.
[49]Pseudo-Dionysius, 'On the Heavenly Hierarchy', in *Dionysius the Aeropagite, Works*, 1897, Parker (trans.), p. 110.
[50]Pseudo-Dionysius, 'On the Heavenly Hierarchy', in *Dionysius the Aeropagite, Works*, 1897, Parker (trans.), p. 121.
[51]Pseudo-Dionysius, 'On the Heavenly Hierarchy', in *Dionysius the Aeropagite, Works*, 1897, Parker (trans.), p. 124.

Virtues, from the Greek *dynamis*, meaning 'power', 'force' or 'virtue'.
Authorities, from the Latin *potestas*, meaning 'powers'.

The Third Triad.[52]
Principalities, from the Latin *principatus*, meaning 'rulers'.
Archangels, from the Greek *archangelos*, meaning 'chief or principal angel'.
Angels, from the Greek *angelos*, meaning 'messenger' or 'one that announces'.

This proved to be such an influential schema that it was adopted by Thomas Aquinas in his *Summa Theologica*, thus becoming canon.[53] While the specific contents of the hierarchical configuration varies from thinker to thinker, the same four-tiered pattern was replicated well into the late medieval and early Renaissance grimoires, such as the *Lemegeton*, which provided the theurgist with exhaustive lists of individual angels within these hierarchies and detailed rites to attract their influence and cajole them into descending to the material plane.[54]

It was the last member of the hierarchy that was, under the moniker of the 'guardian' angel, to become one of the most important points of focus in the theurgical practices which were later derived from the Pseudo-Dionysius' works. For it was this class of tutulary angels which were closest to men and who were able to facilitate "the elevation, and conversion, and communion, and union with God,"[55] that was the goal of all theurgists. One of the most famous texts to deal specifically with the theology and methodology behind the attainment of the Knowledge and Conversation of the Holy Guardian Angel is *The Book of the Sacred Magic of Abramelin the Mage*. This text details a six month extended theurgic operation designed to elevate the soul of the aspirant so that he might become a receptacle for the protective angel that inhabits the mode of being henologically prior to him.[56] With the attainment of this *apotheôsis*, 'to become divine', came access to a whole host of abilities described as magic or sorcery, for it was through the perfection of the 'higher' art of theurgy that the gates to the 'lower' art of goetia were opened.

It is in the inclusion of a 'demonic', as opposed to 'daemonic' counterpart to the angelic hierarchy, that the medieval theurgists distinguished themselves from their late Classical forefathers. What occurred was the development of what C.S. Lewis jokingly termed

---

[52]Pseudo-Dionysius, 'On the Heavenly Hierarchy', in *Dionysius the Aeropagite, Works*, 1897, Parker (trans.), p.126.
[53]Aquinas, Fathers of the English Dominican Province (trans.), *Summa Theologica*, Volume 1, Part 1, p. 533.
[54]Peterson, *The Lesser Key of Solomon: Lemegeton Clavicula Salomonis*, p.57-58.
[55]Pseudo-Dionysius, 'On the Heavenly Hierarchy', in *Dionysius the Aeropagite, Works*, 1897, Parker (trans.), p.127.
[56]Abraham of Worms, Mathers (trans.), *The Book of the Sacred Magic of Abramelin the Mage*, p. 49.

a 'lowerarchy' to mirror the emanative layers above.[57] This infernal court was seen as a mocking mirror of God's hierarchy that descended towards the Devil, just as the celestial ladder ascended towards God. Initially derived from lower elemental classes of daemons in Proclus' cosmology, "Psellus[58] added lucifuges, or light-fleeing demons, and Johannes Trithemius[59] lent the weight of his authority to the system," which later "became part of mainstream theological tradition."[60] By the time of Aquinas the idea of an infernal demonic counterpart to the angelic was commonplace. Developing parallel to these philosophical conceptions was a stream of mythic tales about the biblical figure King Solomon.[61] It was the coming together of these Solomonic tales with the Neoplatonic cosmologies that evolved into the particular mythology and lexicology that surrounded the goetic literature of the Middle Ages.[62] One of the first demonological catalogues to appear was the sixteenth century *Pseudomonarchia Daemonum*, whose sixty-nine demons were soon adapted into the renowned seventy-two-fold hierarchy of the *Lemegeton*. The *Abramelin* text expanded and systematized the hierarchy further, extending the number of demons and presenting them in a monarchical schema,[63]

> The Four Princes, Lucifer, Leviathan, Satan, and Belial.
> The Eight Sub-Princes, Astarot, Magot, Asmodee, Belzebud, Oriens, Paimon, Ariton, and Amaimon.
> The Three Hundred and Sixteen Servient Demons, Groupings of Servitors Proper to Each of the Eight Sub-Princes.

What this mirror image of the celestial hierarchy created was something of a diamond shaped universe with God, or the One, at the top, man in the middle, the Devil at the bottom, and a plenary continuum of intermediary angels and demons set betwixt the three. Whereas the Neoplatonic cosmos ended with man as the lowest member of the emanative chain, the reformulations of the medieval magicians brought the Neoplatonic schema more in line with the archaic shamanic conception of the world as consisting of a celestial over-world, a material middle-world, and an infernal under-world.[64] However, unlike the shamanic world where there was a balance between the upper and lower realms, neither of which held metaphysical primacy over the other, the medieval theurgists saw the infernal realms and demons as distinctly inferior to both the celestial angels and to themselves. It was this spiritual inferiority of the demons that

---

[57] Kieckhefer, *Forbidden Rites: A Necromancer's Manual of the Fifteenth Century*, p. 155.
[58] Michael Psellos was an eleventh century Byzantine monk.
[59] Johannes Trithemius was a fifteenth century German abbot. Steganographia 1500 AD.
[60] Kieckhefer, *Forbidden Rites: A Necromancer's Manual of the Fifteenth Century*, p. 155.
[61] The Solomonic cycle of legends revolve around accounts of King Solomon of Israel, 1011-931 B.C., capturing and imprisoning a multitude of demons and bending them to his will. The accounts slowly grew into a folk mythology that accompanied the low goetic magic that was to be paired with the high theurgy. See Butler, *Ritual Magic*, p. 47. Starts with Testament of Solomon 2nd century AD.
[62] Butler, *Ritual Magic*, p. 35.
[63] Abraham of Worms, Mathers (trans.), *The Book of the Sacred Magic of Abramelin the Mage*, p. 104-109.
[64] Eliade, *Shamanism: Archaic Techniques of Ecstasy*, p. 182.

1 - This is probably where the Masonic ideal of Solomon's trans. tradition, the worship of Solomon at his temple.
2 - Blavanfliade', this idea is not 'Shamanic' 6 - impossible, as it pieced and the Legameton by 200 years.
3 - 1563 or 1583 AD 7 - Ashteoth, Magog, Asmodeus, Beelzebub, Orien, _____, _____, Mammon
4 - 11 AD 8 - Syriac
5 - c.1400-1427 AD 9 - or Mot, Syriac death god,

gave the goetic magician the ability to exert his will upon them, for we must remember, in the Neoplatonic cosmos the vector of contingency, and thus of spiritual authority, is unidirectional flowing from top to bottom. Thus does the adept, who elevates his soul by theurgical means, gain ever more power and influence over both the infernal and material realms below. Indeed, after the culmination of the Abramelin operation with the attainment of the Knowledge and Conversation of the Holy Guardian Angel, the mage is instructed to engage in a convocation of the demonic spirits in order to assert his newly gained authority over them.[65] In doing so, he establishes his position in the hierarchy and gains dominion over the realms below.

In closing, we have explored the *doxa* and *praxês* of Neoplatonism as direct predecessors to the angelologies, demonologies, and accompanying theurgical and goetic rites of the late Middle Ages and early Renaissance, and found a direct genetic link between the two. We began by examining the Platonic roots of the two fold emanative scheme of the doctrine of the Forms and the idea of the demiurge. We saw how this was developed into the four-tiered system of Plotinus, where the One is reflected downwards into the Intellect, the Soul, and the Physical. This was followed by an examination of Iamblichus' theurgical innovations within the Neoplatonic framework and the ensuing theological hierarchy that stemmed from the same. We then followed through to Pseudo-Dionysius' Christianization of Neoplatonic thought, which resulted in the substitution of an angelic hierarchy for Iamblichus' classes of gods, daemons, heroes, and pure souls. This angelic ladder of descent was then mirrored with an infernal inverted pyramid of demons, and the two hierarchies, the upper and lower, became the exclusive domains of theurgy and goetia. The synthesis of this whole stream of occult philosophy's development culminated in the various systems of magic exemplified by Abraham of Worms' *Abramelin* grimoire. The synthetic methodology which incorporated theurgy, goetia, and the Christianized Neoplatonic cosmos was transformed into a coherent system that has endured in belief and practice to the present day. And thus are the occult philosophies that grew to fruition during the transitional period between the Medieval and Enlightenment eras the direct heirs to the Neoplatonic legacy.

---

[65] Abraham of Worms, Mathers (trans.), *The Book of the Sacred Magic of Abramelin the Mage*, p. 86-88.

BIBLIOGRAPHY

Abraham of Worms, Mathers, Macgregor S. L. (ed.), *The Book of the Sacred Magic of Abramelin the Mage*. New York: Dover Publications Inc., 1975.

Aquinas, Thomas, Fathers of the English Dominican Province (trans.), *Summa Theologica*, Volume 1, Part 1. New York: Cosimo Classics, 2007.

Aristotle, Hicks, R. D. (trans.), *De Anima*. New York: Cosimo Classics, 2008.

Aristotle, 'Metaphysics'. In *Introduction to Aristotle*, edited by Richard McKeon. New York: The Modern Library, 1947.

Butler, E. M., *Ritual Magic*. Hollywood: Newcastle Publishing Company Inc., 1949.

Copleston, Frederick, *Greece and Rome*, Volume 1 of *A History of Philosophy*. London: Search Press, 1946.

Copleston, Frederick, *Medieval Philosophy: From Augustine to Duns* Scotus, Volume 2 of *A History of Philosophy*. New York: Image Books, 1993.

Crowley, Aleister, Hymenaeus Beta (ed.), *Magick: Liber ABA, Book 4*, Parts I-IV. Maine: Weiser Books, 2000.

Dillon, John M. (ed.) (trans.), 'Introduction to Iamblichus'. In *Iamblichi Chalcidensis in Platonis Diologos Commentariorum Fragmenta*. Leiden: Brill, 1973.

Eliade, Mircea, *Shamanism: Archaic Techniques of Ecstasy*. Princeton: Princeton University Press, 2004.

Hesiod, 'The Theogony of Hesiod'. In *Hesiod, Homeric Hymns, Homerica*, translated by Hugh G. Evelyn-White. Cambridge: Harvard University Press, 1995.

Iamblichus, *On the Mysteries of the Egyptians*. In *Neoplatonic Philosophy: Introductory Readings*, edited by John Dillon and Lloyd P. Gerson. Indianapolis: Hackett Publishing Company, Inc., 2004.

Kazlev, M. Alan, *Iamblichus' Hierarchy of Spiritual Entities*, http://www.kheper.net/topics/Neoplatonism/Iamblich-beings.htm.

Kieckhefer, Richard, *Forbidden Rites: A Necromancer's Manual of the Fifteenth Century*. University Park: Pennsylvania State University Press, 1998.

Liddell, H. G. and Scott, Robert, (eds.) *An Intermediate Greek-English Lexicon: Founded upon the Seventh Edition of Liddell and Scott's Greek-English Lexicon*. Oxford: Oxford University Press, 2000.

Loux, Michael J., *Metaphysics: A Contemporary Introduction*. New York: Routledge, 2010.

Peterson, Joseph, *The Lesser Key of Solomon: Lemegeton Clavicula Salomonis*. Maine: Weiser Books, 2001.

Plato, Grube G. M. A. and Reeve C. D. C. (trans.), *Republic*. Indianapolis: Hackett Publishing Company Inc., 1992.

Plato, 'Timaeus'. In *Greek Philosophy: Thales to Aristotle*, edited by Reginald E. Allen. New York: The Free Press, 1991.

Plotinus, 'Enneads'. In *Neoplatonic Philosophy: Introductory Readings*, edited by John Dillon and Lloyd P. Gerson. Indianapolis: Hackett Publishing Company, Inc., 2004.

Pseudo-Dionysius, 'On the Heavenly Hierarchy'. In *Dionysius the Aeropagite, Works*, 1897, translated by John Parker. London: James Parker and Co., 1987.

Remes, Pauliina, *Neoplatonism*. Berkeley: University of California Press, 2008.

Shaw, Gregory, *Theurgy and the Soul: The Neoplatonism of Iamblichus*. University Park: Pennsylvania State University Press, 1995.

Skrbina, David, *Panpsychism in the West*. Cambridge: The MIT Press, 2007.

From Roots to Fruits
A History of the Grimoire Tradition

BY

David Rankine

In the inner Circle let there be written four divine names with crosses interposed in the middle of the Circle; to wit, towards the East let there be written *Alpha*, and towards the West let there be written *Omega*; and let a cross divide the middle of the Circle. When the Circle is thus finished, according to the rule now before written, you shall proceed.

Peter de Abano, *Heptameron or Magical Elements*

The origins of the grimoires are often shrouded in mystery, due to the authors of most of the texts being unknown, making it very difficult to place the texts in the correct context and determine their provenance. In this paper I propose to trace the development of the grimoires through the period from the thirteenth to the eighteenth century C.E. To do this I will look at earlier texts which had a significant input on the material and practices contained in the grimoires, and also touch on the so-called 'black magic' grimoires of the nineteenth century, which were largely derivative of grimoire material from the period discussed. Whilst texts contemporary with the grimoires, such as significant Kabbalistic works and the Hermetic corpus, undoubtedly contributed to some of the ideas and material found in them, this paper concentrates on the grimoires themselves and their internal influence within the grimoire tradition. Of necessity, the discussion of specific techniques will be brief, as to explore this fully is beyond the scope of this paper and would require several volumes to do the topic justice.

What is a Grimoire?

The word 'grimoire' is derived from the root *grammar* and is used to literally represent a 'grammar of magic', or 'workbook of information and techniques'. The books or manuscripts commonly known as 'grimoires', were generally written in the period from the thirteenth to eighteenth century. The grimoires were essentially a European phenomenon, despite the external influences which contributed to their creation. Thus the grimoires are usually found in English, French, German, Greek, Hebrew, Italian, or

Latin versions, with occasional texts in other languages such as Arabic, Czech, Dutch, and Spanish.

The grimoires discussed in this paper are those which occur in more than one manuscript, demonstrating the continuity of tradition. This precludes some interesting lesser known texts on the basis that their contribution to the tradition cannot be demonstrated through a single manuscript, such as the fifteenth century Latin text of CLM 849 and English *Liber de Angelis* attributed to Osbern Bokenham,[1] as well as the ciphered *Clavis Inferni*[2] and the particularly interesting late sixteenth century Folger Vb.26.[3] The reader will note that the works of Dr John Dee are not included in this paper. This is because although much of Dee's material was derivative of earlier grimoires, his practices were more focused on spirit communication than grimoire conjuration, as his diaries clearly demonstrate.

The core components usually found in grimoires are the creation of the magic circle, consecration of the magic tools, spirit lists, being the angels, demons, or other creatures summoned, conjurations of the said spirits, and other correspondences or pertinent information, such as details of purification of the practitioners and their paraphernalia. Some works, like a number of the variants of the *Key of Solomon*,[4] replaced spirit lists and conjurations with lists of amulets and talismans, with details of their creation and consecration. Nonetheless there are still common themes with the conjurations, amulets, and talismans being used for similar purposes, such as protection and acquisition. Both these terms encompass a range of purposes, with protection including health, property, person whilst travelling, protection from attacks, and so on. Likewise, acquisition may include wealth, success, love, sex, favour with a powerful figure, knowledge, good harvest, and so on.

Although the popular perception of the grimoire tradition is of a heavily Judeo-Christian framework, upon inspection of different grimoires it is clear that in addition to the earlier texts which influenced the practices there are also many influences from the classical religions and folk practices. The clearest indicator of this influence is the number of deities from old religions who occur in the grimoires, sometimes by their own names and at other times in bastardised forms, such as Roman and Greek deities like Apollo, Diana, Hades, Pluto, Python, and Serapis, as well as other ancient deities

---

[1] See Fanger, *Conjuring Spirits: Texts and Traditions of Medieval Ritual Magic*, p. 32-75.
[2] Skinner, Stephen and Rankine, David, *The Grimoire of St Cyprian – Clavis Inferni*. Singapore: Golden Hoard Press, 2009.
[3] Available at http://www.folger.edu/Content/Collection/Digital-Image-Collection/
[4] See Skinner, Stephen and Rankine, David, *The Veritable Key of Solomon*. Singapore: Golden Hoard Press, 2009.

like Astarte,[5] Baal,[6] and Horus,[7] and classical mythical creatures like Cerberus and the Phoenix.[8]

The Roots
Proto-Grimoires and Early Magical Texts

A number of works spanning the period from the second century B.C.E. to the twelfth century C.E. may be seen as major influences on the material subsequently found in the grimoires. The ongoing and derivative nature of such magical texts and the amuletic tradition which was interconnected with them is also significant in the diversity of material which they incorporated.

The *Greek Magical Papyri* is the name given to a collection of magical texts found together which span the period from second century B.C.E. to the fifth century C.E. To these are added the collection of texts in *Supplementum Magicum*, Volumes 1 and 2, which contain contemporary material. The *Greek Magical Papyri*, which is often abbreviated to *PGM*, are characterised by the syncretisation of deities and spiritual creatures from numerous ancient pantheons including Babylonian, Christian, Egyptian, Gnostic, Greek, Jewish, and Mithraic. They also contain practices which are seen as key components of the grimoires, particularly the conjuration of spiritual creatures through repeated coercion, followed by a dismissal when the task is completed. Another theme seen in many of the charms and spells is that of planetary and zodiacal attributions, such as the thirty-six decans, which would also later feature prominently in some of the grimoires. Another significant collection of material is that published by Meyer and Smith in *Ancient Christian Magic*.[9] This work spans the period from the second to the twelfth century C.E. and contains numerous charms, spells, and conjurations written in Coptic and Greek. The flavour of the material is more Christian, with heavy Gnostic and Jewish influences. However, there is also a crossover with the material found in the *PGM*, such as the use of the seven Greek vowels and some of the same *voces magicae*.[10] There are also long angelic conjurations and phrases which hint at the influence of the Jewish system of Merkavah mysticism.

Two early Jewish texts of particular note are the second century C.E. *Testament of Solomon* and the fourth century C.E. *Sepher ha-Razim* or *Book of the Mysteries*. The

---

[5]Ashtoreth.
[6]Bael.
[7]Hauros.
[8]Phenex.
[9]Meyer, Marvin W. and Smith, Richard, *Ancient Christian Magic: Coptic Texts of Ritual Power*. Jersey: Princeton University Press, 1999.
[10]*Voces magicae* are words of unknown origin and meaning, which are often included in charms to focus power and heighten the awareness of the practitioner.

Testament of Solomon tells the story of the subjugation of sixty-one demons by King Solomon, who uses a magical ring given to him by the archangel Michael to bind them and learn the name of their controlling angels. The *Testament of Solomon* not only includes spirits of all thirty-six decans, but also emphasises the use of a controlling angel to bind the more chaotic nature of the demon to the service of the magician. *Sepher ha-Razim* is largely planetary in nature and contains conjurations of numerous angels, and also the use of a wide range of paraphernalia including engraved metal lamellae, an ancient Greek practice which can be seen later in the grimoires in the form of the engraved pentacles. Another feature of *Sepher ha-Razim* is the use of the so-called Celestial Script, which is also found on contemporary amulets from this period and the following centuries.

A theological text from the late fifth century C.E. would also have a significant effect on the grimoire tradition. *The Celestial Hierarchy* of Pseudo-Dionysus the Areopagite was the first text to detail the hierarchy of nine orders of angels which would form the basis of the hierarchies found in Orthodox Christianity, the grimoires, and the Kabbalah. The *Sword of Moses* may also be mentioned here, as this tenth century C.E. text, which may date back as far as the fourth century C.E., has some similarities with the grimoires that would follow, with numerous angels to be conjured to gain the sword, a long string of divine names used in the charms, and a long list of possible acquisitive and protective results which can be achieved using the text.

Early Flowers
The Thirteenth and Fifteenth Centuries

Although there may be earlier versions of some of the grimoires which have not been discovered, the first major grimoires occur in the thirteenth century. These are *Liber Juratus*, also known as *The Sworn Book of Honorius*, the *Ghâyat al-Hakîm*, better known as the *Picatrix*, or *The Goal of the Wise*, and the *Ars Notoria* or *Notary Art*. *Liber Juratus* sets the tone for most of the subsequent grimoires by placing a mystique around its creation. The work begins with the tale of eight-hundred and eleven, or eighty-nine depending on the version, magicians gathering to ensure their knowledge is not lost, and *Liber Juratus* being the result. It is essentially an angelic work of a planetary nature, with the magic sword and magic circles as part of its structure, which significantly also includes the seventy-two *Shem ha-Mephorash* angels in an early chapter. It is noticeable that some of the orations in *Liber Juratus* seem to be derived from those in the *Ars Notoria*, which also dates to the thirteenth century. *Liber Juratus* is the first known source for the *Sigillum Dei Aemeth*, which would form such a significant part of John Dee's workings centuries later, and indeed Dee owned a copy of this grimoire.[11]

---

[11]Sloane MS 313.

The *Ars Notoria* is distinct from the rest of the grimoires in its style and practice. It is alleged that an angel gave the *Ars Notoria* to King Solomon in a dream as a method of gaining the liberal and mechanical arts in a very short time. The most complete versions of the text include numerous figures, or *notae*, of angels combined with geometric shapes and writing, from whence the name of the book is derived. The methodology is a combination of prayers to God and the angels, which include strings of "strange words, supposedly derived from Hebrew or Chaldaic, and other gibberish,"[12] for example *voces magicae*. There are numerous versions of the *Ars Notoria* dating from the thirteenth to the seventeenth century C.E., which all seem to be incomplete.[13] The *Ars Notoria* would undergo a number of revisions and transformations, ending up as the fifth unillustrated book of the *Lemegeton* in the seventeenth century.

The *Picatrix* is a major work of Arabic magic, with a heavy focus on planetary and zodiacal amulets and talismans. There is also an emphasis on the use of incense, which recurs in some of the later grimoires. The first known Latin edition of the *Picatrix* dates to 1256, from the court of Alphonso the Wise in Castille, and whilst the Arab version is undoubtedly older, it does not form part of the grimoire tradition until its Latin form arrives in Europe.

The fourteenth century saw the probable creation of one of the most significant of all texts within the grimoire tradition, the *Heptameron*, or *Seven Days* of Peter de Abano, 1250-1316, which is a manual of planetary magic with the planetary archangels. This book was first published in 1496, and then published as an appendix to Agrippa's *Fourth Book of Occult Philosophy* in 1554, and then in Latin in 1600 before being subsequently translated into English by Robert Turner in his 1655 edition of the *Fourth Book*. The disparity between the publication date and the earlier lifetime of Peter de Abano has been taken by some as demonstrating that it was not his work, and it has been suggested he was not a magician. However, not only were magical books frequently published posthumously, but de Abano was twice tried unsuccessfully by the Inquisition as a magician and significantly mentioned grimoires in his 1310 work *Lucidator*.[14] The conjurations in this book are extremely important, having influenced the later *Key of Solomon* and *Lemegeton*. Included in its contents are the creation of the magic circle, the consecrations of salt, water and incense, and planetary hours. This is all material which would be repeated and adapted throughout the subsequent grimoires.

A significant work dating to the fifteenth century is the German *Book of Abramelin*, 1400-1427. This Jewish magic grimoire is now available in a more complete form, with charms

---

[12] Thorndike, A History of Magic and Experimental Science Vol 2: The First Thirteen Centuries, p. 286.
[13] Thorndike, A History of Magic and Experimental Science Vol 2: The First Thirteen Centuries, p. 279-289.
[14] There is also good evidence to support his authorship, see Skinner and Rankine, *The Goetia of Dr Rudd*, p. 31.

not found in the previous edition, as well as the complete magic squares and full ritual sequence of the eighteen month practice of contacting the guardian angel and not six as given in the incomplete manuscript.[15] This practice is unique amongst the grimoires as a more theurgic practice of great length rather than the usual conjurations for immediate results. There is an interesting parallel between this work and the *Hygromanteia*, as the *Abramelin* contains a section of advice from the author Abraham to his son Lamech, akin to the advice given by Solomon to Rehoboam in the *Hygromanteia*, sometimes called the *Epistle*. However, as this is one of the oldest sections of the *Hygromanteia*, it is more likely that the *Abramelin* section is derived from it or copies the idea, rather than the other way around.

Missing Links
The *Hygromanteia*

The period from the fifteenth to seventeenth century can be described as the heyday of the grimoires, with the best known works being produced during this time. The first of these is the extremely significant *Hygromanteia*, which is only now starting to receive the attention it deserves as a key link in the transmission of material within the grimoire tradition. There are twenty known manuscripts of this grimoire, all in Greek, which date from 1440 right through to the nineteenth century, though significantly seven of them are from the fifteenth century.[16] Also known as *The Magical Treatise of Solomon*, or the *Solomonikê*, the manuscripts are characterised by an introduction from Solomon to his son Rehoboam and a section describing the auspices and malefices of every planetary hour in a week. The material is planetary in nature and includes prayers to the planets and planetary gods from the Greek pantheon, which are followed by prayers to the appropriate angels and then demons, with details of the appropriate incenses to cense with.[17] There is also a section on the planetary and zodiacal attributions of plants and their uses, which may have influenced subsequent works like *The Book of Secrets of Albertus Magnus*. Descriptions of the creation and consecration of the magical tools and circle, along with the use of the pentacles, can all be seen as preceding and influencing the subsequent *Key of Solomon* manuscript tradition.

---

[15] *The Book of Abramelin*, edited by George Dehn and translated by Steven Guth, 2006, has superseded the earlier Mathers edition of *The Sacred Magic of Abra-Melin the Mage* based on a later incomplete French version of the manuscript. In a similar fashion *The Veritable Key of Solomon* by Stephen Skinner and David Rankine, 2008, has superseded Mathers incomplete cut-and-paste *The Key of Solomon the King*; and Joseph Peterson's *The Lesser Key of Solomon*, 2001, and Stephen Skinner's and David Rankine's *The Goetia of Dr Rudd*, 2007, have superseded the Mathers translation of *The Goetia*.

[16] The earliest being Bononiensis' MS Gr. 3632 dating to 1440. See next chapter.

[17] For a partial translation of one version of this text, see Torijano, *Solomon the Esoteric King: From King to Magus, Development of a Tradition*, p. 231-253. An eagerly awaited work including translations of a number of the *Hygromanteia* texts is forthcoming from Ioannis Marathakis. Also now appears in the current chapter. The angels command the demons.

In his work *Solomon the Esoteric King*,[18] Torijano argues convincingly for the early roots of the *Hygromanteia* material, possibly as far back as the fourth to fifth century C.E. Torijano demonstrates some of the many similarities between this material and that in *Sepher ha-Razim* and the *Greek Magical Papyri*, establishing a strong likelihood of transmission. Torijano also postulates the entry of the *Hygromanteia* material from the Byzantine Empire into Italy, where the first known manuscripts of the *Key of Solomon* occur in Italian and Latin. Significantly a number of the *Hygromanteia* manuscripts were also bound together with copies of the *Testament of Solomon*.

Full Bloom
The Sixteenth and Seventeenth Centuries

An interesting work from the early sixteenth century is the German *Magia Naturalis et Innaturalis*, 1505, one of the first texts in the Faustbook tradition of German grimoires. Like many other grimoires it includes a complex magic circle, conjurations, and a spirit list including seven Electors.[19] The *Liber Spirituum*, or *Book of Spirits*, is also found in this work, which the magician used as the repository of signatures and thus confirmed obedience from conjured spirits. Such spirit contracts are also seen in some English works, for example the proto-goetic Sloane MS 3824.[20] From this root of German texts came the idea of the Faustian pact, which is entirely at odds with the whole ethos and practice of grimoire magic, which is about purification of the practitioner and subsequent control of spirits, and entirely contrary to the notion of subservience through signing away your soul or liberty!

The early sixteenth century was a particularly fertile period for the German contribution to the grimoire tradition. The works of the German Abbot Johannes Trithemius, 1462-1516, played a significant part in influencing both subsequent grimoires and also some of the great known contributors to the tradition, providing a direct line of magical continuity. In 1500 Trithemius wrote the *Steganographia*, which was published posthumously in 1606 and contributed directly to the *Lemegeton* as the sub-books of the *Theurgia-Goetia* and the *Ars Paulina*. John Dee also used a copy of the *Steganographia* as part of the inspiration for his Enochian system, along with the *Sigillum Dei Aemeth* of *Liber Juratus*. Trithemius was not only a significant magical scholar, but also a teacher, with his two most significant students being Henry Cornelius Agrippa, 1486-1535, and Paracelsus, 1493-1541.

Henry Cornelius Agrippa produced the seminal three volume *Three Books of Occult Philosophy*, which were distributed privately as manuscripts around 1510 and then

---

[18] Torijano, *Solomon the Esoteric King: From King to Magus, Development of a Tradition*, p. 231-253
[19] Planetary spirits.
[20] Reproduced in Rankine, David, *The Book of Treasure Spirits*. London: Avalonia, 2009.

printed in 1531-33. This work is a huge collection of material from natural magic to Kabbalah and sigilisation, with parts of it being copied into numerous grimoires, books of practice and books of secrets in the subsequent centuries. The other classic Agrippa work is the posthumously produced *Fourth Book of Occult Philosophy*. There are claims that Agrippa did not write this work and indeed, of the six parts, Agrippa wrote only the first two sections, 'Of Geomancy', and 'Of Occult Philosophy, or Magickal Ceremonies'. The latter contains significant material on creating the magic circle, the *Liber Spirituum*, consecrations, and invocations. The remainder of the book includes the *Heptameron* of Peter de Abano and the *Arbatel of Magick*, which was first produced in Latin in 1575, with its forty-nine aphorisms which set the moral code for the practising Christian magician and also covers the conjuration of the planetary Olympic Spirits.

Philippus Aureolus Theophrastus Bombastus Von Hohenheim, better known as Paracelsus, is best known for creating Paracelsian medicine. Amongst his works, however, is the classic *Archidoxes of Magic* that was published posthumously in 1589, a work which introduced the Doctrine of Signatures, being the symbolic association of plants by colour and appearance, as well as numerous amulets and talismans for magical results.

Continuing the line of descent from Trithemius, Johann Weyer, 1515-1588, was a student of Agrippa's whose book *Praestigiis Daemonum* was published in 1563. The 1583 edition of this book contained an appendix of sixty-nine demons called *Pseudomonarchia Daemonum*, which was almost identical to the list of seventy-two demons subsequently found in the *Goetia* and was reproduced by Scot in his *Discoverie of Witchcraft* a year later.

English Member of Parliament Reginald Scot, 1538-1599, produced a grimoire unintentionally! Scot wrote the book *The Discoverie of Witchcraft* in 1584 to diminish fear and belief in witches. However, by collecting together material and making it more easily available in a printed form, he effectively created a standard manual for those seeking to learn more of the practices of magic and witchcraft. Thus, for example, we see the recipe given by Scot for flying ointment being copied in Thomas Middleton's 1613 play *The Witch*. It is ironic to note that later versions of the book included even more grimoire material, adding further to the sources available to its readers. The third edition in 1665 gained a second book to the *Discourse of Devils and Spirits* and nine extra chapters on conjurations. Scot listed many of the grimoires in his book, as can be seen in the list below,[21] perhaps unintentionally, providing a reading list for his readers,

These conjurors carrie about at this daie, bookes intituled under the names

---

[21] My notes in square brackets.

of Adam, Abel, Tobie, & Enoch... Abraham, Aaron and Salomon [*Key of Solomon*]... Zacharie, Paule [*Ars Paulina*], Honorius [*Book of Honorius*], Cyprian [probably *Clavis Inferni*], Jerome, Jeremie, Albert [*Albertus Magnus*], and Thomas: also of the angels, Riziel, Razael [*Sepher Razael*], and Raphael... Ars Almadell [*Almadel*], ars Notoria [*Notory Art*], ars Bulaphiae, ars Arthephi, ars Pomena, ars Revelationis, &c.[22]

The *Key of Solomon*, or *Clavicula Salomonis*, is the best known and most prolific of all grimoires. During the research I conducted with Stephen Skinner whilst working on *The Veritable Key of Solomon*, we located one hundred and twenty-six manuscripts in nine different languages, not including the twenty Greek *Hygromanteia* manuscripts. The earliest actual date on a *Key of Solomon* manuscript is 1572, for an English manuscript, with two undated sixteenth century Italian manuscripts which may well be older. The *Key of Solomon* manuscripts fall into three main families of manuscripts, which may be further divided into ten text groups. Each of these has a core of chapters, with specific additional chapters and material characterising the different groups. Considering the scope of practical material found in the *Key of Solomon*, particularly regarding preparation, purification and consecration of the practitioners, magic circles, paraphernalia, and the sheer numbers, it seems likely that the *Key of Solomon* was distributed as the 'grimoire primer' of the Renaissance. An example which supports this idea is the Catholic six-hundred and ninety-five page manuscript dealing entirely with accusations against monks for using the *Key of Solomon*.[23] Most copies of the *Key of Solomon* contain large numbers of planetary pentacles for different results that form a substantial part of their material. A Hebrew version of the *Key of Solomon*, called *Sepher Maphteah Shelomoh*, or *Book of the Key of Solomon*, appeared around 1700, which curiously was clearly derived from the European language versions and translated back into Hebrew, rather than continuing an earlier tradition for which there is no evidence.

A pseudo-Solomonic work from this period is *Sepher Raziel*, an English grimoire dating to 1564, derived from thirteenth century Latin sources and not to be confused with the Hebrew *Sepher Raziel ha-Melakh*. The text is divided into seven sections, covering different topics including the use of astrology, incense, timings, purity, and the seven heavens and their angels. As can be seen from the sevenfold emphasis, this is another essentially planetary grimoire.

The other best known grimoire that dates to this period, the *Lemegeton*, comprises five parts known respectively as the *Goetia*, *Theurgia-Goetia*, *Ars Pauline*, *Ars Almadel*, and *Ars Notoria*. Of the four manuscripts dating to this period around the seventeenth century, all of them are written in English and the earliest *Lemegeton* dates to around

---

[22]Reginald, 'Book 15, Chapter 31', in *Discoverie of Witchcraft*.
[23]MSS Busta 102.

1641,[24] with the latest being dated to 1712.[25] However, the sources for the *Lemegeton* date back earlier to the early fourteenth century with the *Heptameron*, and to the fifteenth century through sources such as the French *Livre des Esperitz*[26] and the *Steganographia* of Trithemius.[27] Of the books, the *Goetia* deals with the conjuration of seventy-two demons and fallen angels; *Theurgia-Goetia* deals with conjurations of spirits corresponding to all points on the compass; the *Ars Pauline* deals with conjurations of angels corresponding to the hours of the day and night, and also to each of the three-hundred and sixty degrees of the twelve signs of the zodiac. The *Ars Almadel* deals with the conjuration of four angels of the Ayres using wax tablets and clearly influenced the practices of John Dee; and the *Ars Notoria* has already been discussed previously. It is interesting to note that the term 'goetia' was already in common use around the time that the first known *Lemegeton* was compiled, as seen when the French librarian and bibliographer Gabriel Naudé wrote in the seventeenth century distinguishing four types of magic: divine, theurgic, goetia or witchcraft, and natural magic.[28]

One last significant grimoire from the mid-seventeenth century is *The Nine Keys* of Dr Thomas Rudd. This grimoire is essentially conjurations of the major archangels associated with the hierarchy of nine angelic orders first recorded more than a thousand years earlier by Pseudo-Dionysus.[29] Dr Rudd's material was very practical in style and his version of the *Lemegeton* is characterised from the other manuscripts by a number of practical additions, including the inclusion of the seventy-two *Shem ha-Mephorash* angels as controlling angels for the seventy-two demons in the *Goetia*, continuing the tradition seen in the *Testament of Solomon* and the *Hygromanteia*.

Noir et Rouge
Later Derivatives

The period from the late seventeenth century through to the nineteenth century is the derivative period marking a degeneration of the material in the earlier grimoires. The grimoires produced during this time were almost all in French and can be described as works of 'black magic', which emphasise demonic conjuration, results magic, and pacts. The one major exception to this is the *6th and 7th Books of Moses*, which first appeared in 1734. This work of planetary conjurations and talismans is largely derived from the

---

[24]Sloane MS 3825.
[25]Harley MS 6483.
[26]Trinity MS 0.8.29, circa fifteenth century.
[27]For a discussion of the origins of the *Lemegeton*, see Skinner, Stephen and Rankine, David, *The Goetia of Dr Rudd*. Singapore: Golden Hoard Press, 2007.
[28]Naudé, Gabriel, *Apologie pour tous les grands personages qui ont esté faussement soupçonnez de magie*. La Haye: A.Vlac, 1653.
[29]Reproduced as Skinner, Stephen and Rankine, David, *The Keys to the Gateway of Magic*. Singapore: Golden Hoard Press, 2005.

Latin *Liber Raziel*, which appeared in English as *Sepher Raziel*. This popular work would subsequently be reproduced many times, and have an influence on the traditions of Voodoo and Pennsylvania Dutch or Braucherei.

The *Grimoire of Pope Honorius*, which is not to be confused with the *Sworn Book of Honorius*, appeared around 1670 with several variants manifesting in the subsequent two centuries. It is a mixture of derivative material from some of the *Key of Solomon* manuscripts with Catholic ritual, which may be why it has received so much and excessively negative comments from writers like A.E. Waite and Eliphas Levi. In fact, the *Grimoire of Pope Honorius* contains a number of components in common with the more recent Wiccan tradition, which it may well have influenced, including the calling of spiritual creatures at the cardinal points of the magic circle and the double-edged black-handled knife, whereas most images in the *Key of Solomon* and other grimoires are of a single-edged blade.[30]

Contemporary with the *Grimoire of Pope Honorius* was *Le Petit Albert*, or *The Little Albert*, which was published in 1668. Although often described as a black magic grimoire, in fact it is not and rather *Le Petit Albert* belongs more accurately in the Book of Secrets tradition which ran parallel to the grimoire tradition from the mid-sixteenth century. Books of Secrets often drew material from earlier authors, such as Agrippa and Albertus Magnus, and combined simple charms, which required little or no preparation, with folk medicine and practical DIY recipes for everything from making dyes to metalwork. As well as being widely sold, some Books of Secrets were personal collections of charms, and these have been found bound in with grimoires as an addendum of practices which could be conducted quickly and easily. An example of this is the eighteenth century text *A Collection of Magical Secrets*,[31] which was bound in with a copy of the *Key of Solomon*.

One of the most infamous of the black magic grimoires is the *Grimorium Verum*, or the *True Grimoire*. The *Grimorium Verum* first appeared in 1817 in French, with subsequent Italian editions as well. The material is heavily derivative of the *Universal Treatise of the Keys of Solomon*, one of the Key of Solomon families of manuscripts, with large chunks of near verbatim material lifted from manuscripts, such as Wellcome MS 4669.[32] The reputation of the *Grimorium Verum* is largely based on the infernal trinity of Lucifer, Beelzebub, and Astaroth, who are called upon for assistance. The Italian editions of the *Grimorium Verum* have an additional section of 'Other Secrets' added, which is simple charms and rites of a Book of Secrets nature. Another heavily derivative

---

[30]See D'Este, Sorita and Rankine, David, *Wicca Magickal Beginnings: A Study of the Possible Origins of the Rituals and Practices found in this Modern Tradition of Pagan Witchcraft and Magick*. London: Avalonia, 2008.
[31]Skinner, Stephen and Rankine, David, *A Collection of Magical Secrets*. London: Avalonia, 2008.
[32]For more detail of this see Skinner, Stephen and Rankine, David, *The Veritable Key of Solomon*. Singapore: Golden Hoard Press, 2009.

black magic grimoire from the early nineteenth century, possibly as late as 1845, is *Le Grand Grimoire* or *The Great Grimoire*, also known as *Le Dragon Rouge*, or *The Red Dragon*. This work contains the Faustian 'pact with the devil' to gain twenty years of service in exchange for your soul, a practice which only a desperate man without magical experience would consider.

Conclusion

In 1801 Francis Barrett published *The Magus*, a compilation of material which drew heavily on the works of Agrippa and Trithemius. Indeed it could be seen as a duplication of the idea of Agrippa's *Three Books of Occult Philosophy*, collating a wide range of magical material, though in this case from known earlier sources. Following on from Barrett, the nineteenth century saw the complexities of the grimoires reduced to simplified degenerate works of self-gratification through controlling others and attempting to locate treasure. By the mid to late nineteenth century the appearance of works such as the *Verus Jeuistarum Libellus*, or *The True Petition of the Jesuits*, the *Secret Grimoire of Turiel*, 1850, and the *Black Pullet*, late nineteenth century, heralded the end of the creative development of the grimoire tradition. However, the work of figures such as MacGregor Mathers, 1854-1918, and A.E. Waite, 1857-1942, served to draw public attention back to the grimoires, albeit in a very biased and often inadequately translated and contextualised manner.

Of necessity I have kept my description of this complex and rich tradition brief, and have not covered numerous minor works which occurred in single editions. However, with the research now being conducted by magical scholars and academics alike, a clearer picture of the scope, depth, and importance of the grimoire tradition as a corpus of practices and the foundation of the modern magical revival is now becoming apparent to a wider audience, with original rare texts being made available in a way never before seen.

BIBLIOGRAPHY

Agrippa, Henry Cornelius, *Three Book of Occult Philosophy*. Minnesota: Llewellyn, 2005.

Agrippa, Henry Cornelius, *The Fourth Book of Occult Philosophy*. London: Askin Press, 1978.

Alexander, Philip S., 'Sepher ha-Razim and the Problem of Black Magic in Early Judaism'. In *Magic in the Biblical World: From the Rod of Aaron to the Ring of Solomon*, edited by Todd Klutz. London: T & T Clark International, 2003.

Atallah, Hashem, Holmquest, Geylan (trans.) and Kiesel, William (ed.), *Picatrix (Ghayat Al-Hakim)* Vols 1 & 2. Seattle: Ouroboros Press, 2007.

Barrett, Francis, *The Magus or Celestial Intelligencer: A Complete System of Occult Philosophy*. Charleston: Forgotten Books, 2008.

Betz, Hans Dieter (ed.), *The Greek Magical Papyri in Translation including the Demotic Spells,* Chicago: University of Chicago Press, 1992.

Bilardi, C. R., *The Red Church or The Art of Pennsylvania German Braucherei*. California: Pendraig, 2009.

Butler, Elizabeth M., *Ritual Magic*. Pennsylvania: Pennsylvania State University Press, 2002.

Conybeare, F. C., 'The Testament of Solomon'. In *Jewish Quarterly Review*, October, 1898.

Couliano, Ioan P., *Eros and Magic in the Renaissance*. Chicago: Chicago University Press: Chicago, 1987.

Daniel, Robert W. and Maltomini, Franco, *Supplementum Magicum* Volume 1. Koln: Westdeutscher Verlag, 1990.

Daniel, Robert W. and Maltomini, Franco, *Supplementum Magicum* Volume 2. Koln: Westdeutscher Verlag, 1992.

D'Este, Sorita and Rankine, David, *Wicca Magickal Beginnings: A Study of the Possible Origins of the Rituals and Practices found in this Modern Tradition of Pagan Witchcraft and Magick*. London: Avalonia, 2008.

Eamon, William, *Science and the Secrets of Nature: Books of Secrets in Medieval and Early Modern Culture*. New Jersey: Princeton University Press, 1994.

Fanger, Claire (ed.), *Conjuring Spirits: Texts and Traditions of Medieval Ritual Magic*. Stroud: Sutton Publishing Ltd, 1998.

Flint, Valerie I. J., *The Rise of Magic in Early Medieval Europe*. New Jersey: Princeton University Press, 1991.

Gollancz, Herman, *Sepher Mafteah Selomoh (Book of the Key of Solomon)*. London: David Nutt, 1903.

Greenfield, Richard P. H., *Traditions of Belief in Late Byzantine Demonology*. Amsterdam: Hakkert, 1988.

Hedegård, Gösta, *Liber Iuratus Honorii*. Stockholm: Almquist & Wiksell, 2002.

Karr, Don and Skinner, Stephen (eds.), *Sepher Raziel: Liber Salomonis*. Singapore: Golden Hoard Press, 2010.

Kieckhefer, Richard, *Forbidden Rites: A Necromancer's Manual of the Fifteenth Century*. Stroud: Sutton Publishing Ltd., 1997.

King, B. J. H. (trans.), *The Grimoire of Pope Honorius III*. Northampton: Sut Anubis Books, 1984.

Luibheld, C. (trans.), *Pseudo-Dionysus: The Complete Works*. New York: Paulist Press, 1987.

McLean, Adam (ed.), *The Steganographia of Johannes Trithemius. Book I & III*. Edinburgh: Magnum Opus Hermetic Sourceworks 12, 1982.

Meyer, Marvin W. and Smith, Richard, *Ancient Christian Magic: Coptic Texts of Ritual Power*. New Jersey: Princeton University Press, 1999.

Morgan, Michael A., *Sepher ha-Razim: The Book of the Mysteries*. USA: Society of Biblical Literature, 1983.

Naudé, Gabriel, *The History of Magick*. London: John Streater, 1657.

Paracelsus and Skinner, Stephen (eds.), *The Archidoxes of Magic*. London: Askin Publishers, 1976.

Naudé, Gabriel, *The History of Magick*. London: John Streater, 1657.

Peterson, Joseph (ed.), *The Sixth and Seventh Books of Moses*. Florida: Ibis Press, 2008.

Peterson, Joseph (ed.), *Grimorium Verum*. California: CreateSpace Publishing, 2007.

Peterson, Joseph (ed.), *The Lesser Key of Solomon: Lemegeton Clavicula Salomonis*. Maine: Red Wheel/Weiser Books, 2001.

Rankine, David, *The Book of Treasure Spirits*. London: Avalonia, 2009.

Scot, Reginald, *Discoverie of Witchcraft*. London: Dover Publications, 1989.

Skinner, Stephen and Rankine, David, *A Collection of Magical Secrets*. London: Avalonia, 2009.

Skinner, Stephen and Rankine, David, *The Veritable Key of Solomon*. Singapore: Golden Hoard Press, 2009.

A SOURCE OF THE KEY OF SOLOMON THE MAGIC TREATISE OR HYGROMANCY, OR EPISTLE TO REHOBOAM

BY

IOANNIS MARATHAKIS

Pay attention, my dearest son Rehoboam, to the details of this art, regarding the things in which the entire interest of the Hygromanteia lies. First of all, you must always observe the rulerships of the planets and of the signs of the Zodiac, and then use them in order to do what you want.

MS Athonicus Dion. 282, folio 28v.

W hen S. L. MacGregor Mathers released his edition of the relatively unknown, at the time, *Key of Solomon the King*, or *Clavicula Solomonis*, in 1888, he seemed convinced that this grimoire was based on or even translated from an ancient Hebrew original.[1] The *Key of Solomon* indeed contained several Hebrew words and Qabalistic references that could lead a non-scholar to the same conclusion, especially if he was romantically attached to the belief of an ancient magical and initiatory tradition. But although Mathers did not even question the authorship of this text, ascribing it to the Hebrew King Solomon himself, there are indications leading to different conclusions.

These indications cannot be discussed here in detail, as they are beyond the scope of this paper, but they can be mentioned epigrammatically. Firstly, there was no Hebrew original, since the actual Hebrew versions of the *Key of Solomon* are not older than the eighteenth century. The Hebrew manuscripts were probably translated from Italian or Latin into Hebrew, rather than the opposite.[2] Secondly, the logical gaps, overlapping elements and incongruities within the text itself show that the author was in fact trying to incorporate different, and in some cases, contradicting older material. The Qabalistic references were probably added during the revision of this material, something that must have happened not earlier than the sixteenth century, when interest in the Qabalah started to rise within the intellectual circles of Italy and Europe in general. It

---

[1]MacGregor, *The Key of Solomon the King (Clavicula Salomonis)*, p. vii-viii.
[2]Scholem, 'Some Sources of Jewish-Arabic Demonology', in *Journal of Jewish Studies*, p. xvi. See also Peterson, J. (ed.), *The Key of Solomon*, at http://www.esotericarchives.com/solomon/ksol.htm.

is to be noted that this date matches the dates of the oldest manuscripts of the *Key of Solomon*.[3]

If this is the case, there remains to name the main source of the *Key of Solomon*. In 1898, began the publication of a major scholarly work, the *Catalogus Codicum Astrologorum Graecorum*, which was concluded in 1936, numbering twelve volumes. As the name implies, this series contained partial transcriptions of Greek astrological and magical manuscripts scattered throughout the libraries of Europe. The fragmentary nature and astrological orientation of this series, excluding most of the magical material, led Armand Delatte, a contributor of the *Catalogus*, to edit a volume containing some of the excluded material in 1927, under the title *Anecdota Atheniensia I*.

From the aforementioned editions, it became apparent that there was a work on magic that survived mostly in fragmentary form and with numerous variations, as Richard Greenfield puts it, "in a number of manuscripts of which the earliest date to the fifteenth century."[4] There is a list of these manuscripts, originally given by Delatte and repeated by Greenfield, which is the following,[5]

A: Atheniensis, National Library 1265 (16th century).
B: Atheniensis, Greek Historical and Folkloric Society 118 (18th century).
B2: Bononiensis 3632 (15th century).
D: Dionysiou Convent Library 282, Mount Athos (16th century).
H: Harleianus, British Library 5596 (15th century).
M: Monacensis 70 (16th century).
M2: Mediolanensis H2 infer. (16th century).
M3: Mediolanensis E37 sup. (16th century).
N: Neapolitanus II C 33 (15th century).
P: Parisinus 2419 (15th century).
P2: Petropolitanus, Academic Paleographic Museum (17th century).
P3: Petropolitanus, National Library 575 (17th century).
P4: Petropolitanus, National Library 646 (18th century).
T: Taurinensis C VII 15 (15th century).
V: Vindobonensis Phil. Gr. 108 (15th century).

Greenfield adds to this list the following two manuscripts,

---

[3] The oldest manuscripts of the *Key of Solomon* from the sixteenth century are the Sloane 3847 and the Additional MS 36674 of the British Library. Both are edited by Joseph Peterson. The first is included in *Twilit Grotto: Esoteric Archives on CD*, while the second can be found online at http://www.esotericarchives.com/solomon/ad36674.htm.
[4] Greenfield, *Traditions of Belief in Late Byzantine Demonology*, p. 159.
[5] Greenfield, *Traditions of Belief in Late Byzantine Demonology*, p. 159-160, together with the references of their editions. Originally in Delatte, 'Le Traité les Plantes Planétaires d'un manuscript de Leningrad', in *Annuaire de l'Institute de Philologie et d'Histoire Orientales et Slaves*, IX., p. 148-149.

G: Gennadianus, Gennadeios Library 45, Athens (16th century).
M4: Metamorphoseos Convent Library 67, Meteora (16th century).

I would add that this list is not exhaustive, as small fragments of this work survive in many other magical and *iatrosophical*, meaning 'magical-medical', Greek manuscripts. I must also repeat that the variations of the text are numerous, thus basing the work on a complete critical edition is almost impossible. So, following Greenfield and Torijano,[6] I will for the moment limit myself to the examination of the Harley 5596 manuscript, as it is the oldest and most extensive text at our disposal. The manuscript does not number the chapters, but they are numbered here for convenience. In this examination I will try to indicate the similarities between this text and the *Key of Solomon*.[7]

Chapter One
Solomon's Address to Rehoboam

Solomon explains to his son Rehoboam that this book contains knowledge which will enable him to use the powers of the planets for whatever aim he wants. This short address is divided into two paragraphs. The first is similar to the first sentence on page two of the Add. MSS. 10862 Introduction, while the second is similar to the last paragraph on page seven of the Lansdowne MSS. 1203 Introduction.

Chapter Two
Of the Seven Days of the Week

The author cites a list of the operations attributed to the seven planets, along with the method for calculating the planetary hours. The author is evidently drawing from older material of talismanic nature. This chapter is similar to pages eleven to thirteen in 'Book I Chapter II' of Mathers' edition, although the two lists of operations are somewhat different.

Chapter Three
The Prayers of the Planets

---

[6] Portions of this manuscript have been translated in Torijano, Pablo A., *Solomon the Esoteric King: From King to Magus, Development of a Tradition (Supplements to the Journal for the Study of Judaism)*. Leiden: Brill, 2002.
[7] I will for this purpose refer to MacGregor, Mathers S. L. (ed.), *The Key of Solomon the King (Clavicula Salomonis)*. London: Kessinger Publishing Co., 1888, regarding the division of the chapters and the numbering of the pages.

A preliminary operation is described here, during which the sorcerer is instructed to recite one of the seven planetary prayers, depending on the spirit he wants to evoke. After the planet is submitted, he addresses a prayer to the planetary angel, in order to bind the corresponding planetary demon. After these prayers, the sorcerer must offer the appropriate planetary incenses. Finally, the author cites the seven planetary prayers. This chapter is not related to the *Key of Solomon*.

Chapter Four
Of the Signs of the Zodiac

This chapter includes general observations on the twelve signs of the zodiac, instructions for calculating the position of the moon in the zodiac and finally instructions for constructing zodiacal talismans. The first two parts are similar to page thirteen in 'Book I Chapter II' of Mathers' edition.

Chapter Five
Conjuration of the Angels

This is a general conjuration to the angels of the day in order to bind the demons. It must be recited after the prayers of the planets, as indicated in 'Chapter 3'. There is no relation between this conjuration and the *Key of Solomon*.

Chapter Six
Angels and Demons of the Days

This chapter names the angels and the demons of each planet. Three of the angels of our text correspond to the angels given in page eight from Mathers' edition, namely *Mikhaêl*, Sun; *Gauriêl*, Moon; and *Anael*, Venus. *Raphaêl* is here curiously attributed to Jupiter instead of Mercury.

Planetary Angels according to the Harley 5596

Sun	Moon	Mars	Mercury	Jupiter	Venus	Saturn
Mikhaêl	Gauriêl	Ouril	Madadoel	Serpepheêl	Anael	Beel
Ariêl	Salouêl	Sabeel	Peretjkeel	Raphaêl	Gathouel	
Phylonel	Kharjel		Apodokiel		Pêlakouel	
Saüriêl	Emphjloel				Kyrsoel	
Douniel	Spendonim					
	Perdikoim					
	Ougariel					

Planetary Demons according to the Harley 5596

Sun	Moon	Mars	Mercury	Jupiter	Venus	Saturn
Khthouniêl	Tartarouel	Sbirouel	Khalib	Podékoulator	Babet	Zeboul
Ariaêl			Silouanil	Orniel	Baltasar	
Epithouanon					Protizékatour	

Chapter Seven
Planetary Characters, Seals, and Incenses

While the use of the incenses is mentioned in 'Chapter 3' of our text, the planetary characters and the seals described in this chapter have no apparent use in the act of evocation. They are remnants of older material of talismanic nature. Both the characters and the seals do not bring to memory any other magical book and the incenses are similarly unique.

Chapter Eight
Concerning the Construction of the Knife

The text describes the knife with the black hilt. It has only one sharp edge and one has to forge the blade from iron by which a murder has been committed, for example from an older knife or sword. Its handle must be constructed from a horn of a black male goat. It brings to mind the similar black handled knife from 'Book II, Chapter VIII' of the *Key of Solomon*, but its construction is quite different.

Chapter Nine
Concerning the Construction of the Pen

A reed must be cut with a single strike by means of the aforementioned knife. During the strike, the sorcerer must be on his knees reciting a short prayer. The reed must be pointed by means of the same knife, in order to be used as a pen for the various magical characters. There is no exact parallel in the *Key of Solomon*.

Chapter Ten
Concerning the Construction of the Feather Quill

This quill must be constructed from the feather of a goose, crow, or vulture, and it must be plucked from the right wing of the bird. When the sorcerer plucks it he must recite a short conjuration. Afterwards he must point it by means of the black handled knife and wash it in spring water. The feather quill is probably to be used as an alternative to the reed pen and there does not seem to be any difference in their usage. The sorcerer probably chooses the most convenient between the two. This chapter is very similar to 'Book II, Chapters XIV and XV' of the *Key of Solomon*. The short conjuration of Harley 5596 corresponds to the conjuration of 'Chapter XIV'.

Chapter Eleven
Concerning the Construction of the Virgin Parchment

Harley 5596 insists on the use of virgin parchment and it describes its construction. The virgin parchment is made from the skin of a male animal that has not suckled yet. The animal is slain with the black handled knife, while the sorcerer recites a conjuration for cleansing the skin from every possible contamination. Then one has to skin the animal, to wash the skin seven times in running water, and to place it in quicklime. Both this and the next chapter have great similarities with 'Book II, Chapter XVII' of the *Key of Solomon*.

Chapter Twelve
The Unborn Parchment

The unborn parchment is constructed from the skin of a newborn animal that has not yet touched the ground and is taken directly from its mother's belly. The black handled knife is not to be used for the skinning, but instead a sharpened reed is. In all respects apart from that, the method of its construction is exactly the same.

Chapter Thirteen
Concerning the Inks made from the Blood of a Bat, a Swallow, a Dove, and an Ox

The instructions are almost the same for all four animals. One has to recite a certain conjuration, which is different for each animal, the animal is slain with the black handled knife and finally its blood is collected in a glass vessel. The only difference in the instructions is that the ox must be healed in order not to die. There is no difference in the use of these four kinds of ink. They are probably four alternatives, according to which kind of animal is available at the time. This chapter corresponds to 'Book II, Chapter XVI' of the *Key of Solomon*.

Chapter Fourteen
Concerning the Images made of Beeswax

Beeswax is necessary for the sorcerer, since he must use it to construct the ring, as well as various images not defined by the text. It must be taken directly from the beehive and placed in a church. After three masses have taken place in this church, the sorcerer must recite a conjuration for the cleansing of the beeswax. Both the present and the next chapter correspond to 'Book II, Chapter XVIII' of the *Key of Solomon*.

Chapter Fifteen
Concerning the Images made of Clay

It is possible for one to use clay instead of beeswax in order to make the aforementioned undefined images. The text instructs that the clay must be collected from a river, into which the sorcerer must walk upstream, since otherwise there is danger that he will collect clay previously trodden by him, that is to say, contaminated.

Chapter Sixteen
The Knowledge of the Time when some Operations must take place

This chapter refers to the construction of talismans in relation to the phases of the moon, and it is irrelevant to the act of evocation. It has no parallel in the *Key of Solomon*.

Chapter Seventeen
Instructions concerning the Making of the Garments

This chapter begins with the preparation of the sorcerer, who has to fast and remain pure for two weeks to confess his sins and to have a bath. For three days before the evocation he must not eat anything at all from sunrise until sunset, while after the sunset he is allowed to eat only bread and water. The garments, which are an inner tunic, robe, cloak, gloves, socks, and shoes, must be new. With the exception of the gloves that have to be leather, the rest of the garments must be made from white linen weaved by a virgin girl. Various magical symbols are cited, which have to be written on the robe, cloak, gloves, socks, and shoes of the sorcerer, as well as on a cotton cloth that covers the *Ourania*. The ink is made from cinnabar, rosewater, musk, and saffron. This chapter is similar to 'Book I, Chapter III' and 'Book II, Chapters II, IV and VI' of the *Key of Solomon*.

Chapter Eighteen
Concerning the Construction of the Crown

This chapter describes the construction of a headdress made of virgin parchment, similar to the one described in 'Book II, Chapter VI' of the *Key of Solomon*. Upon this headdress one must write various characters and divine names.

Chapter Nineteen
Concerning the Construction of the Heavenly Seal

This is the *par excellence* phylactery of the sorcerer and has to be made of unborn parchment. The *Ourania*, 'Heavenly Seal', of the Harley 5596 MS does not resemble any other symbol found in magical books. Its shape is oblong and includes, among other symbols, ten different talismans enclosed in circles. The ink used is black and red, like the one for the characters on the sorcerer's garments. The *Ourania* must be worn over the sorcerer's chest covered by the cotton cloth that is described in Chapter Seventeen.

Chapter Twenty
Concerning the Ring

Curiously enough, the ring is made of beeswax. The wax ring is swaddled in virgin parchment, upon which the sorcerer must carve a pentagram and write twelve magical names. There is no parallel in the *Key of Solomon*.

Chapter Twenty-one
The Way of Working

The sorcerer must find an isolated place and normalize the ground. During the full moon, he must cleanse the place by means of special composite incense. Then he must trace the circle with the black handled knife. The magical circle consists of two concentric circles within a square. The four angles of the square touch the central points of a greater square, which is the external boundary of the whole design. Between the two circles four pentagrams are traced, one at each cardinal point. Between the pentagrams the sorcerer traces various magical names. Then, he the 'Master', is to enter the circle together with his helper, the 'Disciple'. The Disciple must have a little bell with him in order to ring it before he enters the circle. The image of the circle, with the exception of the magical names, is identical to the one depicted in 'Plate XIV' on page ninety-seven in the *Key of Solomon*. This chapter has many similarities with 'Book II, Chapters VII and IX' in the *Key of Solomon*.

Chapter Twenty-two
Conjurations

This chapter begins with a prayer. The sorcerer asks God to help him in order to submit the demons. After a long list of magical names, the sorcerer recites a conjuration for the visible appearance of the spirits. The spirits are asked to come wherever they may be, with a pleasant form and without harming the sorcerer. The preliminary prayer is similar to the one cited in the *Key of Solomon*, 'Book I, Chapter V'. The conjuration has some small similarities with the one cited in the same chapter, but there is no Qabalistic element in the Greek text. If the spirits do not appear at once, the sorcerer must touch the *Ourania* on his chest and proceed with a second conjuration, full of magical names, that is supposed to bind the demonic kings of the four quarters, namely *Loutzipher, Beelzeboul, Astarôth* and *Asmedai*.[8] By means of this conjuration, the legions of the spirits are expected to appear without delay. The conjurer must not be afraid, but ask them who their king is. When the king is revealed, the other spirits must swear submission to the sorcerer in the king's name. The king himself must swear in his office. Although the action of touching the *Ourania* brings to mind 'Book I, Chapters VI and VII' of the *Key of Solomon*, the conjuration has no resemblance.

Chapter Twenty-three
How to make a Lady love you

When the spirits have given the oath, the sorcerer must state his will in the form of another conjuration. Our text offers two possible requests to the spirits, women and money. This chapter is a conjuration that sends the spirits to a woman in order to make her love the sorcerer.

Chapter Twenty-four
How to send them to bring you a Treasure

As in the previous chapter, when the spirits have given the oath, the sorcerer can send them to bring him a treasure by means of this conjuration.

---

[8]Although the *Key of Solomon* does not cite these names, three of the chief demons of the four quarters seem to have survived in the *Grand Grimoire* and the *Grimorium Verum*. See Peterson, J. (ed.), *Grimorium Verum*. California: CreateSpace Publishing, 2007.

Chapter Twenty-five
Another Method of Spirit Evocation

From this point begins a slightly different method of evocation. It seems that one copyist included two separate but similar methods in the same book and the posterior copyists continued to cite them both. This second method, like the first, begins with the preparation of the sorcerer, who must fast and remain pure for two weeks. Again, before the evocation he must consume only bread and water. His garments must be new and made from white linen, but this time there is no mention of magical symbols written upon them. The headdress is a piece of cloth, probably something like a turban, while the phylactery, which is again made of unborn parchment, consists of twenty-four symbols enclosed in separate circles.

Chapter Twenty-six
The Way of Working

As in the previous method, the sorcerer must find an isolated place. During the full moon he must be washed, anointed with some kind of fragrant oil, and wear the garments. Then he must trace the circle with the black handled knife and offer a special composite incense from four censers located at the four cardinal points.

Chapter Twenty-seven
Conjurations towards the Four Quarters

This chapter consists of four conjurations that contain the names of all the spirits of the four quarters. There are about thirty demons ascribed to each quarter, that is to say we have about one hundred and twenty names of demons in all. Some of them are taken from the *Testament of Solomon*, since the author could probably not make them up by himself. The text is not clear-cut as to whether there must be a conjuration of all four quarters together, or that the sorcerer has to choose beforehand which of the four quarters to evoke.

Chapter Twenty-eight
The Conjuration

This conjuration resembles the first method. After it is recited, the sorcerer is supposed to see the legions of the spirits and ask what he wants. At this point, the author informs us that here ends the book concerning the evocation of demons.

After two somewhat irrelevant recipes relating to water divination, there is a belated addition of longer lists of the horary angels and demons, and of the hours appropriate for the construction of the planetary talismans. They are followed by a chapter concerning the planetary herbs. The existence of two separate lists of angels and demons has been briefly discussed by Greenfield. The two lists seem to be distantly related to each other, "the first being but a fragment which was similar in content as well as method and so probably equally extensive at one time."[9] I would add that the short list is an abbreviated form of the long list and that the whole text is but a recension uniting at least two irrelevant books. This hypothesis explains the aforementioned belated addition of the long list of horary spirits. The recensionist probably regretted changing the older text, thus losing a variety of information. If this is the case, we seem to face a very complicated situation. Not only was the *Key of Solomon* a recension of the Greek text, but also the Greek text itself was a recension of older magical books.

Various other indications lead to the same conclusion, since this attempt at recension was quite unsuccessful. Firstly, the part concerning planetary magic is totally irrelevant to the part concerning evocation, since the latter pertains solely to the evocation of the demons of the four cardinal quarters. Secondly, there are peculiar chapters related to planetary talismanic magic scattered throughout the text. Those fragments make us suspect that the first part, a work regarding planetary talismans, was actually transformed to fit the second part, being originally a work on evocation. Moreover, the second part consists of two versions, a long, which are chapters eight to twenty-four, and a short one, which are chapters twenty-five to twenty-eight.

Scott Carroll detects five extant recensions of the text among the various manuscripts, which fall under three textual traditions. Although he admits that it is futile to discern which textual tradition is the closest to the original, he prefers to examine the Monacensis 70 MS, since he maintains that it is less fragmentary.[10] After his examination he concludes that the author was probably Jewish from Alexandria, and that the latest probable date of the text's compilation was the end of the second century A.D. Although a discussion on Carroll's conclusions falls out of the scope of the present article, it seems that his selection of the Monacensis 70 MS was extremely felicitous. This text cites the long lists of the planetary hours and horary spirits in their proper place, that is to say immediately after Solomon's address to Rehoboam, and it generally presents a logical and comprehensive system of talismanic magic free from passages related to evocation.

I feel it somewhat lacking to conclude this paper without a few words on the various titles given to this text. The majority of the manuscripts are untitled. Some are headless,

---

[9]Greenfield, *Traditions of Belief in Late Byzantine Demonology*, p. 338-346.
[10]Carroll, 'A Preliminary Analysis of the Epistle of Rehoboam', in *Journal for the Study of the Pseudepigrapha* 4, p. 91-103.

while others begin with phrases such as "O my dearest son Rehoboam, be attentive to the accuracy of this art." Taurinensis C VII 15 bore the simple title *Solomon's instructions to Rehoboam*, but since it is very general it was never used by researchers. Monacensis 70 and Dionysiou 282 have instead *The Key to the whole art of Hygromancy*. Although the name *Hygromantia Salomonis* was used in the *Catalogus* in order to describe the text, it was obviously misleading, since the content was totally irrelevant to divination. This name is probably a subsequent addition pertaining rather to divinatory material annexed at a later time. Delatte in *Anecdota Atheniensia* chose to name the text *Traité de Magie*, translated by Greenfield as *Magic Treatise*, which was probably inspired by the title of Harley 5596. However, the Greek title *Apotelesmatikê Pragmateia* literally means 'Treatise on Astrological Influences', thus bolstering the theory of an early work on planetary talismanic magic. Finally, the artificial title *Epistle to Rehoboam*, not supported by the text, was extensively used by Carroll, as he was trying to incorporate this text in the corpus of the Old Testament Pseudepigrapha.

As a conclusion, I would like to apologise to Greek readers who are familiar with my work on the history of the grimoires from *Anazêtôntas tên Kleida tou Solomonta*.[11] They will probably be at a loss here, since in this book I have used the titles *Hygromancy* and *Epistle* for the earlier talismanic work, following Carroll, and *Magic Treatise* for the posterior work on evocation, following Greenfield. This was a choice based solely on my feeling that it was essential to use titles based on the existent bibliography.

---

[11]Marathakis, Ioannis, *Anazêtôntas tên Kleida tou Solomônta*. Athens: Eidikos Typos, 2007.

BIBLIOGRAPHY

Carroll, S., 'A Preliminary Analysis of the Epistle of Rehoboam'. In *Journal for the Study of the Pseudepigrapha* 4. London: Sage Publications, 1989.

Delatte, Armand, 'Le Traité les Plantes Planétaires d'un manuscript de Leningrad'. In *Annuaire de l'Institute de Philologie et d'Histoire Orientales et Slaves,* IX. Universite libre de Bruxelles, 1949.

Greenfield, Richard, *Traditions of Belief in Late Byzantine Demonology.* Amsterdam: Hakkert, 1998.

MacGregor, Mathers S. L. (ed.), *The Key of Solomon the King (Clavicula Salomonis).* London: Kessinger Publishing Co., 1888.

Marathakis, Ioannis, *Anazêtôntas tên Kleida tou Solomônta.* Athens: Eidikos Typos, 2007.

Marathakis, Ioannis, *The Magical Treatise of Solomon or Hygromanteia.* Singapore: Golden Hoard Press, 2011.

Peterson, J. (ed.), *Grimorium Verum.* California: CreateSpace Publishing, 2007.

Scholem G. (ed.), 'Some Sources of Jewish-Arabic Demonology'. In *Journal of Jewish Studies.* Oxford Centre for Hebrew and Jewish Studies, 1965.

THE ICELANDIC TRADITION OF MAGIC ANALYSIS OF A LATE-EIGHTEENTH CENTURY ICELANDIC GALDRABÓK

BY

CHRISTOPHER A. SMITH

A Thurs I carve on thee, and three staves,
Perversion and madness and lust;
But I may scrape off that which I carved
If I find need for that.

Skírnir, *Skirnismal*

The Status of Iceland in Modern Northern Magic

It goes without saying that interest in rune magic, *seiðr*, and the old gods of the North has experienced an unprecedented upsurge since 1970. The revival has gone through a number of phases, been driven by several charismatic characters and writers, undergone schisms, and seen the rise and decline of organizations. In attempting to make sense of the enigmatic Futhark rows and the remaining fragments of northern European lore, and turn these into some coherent system of magic, writers, and experimenters have frequently looked outside of the tradition itself, taking their inspiration from Wicca, pan-Germanic nationalism, oriental yogic practices, and the Western Occult Tradition.[1] Fortunately, there has recently been a trend towards greater purism so that the more fantastic concepts are eschewed and some intellectual honesty, at least, is applied when occult practices from other parts of the world are co-opted.

One thing that has justifiably stayed fairly constant is an appreciation and reverence of Iceland, its people, and its culture for their role in conserving such lore as now exists. After all, it was mainly down to the efforts of the skald and historian Snorri Sturlusson, the collector Arni Magnusson, Jón Árnason, and other anonymous writers that a large body of lore was preserved in writing in the form of folk tales, sagas, and mythology. Furthermore, the Icelandic language has changed much less than its Scandinavian cousins over the years and is still a good basis for mastering the intricacies of Old

---

[1] This is understandable. Given the sketchy nature of the extant sources, it is difficult to build up anything coherent without 'outside help'.

1- Its really not that fragmented. Egg People are just lazy and want to play "magic".

Norse.[2] Even today, Icelanders regularly choose names that are familiar in the sagas when naming their children, such as Gisli, Sigurður, and Brynhildr, for example, and they retain the ancient patronymic system of surnames, whereby Sigurður, son of Gisli, is officially known as 'Sigurður Gislason'. Outside of the capital area, people are still very close to the land and the sea in their daily economic activities, and there is still a very real, underlying belief in the existence of elves, trolls, and ghosts. Geographically, it is always a land of fire and ice, of the midnight sun in summer and long, long darkness in the winter, and the rugged landscape has a distinctly 'heroic' quality about it. Iceland was also the first country to officially recognize *Ásatrú* as a religion. For modern adherents of the Northern magical tradition, a trip to Iceland takes on the nature of a pilgrimage.

It is therefore strange that so little attention has been paid up to now to indigenous Icelandic magical practices that post-date the Viking Age. There seems to be little inclination to look for evidence of continuity, or seek out indications that we might have to revise our conceptions of Viking-age magic. There are few published works, of which I have been able to track down only nine so far, and of these only two are in English. In his book *The Galdrabók: An Icelandic Grimoire*,[3] Stephen E. Flowers translated an earlier work in Swedish[4] and added some commentary on the historical background and the methods of magic that were employed in the grimoire. The other work available in English is *Tvaer galdraskræður: Two Icelandic Books of Magic*[5] and this publication will form the basis for this paper.

Gadrasýning á Ströndum

In the year 2000, the Icelandic museum of Sorcery and Witchcraft was established at the small village of Hólmavík in the Westfjords province of Iceland, and it has done much to promote interest in Icelandic magic. It was to this museum that I travelled in October 2008 and to which I returned for a much longer period beginning in August 2010 with the aim of learning the Icelandic language and studying the true nature of Icelandic folk beliefs. The museum itself focuses on the seventeenth century, when the European fashion for persecuting witches and sorcerers found its way to Iceland, with the result that a number of individuals were tried, convicted, and punished with

---

[2]It is often stated that the written Icelandic language has not changed in a thousand years and that only the pronunciation has changed. Guides in the National Cultural Museum in Reykjavik avidly peddle this story to foreign visitors. It is not true. Very few Icelanders today can read the mediaeval texts without specialised tuition.

[3]Flowers, Stephen E., *The Galdrabók: An Icelandic Grimoire*. Austin: Runa-Raven Press, 2005.

[4]Lindqvist, Natan, *En Isländsk Svartkonstbok från 1500 talet*. Uppsala: Appelbergs boktryckeri aktiebolag, 1921. This is also counted among the nine published works.

[5]Rafnsson, Magnús (trans.), *Tvaer galdraskræður: Two Icelandic Books of Magic*. Hólmavík: Strandagaldur, 2008.

various degrees of severity. The museum houses an eclectic and fascinating collection of exhibits illustrating magical practices at that time, such as the *Tilberi*, a kind of vampiric worm; the 'sea mouse', which was captured in order to gain money; a fish's head raised on a pole in order to control the winds; and, of course, the world-famous *Nábrók* or 'necropants'. It also has a display of reproductions of the grimoires that have survived the age of persecution and are now preserved in the National Library and the Arni Magnusson Institute in Reykjavik.

The Grimoires

There are dozens of Icelandic grimoires in various collections and others are still coming to light. Some are fairly extensive, while others consist only of a single page. All of them are, of course, handwritten and in the Icelandic language. I still lack the necessary knowledge and skills[6] to decipher the manuscripts themselves, so for my present purposes I have concentrated on one manuscript only, the Lbs 2413 8vo that has been rendered into print and translated into English by Magnús Rafnsson in *Tvaer galdraskræður: Two Icelandic Books of Magic*, a dual-language book published in 2008. In introducing the work, Magnús Rafnsson confines himself to a brief description of the two grimoires and a summary of the current extent of knowledge about Icelandic grimoires in general. His introduction is followed by a plain exposition of the contents of the grimoires without further comment. He writes,

> The manuscript Lbs 2413 8vo was written ca. 1800 and is the largest collection of magical staves in a single manuscript even when compared to those collected by amateur scholars almost a century later. Many of the magical acts described are the same as those mentioned in court records [of prosecutions for sorcery and witchcraft - CS] and similar ones can be found in the 17th century grimoires. The manuscript itself measures 10 x 8 cm with 74 leaves and nothing is known of its history or how the library acquired it. Apparently a systematic collection was intended, beginning with various acts to prevent theft or find who has stolen, then a collection of love magic, but after that there seems to be no specific order to the staves. After a number of protective staves or sigils there follow a number of invocations against ghosts and evil spirits.

Without detracting in any way from the value of Magnús' painstaking effort to bring these grimoires to the modern public, it is my belief that one can go much further in commenting on this and other works, and to this end the present paper is dedicated.

---

[6]For example, familiarity with the language and styles of handwriting.

Analysis of Lbs 2413 8vo

The grimoire consists of one hundred and eighty-seven separate spells and sigils, covering a wide variety of intentions and purposes. A very few of them are vague in the extreme, offering only a sigil without any further explanation. Most, however, are quite specific as to the purpose, the method, and the instrument to be used for carving the surface to be carved, whether any body fluids are involved, and many other factors. Some are overtly Heathen, others overtly Judeo-Christian, yet others an amalgam of both religious backgrounds. In some cases, certain words are written in a code and we can only speculate as to why this may have been done.

A considerable number of spells, twenty-nine, are general in nature, being for luck, for protection from evil, or to be used for multiple purposes. Not surprisingly, most of these are talismanic in method, that is, they are designed to be carried upon the person permanently. A typical example is spell number 145, "The staves that follow are against all evil on sea and land. Carve them on skin of a heifer's first calf and carry always with you." The second largest category of spells, nineteen, have no specified purpose, although the purpose of some of these can be surmised on the basis of the spells that preceded them. One can only assume that the accompanying sigils and glyphs were collected merely out of curiosity or that, perhaps, the purpose was so well known to the collector as to require no further notes. Nearly half of the sigils that fall into this 'unspecified' category are distinctly Judeo-Christian in character, such as the Seal of the Holy Spirit, the Seal of Jareb son of Solomon, and so on, which prompts one to speculate that the collector came across them and simply added them to the grimoire without understanding their meaning. However, the 'general' and 'unspecified' categories account for only about twenty-six percent of the total. The vast majority are quite specific as to their intention and the purposes open up a fascinating insight into the lives and concerns of Icelanders circa 1800.

Human Relationships

As one might expect, there are quite a few spells relating to love or lust, an eternal and ubiquitous human preoccupation. Take spell number 22 for example, where it states, "That a girl will love you. Carve this stave in the palm of your hand with your saliva and then shake her hand." The interesting thing about the spells of this type is that they all aim to gain the love of a woman, which suggests that the owner of the grimoire was a man. This accords with the male-dominated nature of Icelandic sorcery as recorded in the court records of the seventeenth century witchcraft persecution. Only one woman was executed on charges of witchcraft in Iceland. Of course, it may be that women in Iceland practised witchcraft to an equal degree but were canny enough not to get caught, or that they practised a different type of magic not recognised as such by the authorities. Three more spells are related to the theme of love and lust. Two are intended to test whether a woman is a virgin or not, and the third is intended to ensure that the desired girl is not 'corrupted' by anyone else, of course!

As well as these, there are more spells relating to human relationships of a non-sexual nature. The main themes here are soothing anger, inflicting fear, influencing someone to see your point of view, or gaining general popularity.

If you want to change the views of a man you are disputing with. Carve this stave on the skin of a heifer's first calf and carry on your breast.

Economic

Pastoral farming and sea fishing are important elements of the Icelandic economy even today; in 1800, most Icelanders made their living from fishing or from rearing sheep or more rarely other livestock. This is reflected in the large number of spells designed to protect the magician's own livestock, to harm the livestock of an enemy, to get success in fishing or rowing, or to prevent a competitor from catching fish. There was little arable farming, but it was essential to gather hay for the winter, as can be seen from one spell for keeping the edge of a scythe sharp for this purpose. And of course, having successfully reared one's sheep or caught a good haul of fish, a portion of these would be traded for other necessities, so there are also six spells to ensure a fair or advantageous deal in trading.

To fish, carve this stave on your sinker.

Crime and Civil Disputes

In theory, Iceland was a society governed by law from the very first *Alþingi* in 930 C.E., but given the scattered and fragmented structure of that society with no towns or villages until the late eighteenth century, enforcement of the law was rough and haphazard. There was no established police force. This is reflected in the relatively large body of spells designed to discover who has stolen, to protect from theft, including rustling of livestock, or to win one's case in disputes.

> Item. Carve on red spruce and keep under your head for 6 nights and you will see the thief.

Presumably, given that sorcerous means of discovery could not be presented as evidence in a court of law, the discovery of the thief would be followed by personal retribution without reference to the local magistrate.

While on the topic of crime, there are still more spells that were probably conceived with the intent of committing some crime or other mischief. There are spells to induce sleep in others, to gain invisibility, and to make someone steal. It is interesting, especially given the other options for crime and the moral codes of the times, that theft is the major topic. For example, no spells relating to direct physical violence,[7] deadly or otherwise, are mentioned in the grimoire.

Healing

A surprisingly small number of the spells are dedicated to healing. There are two for healing humans and three for healing livestock, such as horses and cows, but not sheep.

Weather Control

Only two spells, 43 and 126, have the purpose of controlling the weather in some way. Number 43 is "for a favourable wind" and number 126 is "to call up a northern blizzard."

Protection against Ghosts, Spirits, and Magic

---

[7]Except for wrestling.

Fifteen spells are devoted to this purpose. Nearly all of those intended to ward against hostile magic are talismanic in method.

Advantage in Sports and Games

Two of the listed spells are intended to help the user win at games of cards and three are intended to gain victory in the traditional Icelandic sport of wrestling.

Purely Malicious Intentions

Some of the spells have the purely malicious intention of making someone else's life a misery in some way or other, whether by influencing their bodily functions, such as inducing vomiting or unstoppable farting, making a rider fall from a crippled horse, or causing someone to lose his way. Interestingly, none of these spells have an overtly deadly intent towards humans, although getting lost in winter could have fatal results! The reason for this is obscure. It may be that the collector eschewed spells designed to kill or inflict serious, lasting harm. Alternatively, it is possible that the possession of deadly spells in written form was likely to guarantee ultimate condemnation of the owner if found out, so such spells may have been memorised rather than committed to writing. A kindly interpretation is that spells designed to kill or inflict serious injury were simply beyond the pale in the society in which this magic was generated.

Method

So far, the analysis of the manuscript has mainly been of historical and anthropological interest. The practical magician will, however, be more interested in the methods of application. After all, what is the use of analysing such ancient manuscripts, unless one can learn from them in order to promote the science and art of magic, draw general conclusions, and move on to invent new spells more relevant to modern circumstances?

Prayer

Only seven of the one hundred and eighty-seven spells in Lbs 2413 8vo consist of simple prayers to a higher power. All of these are overtly Judeo-Christian in content, even where in a single example reference is made to the old, Heathen gods. Although I do not discount theurgy as a valid magical method, these prayers hardly count as aligning oneself with divine forces as they are merely pious words uttered in the hope and faith of divine help. They can therefore be disregarded as examples of real magic.

Talismans

By far the largest category of the spells included in the manuscript, seventy-one out of one hundred and eighty-seven, involves the creation of a talisman of some description. The talisman is then carried upon the person until its aim is achieved. This could be virtually for life if the aim is to achieve good luck in general or to permanently ward against evil, although many have a much more limited aim, such as to find out who has stolen from you or simply 'to get your wish'. A good example of such a talisman is contained in number 141,

> This is the luck-knot of a man. It should always be carried on one's body.

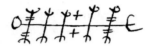

Note that there are no instructions regarding what is to be done with the talismans once their intention is achieved.

Contact, Proximity, and Feeding

The next most common method of bringing about a magical intention is by carving a stave on one object and then bringing that object into contact with the target person or animal. One might also carve the staves on food, such as bread or cheese, and feed it to the intended victim. Closely related are spells that work in proximity to the victim. The stave is either carved on an object and then brought close to the victim, or carved in a place that the victim will have to approach, such as her bedpost. Some spells even involve carving a stave directly onto the target person, animal, or object. It should be mentioned at this point that the word 'carve', *rist*, is used fairly indiscriminately throughout the grimoire to mean 'writing' or merely 'tracing characters', as well as actually 'carving', and I will return to this matter later. The spells that operate by contact, proximity, or feeding often seem to assume a surprising freedom of access to the intended victim. Take, for example, spell number 42,

> To prick with a sleep thorn. Carve on a beech tablet with steel and lay under or on top of the head of the sleeper and recite: I invoke the Devil that he put power into these staves so whether I lay them under or over the head, that this man (and name him) will sleep as the stones lying in the streets.

The ease of access to the victim is more understandable when one realises that there were few locks on doors and that people, including servants, often slept crowded together under the same roof.

Divination

Many of the spells mentioned in the grimoire are methods of divination, usually in order to find out who has stolen goods. Some of these involve scrying into a bowl of water in order to see the face of the thief, while others operate by inducing dreams that will reveal who the thief is. In one case, slips of paper bearing the names of suspects are floated on water where the first one to sink reveals the name of the thief.

Materials Used

Although there are some spells that do not require the carving of a stave, simple prayers being a good example, the majority involve carving, writing, or tracing a stave on some surface or other. The majority fail to specify one or more of the materials that are to be used, but this still leaves us with many in which the carving instrument, the carved surface, body fluids, and sometimes additional materials such as herbs are laid down.

Carving Instrument

As mentioned previously, the word 'carve', *rist*, is used indiscriminately to mean writing and tracing, as well as actual carving. The instrument most frequently prescribed is the knife, *mathnif,* which the magician habitually uses when eating. This would have the advantages of being readily available and having an established psychic link with its owner through daily use. Ten of the spells call only for the stave to be traced with one's own finger, three of them naming a specific finger.[8] Again, this would have been an easy and convenient method of 'carving' when a quick, single result is required. In other cases, the spell names a certain material that is to be used for the carving or writing. These include steel, brass, copper, lead, silver, wood, with juniper being mentioned in one, basalt, and human bone. Amazingly, one spell for skill in wrestling says, "Carve these staves on your shoe with human bone or a bone from the toe of your wrestling foot." Quite how one is supposed to extract a bone from one's own foot is not mentioned, and it is hard to see how this potentially crippling procedure would enhance wrestling skills.[9]

---

[8]One specifies "the long finger on the left hand" and two specify "the left leech-finger", more commonly known as the 'ring-finger' these days.
[9]I strongly suspect that some misinterpretation has crept in at some point, although the translation from the

Instruments other than knives or fingers are also sometimes called for, such as scissors, awls, finger bones that are presumably whittled to a point first, pens, pencils, the spine of a dogfish, and a raven's feather. Unfortunately, the grimoire does not mention why it is important to use a particular instrument or material for carving. All of the materials and implements, with the exception of silver,[10] lead and, human bone, would have been commonly available. This forms a sharp contrast with the surface to be carved, as we shall see.

The Carved Surface

As with the carving instrument, the surface to be carved is often not specified, but this still leaves us with many cases where it is and a wide variety of objects and materials we see here too. Sometimes these are easily explicable, being themselves in some way the target of the spell, such as the bowl that is to be used for scrying, the tool that is to be charmed, or the animal that is to be harmed or healed. Other obvious cases include many of the 'proximity' type spells, such as the bedpost of the girl one intends to seduce, the saddle cloth of the horse that is to be harmed, and so on. At other times we are presented with a variety of materials, some of them easily available and others less so. Baleen, for example, might seem quite an exotic material these days, but in eighteenth century Iceland it would have been fairly common. On the other hand, many of the staves are to be carved on oak, where sometimes 'splintered oak' or 'killing oak'[11] is specified, and this would have been extremely rare in Iceland's relatively treeless environment. Beech, rowan and, red spruce are also used.[12] Another favourite surface for carving is heifer's skin or the skin of a heifer's first calf. Again, I suspect that something may be lost in translation here, as a heifer is a virgin cow and therefore is no longer a heifer when it has calved. Such material would also have been relatively rare. Most farmers were very poor and would only have owned a single cow for its milk yield. Beef was a luxury and it would be unusual to slaughter a heifer or its first calf. Perhaps the rarity of such materials was intended to enhance the power of the spell. Sanctified paper is also specified in many of the spells, though they do not specify by whom or by what means the paper had to be sanctified.

Icelandic is quite accurate.

[10]Iceland had no towns and few villages before 1780. Barter was common and many farmers rarely handled a coin in the whole of their lives. It has been truly said that the country only began to emerge from the Middle Ages towards the end of the nineteenth century.

[11]Magnús Rafnsson has informed me that oak and beech could be used to refer to any substantial tree, including birch, and that the former species were indeed unknown in Iceland. I have yet to establish what is meant by 'killing oak' or why the oak should be splintered. I advanced the idea that splintered oak might be from a lightning-blasted tree, which is a powerful association with Thor, but I was told that thunderstorms are very rare in Iceland.

[12]Beech does not grow in Iceland, while rowan and spruce grow quite abundantly.

Bodily Fluids

Having carved the stave, or while carving it, if writing is actually intended, it frequently had to be charged with a bodily fluid. In the manuscript only blood and saliva are mentioned. Blood is used in twenty-six of the spells. This was most usually the magician's own blood, but three specify calf's blood. Saliva is used in eleven spells and a single spell says that either blood or saliva may be used. Human excrement, preferably from a dead man, is specified in spell number 59 to make someone sleep, but this is not used to charge a stave.

Other Significant Elements of the Spells
Heathen Elements

Although only six, or possibly seven, of the one hundred and eighty-seven spells listed in the manuscript have overtly Heathen references, for example to the pre-Christian deities of Iceland, one should rather be surprised that there are any such references at all rather than dismayed at the lack of them. After all this manuscript dates from the year 1800, eight hundred years after the official conversion of Iceland to Christianity. Most often, the Heathen references fall among other Judeo-Christian invocations. Number 181, the *Byrnie Prayer, Brynjubæn*, is a case in point. It begins, "I entrust myself today and every other day to the name and graceful power of God, the Father, the Son and the Holy Spirit." It then rambles on for another four pages, calling on John the Baptist, Jesus Christ, angels, archangels, and so on for protection. Then, towards the end of the prayer, we come across the following intriguing words, "When they want to do me evil may the ancient Satan and the cunning Óðinn look at me with the eyes of wolf and eagle... Óðinn with the elfs will make them mad...." Presumably the author still had enough faith in the old gods and the elves to hedge his bets. Spell 75 is punchier and makes no concessions to Christianity, "Write nine[13] ása and þursa 30.[14] I invoke þór and Óðinn so he will shit as many farts as the vein lies in his arse, all my enemies will feel shame and become afraid, they will retreat and be disgraced...." The invocation accompanying spell 45 for invisibility contains so many Heathen references that it is worthy of further study in its own right and is worth quoting in full,

> Strike thou þór,
> Fog thou hast,
> And even in fog
> far and wide walked
> with the daughters of Jöfrir

---

[13] The English translation in *Tvær galdraskræður* gives eight, but this is a mistranslation. The original Icelandic is *níu*, which is clearly nine.
[14] These are Futhark runes.

and in the fog of Þórir
fog of Þumill
fog of Örvandill
fog of Baldur
and the fire of Óðinn;
Come now Lord
around the dark head
that Hringþornir
pushed to sea.
All then became afraid
Fire then rose
into the air
nowhere were seen
the sky, the moon
nor the stars.
Cover my head
Hliðskjálfargramur
body with bones,
breast with bones,
cartilage with feet
so no man will see me.[15]

In reversal of the concept of the *Byrnie Prayer*, in which Odin and the elves are called upon almost as an afterthought, this very Heathen invocation ends in, "In Nomine pater et filius et Spiritus Santus Amen!"[16]

Mention of Runes

It is not the purpose of this paper to define exactly what a 'rune' is. At present, I refer only to cases where runes are mentioned in some way or where identifiable Futhark runes are used. Surprisingly, considering Iceland's heritage, this occurs in only five of the one hundred and eighty-seven spells. One of them is the spell to inflict farting quoted in the previous section. Another farting spell, number 67, also says, "I carve you 8 ásar, 9 nauðir, 13 þursa." Interestingly, characters in the given numbers are shown in this spell, but these characters bear little resemblance to the relevant runes of either the Elder or the Younger Futhark rows,

---

[15]Quoted verbatim from the text without alteration of the punctuation.
[16]Note the corrupted and incorrect Latin.

Spell 117, "If you want to hide something. Carve this stave, augnaþurs, over it", has only a tenuous connection with the Futhark runes. It literally means 'eye-thurs', but at least it has an element of connection with the third rune of the Futhark. It is relatively easy to decipher in its intention, where the Thurs-force strikes the eye, rendering it blind. The illustrated stave does not resemble the Thurs-rune, however. Spell 168 mentions "the greater Hagall" that should be carved on one's headgear in blood from the left arm "against all evil." The stave itself consists of two concentric circles with twenty-three radiating tridents,[17] all very crudely drawn. The fifth is actually the final spell in the grimoire. It is mainly Christian in sentiment but ends, without further explanation, with "og skrifa í málrúnum," which means 'and write in speech runes'.

The SATOR Square

One of the spells, number 115, concerns the ancient SATOR square, illustrating it accurately and saying, "The following they call Sator verse. It can be read every way and is good for many things. Some call it a releasing verse and say that it should be read over a woman giving birth and over a tackle when it becomes stuck in the bottom." Another spell, number 165, is against sorcery and calls for the magician to read "Sator a,r,e,p,e, t,e,n,a,t, o,p,e,r,o, n,o,t,a,s, Eli Eli Lamani Sabatini." Apart from the superstitious quoting, or misquoting, of Jesus' words on the cross,[18] the spell actually gets the SATOR rebus wrong. One can only suppose that it was handed down and transcribed with errors. I will return to the subject of error and superstition later.

Use of Code

A significant number of the spells, twenty-five in all, have certain words in a code. The code words include letters that do not occur in Icelandic, such as c, q, and x. It is quite a simple code, once deciphered, in which letters of the alphabet are consistently transposed. Having said that, credit is due to the author of *Tvær Galdraskræður* for cracking the code in the first place. One can only guess why certain words are in code while others are not. Just over half of the spells that use coded words relate to sex and prevention of seduction. The words that are in code, in these cases, are mainly 'woman' or 'maiden'. The spells to make someone sleep or fart also contain coded words. It

---

[17] *Elhazl/Maður* staves?
[18] *Eli Eli lama sabachthani*, which means "My God, my God, why have you forsaken me."

may be that the recorder of the spells felt that these particular ones were sufficiently disreputable as to require some kind of disguise.

Time and Direction

A few of the spells also include specific instructions relating to time and direction. Some of them specify the number of days or nights over which the operation is to be performed and, notably, the numbers are always three or its multiples. Others relate to the state of the moon. "One night old," "three nights old," "full," and "waxing" are variously specified, although one spell gives a more complex formula, "Carve these staves on splintered oak with a pencil when a Saturday moon is 5 nights old according to German numbers and keep under your head: to dream what you want." Another two spells name days of the week, such as in spell 39, the 'rowing staves' are to be carved on a Friday, and the second part of spell 9 stipulates the use of "an unused steel knife that was made between daybreak and matins on a Sunday." Three of the spells give solar timings, which are "the eve of St John's Mass,[19] when the sun is at its highest or while the sun is directly in the east." Finally, one spell instructs, "Walk fasting along the burn that runs from east to west before a bird flies over it." The meaning of this is somewhat mysterious; it may simply mean 'before dawn'.

Direction is also important in six of the spells. In only two cases is there an overlap between time-specific and direction-specific spells. One of these has been quoted above and the other, which is to be performed "while the sun is directly in the east", simply says that one should walk in the direction that you want the wind to come from. Spell 2, which is a spell for scrying to find a thief, requires water from a spring "that comes up facing east and north." Spell 72, a spell for acquiring skill in wrestling instructs, "and turn your face to the north-west" after a prayer to Thor and Odin. Spell 126 has "To call up a northern blizzard. Carve this stave on the head of a ling and walk northwards and wave it in the air." Spell 33, which is for trading, only specifies *öfugt*, 'in the wrong direction', which may mean 'anti-clockwise'.

The Form of the Staves

For the practising magician, the staves themselves are perhaps the most interesting aspect of the grimoire. At the same time, they are the hardest aspect to comment on. As anyone will know who has constructed bindrunes or other magical sigils, the object is to devise a glyph that embodies the magical intent in a way that bypasses even one's own conscious mind, thereby harnessing the enormous power of the subconscious, as

---

[19]St John's Mass fell on the twenty-fourth of June, known in England as Old Midsummer's Day.

well as other extra-personal forces. Deconstructing the staves contained in Lbs 2413 8vo might therefore seem a nearly impossible task. Nevertheless, it must be attempted and the present paper would not be complete without at least some remarks on the forms they take. Detailed analysis and deconstruction of these intriguing glyphs will have to wait, however, and will form the subject of a further paper.

The staves range from very simple forms to highly complex ones, and from poorly executed with some even resembling the inexpert doodling of a child and the kind of work one might expect from a moderately accomplished calligrapher.

The staves frequently consist of a number, usually four or eight, of spokes radiating from a central point or circular hub, terminating in a trident, a cross, or a circle. In this respect, they resemble the familiar *Ægirshjálmur* or 'Helm of Awe'. Spell 114, which is not actually a spell as such, illustrates a number of staves of this type and says, "These are the nine Helms of Awe that no-one can be without who will handle knowledge and each one should be used 99 times."

Some spells employ a single stave, while others call for multiple staves to be carved to achieve the desired effect. In many cases, the same intent, to get a girl for example, is served by very different staves in different spells. Conversely, one stave is used in spells 1 and 26 for quite different purposes.

Where Futhark-type runes, such as *ás*, *þurs*, and *nauð* are mentioned by name, the associated staves in the manuscript bear no resemblance to the Futhark staves. Nevertheless, the staves that are illustrated do crop up in other spells where runes are not mentioned, so it may be possible to extract some system from these with further study.

In five of the spells, the familiar trident form is reversed so that the 'horns' point inward towards the hub. Four of these spells are designed to have some kind of restrictive effect, so it is tempting to think that a pattern may be emerging here, albeit a small one. All in all, I have the impression that there is an underlying system to the form of the illustrated staves, but it may take many years of study, pondering, and comparison with other grimoires before this system can be discerned.

Time and Space

It is clear that time and space are important factors in the operation of many of the spells. It is frequently necessary to have direct contact with the person or object that is to be influenced, or at least be in close proximity. As outlined above, direction in terms of the points of the compass is sometimes also important. This is an important factor in the Western tradition of magic, and from the *Eddas* and sagas we can adduce that compass directions had esoteric importance in the sphere of the North.[20] The examples given above in the section on time and direction indicate that the time of day, the day of the week, the phase of the moon, the position of the sun, and the time of year could also play a role.

Use of Bodily Fluids

The use of blood to 'redden' runes after they had been carved is well attested in the *Eddas* and sagas, and this tradition has clearly survived into the late eighteenth century. Saliva is another frequently used body fluid. Semen is not mentioned at all in the manuscript, but there is evidence from seventeenth century court records that this was also used.[21] A rationale advanced for this is that the bodily fluid magically brings the stave to life and that the fluid is furthermore 'charged' with the will and intent of the magician if his own blood, saliva, or semen is used.

---

[20]Niflheimr is to the north, Muspelsheimr to the south, and Jötunheimr to the east. There is also evidence that Vanaheimr was thought of as being to the west. Rydberg would disagree sea.
[21]The case against Sigurður Jónsson of the Westfjords, 1671.

Tools and Materials

The most common tool prescribed for carving is the magician's own eating-knife. As pointed out earlier, this would have the practical advantage of always being easily to hand, but it may have been felt that a magical link existed between the knife and the owner due to frequent use. In some cases specific metals or other materials are specified for carving, steel being the most common, but no reason is given for the specification. Some would have been harder to come by than others, such as human finger bones, and some would even have been quite impractical, for example carving a washing bowl using an implement of wood or lead would seem quite a difficult undertaking. There is no evidence in the Viking-age sources that metals, other than gold, had specific correspondences with certain deities. No authenticated 'tables of correspondences' exist for the Northern tradition of magic, but the eighteenth century descendants of the Vikings clearly had reasons for associating certain carving materials with certain magical purposes. Perhaps further study of this and other manuscripts will eventually lead to the creation of a table of correspondences.

As for the surface to be carved, where it is not already obvious by prior intent, for the tool that is to be charmed, the animal to be healed, or the maiden to be seduced, the spells often seem to go out of their way to make life difficult. Materials such as the skin of a first-born calf, sanctified paper, and woods not commonly available in Iceland are called for. One can only speculate that the intention is to make the spell more 'special' and to call for additional effort from the person who would cast it. The unusual nature of the material and the effort required to obtain it would help to focus the mind of the magician and give him confidence that extraordinary power was being brought into the spell.[22]

Heathen Influences, Runes, and the Stave-forms

Although the general religious tenor of the manuscript is overwhelmingly Christian, the fact that the old gods of the North are mentioned at all is quite exciting if you consider that Iceland had officially adopted Christianity eight hundred years earlier. In an effort to consign the Aesir and Vanir to oblivion, even the names of the days of the week had been changed by the early part of the twelfth century, eliminating links to Tyr, Odin, Thor, Freyr/Freya, and *Loður*.[23] Despite this, belief in the Heathen gods clearly lived on in half a dozen of the spells. There are also some references to Futhark runes, as known

---

[22]I can remember wondering, at the age of about eighteen, where I was going to find the 'virgin parchment' called for by Renaissance grimoires. I later realised that this should be interpreted as 'a clean piece of paper' but it certainly made my efforts seem more significant!
[23]The Icelandic day names are *Sunnudagur*, Sun-day; *Mánudagur*, Moon-day; *Þriðjudagur*, third day; *Miðvikudagur*, midweek-day; *Fimmtudagur*, fifth day; *Föstudagur*, fast-day; and *Laugardagur*, bath-day.

from the Old Icelandic Rune Poem, but the fact that these references are so few has to be a little disappointing to modern-day magicians who base almost their entire system of magic on the Futhark rows. Where characters are illustrated in connection with these rune-names, they do not resemble the familiar, angular characters of the Viking-age runes. As a worst-case scenario, it makes one wonder whether R. I. Page is right after all when he asserts that the individual Futhark runes have no inherent magical value and that they were employed in just the same way as our modern alphabet simply as a system of writing.[24] Having said that, the runes could be carved or written and were in many different ways even before 1100 C.E. There was no 'standard' Futhark. Scripts also develop over time, and it may be that the characters evolved into new forms as they were copied again and again in this small and isolated community. Furthermore, runes have been expressed in many coded ways based on their positions in the three *ættir* or 'divisions' of the row. I suspect that they have been incorporated in this form into some, at least, of the magical staves in the manuscript.

As already stated, the staves themselves can be extremely complex, but we need not be daunted by this. Certain patterns are present and with knowledge of mythology and cultural background, plus some lateral thinking, it should be possible to deduce why the staves take particular forms. The eight-spoked *Ægirshjálmur*, for example, with outward-pointing trident terminations and three cross-bars on each spoke, could be interpreted as drawing protection from all the eight outer worlds into the central world of Midgard, plus a twenty-four-fold invocation of the Need-rune.

The *Galdrabók* designated Lbs 2413 8vo is essentially a book of 'low' folk magic for entirely practical purposes, such as winning love, finding who has stolen goods, performing tasks more effectively, or gaining protection from hostile supernatural forces. The collector's motivation for amassing these one hundred and eighty-seven entries is unknown, and he or she may not have been a practising magician at all and may have collected them purely out of curiosity. There are certainly no comments of any kind regarding the system of magic and the various spells seem to have been gathered with more enthusiasm than discernment. There are clearly identifiable errors of transcription, as shown in one of spells using the SATOR formula, which leads one to wonder how many more errors may have been made in recording the staves and the instructions that accompany them. Also, the fact that the same stave is used for two entirely different purposes inclines one to think that the spells were employed[25] in a fairly superstitious and undiscerning manner, with no thought given to their method or structure. Nevertheless, the manuscript offers the modern analyst a revealing view of the life and concerns of Icelanders around the end of the eighteenth century and the methods of magic that were used.

---

[24]Page, R. I., 'Runes'. The British Museum Press, 1987.
[25]If they were used at all by the person who wrote the manuscript.

BIBLIOGRAPHY

Rafnsson, Magnús, *Angurgapi: The Witch-hunts in Iceland*. Hólmavík: Strandagaldur: 2003.

Rafnsson, Magnús (trans.), *Tvaer galdraskræður: Two Icelandic Books of Magic*, Hólmavík: Strandagaldur: 2008.

Flowers, Stephen E., *The Galdrabók: An Icelandic Book of Magic*. Austin: Runa-Raven Press, 2005.

Page, R. I., *'Runes'*. The British Museum Press, 1987.

FROM CONJURER TO PHILOSOPHER
A COMPARATIVE ANALYSIS OF MEDIEVAL
AND RENAISSANCE ANGEL MAGIC

BY

CHRISTOPHER A. PLAISANCE

It is no more than Solomon's due that his is the name which carries the guns in the rituals of ceremonial magic; for his world-wide reputation as the master of legions of spirits has endured for at least two thousand years.

Elizabeth M. Butler, *Ritual Magic*

This is a paper in the history of Western esotericism with the purpose to argues that the process of evolution from medieval to Renaissance forms of angel magic, as specifically embodied in *Liber Juratus Honorii* and *De Occulta Philosophia Libri Tres*, is more accurately characterized as one of a developmental continuum, rather than a discontinuous break made by the fifteenth century reintroduction of the Neoplatonic and Hermetic corpora. It proceeds by examining, firstly, what precisely angel magic is, how it can be placed with in an etic explanatory matrix, and what its relation to concurrently practiced forms of magic is. This is followed by an explication of both ritual magic in general, and angel magic in particular, as practiced during the medieval and Renaissance periods. This is done by appealing both to the two aforementioned texts, as well as works from the various traditions from which they evolved. The paper then concludes with a cautiously suggestive analysis of the possible reasons as to why the great gap that seemingly exists between medieval and Renaissance forms of angel magic is more apparent than real.

The image of the medieval conjurer is one which is so striking that it has imprinted itself upon Western man's imagination up until this present day. The necromancer[1] enters into his oratory, clothed in ceremonial vestments, and adorned with all manner of sigils and talismans. He bears a veritable arsenal of weapons, and protects himself

---

[1]Although the term 'necromancy', stemming from the Latin *necromanteia*, literally refers to 'divinatory communication with the dead', medieval writers later came to interpret all alleged dealings with the dead as actually being the magicians entering into congress with demons pretending to be the deceased. Thus, necromancy became the preferred term for demonic evocation, and it is in this sense that the term is used in this paper. See Kieckhefer, *Magic in the Middle Ages*, p. 152.

within a complex circle constructed from divine names of power. So armed and defended, he calls upon God and his angels to lend him their authority that he might evoke a hideous demon to appear within his suffumigated triangle and grant him all manners of material and carnal gifts.[2] How different is this from the cultivated, might we even say, 'constructed' image of the Renaissance magus. He often assumes the roles of courtly scholar, mathematician, natural philosopher, or medical doctor. He is a man who invokes the hieratic powers not for material gain, but rather for the 'higher' goals of increased knowledge and spiritual transformation.[3] Are these two polarized representations, however, wholly accurate characterizations of the magical practices and theories of these respective ages? Is there really such a vast gap between the stereotypical Solomonic conjurer of the Middle Ages and the sophisticated magus of the Renaissance?

This paper's purpose is to argue that the process of evolution from medieval to Renaissance forms of angel magic, as specifically embodied in *Liber Juratus Honorii* and *De Occulta Philosophia Libri Tres*, which hereafter I shall refer to as *Liber Juratus* and *De Occulta*, is more accurately characterized as one of a developmental continuum than a discontinuous break made by the fifteenth century reintroduction of the Neoplatonic and Hermetic corpora. This proposed notion of a degree of continual fluidity mirrors in many ways contemporary reevaluations of a similar continuity between the historical periods themselves. The term 'Renaissance', which comes from the French *rinascere* and means 'to be reborn', was constructed during the nineteenth century to demarcate the fifteenth and sixteenth centuries as being qualitatively different from the preceding Middle Ages as a literal 'rebirth' of cultural, literary, and philosophical themes from the classical world.[4] As Kocku von Stuckrad identifies, although thinkers such as Petrarch, 1304-1374, had taken steps towards identifying this time period as such, it was "the cultural circumstances of the nineteenth century [that] first produced the concept of the Renaissance as a prominent and unique cultural age of preparation for 'modernity'"[5] as particularly established by Jacob Burkhardt's, landmark study, *Die Kultur der Renaissance in Italien*, 1860. While this modern reexamination of the Renaissance as a polemic construction will be examined in depth at a later point, it will suffice at this point to note that although there were major social, philosophical, scientific, and religious changes that occurred during this time, the degree to which these distinctions were owed to intentional revivals of classical themes did not have a distinct primacy over the medieval sources of the types of ideas that we generally

---

[2] This depiction of the appearance and action of the medieval conjurer is culled from both the descriptions of the demons and the methods for their summoning in the goetic manuscripts. See Peterson (ed.), *The Lesser Key of Solomon: Lemegeton Clavicula Salomonia*, p. 7-56. a post-medieval work

[3] This counter-example is culled from the lives and works of Renaissance magicians such as Cornelius Agrippa, 1486-1553, and John Dee, 1527-1608, as decribed in Yates, *The Occult Philosophy in the Elizabethan Age*, p. 43-56, 92-110.

[4] von Stuckrad, *Western Esotericism: A Brief History of Secret Knowledge*, p. 44.

[5] von Stuckrad, *Western Esotericism: A Brief History of Secret Knowledge*, p. 44.

associate with both the Renaissance in general, and with esotericism in particular.

In defining our terms, we find that angel magic is best understood in contradistinction to other historical forms of magic. This is accomplished by placing it within the larger context of ritual magic, a term which can generally be used to describe practices composed of complex and lengthy rituals for the purposes of obtaining varieties of material, intellectual, or spiritual benefits through the intercession of conjured spirits.[6] Within this genre, angel magic can be defined by contrasting it with its sister subgenre, demonic magic. Though both forms of magic involve the magician entering into congress with supernormal intelligences and appear as aspects of Solomonic ritual magic, the methodologies involved and the purposes for engaging in the two practices were quite different. Following the classical distinction between *theourgia* and *goêteia* as diametrically opposed forms of 'higher' and 'lower magic',[7] we find in the medieval *Lemegeton Clavicula Salomonis*, which hereafter I shall refer to as the *Lemegeton*, two very different types of magic as represented by the 'Of the Arte Goetia' and 'Ars Notoria' sections.[8] While in the former chapter the type of magic can be characterized as one in which the magician invokes divine powers so that he can be lent authority over infernal spirits for the varied purposes of obtaining such things as material wealth or power over his friends and enemies,[9] the latter is more concerned with bettering the intellectual and spiritual state of the magician.[10] We find that the praxis in the first section is principally concerned with magic circles, sigils of the spirits being evoked, as well as a series of conjurations and threats designed to, at once, insulate the magician from the harmful powers of the demon being dealt with while at the same time impelling it to do his will.[11] With the second section, however, "rather than the magic circles, sacrifices, conjurations and bindings that we find in demonic texts, the angelic operations involve lengthy prayers to God," with the overall character of the rites being thoroughly infused with "fasting, confession, and periods of silence and meditation."[12]

As a further way of defining ritual magic, it may be contrasted against image magic.

---

[6] Fanger, 'Medieval Ritual Magic: What it is and Why We Need to Know More About it', in *Conjuring Spirits: Texts and Traditions of Medieval Ritual Magic*, Fanger (ed.), p. vii.

[7] Shaw, *Theurgy and the Soul: The Neoplatonism of Iamblichus*, p. 169.

[8] See Peterson, Joseph H. (ed.), *The Lesser Key of Solomon: Lemegeton Clavicula Salomonis*. York Beach: Weiser Books, 2011. But this is a bad text!

[9] The fifty-sixth goetic demon, Gemory, is exemplary of this, "his office is to tell of all Things past present & to come, and of Treasure hidden and wit layeth in, & procureth ye love of women, both young & old." Peterson (ed.) *The Lesser Key of Solomon: Legemeton Clavicula Salomonis*, p. 32.

[10] The Notory Art is described as the means by which Solomon "in a short time knew all Arts and Sciences, both Liberal and Mechanick, with all the Faculties and Properties thereof: He had suddenly infused into him, and also was filled with wisdom, to utter the sacred mysteries of most holy words." Peterson (ed.) *The Lesser Key of Solomon: Legemeton Clavicula Salomonis*, p. 163.

[11] Peterson (ed.) *The Lesser Key of Solomon: Legemeton Clavicula Salomonis*, p. 41-55.

[12] Fanger, 'Medieval Ritual Magic: What it is and Why We Need to Know More About it', in *Conjuring Spirits: Texts and Traditions of Medieval Ritual Magic*, Fanger (ed.), p. viii.

The dichotomy between the previously described ritual magic texts and those of the image variety can be understood as being medieval representatives of two streams of practice and thought that first began fermenting in the carboy of second century Alexandria. The traditions of ritual magic emerged as the successors to the *Testament of Solomon*, a first to third century koine Greek document which purports to be a narrative record of King Solomon's trapping of a number of demons in a brazen vessel. It is the source for the rich demonological traditions which subsequently took root in Western magical grimoires.[13] On the other hand, we have the *Picatrix* as the fountainhead of astrological image magic. An Arabic text, the *Picatrix* entered Europe in 1256 with a Latin translation and gifted to the West a richly developed system of talismanic magic, which was guided by an underlying Platonic theory of a universe governed by an occult system of harmonic correspondences.[14]

The gulf that separates ritual from image magic has been analyzed by Nicolas Weill-Parot, who describes the situation in terms of 'addressative' versus 'non-addressative' magic. Addressative magic "can be defined as an act by means of which the magician addresses a sign to a separate intelligence (a demon, an angel or some other spirit intelligence) in order to obtain its help to perform the magical operation."[15] This is the style and theory of magic in which supernormal events are actualized by means of the intercession of supernormal intelligences in the magician's affairs. Non-addressative magic proposes that "since the agent governing all events is not a particular intellectual agent (a spirit), but the universal and celestial harmony,"[16] then even in situations where the magician believes himself to be addressing spirits, he is simply actualizing occult harmonic principles in nature. Thus, between ritual and image magic, we see a rather severe philosophical differentiation, all of which, however, takes place within a Hermetic framework, with the Solomonic world of spiritual hierarchies resting upon the Iamblichean and Proclean theologies, which were later diffused into the West by Pseudo-Dionysius' *De Coelesti Hierarchia*, and the astrological image magic of the *Picatrix* wholly built upon the intricate networks of correspondences between the ideal and actual developed by centuries of preceding Stoic, Platonic, and Hermetic philosophers. In addition, it was the Church's position that, in theory, image magic was licit, while ritual magic was illicit. However, in practice, as the Church managed to find "implicit addressativity unavoidably hidden behind all magical practices,"[17] and since "the Christian Church had a monopoly on 'addressativity,'" magic,

---

[13]Johnston, 'The Testament of Solomon from Late Antiquity to the Renaissance', in *The Metamorphosis of Magic from Late Antiquity to the Early Modern Period*, Bremmer and Veenstra (eds.), p. 36-37.

[14]Plessner, *Picatrix (The Aim of the Sage)*, http://www.esotericarchives.com/picatrix.htm.

[15]Weill-Parot, 'Astral Magic and Intellectual Changes (Twelfth–Fifteenth Centuries): 'Astrological Images' and the Concept of 'Addressative' Magic', in *The Metamorphosis of Magic from Late Antiquity to the Early Modern Period*, Bremmer and Veenstra (eds.), p. 169.

[16]Weill-Parot, 'Astral Magic and Intellectual Changes (Twelfth–Fifteenth Centuries): 'Astrological Images' and the Concept of 'Addressative' Magic', in *The Metamorphosis of Magic from Late Antiquity to the Early Modern Period*, Bremmer and Veenstra (eds.), p. 177.

[17] Weill-Parot, 'Astral Magic and Intellectual Changes (Twelfth–Fifteenth Centuries): 'Astrological Images'

ritual or image, was always considered addressative, and thus illicit.[18]

Within the Solomonic genre of ritual texts, it was the Notory books that exerted the strongest influence upon the *Liber Juratus.* Seeking "*sapientia, scientia et intelligencia...* through the use of prayers and figures,"[19] texts within the Ars Notoria genre formed the early background from which later medieval texts on angel magic emerged. *Liber Juratus*, however, was "clearly not a translation from Arabic, Hebrew or Greek," as were so many of the Solomonic grimoires, but was "an original composition in Latin"[20] by a magician known pseudonymously as Honorius of Thebes, a man who, judging from his conversancy with the Church's liturgy and ritual, was likely a part of the "clerical underworld"[21] that Richard Kieckhefer describes as being the center of ritual magic in the medieval world.

The centerpiece of *Liber Juratus* is "an elaborate ritual to obtain... what Catholic theologians term the Beatific Vision, that is, a vision of God Almighty in all His Glory, during which the viewer can... participate to some extent in God's omniscience."[22] Twenty-eight days of purification and prayer comprise the operation, the culmination of which is the magician being able to "see the celestial palace and the majesty of God in his glory, and the nine orders of angels, and the companies of all blessed spirits."[23] This Beatific Vision is not without precedent in the Western esoteric tradition. We find the likely source in Plato's soteriology as participation in the Form of the Good.[24] In Plotinus, we again find it explicitly taught that "knowing of The Good or contact with it is the all-important" and that through this process of *henôsis*, one becomes "identical with Being and Intellectual-Principle and the entire living all."[25] Thoroughly conversant with Plotinian philosophy, it is Augustine's 'Of the Beatific Vision' in

and the Concept of 'Addressative' Magic', in *The Metamorphosis of Magic from Late Antiquity to the Early Modern Period*, Bremmer and Veenstra (eds.), p. 177.

[18]Weill-Parot, 'Astral Magic and Intellectual Changes (Twelfth–Fifteenth Centuries): 'Astrological Images' and the Concept of 'Addressative' Magic', in *The Metamorphosis of Magic from Late Antiquity to the Early Modern Period*, Bremmer and Veenstra (eds.), p. 169.

[19]Klassen, 'English Manuscripts of Magic, 1300–1500: A Preliminary Survey', in *Conjuring Spirits: Texts and Traditions of Medieval Ritual Magic*, Fanger (ed.), p. 15.

[20]Mathiesen, 'A Thirteenth-Century Ritual to Attain the Beatific Vision from the Sworn Book of Honorius of Thebes', in *Conjuring Spirits: Texts and Traditions of Medieval Ritual Magic*, Fanger (ed.), p. 145.

[21]Kieckhefer, *Magic in the Middle Ages*, p. 153-156.

[22]Mathiesen, 'A Thirteenth-Century Ritual to Attain the Beatific Vision from the Sworn Book of Honorius of Thebes', in *Conjuring Spirits: Texts and Traditions of Medieval Ritual Magic*, Fanger (ed.), p. 150.

[23]Peterson (ed.) (trans.), *Liber Juratus Honorii or The Sworne Book of Honorius*, http://www.esotericarchives.com/juratus/juratus.htm.

[24]Plato, 'Republic', in *Complete Works*, Grube (trans.), Cooper and Hutchinson (eds.), p. 517b–c, "In the knowable realm, the form of the good is the last thing to be seen, and it is reached only with difficulty. Once one as seen it, however, one must conclude that it is the cause of all that is correct and beautiful in anything, that it produces both light and its source in the visible realm, and that in the intelligible realm it controls and provides truth and understanding."

[25]Plotinus, Mackenna (trans.), *The Enneads*, VI.7.36.

De Civitate Dei Contra Paganos that we find both the introduction of the idea into Catholic theology and the naming convention found in *Liber Juratus*.[26] The difference, however, in *Liber Juratus* is that rather than simply describing the result and giving vague hints as to how one might attain it, we find excruciatingly detailed instructions on exactly how a magician is to go about doing so. Nor was this tradition to end with *Liber Juratus*. As "one of the oldest and most influential texts of medieval magic," the "legendary reputation"[27] bears striking similarities to later fourteenth century works on angel magic, such as the *Book of Abramelin*, which describes a six-month operation designed to achieve Knowledge and Conversation of one's Holy Guardian Angel,[28] and the *Almandal*, which centers around "a ritual of redemption and the perfection of human nature."[29] In short, we find in medieval angel magic a widespread tradition drawing upon classical sources, whose central goal is to better the intellect and soul of the magician.

The key event in the emergence of distinctly Renaissance forms of magic was the rediscovery of the Neoplatonic and Hermetic corpora. Through the Byzantine Neoplatonist, Georgios Gemistos Plethon, 1355-1452, Cosimo de' Medici, 1389-1464, came to be in possession of an extensive collection of Greek manuscripts containing previously unknown to Western audiences works of Plato, Plotinus, Iamblichus, Proclus, as well as the group of Alexandrian texts later known as the *Corpus Hermeticum*.[30] Many of these manuscripts were then translated by Medici's subject, Marsilio Ficino, 1433-1499, and later disseminated widely throughout Europe. With this resurrection of late classical material, we see a 'newness' in Renaissance magic, which demonstrates this by means of its "urbane language, its philosophical and religious character, and its attempt to recover the original magic of a pristine past through the use of ancient texts."[31] While this paper will later make a case for a greater degree of continuity, the Renaissance magicians themselves uniformly described their work in opposite terms as a revival of the *prisca theologia*, handed down to mankind from the legendary magus, Hermes Trismegistus.[32] Though, thanks to Isaac Casaubon's, 1559-1614, dating, we now know that the Hermetic corpus was composed between the second and third centuries in Hellenistic Alexandria, whereas Renaissance Hermeticists believed them to have been pre-Judaic works of ancient Egyptian origin.[33] Thus, the largely Platonic character of the *Corpus Hermeticum* was misconstrued as the latter having been the

---

[26]Augustine, Dodds (ed.) (trans.), *The City of God*, p. 534-540.
[27]Peterson (ed.) (trans.), *Liber Juratus Honorii or The Sworne Book of Honorius*, http://www.esotericarchives.com/juratus/juratus.htm.
[28]Abraham of Worms, Mathers (trans.), *The Book of the Sacred Magic of Abramelin the Mage*, p. 49.
[29]Veenstra, 'The Holy Almandal and the Intellectual Aims of Magic', in *The Metamorphosis of Magic from Late Antiquity to the Early Modern Period*, Bremmer and Veenstra (eds.), p. 196.
[30]Goodrick-Clarke, *The Western Esoteric Tradition*, p. 35-36.
[31]Klaassen, 'Medieval Ritual Magic in the Renaissance', in *Aries 3*, p. 166.
[32]Voss, 'Introduction', in *Marsilio Ficino*, Voss (ed.), p. 16.
[33]Yates, *Giordano Bruno and the Hermetic Tradition*, p. 398.

1— Rene D'Anjou, Duke of Lorraine, reputedly encouraged Medici. Baigent, *Temple And The Lodge*, p. 138

source of the former, when the converse is the truth of the matter.

Nevertheless, this myth of antiquity lent itself to the reconciliation of the previously compartmentalized forms of astrological image magic and ritual magic into one continuous philosophically oriented praxis. Initiated by Ficino, this breaking down of the barriers between addressative and non-addressative magic was affected by the reintroduction of a theoretical foundation upon which both praxes were founded upon during the late classical period, Neoplatonism, and Hermetism. However, as Ficino was a priest, he greatly desired for his magic to be considered licit and thus attempted to parse the whole of his system as non-addressative.[34] Later Renaissance magicians would adopt a more cavalier attitude towards exposing the addressativity of their systems, while at the same time stressing the holistic relatedness of all forms of magic. Agrippa, in particular, would come to more freely advocate a marriage of addressative and non-addressative magical systems as being two graded manifestations of one hierarchical continuum.[35]

While there is somewhat of a dispute to be explored later in the paper as to exactly how much Renaissance angel magic owes to its medieval predecessors, there can be no doubt that Ficinian magic draws heavily and overtly from two works, the *Corpus Hermeticum* and Iamblichus' *De Mysteriis Aegyptiorum*, which hereafter I shall refer to as *De Mysteriis*. Ficinian magic is, as Walker discusses, angelic magic not so subtly disguised as natural non-addressative planetary magic.[36] In its Ficinian form, planetary influences are seen to act on the imagination of the magician, who then produces effects on either himself or external beings by means of such things as music, talismans, poetry, incantations, and so on.[37] What has this to do with angel magic? Everything. In both the theologies of *De Mysteriis* and the *Corpus Hermeticum*, we find the ubiquitous *arkontos*, or 'archons'. While Iamblichus speaks of both *enyloi*, 'hylic', and *êgemonikoi*, 'sublunary', archons, it is the latter class which is of interest to us here.[38] Thomas Taylor, 1758-1835, describes them as "the *cosmocrators*, or governors of the world, [which are] the *planets*."[39] We find this same type of identification of the archons with planetary intelligences implied in the *Corpus Hermeticum*.[40] While the theologies of

[34]Walker notes that Ficino suggests that "magical practices which are supposed to be non-demonic, to work by the influence of an impersonal planetary spirit on man's spirit and body, but no higher, and not by the influence of a personal "spirit" (i.e. Demon), possessed of a soul, who could act directly on man's rational soul," Walker, *Spiritual & Demonic Magic from Ficino to Campanella*, p. 45. He later notes that Agrippa's appropriation of Fininian magic "exposes what Ficino, rather feebly, had tried to conceal: that his magic was really demonic," Walker, *Spiritual & Demonic Magic from Ficino to Campanella*, p. 96.
[35]Agrippa, Freake (trans.), Tyson (ed.), *Three Books of Occult Philosophy*, p. 3.
[36]Walker, *Spiritual & Demonic Magic from Ficino to Campanella*, p. 76.
[37]Walker, *Spiritual & Demonic Magic from Ficino to Campanella*, p. 76.
[38]Iamblichus, Clarke (trans.), *Iamblichus On the Mysteries: Translated with Introduction and Notes*, II.3.71.3–4.
[39]Iamblichus, Taylor (ed.) (trans.), *On the Mysteries of the Egyptians, Chaldeans and Assyrians*, p. 88ff.
[40]Copenhaver (trans.), *Hermetica: The Greek Corpus Hermeticum and the Latin Asclepius in a new English*

the Renaissance Neoplatonists make no mention of archons, what are mentioned in exquisite detail are the "intelligences, spirits and angels" who govern "every heaven and star,"[41] to include planets such as Saturn and Jupiter, as well as zodiacal signs, decans, and elements. Thus, it is with the planetary angel magic of the Renaissance that we see a distinct union of the heretofore separate disciplines of astrological and angel magic.

It is against this background of Hermetic revivalism and Ficinian planetary angel magic that we come to Agrippa. A minor noble of the von Nettesheim family, Agrippa was born in the German city of Köln, and developed an early interest in Latin and Hebrew.[42] His magical magnum opus, De Occulta, was dedicated to his teacher, the cryptographer, lexicographer, and occultist, Johannes Trithemius, 1462-1516.[43] In this work, Agrippa began by defining magic as "the most perfect, and chief science, that sacred, and sublimer kind of philosophy, and lastly the most absolute perfection of all most excellent philosophy."[44] In a later apologetic commentary on De occulta, he supplements this definition with the statement that "magic therefore comprehending all philosophy, natural and mathematical, joins the powers of religions to them."[45] What both definitions highlight is that, from the very beginning, Agrippean magic is chiefly concerned with the same kinds of things that medieval angel magic dealt with, the intellectual and religious development of the magician. This was not to be in any way confused with the goetic sorcery that Agrippa lambasts as being "unfortunate" and "unlawful," as it involves "commerces of unclean spirits... and is abandoned and execrated by all laws."[46]

Agrippa understood the hierarchical continuum of magical practices as intimately connected to the metaphysical hierarchy that leads from nature up to God. In both cases, he broke these continua down into groups of three. The lowest hypostasis is the elemental world, which is the sublunary sphere of the Neoplatonists that encompasses mankind as we are sheathed in gross matter.[47] To this sphere Agrippa associated natural magic, what we have previously referred to as non-addressative, or image magic, which is principally concerned with the discovery and exploitation of the occult virtues of material things due to their harmonic resonance with intelligences higher up on the emanative hierarchy.[48] The medial hypostasis is the celestial world, which is the realm

translation with notes and introduction, p. 116-117.
[41]Agrippa, Freake (trans.), Tyson (ed.), Three Books of Occult Philosophy, p. 499.
[42]Tyson, 'The Life of Agrippa', in Three Books of Occult Philosophy, Agrippa, Freake (trans.), Tyson (ed.), p. xv.
[43]Tyson, 'The Life of Agrippa', in Three Books of Occult Philosophy, Agrippa, Freake (trans.), Tyson (ed.), p. xviii.
[44]Agrippa, Freake (trans.), Tyson (ed.), Three Books of Occult Philosophy, p. 5
[45]Agrippa, Freake (trans.), Tyson (ed.), Three Books of Occult Philosophy, p. 689.
[46]Agrippa, Freake (trans.), Tyson (ed.), Three Books of Occult Philosophy, p. 695.
[47]Agrippa, Freake (trans.), Tyson (ed.), Three Books of Occult Philosophy, p. 3.
[48]Agrippa, Freake (trans.), Tyson (ed.), Three Books of Occult Philosophy, p. 39.

wherein dwell the planetary and stellar angels and intelligences.[49] The corresponding form of magic to the celestial realm is celestial magic, something in between addressative and non-addressative magic, which deals primarily with mathematical[50] and planetary magic,[51] all of which is accomplished through the mediating function of the "Soul of the World."[52] The metaphysically highest and ontologically primary hypostasis is the intellectual world, which is composed of properly religious beings, such as various orders of angels and God.[53] To this world ceremonial magic, properly addressative magic, is correlated. It is this part of Agrippa's magic that focuses most strongly on the invocations of angelic and divine powers.[54] Logically, the three divisions of the world and its magic are mirrored in the three books that comprise *De Occulta*.

Within this pansophic system, the central focus of Agrippean magic is, unsurprisingly, remarkably similar to those of the medieval works on angel magic previously discussed. Indeed, the end goal of Agrippa's system is characterized by the same kind of apotheotic transformation of the soul that distinguished the results of *Liber Juratus*, the *Book of Abramelin*, and the *Almandal*. Explicitly noting the similarities between his magic and that of the *Corpus Hermeticum*,[55] Agrippa spoke of how by means of training the soul to transcend the bodily confines that the ancients were able "to learn the knowledge of many things," and that the magician "by leaving the body shalt pass into the spacious heavens" and "become an immortal god."[56] What he described is precisely the kind of ascent of the soul that marked the theurgical system of Iamblichus, who Agrippa constantly referenced throughout *De Occulta*.[57] Agrippa described the experience as when the soul,

> Hath obtained its own nature, and is not oppressed by the allurements of the senses, that by its own power it suddenly ascendeth, not only remaining in the body, but even sometimes loosed from its fetters, and flyeth forth of the body to the supercelestial habitations, where now it being most nigh, and most like

[49] Agrippa, Freake (trans.), Tyson (ed.), *Three Books of Occult Philosophy*, p. 3.

[50] Agrippa, Freake (trans.), Tyson (ed.), *Three Books of Occult Philosophy*, p. 233.

[51] Agrippa, Freake (trans.), Tyson (ed.), *Three Books of Occult Philosophy*, p. 426.

[52] Agrippa, Freake (trans.), Tyson (ed.), *Three Books of Occult Philosophy*, p. 421.

[53] Agrippa, Freake (trans.), Tyson (ed.), *Three Books of Occult Philosophy*, p. 3.

[54] Agrippa, Freake (trans.), Tyson (ed.), *Three Books of Occult Philosophy*, p. 587.

[55] The Hermetic process of *theôsis* is described as such, "Thus, unless you make yourself equal to god, you cannot understand god; like is understood by like. Make yourself grow to immeasurable immensity, outleap all body, outstip all time, become eternity and you will understand god," Copenhaver (trans.), *Hermetica: The Greek Corpus Hermeticum and the Latin Asclepius in a new English translation with notes and introduction*, p. 41.

[56] Agrippa, Freake (trans.), Tyson (ed.), *Three Books of Occult Philosophy*, p. 629.

[57] Iamblichus says of *theôsis*, "The more we ascend to the heights and to identity with the primal entities in form and essence, and the more we raise ourselves up from particulars to universals, the more we discover the eternal union that exists there, and behold it as pre-eminent and dominant and containing about it and within it otherness and multiplicity," Iamblichus, Taylor (ed.) (trans.), *On the Mysteries of the Egyptians, Chaldeans and Assyrians*, p. 73.

to God, and made the receptacle of divine things, it is filled with divine light and oracles.[58]

Thus, we find in Agrippa's magic the same lofty spiritual overtones that so characterized the Beatific Vision of *Liber Juratus*. It is an utterly theurgic form of magic that is ultimately concerned with the obtaining of a perfect knowledge of the universe and of God by means of transforming one's soul into a vessel that is godlike enough to effect the transmission of such knowledge. As with his medieval predecessors, Agrippa is not alone in the Renaissance. In John Dee's and Edward Kelley's, 1555-1597, system of angel magic, we see a similar "quest for a universal science based on the unity of all knowledge"[59] achieved by means of an extensive series of angelic revelations revealed to the two during sessions in which they scryed through mirrors and crystals.

Through the course of this investigation of medieval and Renaissance angel magic, it becomes apparent that the principal differences only exist insofar as Renaissance forms were explicitly impregnated with the philosophies that were lying implicitly dormant during the Middle Ages. We are able to see the two periods not as discretely divided epochs separated by the reintroduction of the Hermetic and Neoplatonic corpora by Ficino, but rather as a continuum. Why then did nineteenth century historiographers seek to bifurcate the two? Von Stuckrad identifies two prejudices that aided in this artificial construction. The first is the widespread myth concerning the Middle Ages as a negatively valued incubatory period between the positively valued classical and Renaissance periods. It treats the medieval period as one of darkness and ignorance, a "deep slumber" that was only shaken off with the recollection of "the sciences and culture of the ancient world."[60] This is simply a polemic device used to support the view that the 'modern age' is the culmination of a process that is characterized not only by change but by progress, a notion which reeks of the worst excesses of Hegelian dialectic.¹ "The second prejudice… is the assumption that the West is Christian."[61] In this he sees the mistaken perception of intrinsically separate 'Eastern' versus 'Western' spheres as another myth that hinders an accurate understanding of cultural pluralism. In this way, the Middle Ages may be regarded as a shared cultural space in which several interacting religions gave rise to a distinct pluralism, rather than a dumbed down narrative of the Christian West standing in opposition to the Islamic East.

We can see that while the reintroduction of the Neoplatonic and Hermetic corpora was an extremely important event for the history of esotericism, it was not as big of a defining point as we have been led to believe. Firstly, the idea that Platonism and Hermetism were suddenly reintroduced to Western Europe is demonstrably

[58]Agrippa, Freake (trans.), Tyson (ed.), *Three Books of Occult Philosophy*, p. 629.
[59]Goodrick-Clarke, *The Western Esoteric Tradition*, p. 63-64.
[60]von Stuckrad, *Western Esotericism: A Brief History of Secret Knowledge*, p. 45.
[61]von, Stuckrad, *Western Esotericism: A Brief History of Secret Knowledge*, p. 45.

¹-i.e., Marxism

false. Classical Platonism was known through the *Timaeus* throughout the Middle Ages.[62] Neoplatonism was known principally through the Christianized Procleanism of Pseudo-Dionysius and Johannes Scotus Erigena from the early Middle Ages onward.[63] Likewise, Hermetism was known during the medieval period through the *Asclepius*.[64] Secondly, Hermetic magic and Neoplatonic theurgy were implicitly present in both the Solomonic and astrological image magic systems. The archetypal grimoire of image magic, the *Picatrix*, is littered with pieces of text attributed to Plato and "echoes of Neo-Platonic and pseudo-Empedoclean propositions."[65] In dealing with the nature of man, it begins with the premise that man is a microcosm, and from there develops a non-addressative theory of magic whose occult harmonics reek of Hermetism and Neoplatonism. Likewise, the spiritual hierarchies found in the Solomonic grimoires echo strongly the emanative theologies of the Alexandrian Neoplatonism, with which the Judaic demonologies were mixed to create the Solomonic tradition. Thirdly, the angel magic, as represented by the various central rites of *Liber Juratus*, the *Book of Abramelin*, and *De Occulta*, are nearly identical in both the methodologies and results. Indeed, in Dee's case, although "it seems unlikely that Dee ever used or knew the *Almandal*, his angelic magic does not differ significantly from that of the medieval text."[66]

Finally, we come to the issue of why the Renaissance magicians themselves denied the continuity between their systems of magic and that of the Middle Ages. A chief culprit may be Petrarch's origination of the conception of the preceding era as a 'dark age'. It was with Petrarch that we see the genesis of the idea that antiquity, rather than being a 'dark age', was rather the light of civilization that was being restored by the Renaissance, and it was the medieval period that was truly 'dark'.[67] This prejudicial outlook was further compounded by an all too rational fear of evoking the ire of the Church. As Fanger notes, "the rise in witchcraft accusations in the early modern period is ~~not un~~connected to the problematic status of medieval ritual magic and the unsavory mythical aroma which surrounds the medieval necromancer in literary sources."[68] She suggests that this was a contributing factor to the list of reasons "why the intellectual magicians of the early modern period might have been unwilling to

---

[62]Faivre, 'Ancient and Medieval Sources of Modern Esoteric Movements', in *Modern Esoteric Spirituality*, Faivre and Needleman (eds.), p. 26.
[63]Faivre, 'Ancient and Medieval Sources of Modern Esoteric Movements', in *Modern Esoteric Spirituality*, Faivre and Needleman (eds.), p. 26.
[64]Faivre, 'Ancient and Medieval Sources of Modern Esoteric Movements', in *Modern Esoteric Spirituality*, Faivre and Needleman (eds.), p. 23.
[65]Plessner, *Picatrix (The Aim of the Sage)*, http://www.esotericarchives.com/picatrix.htm.
[66]Veenstra, 'The Holy Almandal and the Intellectual Aims of Magic', in *The Metamorphosis of Magic from Late Antiquity to the Early Modern Period*, Bremmer and Veenstra (eds.), p. 215.
[67]Mommsen, 'Petrarch's Conception of the 'Dark Ages', in *The Italian Renaissance*, Findlen (ed.), p. 220.
[68]Fanger, 'Medieval Ritual Magic: What it is and Why We Need to Know More About it', in *Conjuring Spirits: Texts and Traditions of Medieval Ritual Magic*, Fanger (ed.), p. x.

profess an open debt to their medieval antecedents."[69] This is particularly evident in Agrippa's forced retraction of *De Occulta*. Although, as we have explored, his system of magic is eminently theurgic, in the section of his retraction entitled 'Of theurgia', he mentions the "Art Almadel, the Notary Art, the Pauline Art, the Art of Revelations" as "superstitions, which are so much the more pernicious, by how much they seem the more divine to the ignorant."[70]

It now becomes clear that the compounded factors of prejudicial historiography, Petrarch's foundational myth of the Renaissance as an age of light being reborn out of the medieval darkness, and the Church's outright oppression of illicit magical practices and philosophies likely led to a situation in which medieval and Renaissance forms of angel magic were falsely seen as being representative of two disconnected traditions. Rather, the truth of the matter seems to be that the transition from the prior to the latter can be most accurately described as that of a developmental continuum rather than a discontinuous break affected by Ficino's reintroduction of his patron's collection of Neoplatonic and Hermetic texts. In this light, it is my hope that the medieval magicians who committed so much of themselves in developing their praxes might be given their proper place in the grand narrative of the history of Western esotericism. No more should they be seen as purveyors of "silly secrets, ragtags and bobtails of folklore dressed up in Kabbalistic shreds and patches,"[71] but rather as the important links in the 'golden thread' of esotericism from antiquity to modernity that they are.

---

[69] Fanger, 'Medieval Ritual Magic: What it is and Why We Need to Know More About it', in *Conjuring Spirits: Texts and Traditions of Medieval Ritual Magic*, Fanger (ed.), p. x.
[70] Agrippa, Freake (trans.), Tyson (ed.), *Three Books of Occult Philosophy*, p. 699.
[71] Butler, *Ritual Magic*, p. 60.

BIBLIOGRAPHY

Abraham of Worms, Mathers, Macgregor S. L. (ed.), *The Book of the Sacred Magic of Abramelin the Mage*. New York: Dover Publications Inc., 1975.

Agrippa, Henry Cornelius of Nettesheim, Freake, James (trans.), Tyson, Donald (ed.), *Three Books of Occult Philosophy*. Minnesota: Llewellyn Publications, 2010.

Augustine, Dodds, Marcus (ed.) (trans), *The City of God*. Edinburgh: T. & T. Clark, 1888.

Betz, Hans Dieter (ed.), *The Greek Magical Papyri in Translation including the Demotic Spells*. Chicago: University of Chicago Press, 1992.

Butler, E. M., *Ritual Magic*. Hollywood: Newcastle Publishing Company Inc., 1971.

Conybeare, F. C. (trans.), *The Testament of Solomon*. http://www.esotericarchives.com/solomon/testamen.htm.

Copenhaver, Brian P. (trans.), *Hermetica: The Greek Corpus Hermeticum and the Latin Asclepius in a new English translation with notes and introduction*. Cambridge: Cambridge University Press, 1992.

Faivre, Antoine, 'Ancient and Medieval Sources of Modern Esoteric Movements'. In *Modern Esoteric Spirituality*, edited by Antoine Faivre and Jacob Needleman. New York: The Crossroad Publishing Company, 1992.

Fanger, Claire, 'Medieval Ritual Magic: What it is and Why We Need to Know More About it'. In *Conjuring Spirits: Texts and Traditions of Medieval Ritual Magic*, edited by Claire Fanger. University Park: The Pennsylvania State University Press, 1998.

Goodrick-Clarke, Nicholas, *The Western Esoteric Tradition*. New York: Oxford University Press, 2008.

Iamblichus, Clarke, Emma C. (trans.) *Iamblichus On the Mysteries: Translated with Introduction and Notes*. Atlanta: Society of Biblical Literature, 2003.

Iamblichus, Taylor, Thomas (trans.), *On the Mysteries of the Egyptians, Chaldeans and Assyrians*. London: Bertram Dobel, 1821.

Kieckhefer, Richard, *Magic in the Middle Ages*. Cambridge: Cambridge University Press, 1989.

Klaassen, Frank, 'English Manuscripts of Magic, 1300-1500: A Preliminary Survey'. In *Conjuring Spirits: Texts and Traditions of Medieval Ritual Magic*, edited by Claire Fanger. University Park: The Pennsylvania State University Press, 1998.

Klaassen, Frank, 'Medieval Ritual Magic in the Renaissance'. In *Aries* 3, 2003.

Mathiesen, Robert, 'A Thirteenth-Century Ritual to Attain the Beatific Vision from the Sworn Book of Honorius of Thebes'. In *Conjuring Spirits: Texts and Traditions of Medieval Ritual Magic*, edited by Claire Fanger. University Park: The Pennsylvania State University Press, 1998.

Mommsen, Theodor E., 'Petrarch's Conception of the 'Dark Ages'. In *The Italian Renaissance*, edited by Paula Findlen, Oxford: Blackwell Publishing Ltd., 2002.

Peterson, Joseph H. (ed.) (trans.), *Liber Juratus Honorii or The Sworne Booke of Honorius*. http://www.esotericarchives.com/juratus/juratus.htm.

Peterson, Joseph H. (ed.), *The Lesser Key of Solomon: Lemegeton Clavicula Salomonis*. York Beach: Weiser Books, 2011.

Plato, Grube G. M. A. and Reeve C. D. C. (trans.), *Republic*. Indianapolis: Hackett Publishing Company Inc., 1992.

Plato, 'Timaeus'. In *Complete Works*, edited by John M. Cooper and D. S. Hutchinson, translated by Donald J. Zeyl. Indianapolis: Hackett Publishing Company Inc., 1997.

Plessner, Martin, *Picatrix (The Aim of the Sage)*. http://www.esotericarchives.com/picatrix.htm.

Plotinus, Mackenna, Stephen (trans.), *The Enneads*. New York: Larson Publications, 1992.

Shaw, Gregory, *Theurgy and the Soul: The Neoplatonism of Iamblichus*. University Park: The Pennsylvania State University Press, 1995.

Stuckrad, Kocku von, *Western Esotericism: A Brief History of Secret Knowledge*. London: Equinox Publishing Ltd., 2005.

Veenstra, Jan R., 'The Holy Almandal: Angels and the Intellectual Aims of Magic'. In *The Metamorphosis of Magic from Late Antiquity to the Early Modern Period*, edited by Jan N. Bremmer and Jan R. Veenstra. Leuven: Peers, 2001.

Voss, Angela, 'Introduction'. In *Marsilio Ficino*, edited by Angela Voss. Berkeley: North Atlantic Books, 2006.

Walker, D. P., *Spiritual & Demonic Magic from Ficino to Campanella*. University Park: The Pennsylvania State University Press, 2000.

Weill-Parot, Nicolas, 'Astral Magic and Intellectual Changes (Twelfth-Fifteenth Centuries): 'Astrological Images' and the Concept of 'Addressative' Magic'. In *The Metamorphosis of Magic from Late Antiquity to the Early Modern Period*, edited by Jan N. Bremmer and Jan R. Veenstra. Leuven: Peers, 2001.

Yates, Frances A., *Giordano Bruno and the Hermetic Tradition*. New York: The University of Chicago Press, 1969.

Yates, Frances A., *The Occult Philosophy in the Elizabethan Age*. New York: Routledge Classics, 2001.

DINING WITH THE DEAD
A CANAANITE VIEW OF DEATH AND NECROMANCY

BY

TESS DAWSON

O Baʿal, if you drive the Shade from me and bring it to rest in the underworld,
The Rapiu from my house and bring it to the House of Freedom,
A sacrifice I shall make,
A meal in your honor;
A vow I shall take,
A promise I shall fulfill.
These actions, O Baʿal, I shall do.

A Prayer to Baʿal, *The Ugaritic Texts*

The venerated father, Yatni-ilu, lay in the comfort of rush mattress. An open-saucer pottery lamp cupping olive oil and a linen wick light the small mudbrick room. Shadows and light flicker across the angles of his weathered face. His children and his grandchildren gather around him and hold his calloused hands, comforting him. He has reached the sunset of his life and soon he will join the ancestors, those who went before him. Yatni-ilu will become one of the *rapiuma*, the 'shades of the dead' in the House of Freedom. His breathing had become ragged and labored when he breathes at all. They wait. Gently, finally, it happens. In his last breath, his *napshu* slips through his nostrils like vapor and journeys to the underworld, leaving behind his body. The family wails in grief; they tear their clothes, and gash themselves.

The Path of the Body

The family hires professional mourners to help them keen for their lost father. Women gather his body, wash him, and prepare him for burial by anointing him with myrrh-laced olive oil and gently wrapping him in handspun, handwoven crisp white linen cloth. They bury Yatni-ilu in a cave or a small crypt under a house used as a burial site, where his physical remains will join with other family members' remains. The terrible Mot, god of the dead, will open his mouth, the grave, and receive the offering of Yatni-ilu. Mot does not receive offerings like the other deities since his gaping maw will in time devour us all. Yatni-ilu's body will be positioned lying flat on his back, slightly curved, or in a fetal position.[1] Lime glaze or powdered lapis the family will sprinkle on Yatni-ilu's dear head. The Natufians, ancestors of the Canaanites, would plaster over the skulls of the dead and recreate their features with paint and install cowrie shells in the eye sockets.[2] Yatni-ilu's family will mourn his death from seven days[3] to seven years.[4] At the end of mourning, they will wear clean whole clothing again and they will play music, but they must always ensure Yatni-ilu's comfort in the afterlife.

The Path of the *Napshu*

Yatni-ilu's *napshu* is his soul, vitality, strength, and appetite.[5] It is his essence. In life, this *napshu* is connected to his body through his throat. In his last breath, this misty force separates from his body through his nose and journeys to the edge of the earth to lift up the mountains Tarjazazu, Tharmagu, and Kankanyu[6] to reach the *Betu Khapthati*, the 'House of Freedom'.[7] Once there, he will feast when with his loved ones who have made the journey before him. Sometimes Ba'al Hadad, Ilu, Shapshu-Pagri, or another chthonic deity will visit the dead. Yatni-ilu's *napshu* is sustained and strengthened through the offerings that his still-living loved ones make in his honor with incense, food, libation, and the repeated memory of his name and deeds. In the afterlife, Yatni-ilu's *napshu*, becomes known as a *rapiu*, a 'shade of the dead', and he becomes one of the *rapiuma*, the 'shades'. This term is perhaps better known by its Hebrew counterpart, *rephaim*.

The Responsibility of the Living to the Dead

The chief responsibility of caring for Yatni-ilu falls to his eldest son. If he had no sons, or if his son cannot fulfill this role, another would take his place. Gender roles were fixed but not rigid, so the next in line to care for the dead could be a wife or a daughter. Upon death, the family holds a feasting rite in Yatni-ilu's honor and afterwards they will care for his shade with periodic rites to ensure his wellbeing. The person who cares for the dead may have been called in Akkadian *paqid* or *sachir*, meaning 'caretaker', or

---

[1]Bar-Yosef, 'The Natufian Culture in the Levant. Threshold to the Origins of Agriculture', in *Evolutionary Anthropology* Volume 6, Issue 5, p. 164.
[2]Tubb, *Canaanites*, p. 28. See also Wright, *Ritual in Narrative: The Dynamics of Feasting, Mourning, and Retaliation Rites in the Ugaritic Tale of Aqhat*, p. 147.
[3]Del Olmo, *Canaanite Religion According to the Liturgical Texts of Ugarit*, p. 162.
[4]Parker (ed.), Smith (trans.) et al., *Ugaritic Narrative Poetry*, p. 76.
[5]Sasson et al. (eds.), *Civilizations of the Ancient Near East*, p. 2063.
[6]Parker (ed.), Smith (trans.) et al., *Ugaritic Narrative Poetry*, p. 138, 147.
[7]Parker (ed.), Smith (trans.) et al., *Ugaritic Narrative Poetry*, p. 138, 147, 172, 149.

⌐Why Akkadian? Is this all in Akkadian? When is this happening?

a *zakir shumi*, a 'person who calls out the name of the deceased'.[8] Here are a few of the rites that could take place for Yatni-ilu, or other beloved dead of the Canaanites.

Pagru Rite[9]

After the body's preparation, the family would have the corpse buried. The rite that has been handed down to us may have involved only deceased kings, but since the rite includes actions customary to kings and citizens alike, non-royal families may have performed similar rites provided they had the means to do so. This rite originates from tribal Amorite custom handed down into Ugaritic tradition. All of the living members of the family would participate in this rite. As a funerary rite, the son of the deceased would erect a memorial stele and hold a sacrifice in his father's honor. The stele would likely contain the deceased's name and a dedication to Dagan, the god of grain. The sacrifice would have involved a sheep or a goat, if possible, or a pigeon if necessary. The sacrifice was completely disposed whole in some way, perhaps by burning or burying.

Seven-fold Rite of Descent[10]

This rite, which also occurred soon after death, probably just involved deceased kings. The ritual text describes the activity as a *dabchu* rite, where a communal feast, a sacrifice, or both accompanied the rite. It begins with an invitation to the *rapiuma* and a summons to mourn the passing of the king as he joins the deceased in the underworld. The *rapiuma* are asked to assist the king as he takes the seven steps into the underworld. Seven offerings accompany this rite. The offerings will atone for misdeeds the king may have accrued. Afterwards, priests offered pigeons for a blessing upon the queen mother of the new king and for the wellbeing of the city.

Kispu Rite[11]

The family of the deceased would meet during new moons, and periodically in addition to new moons, to feast with the deceased family members. The family speaks aloud the names of the deceased and invites the shades to partake of the meal with the living. The living offer food and drink, including water, and music accompanies the rite. It was thought that music would encourage the protective nature of the shades. The rite may have taken place within a corner of the family home set aside for this periodic rite

---

[8]Parker (ed.), Smith (trans.) et al., *Ugaritic Narrative Poetry*, p. 138, 147, 172, 149.
[9]Young (ed.), *Ugarit in Retrospect: Fifty Years of Ugarit and Ugaritic*, p. 159.
[10]Pardee, *Ritual and Cult at Ugarit*, p. 123.
[11]Pardee, *Ritual and Cult at Ugarit*, p. 86.

1- Aren't they from the west, distinct from the Hamites?
2- related to Dagon?
3- presumably means corpse

or perhaps near the gravesite. Other items, such as jewellery and gifts can be presented to the dead during these rites. The living would ask that the new king would have the blessings and strength of the *rapiuma*. The rite comes from Amoritic culture and spread throughout the Near East into parts of Canaan and Mesopotamia. This rite, like the Seven-fold Rite of Descent, may have only occurred for kings, but non-royal citizens likely also honored the dead in a similar fashion.

Marzichu[12]

A *marzichu* referred both to a specific club and a gathering of that specific club. In ancient times, the *marzichu* included only landowning upper class men. They would choose a club member's home to meet in and would draw up a contract for meeting there on a regular basis. The leader of the club usually owned the house in which they met. Club members would drink and feast at a *marzichu*. Texts describe the chief god of the pantheon, Ilu, as overindulging at *marzichu*. Club members would invoke the names of their beloved dead to join them in their feast. Each *marzichu* had its own patron deity with records indicating Ilu in Ugaritic texts, Eshmun and Ba'al Tzapan in Phoenician texts, and Aglibol or Malakbel in Palmyran texts.[13] Biblical accounts represent *marzeach*, which is the Hebrew word for *marzichu*, as events where celebrants would recline on ivory beds, eat rich meat, drink wine until inebriated, play music, and anoint themselves with perfumed oils.

A sample contract for starting a *marzichu* would look like this,

Of the marzichu (chief's name) founded: (chief's name) has set aside a room for the marzichu. If (chief's name) turns out the marzichu from his house, he shall pay the marzichu fifty silver pieces. (Chief's name) shall be the chief of the marzichu. He shall collect one piece of silver from each member of the marzichu. If a member asks for the return of his silver piece, he must pay a fine of two silver pieces to the marzichu. Witnessed by (name of marzichu member #1), son of (name of father of marzichu member #1) and by (marzichu member #2), son of (name of father of marzichu member #2)."[14] The designations of "member #1" and "member #2" are arbitrary. The title of the leader of the marzichu is rabbu, which translates as "great" and "chief;" his role is similar to the president of a club. The fee which the chief collects from the club likely goes to the food and drink that will be served.

[12]Pardee, *Ritual and Cult at Ugarit*, p. 193-195, 205; Lange, Karen E., 'Unearthing Ancient Syria's Cult of the Dead'. In *National Geographic*, February 2005, p. 108-123.
[13]Smith, *The Ugaritic Baal Cycle, Volume I: Introduction with Text, Translation and Commentary of KTU 1.1-1.2.*, p. 141-142.
[14]Smith, *The Ugaritic Baal Cycle, Volume I: Introduction with Text, Translation and Commentary of KTU 1.1-1.2.*, p. 141-142.

1-Again, there is much more that needs to be said here,
2- which one?
3- presumably Osman-Asclepius?

Yanti-ilu's family will likely honor him with a proper burial, feast, and a memorial stele, and Yatni-ilu's son will call his name and invite him to join in the festivities at a *marzichu*. Yatni-ilu's family will make offerings to him and remember his name in feasts to come.

When the Dead are Forgotten

Yatni-ilu's well-being in the afterlife and the well-being of his living family depend on how the family treats Yatni-ilu after he has died. When they keep him strong and sustain his vitality, he can assist his children who are still alive by healing them when they are ill, by offering his sage advice, and by increasing their good luck. Without these offerings, without his name remembered and repeated, he will grow weaker. As a weak shade, he cannot help the living. If he weakens too much, he could become hungry and roam the earth trying to find sustenance to fill his emptiness. Even worse, he could become desperate and angry, and therefore bring harm to the living. As a hungry shade, Yatni-ilu can become a troublesome spirit and find some semblance of peace and fulfilment by possessing a person, entering the person through his ear.[15] In medieval times, the European Jews believed that a *dybbuk* behaved in much the same way, where after the *dybbuk* left the body it would leave behind a drop of blood on the little finger or toe as it passed out of the person's body. Yatni-ilu, whose family buried him and care for him, is much less likely to become a troublesome shade. Woe to those who die suddenly and violently, and woe to those who die with no body left for burial.

If a troublesome shade had re-entered the world and torments a person, the person can create a small effigy of the shade and tell the shade to enter the effigy. The living person would then outfit the effigy with clothes and provisions for a journey and take the effigy westward to an area of desert or wilderness and bury the effigy. This act would serve to give the shade's body a burial and return the shade to the underworld.[16] Mesopotamian custom involves sprinkling flour in a circle around oneself when consulting with, working with, dealing with, or having difficulties with the shades[17] so that the magician might avoid problems of attracting a troublesome spirit.

Deities of the Dead

Canaanite religion had several deities who took care of the dead, but only one deity of death, Mot. As the god of death, Mot's gaping maw remains open to receive offerings

[15]Pardee, *Ritual and Cult at Ugarit*, p. 218.
[16]Black and Green, *Gods, Demons and Symbols of Ancient Mesopotamia*, p. 88.
[17]Black and Green, *Gods, Demons and Symbols of Ancient Mesopotamia*, p. 128.

from all organic beings that have ceased to live. His appetite is insatiable. The Canaanites never made offerings to Mot in ritual, perhaps because they believed that they would give him the ultimate sacrifice, their own bodies, in due time. They never called upon him in ritual setting since this could arouse his interest. Mot lives in the underworld and sits on a low throne in a pit.

Dagan, the god of grain, is Ba'al's father. In Mesopotamia, Dagan bears an association with caring for the dead. In Canaan, the threshing floor and grain metaphors symbolize death.[18] Grain, as a symbol of death, may point to a concept of rebirth or return from death. Canaanite legend has it that the *rapiuma* can return to visit the living through threshing floors.

The storm god, Ba'al Hadad, may appear to have little to do with the dead, however he taunted Mot once and as a result Ba'al died and journeyed to the underworld. Ba'al is called upon to divinize the dead and give them abilities above those of living human beings.[19] In this way, Ba'al helps the shades so that they can help us.

The sun goddess Shapshu-Pagri travels each day high into the sky to light our world and each night she descends in the west to light the day for our beloved dead in the underworld. On Shapshu's travels, she encountered Ba'al's body after he had descended to the underworld. She returned his corpse so that he could have a proper burial. Although most texts refer to her as Shapshu, she also bears the epithet *Pagri*, which means 'corpses'. This epithet points to a role in caring for the dead.

Ugaritic tales talk of Ilu, who is head god of the pantheon, holding a *marzichu* for the shades of the dead.[20] Ilu is known for his compassion, generosity, and hospitality, qualities which he extends on behalf of the well-being of the dead.

The N-word

Biblical tradition, which forbids necromancy, points to the Canaanites as practicing necromancy. Over the ages, this word has become negatively charged and conjures images of the deepest evil. Biblical writers may have feared that seeking the dead for guidance would take the place of trusting in the divine, or they saw it as a challenge to their priestly authority, the authority of their deity, or both. At its core, necromancy as the Canaanites practiced it, simply involved communicating with the dead for guidance. Some would say that necromancy is the 'calling' or 'summoning' of the dead for divining the future. Others might claim that necromancy involves physically

---

[18]Bottéro, Bahrani, and Van de Mieroop, *Mesopotamia: Writing, Reasoning, and the Gods*, p. 284.
[19]Del Olmo, *Canaanite Religion According to the Liturgical Texts of Ugarit*, p. 167.
[20]Del Olmo, *Canaanite Religion According to the Liturgical Texts of Ugarit*, p. 91.

animating the dead, though this was not mentioned in Canaanite texts. Still others confuse necromancy with calling forth demons, but ideally in a rite to converse with ancestors harmful spirits are not present or are divinely guided away from the rite. The Canaanites consulted the dead, especially for purposes of healing and asking guidance.[21] It is likely that they believed the *rapiu*, the 'spirit', would speak aloud or visit in dreams, or perhaps even channel through a person. However, it is unlikely that the Canaanites believed they could unite the spirit and the body, or animate the body without the spirit. The Canaanites may also have found raising a dead body from his proper burial an anathema to their mores since it could weaken the *rapiu* and make him a troubled spirit. The magicians of Mesopotamia did not call upon the dead often, since not only the dead but also unwanted, unhelpful, and even harmful spirits could respond to the call of the magician. Magicians conducted rituals to contact the dead only out of necessity after deep consideration and careful preparation. In Canaanite culture, necromancy was not thought of as evil but was more like asking elders for advice.

Introduction to Ritual

The ritual below is based on a reconstruction of the Ugaritic-Canaanite *pahayu* ritual, the 'ritual of contemplation', as well as Mesopotamian magical practices. Not much about the *pahayu* ritual is known since the ritual texts are scanty, but it seems that the king of Ugarit would have performed this ritual when he wished to look upon a deity, perhaps for guidance.[22] This idea of seeking guidance from a divine or semi-divine source dovetails with the purpose of communicating with the dead. Texts of the *pahayu* include mention of the god Rashap, the goddess 'Anat, and the god Shalim. Rashap and 'Anat are protective warrior deities while Shalim represents west, a direction symbolically associated with death. Offerings included a piece of gold, a piece of silver, animal offerings and seven star-shaped pendants, which were probably eight-pointed stars. In this ritual you will be creating a protective barrier, cleansing yourself and the area, making offerings and engaging in communication or divinatory activity.

Although not a Canaanite technique, the Mesopotamians would create a magical barrier by making a circle out of flour. Since flour is sometimes a difficult substance to manage, you could try whole grain or bulgur, a cracked wheat product. The ancient Egyptians used a substance called natron to purify temples, which was a naturally formed substance comprised of salt and baking soda. Since natron is a substance of purification, baking soda and salt could also be used to make a protective circle. For cleansing purposes, you can use plain spring water, water scented with essential oils, or olive oil infused with myrrh. I suggest using marjoram, or hyssop, myrrh, frankincense, galbanum, or any combination, with myrrh and marjoram as my first choice. For a

---

[21] Parker (ed.), Smith (trans.) et al., *Ugaritic Narrative Poetry*, p. 196.
[22] Pardee, *Ritual and Cult at Ugarit*, p. 171.

bundle of herbs, tamarisk,[23] also known as a salt cedar, works best, or a combination of tamarisk, fruit-bearing date palm stalks and reeds.[24] Alternatively, you could use marjoram, oregano, hyssop, rosemary, thyme, or bay laurel. Oregano and marjoram may have been the 'hyssop' of old, and hyssop was known as a cleansing and protective herb in biblical times.[25] The Egyptians believed thyme brought courage.[26] Tamarisk was known as the 'tree of death' and both Canaanite and Mesopotamian cultures used tamarisk as a tool for exorcism. If you intend to use a broom, make certain that it is clean and fresh, and use it only for cleansing places intended for ritual. If you use a bell to get rid of unwanted entities and call out to desired spirits, use a copper or brass bell. The Mesopotamians used a copper bell for exorcism.[27] Since brass contains copper and zinc, a brass bell could substitute for a copper bell when necessary.

Myrrh is an ideal incense used for healing and blessing in the Canaanite world. An ancient text tells of a *rapiu* who prescribes myrrh for an ailing child. You may want to use two different incenses, one for cleansing the area and one for an offering. Myrrh does well for both. Cedar is excellent for cleansing and encouraging protective forces. Galbanum may have been used in mummification. Mastic is related to the terebinth tree, which was known biblically for sheltering graves. Post-biblical celebrations of the deceased may have involved nuts and fruits, such as pomegranates, strips of purple cloth, myrrh, and fish.[28] Canaanite *pahayu* rituals and funerary rites involved offerings of mutton or beef. For food offerings and libation, I suggest some sort of meat offering if possible, especially mutton, beef or poultry, and red wine to symbolize blood.

Bring a divination device or two to your ritual. A pendulum is easy to use, easy to transport, and hearkens back to the star-shaped pendants. For casting lots, you can bring dice and use techniques of numerology to read the numbers rolled on the dice, or you can bring another tool which shows answers for 'yes' and 'no', as well as 'maybe' or 'uncertain'. Three clean craft sticks or bones can work for this by painting one black for 'no', white for 'yes', and grey or red for 'uncertain' or 'maybe', and close your eyes and draw a stick. If you are high-tech, you can also bring a K-2 meter and ask the spirit to light the LED lights to indicate a 'yes' response. You may want to bring paranormal investigation equipment with you, like a digital voice recorder or a small hand-held cassette recorder. This way, if you wish to ask questions, you can listen for answers later that you may not have heard while you were performing the ritual. You can also bring a video camera or a camera for shooting still photographs. Bring extra batteries because

---

[23]Pardee, *Ritual and Cult at Ugarit*, p. 159, mentions shaking pieces of sacred wood as a protection against venomous bites. See Parker (ed.), Smith (trans.) et al., *Ugaritic Narrative Poetry*, p. 222 and Del Olmo, *Canaanite Religion According to the Liturgical Texts of Ugarit*, p. 367-368.

[24]Zohary, *Plants of the Bible*, p. 96.

[25]Fletcher, *The Egyptian Book of Living and Dying*, p. 20.

[26]Young (ed.), *Ugarit in Retrospect: Fifty Years of Ugarit and Ugaritic*, p. 177.

[27]Winkler, *Magic of the Ordinary: Recovering the Shamanic in Judaism*, p. 90.

[28]Patai, *The Hebrew Goddess*, p. 225.

1 – For which people? The area was under Persian, Macedonian and Roman rule.

the spirits may drain batteries in efforts to manifest themselves.[1]

A Rite of Necromancy

The place should be a neutral location, indoors or outdoors. If you conduct this rite in your own home you may be unhappy if a spirit does not return to the underworld.[2] I also advise against doing this ritual near ruins[29] or archways.[30] These were associated with bad spirits and unfortunate events in later times, and are also associated with the *sheydim* or *lilitu* of Jewish custom. You could perform this in a graveyard if you do obtain permission first,[3] especially if you are visiting at night. If you do a rite in a graveyard respect local custom, like not setting up a circle on someone's grave, especially if you do not know that person or you do not think that person would respond favorably to a pagan rite. The rite should preferably take place at sunset or night. Canaanite lore describes dying as the 'sunset of life',[31] and thus night symbolizes death. Think very carefully about with whom you would communicate and for what reasons you would want to communicate with the individual. If you leave your rite open to contact anyone, you must take extra precautions to ensure that you will not attract unwanted entities.[4] If a person was evil while alive, they are evil when they are dead, and there is every likelihood that you may not want to talk to everyone who wants to talk with you. Also, if you have someone specific in mind with whom you would like to make contact, you could be disturbing someone who does not want to be disturbed. Meditate, pray for guidance, and consult divinatory devices if you are at all in doubt. Avoid conjuring, summoning, evoking, or demanding the presence of anyone from their afterlife, as forcing a spirit from the afterlife is cruel and disrespectful, and it may cause the spirit to become troublesome. Gently contact a spirit with whom you already have a relationship, someone like an ancestor, or perhaps a spirit that is already present in your life. Ask politely if they would speak with you. If a spirit does not desire contact, peacefully and respectfully end the rite.

Supplies should consist of incense and an incense burner or brazier, and for the offerings have available food, wine or juice, two coins, and some fresh flowers; an oil lamp, candle or battery operated camp lantern, and a flashlight; matches, lighter and a fire extinguisher; divination device, pen and paper; flour or salt and baking soda or chalk; scented water or olive oil infused with herbs, and a clean broom used only for exorcism and cleansing of the sacred space; a bell, copper or brass; tamarisk, if possible, and a small bundle of herbs; a list of questions you would like to ask; paranormal investigation equipment; a shovel for burying offerings, a small fire pit for burning offerings; clean dust pan used only for sacred space; and a protective amulet.

[29] Patai, *The Hebrew Goddess*, p. 225.
[30] Parker (ed.), Smith (trans.) et al., *Ugaritic Narrative Poetry*, p. 29.
[31] Pardee, *Ritual and Cult at Ugarit*, p. 75.

1. Is this for real serious?
2. What?
3. Hi, I'd like permission to raise the dead
4. Since westerners don't read the dead, should don't be yell be angry?

Order of Service

Prior to the rite, ensure that you are in a state of emotional and spiritual purity. Atone and cleanse yourself of misdeeds, and ensure that your intentions for this communication are pure. Take a shower or a bath. Make certain that you have no substances or illnesses that might impair your judgment or weaken your vitality before performing this rite. Wear clean clothes. Put on any protective amulet you wish to have with you or bring it with you. Go to the site where you will be holding the rite. The Canaanites most likely took off their shoes prior to ritual,[32] but if you are wearing shoes during this rite cleanse the bottom of your shoes or wear shoes that will only be worn in sacred or temple space.

Although most Canaanite magic does not include creating a protective barrier, sometimes working with the spirits is tricky business. The Mesopotamians would draw a circle with flour prior to working with spirits or performing a healing. Ensure that all the supplies you need are within that circle before you make it. Draw a circle around you with the flour or salt and baking soda. If you wish to draw protective symbols with the flour in your circle, feel free. The *kappu*, palm-of-hand, double zigzags, an upturned crescent or crescent and disk, and an encircled eight-pointed star may afford some protection.

To prepare for the ritual space purify yourself and sweep the area for the ritual space. Fumigate the area with protective incense and make a prayer such as,

> O Choron, god of exorcism, by your grace purify myself and this area of misdeed and undesirable and inappropriate influences and entities. Blessings of wellbeing and wholeness to Choron. I give thanks. O Ba'al, warrior god who has died and returned, protect me and protect this circle from all manner of evil and harm. Blessings of wellbeing and wholeness to Ba'al. I give thanks.

Set up an altar with an altar cloth. Place food offerings, libations, incense and brazier, candle, oil lamp, or camp lantern, bell, flowers, and other items on the altar. Any items you do not wish to place on the altar secure within the circle in an out-of-the-way area. Start up any paranormal investigation equipment, if desired.

Ring the bell a number of times. Three is a number of exorcism, five is a protective number, and seven is a holy number. Ringing the bell sends forth your intention to communicate, whilst driving away unwanted spirits. Present your offerings to the spirits and the deities. Light the offering incense and say a prayer like, "May incense carry my prayers to the heavens, smoke bear my prayer to the stars." Present your food

---

[32]Pardee, *Ritual and Cult at Ugarit*, p. 75.

and drink offerings and say a prayer like, "May the gracious gods and the benevolent shades find strength and wellbeing in these offerings." Make an invocation such as,

> I am (full name); a devotee of (god/goddess) who (list function or epithet of god/goddess). I call upon the benevolent Rapiuma, the helpful shades. Only helpful and benevolent shades may come forth; all other shades are held back by Ba'al's protective hand, by Shapshu-Pagri's intervention, by Rashap's might. O Shade or Shades, I ask you to converse with me and to make my life and the lives of others better through your guidance. I make offerings in your honor and to bring you strength. By the heavens, may you come; by the Deeps may you arrive.[33]

When you give your full name, make sure that it is either your complete birth name or your complete magical name. Include a relationship as part of your full name, such as 'child of...', 'student of...', 'subject of...', or another relationship. If you use a false name, or a name that does not reflect who you truly are, then be aware that the spirit you contact may also use a false name to identify itself.

The deity name that you should use in this invocation is that of a deity with whom you have a solid relationship and who is known as a benevolent deity of protection or powerful beneficial magic. Do not use a deity with whom you have no relationship and do not name a deity who has a malevolent streak. Speak of the deity's sphere of influence or an epithet of the deity. At the end of the invocation you may wish to engage in a Mesopotamian tradition of speaking the word for each magical tool you are using and stating their functions to enchant them, so they shall function more powerfully as magical and protective tools. For instance, "O Censer, you hold the holy incense that it may make an offering to the deities and spirits. O Broom, you sweep away all harm and pollution. O Bell you send any harmful spirits back to the underworld."

Ask your questions and have your pen, paper, and divination tool ready, or you can watch the incense smoke. Write down the outcomes, moments of intuition, and experiences you may have. Leave your expectations open enough so that you can allow yourself to experience nothing. Heavy expectations can hamper what you really might experience, or can clog the channel. Do not make the entire rite from start to finish last more than two hours. The question and answer session should last perhaps an hour, but not longer. It is dangerous to get tired at such a rite, so do not overdo it. Even if a spirit seems not to have made her or his presence known, a spirit may try to communicate with you in a dream later that night or during a night in the week. When the spirit ceases to answer, when you become tired, or when ample time has elapsed with no

---

[33]Black and Green, *Gods, Demons and Symbols of Ancient Mesopotamia*, p. 126. Typical incantations end in "be conjured by heaven, be conjured by the underworld." I choose to change the wording to respect the spirit and allow for the spirit's free will instead of demanding that the spirit appear."

i –what?

response, guide the spirit to the underworld. You may wish to make a prayer such as,

> O benevolent shades, O helpful Rapiuma, I thank you for your kindness. May you be supported and strengthened all the days in the underworld. May your names be remembered, and may you be honored. Return promptly to your resting place, O venerated ones. Return to the underworld, the House of Freedom, all ye spirits who have come forward. Peace and wellbeing to you. Shalam.

Bow in the direction where you perceive the shade, or bow in general towards the west. Visualize a glowing portal in the west leading to the underworld, ask your protective deity or spirit guides to help the shades cross over and tell the shades to follow your guide to the portal in the west to return to the underworld. Perform a divination to see if all have crossed over, and when all have, visualize the portal closed.

Eat the offerings on behalf of the spirit or dig a small hole with the shovel and bury or burn the offerings, including any flowers you brought with you. If you are in a cemetery, respect local customs and bury or burn the offerings off the premises. Raise the cup and drink the libation in honor of the deities.[34] Purify yourself and the space again. Sweep away the circle and any flour should go into dust pan. Bury the sweepings of the circle or toss them into flowing water with a prayer of gratitude for the local deity of the flowing water. Leave the site and do not turn back. In Mesopotamian tradition, you may wish to head to a local tavern or a public place afterwards. Continue to wear your protective amulet for seven days.[35] Be sure to note your dreams for seven days after the rite and carefully review any evidence you may have collected on paranormal investigation equipment. Go back through the notes you made regarding your divinations and experiences from the rite, and try to interpret any meaning or critique the rite. Write down any further insights in your notes.

If you have a troublesome shade that follows and disturbs you in some way, you can follow a couple of Mesopotamian procedures. Make a poppet of the deceased being and declare aloud that this is who the poppet symbolizes. As discussed before, give the poppet proper provisions and take it out to a desert, a wilderness, or a west-lying area and bury it with the provisions. Alternatively, you can make a poppet of the shade and toss the poppet into the river so that the river will carry it away and perhaps back into the underworld,[36] although keep in mind that this is usually for evil spirits. You may also wish to call upon Ba'al in a prayer of protection. This one is based on a prayer

---

[34]Wright, *Ritual in Narrative: The Dynamics of Feasting, Mourning, and Retaliation Rites in the Ugaritic Tale of Aqhat*, p. 72.
[35]Black and Green, *Gods, Demons and Symbols of Ancient Mesopotamia*, p. 127.
[36]Bottéro, Bahrani, and Van de Mieroop, *Mesopotamia: Writing, Reasoning, and the Gods*, p. 284.

found in Ugaritic texts from roughly 1500 B.C.E.,[37]

> O Baʿal, if you drive the Shade from me and bring it to rest in the underworld,
> The Rapiu from my house and bring it to the House of Freedom,
> A sacrifice I shall make,
> A meal in your honor;
> A vow I shall take,
> A promise I shall fulfill.
> These actions, O Baʿal, I shall do.

Make a vow to Baʿal. The vow can include a promise for a gift, community service hours, or resources donated to a worthy community cause. Be sure to follow through with your vow, and to prepare the meal that you promised to make. The sacrifice is a part of the meal and can include a beef dish, since the offering made in this prayer referred to a bull. If you are a vegetarian and you are violently opposed to making a meat offering, it is ultimately up to you and your relationship with the gods as to how you handle the situation. The ancient Canaanites cared deeply for their beloved dead and wanted to ensure that the shade would have a pleasant afterlife. Ensuring a shade's strength helped the shade to take care of the living by providing guidance, healing and good luck. Communicating with the dead was simply a way to make sure the dead were content in the afterlife and gain guidance from elders about difficult situations in life.

[37]Bottéro, Bahrani, and Van de Mieroop, *Mesopotamia: Writing, Reasoning, and the Gods*, p. 284.

BIBLIOGRAPHY

Bar-Yosef, Ofer. 'The Natufian Culture in the Levant. Threshold to the Origins of Agriculture'. In *Evolutionary Anthropology*, Volume 6, Issue 5. New York: Wiley-Liss Inc., 1998.

Black, Jeremy and Green, Anthony, *Gods, Demons and Symbols of Ancient Mesopotamia*. Texas: University of Texas Press, 1998.

Bottéro, Jean, Bahrani, Zainab and Van de Mieroop, Marc, *Mesopotamia: Writing, Reasoning, and the Gods*. Chicago: University of Chicago Press, 1995.

Dawson, Tess, *Whisper of Stone: Natib Qadish: Modern Canaanite Religion*. UK: O-Books, 2009.

Del Olmo, Lete Gregorio, *Canaanite Religion According to the Liturgical Texts of Ugarit*. Indiana: Eisenbrauns, 2004.

Fletcher, Joann, *The Egyptian Book of Living and Dying*. London: Thorsons, 2002.

Pardee, Dennis, *Ritual and Cult at Ugarit*. Atlanta: Society of Biblical Literature, 2002.

Parker, Simon B. (ed.), Smith, Mark (trans.) et al., *Ugaritic Narrative Poetry*. Atlanta: Society of Biblical Literature, 1997.

Patai, Raphael, *The Hebrew Goddess*, 3rd Enlarged Edition. Detroit: Wayne State University Press, 1990.

Sasson, Jack (ed.) et al., *Civilizations of the Ancient Near East*. New York: Charles Scribner's Sons, 1995.

Smith, Mark S., *The Ugaritic Baal Cycle, Volume I: Introduction with Text, Translation and Commentary of KTU 1.1-1.2*. Leiden: Brill, 1994.

Tubb, Jonathan N., *Canaanites*. Oklahoma: University of Oklahoma Press, 1998.

Winkler, Gershon, *Magic of the Ordinary: Recovering the Shamanic in Judaism*. Berkely: North Atlantic Books, 2003.

Wright, David P., *Ritual in Narrative: The Dynamics of Feasting, Mourning, and Retaliation Rites in the Ugaritic Tale of Aqhat*. Indiana: Eisenbrauns, 2001.

Zohary, Michael, *Plants of the Bible*. Cambridge: Cambridge University Press, 1982.

Young, Gordon D. (ed.), *Ugarit in Retrospect: Fifty Years of Ugarit and Ugaritic*. Indiana: Eisenbrauns, 1981.

COMPOSITE INCENSES
AND INCENSE ATTRIBUTIONS
A HISTORICAL SURVEY

BY

IOANNIS MARATHAKIS

Some suffumigations also, or perfumings, that are proper to the stars, are of great force for the opportune receiving of celestial gifts under the rays of the stars, in as much as they do strongly work upon the Air, and breath. For our breath is very much changed by such kind of vapours, if both vapours be of another like: the Air also being through the said vapours easily moved, or affected with the qualities of inferiors, or celestials, daily, and quickly penetrating our breast, and vitals, doth wonderfully reduce us to the like qualities.

Heinrich Cornelius Agrippa, *Three Books of Occult Philosophy*, Book I

It was in 2002 when I rather enthusiastically decided to write a paper on incense, under the title 'Incense: From Papyri to Grimoires'. The paper can still be found on the Internet.[1] However, in the subsequent eight years, more information became available to me. I thus decided that my old paper had to be rewritten.

Kyphi, the Egyptian Sacred Incense

The word *kyphi* is the Greek transliteration of the ancient Egyptian word *kapet*, which means 'incense' in general. Although the word occurs in the *Pyramid Texts*, its first actual recipe is contained in the medical *Ebers Papyrus*, fifteenth century B.C.E. It consisted of nine ingredients boiled in honey. Unfortunately, most of them cannot be identified with certainty, though we know that it contained cinnamon and pine kernels, among others.[2] But about thirteen centuries later, the recipe for *kyphi* changed, containing twelve fragrant ingredients, and the base was not solely honey, but also raisins and wine. There is a recipe inscribed twice in the temple of Edfu and once in the temple of Philae. The ingredients are exactly the same in all three cases and vary only in their

---

[1] http://www.servantsofthelight.org/knowledge/marathakis-incense.html.
[2] Manniche, *Sacred luxuries*, p. 55.

proportions. This is the Edfu 1 version,

Take 273 g each of sweet flag; lemon grass; mastic; pine resin; cinnamon; mint; spiny broom. Place them in a mortar and grind them. Two-fifths of this will be in the form of liquid to be discarded. There remain three-fifths in the form of ground powder. Take 1.5 l each of juniper berries; pine kernels; chervil; common galingale. Reduce the ingredients to powder. Moisten all these dry ingredients with 2.5 l wine in a copper vessel. Leave overnight. Half of this wine will be absorbed by the powder. The rest is to be discarded. Take 3.3 l raisins and 2.5 l oasis wine. Grind together well. Remove the rind and pips of the raisins. Place the rest in a vessel with the herbs. Leave for five days. Mix 1,213 g frankincense and 3.3 l honey in a cauldron. Boil gently until thickened and reduced by one-fifth. Mix with the other ingredients and leave overnight. Grind 1,155 g myrrh and add to the kyphi.[3]

Two centuries later the recipe changed further. The Greek physician Dioscorides, 50-90 C.E., in his work *De materia medica*, gave the following variation,

Kyphi is a composite incense dedicated to the Gods. Egyptian priests use it abundantly. It is also mixed with antidotes and is given to the asthmatic in beverages. It has many methods of preparation, including the following: 0.270 l of common galingale; the same quantity of plump juniper berries; 5,196 g of big stoned raisins; 2,165 g of colophony; 433 g each of sweet flag, spiny broom and lemon grass; 52 g of myrrh; 4.860 l of old wine; 866 g of honey. Stone and chop the raisins and grind with wine and myrrh. Grind and sieve the other ingredients and mix them with the aforementioned mixture. Let steep for one day. Boil the honey until it thickens, melt the colophony and mix them thoroughly. Mix thoroughly with the other ingredients and store in a clay pot.[4]

As Dioscorides implied, it seems that there was more than one recipe for making *kyphi*. A catalogue of different ingredients, rather than a recipe, can be found in a work named *On Isis and Osiris*. The author Plutarch, 46-120 C.E., a Greek historian, writer, and philosopher, who was also a priest of Apollo at the Oracle of Delphi, wrote,

Kyphi is a composition of sixteen ingredients; of honey and wine, raisins and common galingale, colophony and myrrh, spiny broom and shrubby hare's ear;

---

[3]The recipe is rephrased by the present author. I have taken into consideration the translation given in Manniche, *Sacred luxuries*, p. 51; as regards to the chervil, a suggestion by Renate Germer, cited in the Notes; the older translation in Manniche, *An Ancient Egyptian Herbal*, p. 58. Note that the identification of the ingredients is sometimes questionable.
[4]Sprengel (ed.), p. 38-39, *Pedanii Dioscoridis De Materia Medica*, Tomus I, p. 38-39. Translation by the present author. Note that the correspondence of the ancient weights and measures is approximate.

moreover, of mastic and bitumen, thorn apple and sorrel, together with the two kinds of juniper berries (of which one is called major and the other minor), cardamom and sweet flag. And these ingredients are not mixed by chance, but according to instructions contained in holy books, that are read to the incense makers while they mix them.[5]

Some years after Dioscorides and Plutarch, another Greek physician, Claudius Galen, 129-201 C.E., in his work *On Antidotes*, provided the last variation of the ancient world. In fact, Galen cited a poem written by an older physician, Damocrates, who was a contemporary to Dioscorides. The poem reads as follows,

Kyphi is neither a simple mixture,
nor does it grow from earth, nor does it come from a tree.
The Egyptians manufacture it and cense
some of the gods with it. They make it as follows:
They take very plump white raisins
and they discard their skin and all the seeds.
After grinding the flesh well,
they take ninety six grammars of the paste
and the same amount of colophony;
forty eight of myrrh; sixteen of cinnamon;
forty eight of lemon grass; four of saffron;
twelve of bdellium nails, eight of spiny broom;
twelve of spikenard; twelve of good
and pure cassia; twelve of common galingale;
the same amount of big and plump juniper berries;
thirty six grammars of sweet flag;
sufficient honey and very little wine.
They put bdellium, wine and myrrh in a mortar
and they grind diligently, until they become
a honey-thick liquid. Then they add the honey,
they grind the raisins and add
everything else, finely ground. From this
they make small pellets and cense the gods.
That it should be made this way, maintained Rufus,
a great man and master of medicine.
But some who do not have cinnamon
add the same amount of cardamom seed
and proceed the same way, as indicated.
Some give as a beverage for the ulcus of the liver,

---

[5]Bernardakis, *Plutarchi Chaeronensis Varia Scripta*, Tomus I, p. 76. Translation by the present author.

of the lungs or of any of the guts
four grammars of this medicine.[6]

Ketoret, the Jewish Sacred Incense

Kyphi was not the only famous composite incense in the ancient world. The Book of
Exodus informs us about the *ketoret*, the sacred incense used by the Jewish priests for
the worship of Yahweh. It had to be burned every morning and evening on the special
incense altar situated before the curtain of the Most Holy in the Temple of Jerusalem.
Moreover, once a year on the Day of Atonement, the High Priest would to cense the
Ark of the Covenant and the Mercy Seat within the Most Holy. According to the King
James Version,

> And the Lord said unto Moses, Take unto thee sweet spices, stacte, and onycha,
> and galbanum; these sweet spices with pure frankincense: of each shall there
> be a like weight. And thou shalt make it a perfume, a confection after the art
> of the apothecary, tempered together, pure and holy. And thou shalt beat some
> of it very small, and put of it before the testimony in the tabernacle of the
> congregation, where I will meet with thee: it shall be unto you most holy.[7]

Although the Book of Exodus has Yahweh transmitting the recipe to Moses, we have
to note that according to modern biblical exegesis the passage belongs to the priestly
source,[8] a work of writers that were concerned with the ritual of the Second Temple[9]
built in 516 B.C.E. after the return of the Jewish nation from the Babylonian exile.
There is no way to know what kind of incense used to burn in the first Temple of
Solomon.

Regardless of the chronology of the passage though, the first thing we observe in this
recipe is the absence of a base, such as honey or a fruity paste. The reason is probably
the Jewish notion of honey and fruits as being unsuitable for burnt offerings, as another
priestly passage from the Book of Leviticus mentions.[10] This probably means that,
unless one of the ingredients was liquid or syrupy, the *ketoret* would be rather a sticky
powder than shaped into pellets. What we have to do first is to identify the ingredients.
Two of them are quite recognizable, namely frankincense, *lebonah* in Hebrew, and
galbanum, *chelbenah* in Hebrew, but the remaining two are a subject of debate.

---

[6]Kuhn (ed.), *Claudii Galeni Opera Omnia*, Tomus XIV, p. 117-119. Translation by the present author.
[7]Exodus 30: 34-36.
[8]Campbell and O'Brien, *Sources of the Pentateuch*, p. 52.
[9]Bacher, Kaufmann, and McCurdy, 'Bible Exegesis', in *Jewish Encyclopedia*, Volume III, p. 177.
[10]Leviticus 2: 11-12.

According to the *Liddell-Scott Greek-English Lexicon*, the Greek word *staktê* means 'oozing out in drops, trickling, distilling' and it is an adjective that refers to various substances. For instance, *staktê konia*, 'trickling dust', is the lime-water and *staktê almê*, 'trickling salt' is the brine. To my knowledge, the Greek physician Hippocrates, 460-370 B.C.E., was the first who wrote about *staktê smyrna*, 'trickling myrrh', in his work *De Ulceris*, "Grind to powder some trickling myrrh, that is to say myrrh of the best quality."[11] About four centuries later, Pliny the Elder, 23-79 C.E., used the word as a noun to indicate the same thing and explained that this best quality myrrh exudes from the tree spontaneously,

> Incisions are made in the myrrh-tree also twice a year, and at the same season as in the incense-tree, but in the case of the myrrh-tree they are all made the way up from the root as far as the branches which are able to bear it. The tree spontaneously exudes, before the incision is made, a liquid which bears the name of staktê, and to which there is no myrrh that is superior.[12]

But about a century after Hippocrates, the Greek philosopher and botanist Theophrastus, 371-287 B.C.E., in his work *Concerning Odours*, wrote that in his time the word *staktê* as a noun had acquired two more meanings. The first was 'myrrh essential oil', extracted by expression, and in fact the first essential oil extracted in history. The second was 'oil of balanus' perfumed with myrrh essential oil. All three meanings remained in use at least till the first century C.E.[13] According to Theophrastus,

> And from the myrrh when it is bruised flows an oil: it is in fact called staktê (in drops) because it comes in drops slowly. Some indeed say that this is the only simple uncompounded perfume, and that all the others are compound, though made from a larger or smaller number of ingredients, and that iris-perfume is made from the smallest number of all. Some assert this, but others declare that the manufacture of staktê (myrrh-oil) is as follows: having bruised the myrrh and dissolved it in oil of balanos over a gentle fire, they pour hot water on it: and the myrrh and oil sink to the bottom like a deposit; and, as soon as this has occurred, they strain off the water and squeeze the sediment in a press.[14]

However, although it is certain that *staktê* comes from the myrrh tree, it is very problematic as a component of the *ketoret* in all its three meanings. Perfumed oils obviously cannot be incense components at all, because we would then have thick oily mud. Essential oils, on the other hand, have the tendency to evaporate before the rest of the components begin to burn, thus being unsuitable for incense. This leaves us with

[11]Kuhn (ed.), *Hippocratis Opera Omnia*, Tomus III, p. 315. Translation by the present author.
[12]Pliny the Elder, *The Natural History*, p. 130.
[13]Sprengel (ed.), *Pedanii Dioscoridis De Materia Medica*, Tomus I, p. 75-76.
[14]Capps, Page, and Rouse (eds.), *Theophrastus: Inquiry into Plants*, Volume II, p. 353.

the third option, 'best quality myrrh'. Yet, there is already an expression for best quality myrrh, *rosh mor deror*, in some verses earlier[15] and it is very improbable that the author would use different terms for the same substance so close together.

The word 'stacte', as it appears in most modern translations of the Bible, is taken from the Latin Vulgate. St. Jerome, the fifth century C.E. translator, simply latinized the Greek word *stakté* as he found it in the third century B.C. Septuagint translation. One can assume that he would be puzzled with the Hebrew word *nataf* and chose to solve the problem in the easy way. One can also assume that the Septuagint translators found themselves in the same puzzling situation. The Hebrew word *nataf*, as a noun, appears only twice in the Old Testament. Except from the aforementioned passage, it can be found in Job 36: 27, where it is translated as 'drop', since the verb *nataf* means 'to drip'. The Septuagint translators may have chosen the word *stakté* simply because it means 'trickling'.

So, we still have to identify *nataf*. Every now and then there emerges a new theory without serious evidence. Many fragrant gums and resins have been proposed to be *nataf*, for instance benzoin, labdanum, balsam, various mixtures of the above with myrrh, and so on.[16] However, the Hebrew-Aramaic tradition, along with the vast majority of scholars, associates *nataf* with another fragrant substance, *tsori*. This is the root for the Greek word *styrax*, the English 'storax', which is the resinous exudate of *liquidambar orientalis*.[17]

The fourth obscure ingredient of the *ketoret* is onycha. As in the previous case, the word is taken from the Latin Vulgate, which again latinized the Greek word found in the Septuagint. Onycha is the accusative form of the Greek word *onyx*, which means 'fingernail', and also signifies other things that resemble fingernails, such as some forms of agate or a fragrant operculum of a certain sea snail, namely *Strombus lentiginosus*. This operculum is still used in the East for incense and medicine, something that led some scholars to accept it as an ingredient of the *ketoret*.[18] However, this hypothesis is doubtful, since it is counted among the unclean animals by the Jews.[19] [20]

It is not difficult to assume that there has occurred another mistranslation. The Septuagint translators probably did not know how to translate the Hebrew word *shcheleth*, which appears only once in the Old Testament. Strong's *Hebrew Dictionary* associates this mysterious word with *sachal*, "from an unused root probably meaning

[15]Exodus 30: 23.
[16]See entry at http://en.wikipedia.org/wiki/Stacte.
[17]Nielsen, *Incense in Ancient Israel*, p. 61-62, 65.
[18]Benzinger and Eisenstein, 'Incense', in *Jewish Encyclopedia*, Volume VI. p. 570.
[19]Leviticus 11: 9, 12.
[20]Abrahams, 'Onycha, Ingredient of the ancient Jewish incense: An attempt at identification', in *Economic Botany*, vol. 33(2), p. 233-236.

to roar; a lion (from his characteristic roar)." Thus, Strong believes that *shcheleth* is derived from the same root "through some obscure idea, perhaps that of peeling off by concussion of sound".[21] Although exaggerated as a true etymology, this is probably the reason that the Septuagint translators chose to translate it as *onyx*.

The mistranslation hypothesis led to many theories about *shcheleth*. Gums and resins such as labdanum, benzoin, bdellium, and gum tragacanth have been proposed, among other substances, such as cloves or spikenard.[22] But almost the same word, *shchelet*, appears in an Ugaritic text, listed between sesame and raisins. So, it is reasonable to assume that it is some kind of vegetable.[23] If we also take into consideration that the related Hebrew word *shchalim* means 'garden cress', it is easy to suppose that, if not garden cress, *shcheleth* must be another spicy edible leaf. It should be noted that chervil is among the ingredients of the Egyptian *kyphi*.

While during the sixth to fifth century B.C.E. *ketoret* had only four ingredients, later Jewish sources inform us that during the first century C.E. its composition had been dramatically changed, as it now contained eleven spices, with about forty kilograms each of the aforementioned four, nine point one three kilograms each of myrrh, cassia, spikenard and saffron, six point eight five kilograms costus, five point one three kilograms cinnamon, and one point seven one kilograms kinashan, which is a kind of aromatic bark. Other sources add minute amounts of more ingredients, such as a kind of lye, Cyprus wine, Sodom salt and *maaleh ashan*, an unidentified herb that purportedly caused the smoke to rise as a column.[24]

Magical and Sacred Incenses in the Greco-Roman World

The *Greek Magical Papyri* are a corpus of papyri that derive from Greco-Roman Egypt dating from the second century B.C.E. to the fifth century C.E. These papyri cite various magical operations and are something like grimoires of the Greco-Roman world. Many magical operations involve the use of a single gum resin, mainly myrrh or frankincense. But there are also composite incenses reminiscent of *kyphi*, as they contain honey, wine, and some fruity paste. The texts also refer to composite incenses that include animal parts or dung, but we will not expand on these kinds of recipes. There is only one detailed recipe. It is from an operation called *The Sword of Dardanos* that intends to "attract the soul of anybody you want." It involves the construction of a certain talisman, and the incense that ensouls the talisman is the following, "Manna 16

[21] Strong, *A Concise Dictionary of the Words in the Hebrew Bible*, p. 114.
[22] See entry at http://en.wikipedia.org/wiki/Onycha. As far as I know, I was the first to propose bdellium in my aforementioned article.
[23] Nielsen, *Incense in Ancient Israel*, p. 66.
[24] Benzinger and Eisenstein, 'Incense', in *Jewish Encyclopedia*, Volume VI, p. 570.

g, storax 16 g, opium 16 g, myrrh 16 g; 2 g each of frankincense, saffron, and bdellium. Mix with a plump dried fig; add an equal proportion of fragrant wine and use."[25] Other recipes are not so detailed. The following is from a *Slander spell to Selene*, which intends "to attract somebody in one hour, to send dreams, to cause sickness, to kill enemies." The operation lasts three days. The first two days one is to use this beneficent lunar incense, while during the third one is to use a coercive one. "The beneficent incense: frankincense, bay, myrtle, fruit pits, stavesacre, malabathron, costus. Pound all these and mix with Mendesian wine and honey. Shape into pellets the size of broad beans."[26] This is another lunar incense from a *Prayer to Selene, for every magical operation*, "Incense for this procedure. For beneficent deeds: storax, myrrh, sage, frankincense, fruit pits."[27]

Except from magical operations, composite incenses played also a major part in Gnostic rituals. The ritual use of incense among the Gnostics is contained in a third century C.E. text, the 'Second Book of Jeu', contained in the *Bruce Codex*. This text describes how Jesus offered the baptism of water, of fire, and of spirit to the apostles, after which he performs a ceremony for taking away the evil from them. In each of these four initiations, a different fragrant mixture was used. Kasdalanthos remains unidentified,

> It happened furthermore after these words Jesus called his disciples and said to them: "Come all of you and receive the three baptisms before I say to you the mystery of the archons"... Jesus offered up an offering. He placed a pitcher of wine on the left of the offering and he placed the other pitcher of wine on the right of the offering. He laid juniper upon the offering with kasdalanthos and nard... It happened furthermore that Jesus continued with the discourse. He said to his disciples: "Bring me vine branches so that you may receive the baptism of fire". And the disciples brought him vine branches. He offered up incense. He laid there juniper and myrrh and frankincense and mastic resin and nard, kasdalanthos, terebinth and balsam... He offered the incense for the baptism of the Holy Spirit. He laid branches of vine and juniper and kasdalanthos and saffron (residue) and mastic (resin) and cinnamon and myrrh and balsam and honey. It happened moreover after these things Jesus offered the incense of the mystery which took away the evil of the archons from the disciples. He caused them to build an incense-altar upon thalassia plants (?). He laid upon it vine branches, and juniper and betel and kuoschi (?) and asbestos and agate-stone and frankincense.[28]

But besides the recipes, there is much information concerning the attributions of

[25]Preisendanz (ed.), *Papyri Graecae Magicae* I, p. 128.
[26]Preisendanz (ed.), *Papyri Graecae Magicae* I, p. 156-157.
[27]Preisendanz (ed.), *Papyri Graecae Magicae* I, p. 164.
[28]Schmidt (ed.), *The Books of JEU and the Untitled Text in the Bruce Codex*, p. 139-141 for the Baptism of Water, p. 145-147 for the Baptism of Fire, p. 153 for the Baptism of the Holy Spirit, and p. 157 for the mystery that takes away all evil.

fragrant substances in the Greco-Roman times. The oldest information we have is inscribed in the temple of Edfu, second century B.C.E. According to the inscription, there are eleven kinds of resin suitable for the gods, and each one is somehow connected with a specific god. Unfortunately, the inscription is not wholly readable, so we can read only six of these attributions. Moreover, the resins are unidentified, so one can only make assumptions regarding their identity. Three of them, golden in colour, are said to spring from the eye of Ra, and maybe the one is galbanum. Another one, red in colour, is said to spring from the left eye of Osiris, which maybe myrrh. One is said to come from the white of the eye of Thoth, and one from the back of Horus, with no suggestions being indicated.[29]

A similar attribution of incenses to the Greek gods are included in the *Orphic Hymns*, a collection of hymns that date as late as the third century C.E.[30] There are eighty-seven hymns in total, each dedicated to a specific deity, aspect of deity, or group of deities. After their titles, the proper incenses that must be offered to each god follow. Classification of the various gods according to their incense does not offer much, since there seems to be no apparent philosophy in the attribution. Storax is to be offered to Prothyraia, who is an aspect of Artemis; Zeus and Zeus Keraunios, who is Zeus of the Thunderbolts; Proteus; Dionysus; Demeter of Eleusis; Mise, a hermaphrodite deity connected with the Mysteries of Eleusis; Semele; Hipta, the nanny of Dionysus; Hermes Chthonios, who is Hermes of the Underworld; and the Charites. Myrrh is to be offered Protogonus, the firstborn god; Poseidon; the Nephelae; Nereus; and Leto. Frankincense is to be offered to Ouranos; Heracles; Hermes; the Titans; the Kouretes, followers of Rhea; Korybas, a god connected with the Mysteries of Samothrace; Dike; goddess of right; Dikaiosyne, goddess of justice; Ares; Tyche, goddess of luck; Daimon, an aspect of Zeus; the Musae; Mnemosyne, goddess of memory; Themis, goddess of the divine order; Boreas, the north wind; Zephyrus, the west wind; and Notus, the south wind. Manna is to be offered to Nike, goddess of victory; Apollo; Artemis; Liknetes, infant Dionysus; Silenus and the Bacchae; Asclepius; Hygeia, goddess of health; Palaimon, a sea god connected with Dionysus; Eos, goddess of the dawn; and Thanatos, god of death. Libanomanna is to be offered to Helios; Zeus Astrapaios, Zeus of the Lightning; Tethys, consort of Oceanus; and Hephaestus. No incense is mentioned in connection to Hecate; Pluto; Persephone; the Kouretes, as there is another hymn to Kouretes with the indication frankincense; Athena; Dionysus Bassareus Trieterikos, Dionysus celebrated every alternate year; Lysios Lenaios, Dionysus the saviour and Dionysus of the wine; Aphrodite; Nemesis; and Nomus, god of the law.

There are also twenty-one deities whose incenses are described by the general term of 'perfumes'. These deities are the Asteres; Selene; Physis, Nature; Rhea; Hera; the

[29]Manniche, *Sacred luxuries*, p. 27.
[30]Published in Quandt, William (ed.), *Orphei Hymni*. Berlin: Weidmann, 1962.

Nereids; Mother Antaia, an aspect of Demeter; the Horae; Bacchus Pericionius, Bacchus of the Column; Sabazios; the Nymphs; Trietericos, Dionysus celebrated every alternate year, again; Adonis; Eros, Cupid; the Moirae, the Eumenides; the Erinyes; Melinoe, daughter of Persephone; Leukothea, a sea goddess; Oceanus; Hestia; and Oneiros, god of dreams. Apart from these, pine wood is to be offered to Nyx; saffron to Aether; opium to Hypnos, god of sleep; any seed except broad beans to Gaia; any incense except frankincense to Amphietes, Dionysus celebrated annually. A 'variety' of perfumes is to be offered to Pan and to the Mother of the Gods, Rhea.

Attributions of Incenses to the Planets

One of the most important elements concerning incenses during the Roman era was the attributions of odoriferous substances to the seven planets. One of the oldest lists is included in the *Greek Magical Papyri*. The texts inform us that it is taken from "A sacred book called Monad or Eighth Book of Moses, concerning the Holy Name". The mixture of these seven substances provide the composite incense for the magical procedure that follows. The writer claims that "from this book Hermes plagiarized when he named the seven kinds of incense... The proper incense for Saturn is storax, because it is heavy and fragrant. For Jupiter, malabathron. For Mars, costus. For the Sun, frankincense. For Venus, spikenard. For Mercury, cassia. For the Moon, myrrh."[31] Although there are no other contemporary manuscripts containing similar lists, there is evidence that material from those times was preserved in posterior books. One such example is an Arabic magical book, *Ghayat al-Hakim* or *The Goal of the Wise*, which became famous in Europe after it was translated into Spanish, and later into Latin during the thirteenth century C.E. under the title *Picatrix*. It was compiled from several books, some spuriously attributed to Aristotle, Apollonius of Tyana, and even Hermes. There are several lists of planetary incenses, for example,

> When it comes to the planets' incenses, Saturn rules every stinky incense like lynx, army barracks weight lifters and similar; Jupiter rules every good smelling incense like ambergris and aloes wood; Mars rules all incenses mild, spicy and hot like pepper, any other mild pepper flavored spice and ginger; the Sun rules all good smelling incense like musk and ambergris; Venus rules all mild pleasant smelling incense like roses, violet and green myrtle; as for Mercury every pleasant smelling incense mixed like narcissus, violet, myrtle and mallow and the Moon has every pleasant cold smelling incense like camphor, roses and fresh smelling scents.[32]

Some pages before this passage though, the book offers different attributions. For

---

[31] Preisendanz (ed.), *Papyri Graecae Magicae* I, p. 88, 105.
[32] Kiesel (ed.), *Picatrix*, Volume II, p. 16-17.

Saturn wisteria and licorice; for Jupiter saffron, yellow sandalwood, musk, camphor, rose oil, and amber; for Mars red sandalwood; for the Sun aloe wood; for Venus musk and amber; and for Mercury ginger and spikenard. The author probably forgot to cite the attributions of the Moon.[33] Different lists of composite incenses did also exist, thus revealing the great differentiation of the Greco-Roman tradition through the centuries.[34] Another example of this differentiation can be found in a fifteenth century manuscript, Harley 5596, which contains a work known as *Magic Treatise of Solomon*. This work includes an older magicalbook, *Hygromancy* or *Epistle of Rehoboam*, written in the first or second century C.E.[35] and states,

> These are the incenses of Saturn: nigella seeds, nails of a black ass, a head of a snake, pepper, aloe wood... These are the incenses of Jupiter: lignum balsam, cinnamon, opium, camphor, vervain seeds... These are the incenses of the Sun: nutmeg, cassia, roses, storax balls... These are the incenses of Mars: blood of a cat, brain of a vulture, human blood, brain of a crow... These are the incenses of Venus: musk, aloe wood, Armenian bole, Cyprus cumin, civet, fragrant costus... These are the incenses of Mercury: Pure white frankincense, musk, wasp wax, labdanum, sweet flag... These are the incenses of the Moon: Pure white beeswax, saffron, bay root. And if there is not bay root, take the upper part of the evergreen rose and daffodil root.[36]

A third text that depends largely on the Greco-Roman tradition is contained in some manuscripts of the *Sepher Raziel* and *Liber Juratus*,[37] as well as in Agrippa's *Three Books of Occult Philosophy*. However, it is not clear which book is the source of the other two. In this text there are incense attributions to the seven planets, together with a general rule for recognizing the planetary correspondences of aromatic substances. In all three cases the text is followed by instructions on how to make an incense comprised of seven planetary substances. This composite incense, as well as the reference to Hermes, brings to mind the Greek Magical Papyri tradition,

> Besides, to Saturn are appropriated for fumes all odoriferous roots, as pepperwort root, etc. and the frankincense tree: to Jupiter odoriferous fruits, as nutmegs, cloves: to Mars all odoriferous wood, as sanders, cypress, lignum-balsam, and lignum aloes: to the Sun, all gums, frankincense, mastic, benjamin, storax, laudanum, ambergris, and musk: to Venus flowers, as roses, violets, saffron,

---

[33]Kiesel (ed.), *Picatrix*, Volume II, p. 2-10.

[34]Kiesel (ed.), *Picatrix*, Volume II, p. 71-75, 108-113, and 227-230. The last list contains composite incenses with animal parts, such as blood and brains.

[35]At least, according to Carroll, 'A Preliminary Analysis of the Epistle of Rehoboam', in *Journal for the Study of the Pseudepigrapha*, 4, p. 91.

[36]Delatte (ed.), *Anecdota Atheniensia* I, p. 405-406. Translation by the present author.

[37]See Peterson (ed.), *Sepher Raziel*, Sloane 3846,http://www.esotericarchives.com/raziel/raziel.htm#book3. Also, Peterson (ed.), *Liber Juratus*, http://www.esotericarchives.com/juratus/juratus.htm.

and such like: to Mercury all the peels of wood and fruit, as cinnamon, lignum-cassia, mace, citron peel, and bayberries, and whatsoever seeds are odoriferous: to the Moon the leaves of all vegetables, as the leaf Indum, the leaves of the myrtle, and bay tree... But Hermes describes the most powerful fume to be, viz. that which is compounded of the seven aromatics, according to the powers of the seven planets, for it receives from Saturn, pepperwort, from Jupiter, nutmeg, from Mars, lignum-aloes, from the Sun, mastic, from Venus, saffron, from Mercury, cinnamon, and from the Moon, the myrtle.[38]

Other grimoires offer different attributions. The main traditions are summarized in the table below.

Table of Planetary Incenses

Planet	Greek Magical Papyri	Picatrix I	Picatrix II	Sepher Raziel Liber Juratus Agrippa	Heptameron[1] Keys of Rabbi Solomon[2]	Veritable Clavicles of Solomon[3]
Moon	Myrrh		Camphor Rose	Myrtle	Aloe wood	Loadstone
Mercury	Cassia	Ginger Spikenard	Narcissus Violet Myrtle	Cinnamon	Mastic	Juniper
Venus	Spikenard	Musk Amber	Rose Violet Myrtle	Saffron	Costus	Musk
Sun	Frankincense	Lignum aloes	Musk Ambergris	Mastic	Red sandalwood	Bay
Mars	Costus	Red sandalwood	Pepper Ginger	Aloe wood	Pepper	Storax
Jupiter	Malabathron	Saffron	Ambergris Aloe wood	Mace	Saffron	Aloe wood
Saturn	Storax	Wisteria Licourice	Lynx	Costus	Sulphur	Sulphur

The idea of planetary attributions of incenses eventually led to other astrological attributions as well. In some of the aforementioned books there are correspondences to the twelve signs of the zodiac, to the thirty-six decans, and to the twenty eight stations

---

[38]Agrippa, Tyson (ed.), *Three Books of Occult Philosophy*, p. 132-133.

of the Moon. Attributions of incenses to the four elements and to the sub-elements do not appear until the twentieth century with Aleister Crowley's *Liber 777 vel Prolegomena Symbolica*, along with attributions to the ten *sephiroth*. Crowley was generally based on tradition but not restricted by it. For instance, it is the first time that one relates the four ingredients of the *ketoret* to the four elements. His sephirothic attributions remain mainly traditional planetary, while his sub-elemental ones seem to be derived from clairvoyant observation.

Composite Incenses in Evocation

From the fifteenth century and onwards, some grimoires ceased to classify operations under the planets and started to give the same composite incense for all workings of evocation. One famous magical book of the time, *The Book of Abramelin*, contains a magical operation for the achievement of the Conversation with the Holy Guardian Angel, followed by a series of evocations of the 'unredeemed spirits'. This book is preserved in six manuscripts and three editions, the 1725 Peter Hammer's German edition, the 1900 Mathers' edition, and the recent 2006 Georg Dehn's edition. Unfortunately, all three editors disagree in regards the recipe of the proper incense. But since Hammer's edition uses equal parts of storax, onycha, galbanum, and frankincense, it is very probable that the original author tried to duplicate the *ketoret*.[39] Here follow the other two recipes,

> Take of incense in tears (Mathers notes: "Olibanum") one part; of stacte (Mathers notes: "Or storax") half a part; of lign aloes a quarter of a part and not being able to get this wood you shall take that of cedar, or of rose, or of citron, or any other odoriferous wood...[40] Take equal parts of balm, gummy galbanum and pure storax. If you cannot get balm, use cedar or aloe, or other pleasantly-smelling woods.[41]

We spoke earlier of the fifteenth century Harley 5596 manuscript, which contains the *Magic Treatise of Solomon*, in connection with the second century material on planetary magic. However, there is also subsequent material related to evocation. In fact, two different methods of calling the spirits are described, with each method having its own composite incense,

> When it is well swept and appropriate for the Art, take two new and pure

---

[39]According to my translation of a page from Peter Hammer's edition, given in Abraham of Worms, Dehn (ed.), *The Book of Abramelin*, p. 100, these are the four ingredients of the Abramelin incense.
[40]Abraham the Jew, Mathers (ed.), *The Sacred Magic of Abramelin the Mage*, p. 77.
[41]Abraham of Worms, Dehn (ed.), *The Book of Abramelin*, p. 101. Unfortunately, the translator forgets to explain what exactly is meant by the word 'balm'.

earthen vessels, fill them with burning charcoals that do not smoke and place upon them the following incenses: aloe wood, fragrant costus, frankincense, pure musk, cloves, nutmeg and saffron. Add water lily, black cloves, root of daffodil and the blood of a man that was killed undeservedly...[42] You must also have some burning charcoals and four little earthen vessels, new and pure. Place upon them the following incenses: musk, storax, aloe wood ash, spikenard, saffron and nutmeg.[43]

The *Magic Treatise of Solomon* seems to be one of the sources of the famous *Key of Solomon*. The manuscripts of this famous grimoire fall into four distinct families, two of which have been referred to in the planetary incenses table in this paper. The remaining two, namely the Abraham Colorno and the Universal Treatise Family, present simpler incense recipes, "The sweet-smelling perfumes are made with incenses from wood of aloes, nutmeg, benjoin gum and musk...[44] Make some perfumes from aloes, musk and balm."[45] In its turn, the universal treatise family of the *Key of Solomon* served as a source for the last of the grimoires, the nineteenth century *Grimorium Verum*, "You must use lignum aloe, frankincense and mace. Mace is only used in fumigating the circle, while the others serve for all other operations."[46]

Glossary of Substances

Aloe wood: A dark resinous wood that forms in *Aquilaria* trees when they become infected with a type of mold, also known as agarwood.
Amber: See Ambergris.
Ambergris: A fragrant secretion of the sperm whale. It can be found floating upon the sea.
Armenian bole: A red clay native to Armenia.
Balanos oil: Oil pressed from the seeds of the *Balanites aegyptiaca*, also known as the desert date tree.
Balsam: While in later than the twelfth century sources this is identified as the gum resin obtained from *Commiphora gileadensis*, the true balsam of antiquity is probably the tear of a now extinct species of *Persimmon*, native to Palestine.
Bdellium: Gum resin obtained from certain species of the genus *Commiphora*, among others *C. africana*, *C. erythraea*, *C. hildebrandtii* and *C. wightii*. However, it is uncertain which of those gums were regarded as bdellium or as myrrh during antiquity. It should be noted that the gum resin of *C. erythraea* is today known as Opopanax.

---

[42]Delatte (ed.), *Anecdota Atheniensia* I, p. 417. Translation by the present author.
[43]Delatte (ed.), *Anecdota Atheniensia* I, p. 426. Translation by the present author.
[44]Skinner and Rankine (eds.), *The Veritable Key of Solomon*, p. 346.
[45]Skinner and Rankine (eds.), *The Veritable Key of Solomon*, p. 390.
[46]Peterson (ed.), *Grimorium Verum*, p. 29.

Benjamin: See benzoin.

Benzoin: Dried resin of *Styrax tonkinensis*, Siam benzoin, or *Styrax benzoin*, Sumatra benzoin.

Bitumen: A sticky, tar-like form of petroleum that floats on the water of springs and lakes.

Camphor: A waxy, white or transparent solid found in wood of the *Cinnamomum camphora*.

Cardamom: The seeds of *Elettaria cardamomum*.

Cassia: The fragrant bark of the *Cinnamomum cassia* tree.

Cinnamon: The fragrant bark of the *Cinnamomum verum* tree.

Civet: A fragrant secretion of the civet's perineal glands. It is harvested by scraping the secretions from the glands of a live animal.

Cloves: The dried flower buds of the *Eugenia caryophyllata* tree.

Colophony: A solid form of resin, produced by heating fresh liquid resin to vaporize the turpentine. In antiquity, the colophony produced from the resins of *Pistacia terebinthus* and *P. palaestina* was regarded the best.

Common galingale: The herb *Cyperus longus*. Its rhizomes have a violet-like fragrance.

Costus: The herb *Costus speciosus*, very similar to ginger, with a fragrant root.

Evergreen rose: The species *Rosa sempervirens*.

Frankincense: Gum resin obtained from certain *Boswellia* species, mainly *B. sacra*.

Galbanum: Gum resin obtained from *Ferula gummosa*.

Ginger: The rhizome of the plant *Zingiber officinale*.

Gum tragacanth: Gum obtained from several species of the genus *Astragalus*, including *A. adscendens*, *A. gummifer* and *A. tragacanthus*.

Juniper: Various species of the genus *Juniperus*. The 'major' berries probably come from *J. macrocarpa* or *J. drupacea*.

Labdanum: Resin obtained from the shrub *Cistus creticus*.

Laudanum: See Labdanum.

Indum leaf: See malabathron.

Lemon grass: The grass *Cymbopogon citratus*.

Libanomanna: Pounded frankincense.

Licorice: The root of *Glycyrrhiza glabra*.

Lignum aloes: See aloe wood.

Lignum balsam: The wood of the balsam tree.

Malabathron: Leaves of the tree *Cinnamomum tamala*.

Manna: The saccharine exudence of a number of plants, such as *Fraxinus ornus*, *Quercus vallones*, *Alhagi maurorum*, *Tamarix gallica* and *Larix decidua*. It is uncertain which was the one meant by the ancient authors.

Mastic: Resin obtained from the tree *Pistacia Lentiscus*.

Musk: A fragrant substance obtained from a gland of the male musk deer.

Myrrh: Gum resin obtained from certain species of the genus *Commiphora*, mainly *C. myrrha*, but also *C. habessinica*, *C. schimperi*, and *C. molmol*. However, it is uncertain which of those gums were regarded as myrrh or as bdellium during antiquity.

Nard: The plant *Nardostachys jatamansi.* It has a fragrant root.

Olibanum: See frankincense.

Pepperwort: The plant *Lepidium latifolium,* a species of cress. However, judging from the context, it is obvious that Agrippa meant ginger or costus.

Saffron: The flower pistils of *Crocus sativus.*

Sandalwood: The fragrant wood of various trees of the genus *Santalum.* Red sandalwood, however, is the wood of the tree *Pterocarpus santalinus.*

Sanders: See sandalwood.

Sorrel: The plant *Rumex acetosa.*

Spikenard: See nard.

Spiny broom: The plant *Calicotome villosa.* Its root was used in ancient perfumery.

Shrubby hare's ear: The herb *Bupleurum fruticosum.*

Stavesacre: The plant *Delphinium staphisagria.*

Storax: Two different substances, a balsamic oleo-resin obtained from *Liquidambar orientalis,* liquid storax, and a resin obtained from *Styrax officinalis.*

Sweet flag: The plant *Acorus calamus.* Its root was used in ancient perfumery.

Terebinth: Colophony produced from *Pistacia* resin.

Thorn apple: The plant *Datura stramonium.*

BIBLIOGRAPHY

Abano, Peter de, Peterson, Joseph (ed.), *Heptameron, or Magical Elements*. http://www.
esotericarchives.com/solomon/heptamer.htm.

Abraham of Worms, Dehn, Georg (ed.), *The Book of Abramelin*. Florida: Ibis Press,
2006.

Abraham the Jew, McGregor Mathers, S. L. (ed.), *The Sacred Magic of Abramelin the
Mage*, London: John M. Watkins, 1900.

Abrahams, Harold J., 'Onycha, Ingredient of the ancient Jewish incense: An attempt at
identification'. In *Economic Botany*, Vol. 33(2). New York: New York Botanical Garden
Press, 1979.

Agrippa, Cornelius, Tyson, Donald (ed.), *Three Books of Occult Philosophy*. Minnesota:
Llewellyn Publications, 1997.

Bacher, Wilhelm, Kohler, Kaufmann, and McCurdy, J. Frederic, 'Bible Exegesis'. In
Jewish Encyclopedia, Volume III. New York: Ktav Publishing House, 1902.

Benzinger, Immanuel and Eisenstein, Judah David, 'Incense'. In *Jewish Encyclopedia*,
Volume VI. London and New York: Funk and Wagnalls Company, 1904.

Bernardakis, Gregorius (ed.), *Plutarchi Chaeronensis Moralia*, Vol. II. Lipsiae: Teubner,
1829.

Bostock J. and Riley H. T. (eds.), *The Natural History of Pliny*, Vol. III. London: H. G.
Bohn, 1855.

Campbell, Antony F. and O'Brien, Mark A., *Sources of the Pentateuch*. Fortress Press,
Kiesel, William (ed.), Atallah, H. and Holmquest, G. (trans.), *Picatrix*, Volume II.
Seattle: Ouroboros Press, 2007.
1993.

Capps, E., Page T. E., and Rouse, W. H. D. (eds.), Hort, Arthur (trans.), *Theophrastus:
Enquiry into Plants*, Volume II. New York: G. P. Putnam's Sons, 1916.

Carroll, Scott, 'A Preliminary Analysis of the Epistle of Rehoboam'. In *Journal for the
Study of the Pseudepigrapha*, vol. 4. London: Sage Publications, 1989.

Delatte, Armand (ed.), *Anecdota Atheniensia I*. Liege: Imp. H. Vaillant-Carmanne,
1927.

Kuhn, Carolus Gottlob (ed.), *Claudii Galeni Opera Omnia*, Tomus XIV. Lipsiae: C. Cnobloch, 1827.

Kuhn, Carolus Gottlob (ed.), *Hippocratis Opera Omnia*, Tomus III. Lipsiae: C. Cnobloch, 1827.

Marathakis, Ioannis, *Incense: From Papyri to Grimoires*. http://www.servantsofthelight.org/knowledge/marathakis-incense.html

Manniche, Lise, *An Ancient Egyptian Herbal*. London: British Museum Press, 1999.

Manniche, Lise, *Sacred luxuries*. London: Opus Publishing Limited, 1999.

Nielsen, Kjeld, *Incense in Ancient Israel*. Leiden: Brill, 1984.

Peterson, Joseph (ed.), *Grimorium Verum*. California: CreateSpace Publishing, 2007.

Peterson, Joseph (ed.), *Sepher Raziel*, Sloane 3846. http://www.esotericarchives.com/raziel/raziel.htm#book3.

Peterson, Joseph (ed.), *Liber Juratus*. http://www.esotericarchives.com/juratus/juratus.htm.

Peterson, Joseph (ed.), *The Veritable Clavicles of Solomon*. http://www.esotericarchives.com/solomon/l1203.htm.

Pliny the Elder, Riley, H. T. (ed.), *The Natural History*. London: Taylor and Francis, 1855.

Preisendanz, Karl (ed.), *Papyri Graecae Magicae*. Stuttgart: Teubner, vol. I, 1973, vol. II, 1974.

Quandt, William (ed.), *Orphei Hymni*. Berlin: Weidmann, 1962.

Schmidt, Carl (ed.), *The Books of JEU and the Untitled Text in the Bruce Codex*. Leiden:

Skinner, Steven and Rankine, David (eds.), *The Veritable Key of Solomon*. Singapore: Golden Hoard Press, 2008.

Sprengel, Curtius (ed.), *Pedanii Dioscoridis De Materia Medica*, Tomus I. Lipsiae: C. Cnobloch, 1829.

Strong, James, *A Concise Dictionary of the Words in the Hebrew Bible*. New York: Abingdon Press, 1890.

THE SCIENCE OF OMENS
DIVINING THE WILL OF THE GODS

BY

GWENDOLYN TOYNTON

An omen makes it possible to tell what will be one's lot – loss or gain; joy, sorrow, or unalloyed misfortune; long life or death; and the realization of one's wishes and endeavors. When two armies are locked in battle, it can tell which will win the undisputed victory, which will deal the crushing blow. In answer to the question "What is happening in the world?" a mortal may place his trust in the omen creatures.

David Gordon White, *Predicting the Future with Dogs*

The Science of Omens is also referred to as the Mantic Tradition. Principally concerned with omens, portents, and oracles, its ritual specialists were the seers and diviners of the ancient world. The belief that omens and portents foretell the future through natural phenomenon is very old and has its roots deep in primordial history. It still survives today in practices ranging from commonly known forms of divination, such as astrology and palmistry through to the reading of tea leaves. What we shall examine here is the form of divination which utilizes naturally occurring phenomenon, such as the behavior of animals and the weather, rather than using tools such as tarot cards or runes. This form of predicting the future, often referred to as 'augury', is not so common today though a substantial amount of this lost art exists on in customs and folklore. Augury is specifically concerned with the study of omens and portents in the natural world, which are deemed to contain signals from the gods of forthcoming events. Predictions of the future obtained through the divination of omens should not be confused with superstition, which is a 'folk saying' that is not provided by specialists trained in mantic ritual. Divination via omens and portents is an active process, in which signals from the gods are deliberately sought[1] and occurs with no active intent on the part of humans. The study of omens was regarded as a science and its practitioners were accorded the highest degrees of wealth and power by their peers. The lost practices of the Mantic Tradition once ruled the world and the hearts of our ancestors.

---

[1] A superstition is 'passive'.

The 'Science of Omens' is the title of a chapter within a fourteenth century text from India, the *Śārṅgadhara Padhati*, or *Sarngadhara's Guidebook*.[2] This is a well-known work in Hinduism and it contains a wealth of knowledge on divination and esoteric lore. This chapter contains many of the usual forms of augury, such as observing the patterns of birds to predict the future, as well as other animals commonly found in India. It also contains other forms of divination, such as oracular gambling, the throwing of dice, palmistry, astrology, and oneiromancy, which is the interpretation of dreams. What is distinctive about this chapter, however, is that it describes the animal most suitable for augury and using omens to predict the future as the dog. The common canine may not at first appear to be an obvious source of mystic knowledge, but in Hinduism the dog holds a special status which is unique. The dog is what is called a 'liminal' or 'threshold' animal. It is partly domesticated, but also still partially wild like its cousin the wolf. It therefore sits on the boundary of man's world and the world of the animals. Much of the dogs' behavior is like our own and is therefore easier to interpret. However, its links to the natural world still exist and thus it is susceptible to higher powers to communicate and reveal the future through the behavior of the dog under ritual conditions. It is for these reasons that the dog is valued as an 'omen creature' in Hinduism. Sarngadhara almost immediately singles out the dog as the most eminent of all omen creatures. He clearly states that the reason for this choice is the dog's wide variety of behavior patterns, as well as its bark, are easy to understand. Dogs are, moreover, easy to come by and easier to approach and observe than are wild animals or birds.[3]

The rite itself is quite detailed in terms of structure and interpretation, and is preceded by offerings and prayers to the gods. In the rite the dog is ascribed a divine status, and during the rite it will become a medium by which to communicate directly with the will of the heavens. The dog is placed in the middle of a ritual diagram, on a symbolic altar upon which it is itself worshipped like a god, with flowers, incense, and so on, but upon which is also symbolically sacrificed in the form of the baked flour-cake shaped like a brace of dogs.[4] Like the human practitioner in ancient India, the dog is both the victim and the enjoyer of the fruits of the sacrifice. The dog 'dies' symbolically, yet at the same time lives to enjoy the sacrifice, and more importantly for the omen-master who is performing this ritual, lives to communicate future events, that is, what it has 'seen' while passing beyond this world through the world of the dead, and thereby into the future, to people trapped in the present. Oracular rituals of this sort continue to be performed, albeit in simplified form, in modern-day India using rams and mares.[5]

During the rite, the dog is placed upon a traditional *maṇḍala*, which operates as a symbolic representation of the cosmos. Following the preliminary ritual and offerings

[2]White, 'Predicting the Future with Dogs', in *Religions of India in Practice*, Lopez (ed.), p. 288.
[3]White, 'Predicting the Future with Dogs', in *Religions of India in Practice*, Lopez (ed.), p. 289.
[4]Two dogs, like the *Sārameyau*, verses 22-23.
[5]White, 'Predicting the Future with Dogs', in *Religions of India in Practice*, Lopez (ed.), p. 291.

to the gods, the reading of omens commences. The instructions for interpretation are significantly complex in structure and are translated into predictions of the future by reading the actions of the dog at various points within the maṇḍala. This includes such factors as the dog's direction in which it is facing; the movements and gestures it makes with its legs, mouth, and so on; location in which it is found; the direction in which it displaces itself; and finally, utterances, such as barking, howling, crying, and so on.[6]

One specific example of an oneiromantic text from India that survives in full can be found within what is collectively known as the *Six Rites*, which is part of the magico-religious practices of Tantrism. The *Six Rites* is in essence a step by step instruction manual for the practitioners of the magical aspect of Tantrism. The following passage is an extract from the *Mantramahodadhi*, which is a treatise on magic. This passage is a perfect instance of the ritual application of oneiromancy, as in this case the rite is performed to determine the success of a future magical endeavor.

> [The practitioner] who wishes to perform the worship of a deity should first consider the future. Having taken a bath, performed the twilight [ritual] and so on, [and] having collected the lotus like feet of Hari, he should lie down on a bed of Kuśa [grass and] pray to the bull-bannered Śiva.

> O Lord, Lord of the God of Gods, bearer of the Trident, who rides a bull! Announce, O Eternal One, the good and the bad, while I am asleep. Salutation to the Unborn, Three-eyed, Tawny, Great Souled One. Salutation to the handsome, omnipresent Lord of Dreams. Tell me the truth in the dream regarding all matters completely. O Great Lord, by your grace I will accomplish success in the ritual.

> Having prayed to Śiva with these mantras, he should sleep calmly. In the morning he should tell the preceptor the dream he had at night. The connoisseur of the mantra should himself reflect on the [significance] of the dream [without the preceptor if he is unavailable].[7]

The text then continues on to reveal a list of auspicious and inauspicious omens. To receive a dream containing an auspicious omen is an indication that if the ritual is performed it will be a success. The revelation of an inauspicious omen in the dream is indicative of the opposite where Shiva has denied the success of the rite and if it is performed the practitioner will be cursed and will generate negative karmic action. Given the nature of the magic contained within the *Six Rites*, it is necessary to place this limitation upon its practice, as four of the forms of magic contained within can

[6]White, 'Predicting the Future with Dogs', in *Religions of India in Practice*, Lopez (ed.), p. 292.
[7]Bühneman, 'Six Rites of Magic', in *Tantra in Practice*, White (ed.), p. 461.

be easily be described as what is commonly referred to as 'black magic' and hence require sanction from Shiva to prevent their misapplication. The role of the guru is also important for offering advice on how to interpret the omens and portents to the dreamer.

The Hellenic world and Mesopotamia also held omens and divination in high regards, and it is from these regions that the majority of records on divination and the study of portents originate. The Mantic Tradition held great power within the Mediterranean and the Middle East, with soothsayers and seers to be found within the courts of every kingdom. Because of the vast array of different techniques used to predict the future in these geographic regions, I have narrowed down the Mantic Tradition in this paper to specifically those divinatory techniques that rely on the reading of omens. The sibyls and oracles of Rome and Greece utilized trance methods to procure their remarkable visions, which differ in technique from the science of omens that predicts the future from naturally occurring phenomenon and not the production of altered mind states, as was employed by the sibyls and oracles.

Omen texts and inscriptions, such as the *Enuma Anu-enlil* series, are believed to go back to the third millennium B.C. in view of the references to the fourfold division of the world into the lands of Akkad, Elam, Subartu, and Amurru, and to early kings like Rimush and Ibn-sin.[8] Similary, in the Sumerian version of the flood story Ziusudra, or Ut-Napishtim, the Babylonian Noah, is represented as resorting to divinatory practices, and one of the kings of this age, Enmeduranki of Sippur, was alleged to have obtained from the gods the arts and insignia of divination.[9] From this point of origin, the science of omens in the ancient Middle East progressed down many different paths. The Akkadian *barû*, a 'seer', studied oracles, dreams, and visions, they read omens in the movement of water, known as hydromancy, the behavior of oil, known as lecanomancy, celestial phenomenon, and the actions of animals. They also begun to practice what could be seen today as a peculiar and barbaric divinatory technique by reading the liver of a sacrificial animal, hepatoscopy. This form of divination is particularly difficult for us to comprehend in the modern era, yet to the ancient *barû* there was a justification for this form of augury. The liver and entrails of the animal were believed to be the core of the animal's soul and by reading the interior marks and blemishes on the sacrificial animals' 'soul' the *barû* received insights into future events. Also, in Stoic theory, the internal organs were a microcosm of the universe itself, and according to this hypothesis a detailed examination of the liver, which was believed to be the most important bodily organ, could reveal the future. At any rate, the practice of hepatoscopy spread from the Middle East through to the Etruscan diviners, known

[8]James, *The Ancient Gods: The History and Diffusion of Religion in the Ancient Near East and the Eastern Mediterranean*, p. 232.
[9]James, *The Ancient Gods: The History and Diffusion of Religion in the Ancient Near East and the Eastern Mediterranean*, p. 232.

as haruspices, and from there expanded into the Greco-Roman world.[10]

Another form of divination which is found in both the Mediterranean traditions and the practices of the *barû* is a type of divination that is called dream incubation. In dream incubation a ritual sleep is deliberately induced by the practitioner with the sole purpose of forming deep dreams that would initiate the dreamer into special wisdom or get the dreamer to serve as an oracle.[11] The usage of the word 'incubation' here is not a technical term in the study of religion or dreams; it translates into English as a cultic term or phrase in various languages, with very specific associated fields of meaning. One example of this can be seen in the ancient Greek *enkamêxis*, 'sleeping in a sanctuary'.[12] Likewise, the Latin etymology of *incubation* implies 'the act of lying down' and its application of the idea is gestating in the dark, characteristically in a small enclosed space.[13] This time of oneiromantic induction is also known as the 'message dream', in which a dream is experienced during the night after due preparation in the god's sanctuary.[14] This type of dream frequently appears in texts of the ancient Near East as a substitute term for dream incubation. By stressing the importance of the location in which the dream is experienced, the message dream is thus closely linked to the incubation dream, as location is a requirement for both types to successfully induce the dream. Locales in which dream incubation takes place are so closely identified with their respective gods that they are thought to be physically inhabited by the god's actual presence. Because the god inhabits the area, the place is the one in which a dream is most likely to be granted by the god, hence incubated dreams are referred to as *theopemti*, 'god-sent'.[15] To the Greeks the method of incubation was based on the assumption that the daimon, which was only visible in the higher state achieved by the soul in dreams, had his permanent dwelling at the seat of his oracle.[16] The selection of the space in which to provide dream incubation was of paramount importance. The very act of preparation to sleep in such a place is in itself a ritual act, equivalent to any other ritual preparation or sacrifice in its contribution to the sacred. This particular form of divination was sometimes also incorporated with the healing of the sick, and in Greece it is found in the cult of the healer god Asclepius. One of the Epidaurian inscriptions reports an incident in which a man whose fingers were paralyzed had a dream that he was playing dice, and just when he was about to make a throw the god

---

[10]James, *The Ancient Gods: The History and Diffusion of Religion in the Ancient Near East and the Eastern Mediterranean*, p. 233.

[11]Pattern, 'A Great and Strange Correction: Intentionality, Locality, and Epiphany in the Category of Dream Incubation', in *History of Religions* Vol. 43, No. 3, Doniger, Kapstein, and Wedemeyer (eds.), p. 197.

[12]Pattern, 'A Great and Strange Correction: Intentionality, Locality, and Epiphany in the Category of Dream Incubation', in *History of Religions* Vol. 43, No. 3, Doniger, Kapstein, and Wedemeyer (eds.), p. 201.

[13]Pattern, 'A Great and Strange Correction: Intentionality, Locality, and Epiphany in the Category of Dream Incubation', in *History of Religions* Vol. 43, No. 3, Doniger, Kapstein, and Wedemeyer (eds.), p. 196.

[14]Bremmer, *The Early Greek Concept of the Soul*, p. 20.

[15]Pattern, 'A Great and Strange Correction: Intentionality, Locality, and Epiphany in the Category of Dream Incubation', in *History of Religions* Vol. 43, No. 3, Doniger, Kapstein, and Wedemeyer (eds.), p. 205.

[16]Rohde, *Psyche: The Cult of Souls and Belief in Immortality among the Greeks*, Vol. 1, p. 92.

suddenly appeared, jumped on his hand, stretched out his fingers, and straightened them one by one. As the day dawned, he left the temple cured, although at first he had doubted the accounts of the cures he had read on the tablets in the precincts of the sanctuary.[17]

Although the cult of Asclepius eventually also spread to Rome in the form of the Aesculapium, prior to this divination the Romans focused on the reading of omens via the natural world, such as the flight of birds or the behavior of lightening. Roman religion was focused on the belief that the divine will could be ascertained from signs and omens that occurred naturally, but in the form of extraordinary phenomena. This idea is again connected to Stoicism, which held that the universe was composed of a fiery spirit that permeated everything, with human beings being a part of it just as much as birds or cows, and that this rational spirit ordained and controlled everything which happened.[18] One of the official forms of divination in Rome came from the observance of birds.

In Rome there was a special site, the Auguraculum, on the Capital which was reserved for the purpose and the magistrate would be accompanied by one of the college of fifteen augurs, distinguished figures like himself, who pronounced the ceremonial formula for designating the quarter of the sky and would interpret, blind-folded, any signs which the magistrate reported. The practice was regarded so seriously that when in 99 B.C. Claudius Centumalus built a house which obstructed the view from the Auguraculum, he was forced to pull it down.[19]

The practice was not limited to wild birds, for like their Hindu counterparts, the Romans saw the benefits in keeping domesticated livestock for the purposes of divination. Specially raised chickens known as *pullarii* were one of the preferred divinatory tools of augury for the Romans, especially when on military expeditions as the birds could be transported easily. Another method of reading omens which is found amongst the Romans is divination through lightening, which naturally was assumed to reflect the direct will of Jupiter, the king of the gods who ruled over the sky. The place where lightning struck was immediately declared holy, because it seemed that Jupiter had claimed it for himself. The area, called *bidental*, was enclosed and sacrifices and prayers were made there. Thunder was also studied. There survives, at third hand, a calendar which gives the significance of thunder-claps on each day of the year. Thus if it thunders on the third day of December a shortage of fish will make people eat meat; if it thunders on nineteenth day of August, women and slaves will commit murder.[20]

---

[17]Rohde, *Psyche: The Cult of Souls and Belief in Immortality among the Greeks*, Vol. 1, p. 241.
[18]Ogilvie, *The Romans and their Gods*, p. 54.
[19]Ogilvie, *The Romans and their Gods*, p. 56.
[20]Ogilvie, *The Romans and their Gods*, p. 59.

Because the Mantic Tradition was widespread through the Middle East and the Mediterranean regions, we can find many records of its presence, diligently preserved by classical scholars and archeologists. When it comes to studying omens in the European traditions however, the task becomes significantly more difficult due to the gradual erosion of the indigenous European traditions by Christianity over many hundreds of years. The reconstruction of indigenous European beliefs is a challenging task, compounded by the lack of research on this aspect of history. Whilst it is widely known that the both trance work and runes were employed as divinatory techniques in Europe and Britain, the ritual and religious practices of these peoples have not been studied in the same manner as those of Greece, Rome, and the Middle East, and hence there is little conclusive evidence as to how and what techniques were actually used in the Mantic Tradition. Despite this, we can still find instances of divination via omens and portents in the European traditions. A Gaelic rite of divination called *taghairn* was practiced in the following manner,

> A man is wrapt in the warm skin of an animal just killed, he is then lain down beside a waterfall in the forest, and left alone; by the roar of the waves, it is thought, the future is revealed to him.[21]

Like the Indians, the Teutons had complex systems for reading omens from the behavior of animals. Their system differs however, in that rather than recommending domestic livestock as the ideal candidates for ritual divination and oracular readings, the Teutons deemed domesticated animals unsuitable for the purposes of augury. In this regard they also differed from the Greeks and Romans, in that there are also few instances of birds being used for divination, despite the fact the birds were thought to be messengers of the gods and heralds of important tidings in the Northern mysteries.[22] Birds that were studied for signs of omens and portents were frequently birds of prey. Ravens and crows also held a position of prominence. In the same manner as the Romans, the Teutons had provided special titles and authority to diviners. In the old Germanic language we find the words *heilisôn*, *heilisôd*, *heilisari*, and *heilisara*, which are all equivalents to the term 'augury'.[23]

The sacred priestly tradition appears, like the priestly office itself, to have been hereditary in families. A female fortune teller declared that the gift had long been in her family and on her death would descend to her eldest daughter, from mother to daughter therefore, and from father to son. By some it is maintained that soothsaying and the gift of healing must be handed down from women to men, from men to women.[24]

---

[21]Grimm, *Teutonic Mythology*, Volume III, 2004, p. 1115.
[22]Grimm, *Teutonic Mythology*, Volume III, 2004, p. 1128.
[23]Grimm, *Teutonic Mythology*, Volume III, 2004, p. 1106.
[24]Grimm, *Teutonic Mythology*, Volume III, 2004, p. 1107.

OCCULT TRADITIONS

The Science of Omens was at one time employed by the major civilizations of the ancient world, and its techniques were as varied as its practice was widespread. The practitioners of this ancient art were accorded with titles and rank, sometimes with power so great their prophecies and predictions shaped the destinies of empires and the tides of battle. Though some of their techniques may seem unusual, we must ask ourselves how such practices could be relevant today. With our contemporary knowledge of science and advanced understanding of man's role in the natural world, we are once again progressing towards a sense of unity with nature. No longer in opposition to the will of the earth we are learning not to pillage her harvests and are restoring the precocious balance between civilization and nature, which our ancient ancestors already understood by reading the actions of animals. Animals have not lost their natural instincts which tie them closely to the environment in which they live, yet in humanity this instinct is subdued. There are few biologists who would doubt that an animal can foretell the weather or natural events better than a human, and it is precisely for this reason that our ancestors chose to rely upon the study of natural phenomenon for the science of omens. What they were reading was the will of nature, which in many ways is a direct experience of the will of the gods.

BIBLIOGRAPHY

Bremmer, J., *The Early Greek Concept of the Soul*. New Jersey: Princeton University Press, 1983.

Bühneman, G., 'Six Rites of Magic'. In *Tantra in Practice*, edited by David Gordon White. New Jersey: Princeton University Press, 2000.

Grimm, Jacob, *Teutonic Mythology*, Volume III. New York: Dover Publications, 2004.

James, E. O., *The Ancient Gods: The History and Diffusion of Religion in the Ancient Near East and the Eastern Mediterranean*. London: Readers Union Ltd., 1962.

Ogilvie, R. M., *The Romans and their Gods*. London: Pimlico, 2000.

Pattern, K. C., 'A Great and Strange Correction: Intentionality, Locality, and Epiphany in the Category of Dream Incubation'. In *History of Religions* Vol. 43, No. 3, edited by Wendy Doniger, Matthew Kapstein, and Christian K. Wedemeyer. Chicago: University of Chicago Press, 2004.

Rohde, E., *Psyche: The Cult of Souls and Belief in Immortality among the Greeks*, Vol. 1. New York: Harper Torchbooks, 1996.

White, David Gordon, 'Predicting the Future with Dogs'. In *Religions of India in Practice*, edited by Donald S. Lopez. New Jersey: Princeton University Press, 1995.

SETH, THE RED ONE OF CHAOS AND EQUILIBRIUM

BY

DAMON ZACHARIAS LYCOURINOS

Homage to thee, O divine Ladder! Homage to thee O Ladder of Set! Stand thou upright, O divine Ladder! Stand thou upright, O Ladder of Set! Stand thou upright, O Ladder of Horus, whereby Osiris came forth into heaven.

Pepi I, *The Pyramid Texts*

Despite the efforts of various scholars down through the ages endeavouring to provide a tradition for dualist renditions of the universe, the particular emanations of dualist thought still remain aloof to biased revisions and broad generalisations that either celebrate or condemn. Although the term 'dualism' denotes the existence of the state of two parts in the form of binary opposition, the manner in which this idea finds expression differentiates itself to the extent of both embracing opposing doctrines and transcending them. The reason for this is due to the fact that dualism has a different application in philosophical, historical, and cosmological contexts. The term 'dualism', as a distinct area of description for the religious tradition of Manichaeism, was introduced by Thomas Hyde in 1700[1] and then further introduced by Christian Wolff to define philosophical systems that relate to the mind and body as two distinct entities.[2] However, the use of the term 'dualism' in philosophical discourse differs greatly from its examination within a religious context with cosmological and historical references. Although many have argued that dualism within a religious context is the rite of passage from polytheism to monotheism, or a rebellious outcry against monotheistic cosmology, studies in individual religious traditions that have and continue to express dualist tendencies demonstrate that these tendencies exist in polytheistic, monotheistic, and monistic religious traditions, either as metaphysical expressions on the margins or inherent doctrines within the core structure of the religious tradition.

The essence of religious dualism is manifests in the cosmic battle between the forces of good and light against the minions of evil and darkness, which exists as an

---

[1] Hyde, Thomas, *Historia Religionis Veterum Persarum*. Oxford, 1700.
[2] Wolff, Christian, *Psychologia Rationalis*. Frankfurt and Leipzig, 1734.

all-embracing conflict defining arcane mechanisms of the universe. In some traditions, such as Zoroastrianism and Manichaeism, this cosmic struggle is between two distinct and coeternal principles, and the battle is everlasting, for it is the very definition of the universe itself. In more moderate dualistic traditions, such the Gnostic school of Valentinianism, the source of evil and darkness is inferior to the principle of good and light, with the former being an extension of the latter. Some dualist traditions have an eschatological dimension, where at the end of time a purification of the world will take place and all evil will be vanquished. A final difference ~~that takes place~~ between various dualist religious schools is the way in which creation is conceived. In cosmic dualism, such as Zoroastrianism, the created world is not conceived as evil, but instead as a creation of the good principle that has been assaulted by the forces of evil and darkness. However, in more anti-cosmic dualist systems, as presented in the mythologies of some Gnostic schools, the created world is seen as a creation of the Demiurge who opposes the good and light principle ~~that resides~~ within the domain of spirit.

In relation to the diverse types of dualism that can be found in polytheistic, monotheistic and monistic religious traditions, Stoyanov writes,

> In certain religious traditions, diverse types of dualism could coalesce and appear in torturous combinations with monotheistic and polytheistic conceptions. What is more, within the framework of the development of some religious traditions, there can be detected a transition from dualist tendencies or notions of duality to the dualism of the irreconcilable cosmic opposites or a reversal of this process – a neutralization of the dualist elements implicit or developed in earlier stages of religion.[3]

A religio-historical illustration of this pattern of cosmological equilibrium through unified opposites becoming mutually exclusive opponents on the battlefield of cosmic strife is amply portrayed in the development of the opposition of the gods Osiris/Horus and Seth.[1]

As with many ancient religions, the ancient Egyptian religion was preoccupied with the primordial interplay of binary opposites, such as light and darkness. This can be seen from the doctrine of creation at Hermopolis[2] where Kuk and Kauket, who both belonged to the primal Ogdoad, were associated with darkness, but they respectively brought life into light, made the night, and called the day into existence. The cosmogonic doctrine at Heliopolis depicts the shining creator god Atum as emerging from the ocean of Nun and also from darkness. This cosmological struggle between light and darkness also appears prominently in the daily fight between Re and the monstrous Apopis, who emerges from the primordial darkness to threaten Re's solar barque in the mythological

---

[3]Stoyanov, *The Other God – Dualist Religions from Antiquity to the Cathar Heresy*, p. 5.

1-These are two different oppositions.
2-This is a late doctrine - I believe it has origins in the Middle Kingdom, but does not fully develop until the New Kingdom. No no no - they are in the Pyramid Texts; their vocabulary as Ogdoad is Middle Kingdom.

unveiling of the death and rebirth of the Sun.[1] Despite this vicious struggle, darkness was seen by the ancient Egyptians as the source of light. This ~~very~~ understanding of the polarity of light and darkness indicates that they did not suffer from the dogmatic elimination of one of the two opposites, yet remained in favour of a continuum of eternal equilibrium.[4] In ancient Egyptian cosmology, light and darkness were conceived as belonging to the same whole and demonstrated a metaphysical tendency of attaining balance through a system of dualities.[2]

This tendency to apply a duality of principles in active opposition is clearly portrayed in the cosmic struggle of opposition and reconciliation between Osiris and Seth, which, following the unfolding of cosmic events, is continued with the violent antagonism and further reconciliation between Horus and Seth. Various aspects of these mythic unfoldings of violent events between Osiris/Horus and Seth can be collected from a vast array of accounts and fragments in ancient Egyptian religious texts and magical spells, inscriptions on temple walls,[5] and narratives found in classical literature, such as Plutarch's *De Iside et Osiride*.[4] But before I begin exploring and presenting the various elements of these cosmic struggles between Osiris/Horus and Seth, it is necessary to first explore the enigmatic, necessary, and dangerous character of the god Seth.

Seth[6] appeared originally as a desert deity who came to represent the forces of chaos and confusion in the world. His presence is a tumultuous one, ~~where~~ he first appears in the earliest periods and survived well into the Late Dynastic period. Artefacts of him appear from the Naqada I Period, and the god appears on the mace-head of the proto-dynastic ruler Scorpion.[3] He also appears on the *serekh* of Khasekhemwy together with Horus.[4] In the Old Kingdom he appears frequently in the *Pyramid Texts*, and by the Middle Kingdom, he was the god who stood at the bow of the Re's barque and fought off the monstrous serpent Apopis.[5] He was also a part of the Heliopolitan Ennead as the son of Nut and Geb, and brother of Osiris, Isis, and Nephthys.[6] During the Hyksos period he was identified with the foreign god Baal and in the Nineteenth and Twentieth Dynasties he acted as the patron god of the Ramessid rulers.[11] After the Twentieth Dynasty Seth was associated with Egypt's hated enemies as god of the desert and foreign lands, and by the Twenty-fifth Dynasty his worship had declined immensely.[7]

The god Seth was referred to as the 'Red One' and god of the desert, referred to as the

---

[4]For further discussion I recommend Anthes, R., 'Egyptian Theology in the Third Millenium B.C.'. In *JNES* 18: 3, July 1959.

[5]These range from the *Pyramid Texts*, the *Coffin Texts*, the *Shabaka Stone*, the legend known as 'The Contention of Horus and Seth' from the *Chester Beatty Papyrus* No. 1, and the inscriptions on the walls of the temple at Edfu which narrates the 'Legend of the Winged Disc' and 'The Triumph of Horus'.[3]

[6]This name is also spelt as Set, Setesh, Sutekh, Setekh, or Suty, and in Ancient Greek is given as *Sêth*, whilst the occurrence of his name in Egyptian hieroglyphics is *swth*.

[7]Wilkinson, *The Complete Gods and Goddesses of Ancient Egypt*, p. 197.

1-More as king left the sun to live.
2- Not really "Darkness threatened to engulf the kingdom if the Pharaoh did not embrace light.
3-These sources span at least 2400 years, and reflecting a changing view of Seth, or a developing story - next become a fixed myth.
4- Add 300-400 years.
5-While the cult of Seth was still in flux.
6-Add elaborate effort to unify the two.
7-Thought Old Kingdom.
8-Of Sumerian origin.
9-Sothis is where it began!
10-Because of the use of bronze?
11-They were red-headed.

'Red Land', which also signified his connection to rage and violence who opposed Ma'at [anubis] [monkto], and represented the raw and darker forces of the cosmos. As a pure representation of strife and rebellion, he was the eternal foe of his brother Osiris, whom he murdered and then engaged in a fierce struggle with Osiris' son, Horus, which lasted for nearly eighty years.[1] The very fact that Horus castrated Seth in their struggle indicates that he was also associated with acts of sexual violence that needed to be suppressed.[2] In ancient Egyptian funerary literature of the New Kingdom, he was believed to devour the soul of the deceased, and his malevolent character found channels of expression in this world through crime, civil unrest, disease, and violent storms. He was also associated with the chaos serpent Apopis, and later the ancient Greeks identified him with their own chaotic god Typhon.[3] However, despite all these malevolent attributes that his character displayed, the god Seth was also held to be of great cunning and power, which on many occasions was put to magical use for protective purposes. One of his epithets was 'great of strength' and his sceptre was said to weigh two thousand kilograms. Iron, which was the hardest metal for the ancient Egyptians, was referred to as 'the bones of Seth'.[4] Tuthmosis III called himself 'beloved of Seth' and Ramesses II is said to have fought like Seth at the Battle of Kadesh. His strength and magical powers were also clearly demonstrated in how he resisted the evil eye of Apopis and defended the sun god from the monstrous serpent.[5]

Early iconography depicts Seth as an animal with a curved head, tall square-topped ears, and erect arrow-like tail, either standing or crouching. The association of Seth with the Ramessid Dynasty is obvious from monuments, such as the statue in the Egyptian Museum in Cairo, which depicts Seth crouching and overshadowing the pharaoh in a protective stance in the same fashion as the Horus falcon. There are also scenes illustrating the sun god's barque being towed by Seth animals. In later iconography Seth is depicted as a semi-anthropomorphic god with the head of the Seth animal,[8] sometimes wearing the White Crown of Upper Egypt and sometimes the Double Crown of all Egypt. He has also been shown fused with Horus as a two-headed deity, a symbol of the united rulers of Upper and Lower Egypt. Despite his ambiguous character, Seth was venerated considerably throughout ancient Egypt. Many of his cult centres were located in Upper Egypt, where he was often regarded as the patron god balancing Horus in Lower Egypt.[6] His earliest cult centre was probably at ancient Nubt at the entrance to the Wadi Hammamat, which supervised trade to the eastern desert regions. Seth was also said to have been born there. Seth was also venerated in parts of Lower Egypt and especially in the area of the Fourteenth Nome on Egypt's north-eastern frontier. A cult centre of the god also existed at Pi-Ramesses in the Delta. The sacrifice and destruction of various Sethian animals were parts of

[Right margin handwritten: Seth was of the Semites of Lower Egypt, Horus was of the pTfeot Upper Egypt]

---

[8]The Seth animal has no immediate resemblance to any known creature, although some have suggested composite of an aardvark, a donkey, a jackal, or fennec. Early Egyptologists proposed that the Seth animal was a representation of a stylised giraffe but this theory has been refuted as ancient Egyptians clearly distinguished between the giraffe and the Seth animal.

1 - This is from Plutarch, thought he core New Kingdom representations of this story. From where does this date?
2 - Seth explicitly tries to rape Horus. But... does this indicate a second Mesopotamian syncretism?
3 - Second Intermediate Period
4 - Introduced c. 14th century BC but not popular.
5 - Not cont or power, with the negative images.
6 - Damon has invoked Upper and Lower Egypt + perhaps invoked Seth + Horus

religious activities that related to him, such as the sacrificial slaughter of a red ox, but not exactly in the form of official veneration, and in the ancient Egyptian calendar his day of birth was considered an ominous day. The most important rite was the ritualised hunt of the hippopotamus, which the pharaoh hunted as a symbol of Horus' victory over Seth[1]. Despite the acts of ritual destruction in religious activities that surrounded him, another one being the creation of wax models of the god and then the thorough destruction of them, Seth was frequently invoked in magical spells against conditions which were relevant to the god's own mythology.

The early theological reality surrounding the tale of strife between Osiris/Horus and Seth still remains partially unknown due to the obscurities of the early foundations and evolution of the religious cults of Osiris, Horus, and Seth[2]. Both Osiris and Seth belonged to the Ennead and were the sons of Geb and Nut along with Isis, the sister-wife of Osiris, and Nephthys, the sister-wife of Seth. Even from his birth Seth was inclined to violent and disorderly behaviour, and according to Plutarch he tore his way through his mother's side, affecting the process of creation, which made him the 'angry and howling god'[3]. One account of the myth speaks of Seth's envy for Osiris, who was immensely revered and royally married to his sister Isis. His envy, which was fuelled by unholy hatred for Osiris[9] and his raw appetite for violence, inspired him to devise a plot to murder his brother and take Isis as his own wife. Seth tricked Osiris into entering a chest, which Seth then sealed and cast it into the river. Although Isis managed to recover the chest, Seth found the body of his brother again and this time chopped it into fourteen or sixteen pieces which he scattered all over Egypt. With the assistance of her sister, Nephthys, Isis managed to locate the pieces of Osiris and set up temples of Osiris where the remains were found. The myth itself asserts that it was Isis' search and recovery of pieces of Osiris that was responsible for the foundation of the cults of Osiris across Egypt. His body was finally assembled[10] and Osiris was partially resurrected, making him the primordial mummy. Osiris was now lord of the afterlife and judge of the dead. However, Osiris' resurrection was not the final chapter in his strife against Seth, as the composite nature of this myth continued by being superimposed on the tales of struggle between Osiris' son Horus and Seth. Horus, who was either conceived magically by Isis as she journeyed with Osiris, or according to other accounts was conceived before the murder of his father.[11] The struggles between Seth and Horus are recounted in various versions and are referred to as 'The Two Gods', 'The Two Brothers', and 'The Two Great Ones'.[4] When described as 'The Two Brothers', Seth, being the younger brother of Osiris, is presented as the elder brother

[9]Plutarch also mentions that one of the main reasons for his envy and hatred towards Osiris was because of the adulterous affair that Osiris was having with Nephtys.

[10]According to Plutarch's version of the myth presented in *De Iside et Osiride*, the body of Osiris was ultimately reassembled except for his genitals.

[11]Horus, as the son of Isis and the avenger of Osiris, was coalesced with the supreme falcon god of the sky referred to as Horus the Elder. The dynastic and solar attributes of Horus the Elder were also incorporated into the divinity of Horus the Younger.

1 - Seth changed himself into a hippopotamus.
2 - Not really. It's more a question of how Seth-Horus was syncretized into Osiris-Seth.
3 - probably from syncretism with Baal. This is late.
4 - This predates Plutarch maybe 1500 years.

in the struggle, thus perpetuating the mythic cycle through a reversal of the original cosmological situation.[12] Seth and Horus fought many violent struggles hosting armies against each other with Seth facing crushing but not ultimate defeats.[13] Both Seth and Horus displayed much cunning and power in their battles. It is said that Seth injured Horus' lunar left eye, which was restored magically by Thoth, and Horus in return castrated Seth, whose injury was also restored by Thoth.[1] In the original legend, the fight between Set and Horus would continue until the end of time itself, when chaos would overrun Ma'at and the waters of Nun would swallow up the world. It was only when Set was vilified that this altered, with Horus eventually overpowering Seth.[2] Seth was then vanquished and decreed guilty by the tribunal of the Great Ennead. The *Shabaka Stone* recounts[14] that Geb acted as the judge between Seth and Horus. To end their feud, he decided to place Lower Egypt under the sovereignty of Horus and Upper Egypt under Seth.[3] However, instead of bringing peace, Geb followed with a second decision, where he placed Horus as sole ruler over the 'Two Lands', as Horus was the son of Osiris. For this, he was portrayed at times wearing the Double White and Red crown of Egypt, whereas Seth was depicted as crownless.

This division of ancient Egypt between Seth and Horus has been interpreted both within a cosmological and a historico-political context. According to Stoyanov,

> The cosmological reading of the separation of Egypt and of the antagonism between Horus and Seth approaches the myth as if it belonged primarily to the 'sphere of cosmology' from where it was extrapolated to political and geographical realities, as 'a part of the Egyptian concept of life, in which reality is not simple but is built up upon two principles'. This marked Egyptian predilection for and systematic usage of dual symbolic classification is seen as underlying the formation of the concept and reality of the Egyptian dual monarchy, the kingship of Upper Egypt and the kingship of Lower Egypt, establishing perfect harmony between the inherited cosmological and the new political notions, according to which totality is seen as comprising and balancing opposites, and because of which a 'state dualistically conceived must have appeared to the Egyptians the manifestation of the order of creation in human society.[15]

Historical evidence does indicate that there was an actual historic conflict between the Seth-worshipping Upper Egypt and the Horus-worshipping Lower Egypt around the end of the Pre-dynastic Period, 5300-3100 B.C.E.,[4] and before the unification of Egypt

---

[12]Stoyanov, *The Other God – Dualist Religions from Antiquity to the Cathar Heresy*, p. 9.

[13]For further reading I recommend Murray, Margaret A., 'The Battles of Horus'. In *Ancient Egyptian Legends*, edited by L. Cranmer-Byng and S. A. Kapadia. Gloucester: Dodo Press, 2010.

[14]Lichtheim (trans.), 'The Memphite Theology', in *Ancient Egyptian Literature, A Book of Readings, Vol. I, The Old and Middle Kingdoms*, p. 51-58.

[15]Stoyanov, *The Other God – Dualist Religions from Antiquity to the Cathar Heresy*, p. 12.

1- Thoth is present alone & seems "New Kingdom"ish.
2- Seth wasn't vilified long before this alteration"
3- This stone is way late - from the Nubian period. I don't recall if it says this, but, if so, it's another thing the niggers fucked up. However, this is also a Memphite ideology - which was introduced late in the New Kingdom. See n.14.
4- Again, his Egypt's are confused.

under Menes[1], 3100-3050 B.C.E., Seth and Horus were both pre-dynastic gods who both had cults and temples in Upper Egypt, and historic evidence suggests that even in Upper Egypt the followers of Seth and Horus battled each other before the followers of Horus crossed into Lower Egypt[2]. Before this, the rulers of Upper Egypt were seen as the personification of the dual rulership of Horus and Seth,[16] such as the Scorpion King who later invaded Lower Egypt[3]. The historical strife and turbulence between the followers of Seth and Horus can be seen reflected in the mythological cycles of strife between the two gods and as a projection of this cosmological battle into a historical reality, which in the following separated ancient Egypt into two halves, one under Horus and the other under Seth. The amalgamation of Horus and Seth in the status of the dual ruler and the binding power of the rulership over both Upper and Lower Egypt also clearly expressed the process of unifying the two gods, which also appeared in various representations showing a fusion of Seth with Horus as a two-headed god, and then the final unification of Egypt under the adherents of Horus reflecting Geb's final decision.

The concept of the pharaoh assuming the duality of Horus-Seth had a long-lasting tradition in the ancient Egyptian royal ideology. The *Ancient Pyramid Texts* speak of this fusion and how it sought to initiate the good of the pharaoh, as evident from the 'baptism of the pharaoh'.[17] This royal status served as an embodiment of 'The Two Lords and Rivals' that eventually would reverse this rivalry and initiate an equilibrium both within the cosmological dimension and socio-historical sphere vanquishing all conflicting powers with the martial strength of Seth and the kingship of Horus. This embodiment was displayed and demonstrated with the pharaoh sitting upon the throne of Horus and the seat of Seth. The Horus-Seth god that emerged from this amalgamation depicted with a double head of a falcon and the Seth-animal, was a projection of the dual power and divinity inherent in the ruler of Upper and Lower Egypt, also representing the reconciliation of 'The Two Rivals' on a cosmological level. This process of amalgamating inimical gods exemplifies the tendency that ancient Egyptians had to reassert equilibrium between opposites and reinstating a cosmological unity.

Seth was also seen adopting another dual role as the defender of Re's solar barque against Apopis. When Apopis tried to mesmerise the barque's crew, only Seth was magically virile enough to withstand the serpent's gaze, and with the rising of the Sun, Apopis was vanquished, beheaded, and hacked into pieces. His role as the defender of the solar barque of Re gave him the titles of 'Lord of Life' and 'Chosen of Re', and in some cases he and Re appeared as the dual god of Seth-Re. The astrological symbolism of the conflict with Apopis can also be seen when Orion, Osiris' constellation, chained the serpent in the southern sky and the Great Bear, Seth's constellation[4], restrained him

---

[16]Griffiths, *The Conflict of Horus and Seth*, p. 131-136.
[17]Griffiths, *The Conflict of Horus and Seth*, p. 122-123.

1-Namer.
2- The exact opposite of what he just said, and correct.
3- Nono no - Scorpion is a First Dynasty King, I believe.
4- linked to the idea of Anubis?

in the northern sky. This alliance between the constellations of Osiris and Seth again presents another aspect of the duality of Seth. Despite Seth's role as defender against Apopis, his dualistic ambivalence is evident when he inclined again to his inherent violent nature and attacked Horus with the assistance of the seven stars of the Great Bear. However, the ambivalence of the cosmological dualism of Seth reappears when one examines the belief that the stars of the Great Bear had the shape of an adze. The constellation was also believed to be associated with the heavenly adze, its metal being the iron of Seth that Horus used to open the mouth of Osiris. Thus Seth again assumed a dualistic role in the Osirian cycle with his constellation of the Great Bear being both an instrument of destruction and resurrection.[18] Seth's ambiguous nature and role becomes even more complicated when one encounters references in the *Ancient Pyramid Texts* suggesting that Osiris initiated Seth into being, or that Osiris is the *ka*[19] of Seth. According to te Velde, Seth as the demonic initiator performed a dual sacrificial role in the Osirian cycle where by murdering Osiris he offered himself as a sacrifice, and brought about the ultimate resurrection of Osiris,[20] a cosmological event so significant for the ancient Egyptians. From this, Seth, even as vile and evil as he might have been at times, appears to be as crucial as Horus and even Osiris himself in the Osirian cycle.

Despite his hostile and violently ambivalent nature, Seth was still seen as having many beneficent characteristics, such as lord protector of the desert oasis, and was honoured by many rulers in ancient Egypt. The Hyksos dynasts revered Seth[2] and the first pharaoh of the Nineteenth, 1293-1185 B.C.E., and Twentieth Dynasties, 1185-1070 B.C.E. Rameses I, the first pharaoh of the Nineteenth Dynasty, was the son of a military commander named Sety, which means 'He of the god Seth', and two other pharaohs, Sety I and Sety II, adopted the Seth-name. The warrior pharaoh Rameses II, 1279-1213 B.C.E., invoked the strength of Set on the battlefield and referred to himself as 'son of the victory-bringing Seth'.[3]

The presence of Seth featured immensely *prominently* in ancient Egyptian magic, due to him *his* possessing 'mighty magical powers', which is evident from his magical resistance to the evil eye of Apopis. Seth's potency was also present in spells with *where* magicians utilising the *need* 'spear of Seth', a symbol of his wrath and might, against their enemies.[4] The magician sought his assistance in offensive magical attacks for he was renowned for his ferocious fighting nature and his ability to send nightmarish dreams. However, Seth was also called upon as a healer and as a ritual partner of Horus, such as in the Opening of the Mouth ceremony in which both assist each other in the purification rite. And as Stoganov accentuates, "what is more, the two gods may be envisaged as assisting Osiris

---

[18] Faulkner (trans.), 'Pyramid Texts 13-14', in *The Ancient Pyramid Texts*, p. 3-4.
[19] The ancient Egyptian word *ka* is normally translated as 'soul' or 'spirit' in general usage, yet the royal *ka* was shown as embracing the royal ancestors as well as the living pharaoh and was central to the ancient Egyptian's concept of pharaonic accession. *Its more the vehicle by which the ba is manifest.*
[20] te Velde, p. 96, *Seth, God of Confusion: A Study of His Role in Egyptian Mythology and Religion*, p. 96.

1- How could this be in the ⬛⬛⬛ era of the Pyramid Texts when Iron was un known?
2- Are you exceptional case.
3- Both because they were red-haired.
4 - Suggestive of ON Geirrodr, as Geirvandil, or Gendel

to ascend the ladder to the heavenly realm, Seth thus asserting his dual role in the death and resurrection of Osiris."[21]

Despite various cosmic occasions of the Horus-Seth alliance, and even the earlier emergence of the dual god, the more negative attributes of Seth, such as violence, excessive sexuality, and disorder prevailed to the extent of diminishing all beneficent aspects of the god. He began to be increasingly associated in popular theological imagination with foreign lands[22] and the 'Red Land', and along with various trickster characteristics attached to him he was seen as the evil rival in the cosmic struggle of the 'Two Rivals'. The extreme demonization began in the Late Third Intermediate Period, 1069-656 B.C.E.,² and reached its zenith during the Ptolemaic and Roman periods. This theological exile resulted in removing Seth from various depictions in the ceremonies of the purification of the pharaoh and was replaced by Thoth. In addition to this, there is not much evidence in regards to more temples of Seth being constructed. Seth's ultimate demotion occurred during the periods of Ptolemaic and Roman rule in ancient Egypt. The conquerors ironically identified Seth with his former enemy, Apopis, who the ancient Greeks identified with their own vehement serpent, Typhon. Despite his association with Typhon, in the *Greek Magical Papyri*, and especially in *PGM* IV. 154-285,[23] he is invoked as a higher and solar god when the Sun is in the midheaven and is referred to as "ruler of the realm above and master, god of gods,[24] lord, god of gods, master daimon"[25] and "you who did control the god's wrath, you who hold royal sceptre o'er the heavens."[26]

Despite his chaotic cosmic behaviour, vicious outbursts of violence, and strife with Osiris and Horus, Seth always returned as the reconciler and equilibrator. Although he inhabited the desert wastelands both within and beyond the seen world, and initiated many events of turmoil and destruction upsetting the natural order of the worlds of mortals and gods, he was always reconciled by returning order to chaos, as with his role in the resurrection of Osiris. However, this cyclical occurrence of cosmic affairs would eventually come to an end for the 'Red One', with him being denied his reconciliation and branded forever in the minds of the worshippers in the land of the Nile as 'that one' who was the eternal enemy of the gods and creation, a god of dangerous foreigners, 'the wicked one', and the 'son of evil'. Being transposed to the evil dimension of ethical

---

[21] Stoyanov, *The Other God – Dualist Religions from Antiquity to the Cathar Heresy*, p. 17.
[22] This identification first stemmed from the victorious campaigns of the Sethian pharaoh Peribsen over the Asiatic lands, which in extension gave prominence to Seth as ruler over Asian lands. However, in the Late Period when the Egyptians where overrun by Assyrian and Persian invasions, Seth fell victim to a scapegoating rebound where he was now associated as the 'god of foreign lands' with those who had conquered the Egypt. It firststemmed from Seth's role as the Semitic God, be 3000BC.
[23] Betz (ed.), *The Greek Magical Papyri in Translation including the Demotic Spells*, p. 40-43.
[24] *PGM* IV. 180-181.
[25] *PGM* IV. 218.
[26] *PGM* IV. 261-262.

2.- This is a sketch of the Third Intermediate Period. The Third Intermediate Period really ends with the Meshwesh Libyan conquest, c.970 BC.
3.- This started with the Hyksos.

dualism he became associated with his archrival, Apopis. The 'Red One' and the days when his power was invoked by mighty pharaohs, when he stood triumphant on the helm of the solar barque of Re, the manifestation of the dual Horus-Seth god, and the era when reed and papyrus were placed at the entrance to Ptah's dwelling in Memphis symbolising the unity of Horus and Seth over all of Egypt are neglected by many, but like all great gods, his triumphant return one day will be immanent.

BIBLIOGRAPHY

Anthes, R., 'Egyptian Theology in the Third Millenium B.C.'. In *JNES* 18: 3, July 1959.

Betz, Hans Dieter (ed.), *The Greek Magical Papyri in Translation including the Demotic Spells*. Chicago: University of Chicago Press, 1992.

Faulkner, R. O. (trans.), *The Ancient Pyramid Texts*. Oxford: Oxford University Press, 1969.

Griffiths, J. G., *The Conflict of Horus and Seth*. Liverpool: University of Liverpool Press, 1960.

Hyde, Thomas, *Historia Religionis Veterum Persarum*. Oxford, 1700.

Lichtheim, M. (trans.), 'The Memphite Theology'. In *Ancient Egyptian Literature, A Book of Readings, Vol. I: The Old and Middle Kingdoms*. Los Angeles: University of California Press, 1973.

Murray, Margaret A., 'The Battles of Horus'. In *Ancient Egyptian Legends*, edited by, L. Cranmer-Byng and S. A. Kapadia. Gloucester: Dodo Press, 2010.

Stoyanov, Yuri, *The Other God – Dualist Religions from Antiquity to the Cathar Heresy*. New Haven and London: Yale University Press, 2000.

Wilkinson, R. H., *The Complete Gods and Goddesses of Ancient Egypt*. London: Thames & Hudson Ltd., 2003.

Wolff, Christian, *Psychologia Rationalis*. Frankfurt and Leipzig, 1734.

Velde, H. te, *Seth, God of Confusion: A Study of His Role in Egyptian Mythology and Religion*. Leiden: Brill, 1967.

EVOLIAN SEX, MAGIC, AND POWER

BY

DAMON ZACHARIAS LYCOURINOS

At the beginning of orgasm, a change of state takes place… and in an extreme case, during the spasm, the individual undergoes a traumatic experience of the power that 'kills'.

Julius Evola, *The Metaphysics of Sex*

The word 'sex' throughout the history of humanity has always summoned multiple meanings, manifestations, and images expressing the most primal instinct of the human species. For humans, sexuality is a mode of experiencing themselves as sexual beings biologically, emotionally, and in some cases, spiritually. The implications of human sexuality can cover nearly all aspects of the human condition, embracing issues of culture, society, politics, philosophy, and religion. Regarding human sexuality, one must neglect how it is also influenced by superior mental activity and by social, cultural, educational, and normative characteristics of areas where individuals develop. However, apart from being the very essence of the birth of life, it can also mutate into a dimension of demise, degeneration, and even horror. The endless tale of sex is one of pleasure and obsession, invoking both beauty and sorrow. Some of the most wondrous achievements of humanity have been inspired by this primal instinct, and the unfolding of history has been guided by the urges of human sexuality. Its ambiguous nature can be seen in how it serves and unites the two fundamental human drives of reproduction and pleasure. So great is the effect of sexuality on the human psyche and body that it has urged some to manipulate its force either by suppressing it or celebrating it in the pursuit of spiritual paths and exercises endeavouring to transcend and partake in the spiritual dimension. Its power has also been used as the most dreadful weapon to destroy, humiliate, and enslave. Despite these differences and many more, our relationship with it is the one uniting feature of humanity that we all accept and recognise. Even the absence of it is a reaffirmation of its existence.

Sex and magic have long been in a state of constant flirtation. Since the days of Dionysian revelries, the alleged Gnostic heretical acts of worship, the persecutions of the Templars and the Cathars, the witch frenzy of the Middle Ages, and so on, illicit sexual behaviour has always been linked with acts of worship and magic in popular Western imagination. However, beyond misinformed ecclesiastical condemnations and misled renderings of an 'ungodly pagan' past, the essence and effects of human sexuality have been incorporated into various schools of Western esoteric practice and philosophy. This is evident, although not explicitly, in aspects of the Jewish mystical Kabbalah, the Renaissance magic of Marsilio Ficino and Giordano Bruno, the sexual mysticism of Emanuel Swendenborg, and many more, all of which conceived in their own personal and stylised ways the process of the union of male and female sexuality as being a reflection of the union of the active and passive elements of the divine. However, it was not until the middle of the nineteenth century, and following on into the twentieth century, that the relationship between sex and the esoteric actually formed into distinct magical traditions. Despite attempts but some sex magicians to presenting sex magic as being the purest expression of an ancient heritage of Western esoteric practice and philosophy, and a well-guarded occult secret coming to us from the dawn of ages, this distinct practice of magic is not a rejection of modernity in itself. Rather, it can be seen as a reflection of, and, also simultaneously in parts, as a reaction against the dictates and ideals of modernity, with the affirmation of the individual as being an ultimate force in the universe, the recognition of the multidimensional and powerful reality of sex, a scientific endeavour to unravel the secrets of the universe, and the overwhelming potential of free will as a form of liberation from suppressive institutions, all of which coincide with the attempt to re-enchant a demystified and secularised modern industrial world through the occult.

However, the question that remains is, why so much attention has been drawn towards sex magic? According to adherents to this distinct occult tradition, sex magic transcends the principles of hedonism, and, in its unveiled essence, is a powerful manifestation of magic aligned with cosmic forces and correspondences. The rationale behind this is that, if non-spiritual sex can create new life, intentional ritualised form of sexual intercourse can give birth to supernatural and divine effects and results, so much of which centres around a powerful ideal of social, political, and spiritual liberation.

One of the most influential authors of the twentieth century, who sought to employ sex magic as a means of liberation from social and religious decadence and degeneration, and also revolutionise the popular understanding of sexual intercourse by providing it with a more spiritual dimension, was Baron Julius Evola. In his book *The Metaphysics of Sex* he writes,

> Sex is the 'greatest magical force in nature'; an impulse acts in it which suggests the mystery of the One, even when almost everything in the relationship between man and woman deteriorates into animal embraces and is exhausted... in a faded idealizing sentimentality... The metaphysics of sex survives in the very cases where, in looking at wretched mankind and the vulgarity of infinite lives of infinite races – endless masks... of the Absolute Man seeking the Absolute

woman… - it is hard to overcome a feeling of disgust and revolt.[1]

Despite writing extensively about Tantra, Hermeticism, alchemy, and magic, he was also quite influential in the rise of European fascism during the 1920s and is still widely read by neo-fascist groups in the West. However, it must be noted that Evola was never a member of the Mussolini's Fascist Party and remained quite critical of Mussolini.* Closer examination of his works actually indicates that he was more of a Radical Traditionalist aspiring to forms and fashions of Traditionalist Aristocracy.[2]

Barone Giulio Alessandre Evola, also known as Julius Evola, was born 19 May 1898, the son of an aristocratic Sicilian family. Being raised in a conservative Catholic family, he rebelled by first joining a circle of Futurist poets before being introduced to Eastern spirituality and Christian mysticism. After the First World War, in which he served as an artillery officer, he embarked on a spiritual journey seeking to transcend the limitations of the bourgeois by experimenting with yoga, hallucinogenic drugs, and Dadaism. From an early age he was influenced by the philosophy of Nietzsche, and in particular the abolition of Christian morality and the affirmation of the *Übermensch* to take his rightful place as a divine being with divine powers , which is echoed in Evola's words, "No more thirsting of the soul for a hallucinated God to pray to and adore… To soar beyond and above with pure forces."[3]

Like many thinkers who lived and observed the rapid transformations and disintegration that took place in the period between the First and Second World Wars, Evola became a relentless and violent critic of modernity, which he saw as a metaphysical evil. For Evola,

> Present Western 'civilisation' awaits a substantial upheaval without which it is destined, sooner or later, to smash its own head. It has carried out the most complete perversion of the rational order of things. The West has lost its ability to command and to obey… It has lost its feeling for values, spiritual power, godlike men… It has been overwhelmed by the bourgeois misery of a monopoly of slaves and traders.[4]

Inspired by Nietzsche, Evola believed that the origin of Europe's decline and acceptance of slavish morality was Christian theology. Liberation meant abandoning the slavish morality of Christianity and embracing the aristocratic ideals of pre-Christian Europe based on virility and hierarchy. According to Evola,

---

[1] Quoted in Urban, *Magia Sexualis: Sex, Magic and Liberation in Modern Western Esotericism*, p. 140.
[2] An excellent defence of Evola is provided by Joscelyn Godwin in his foreword to Evola, Julius, *Men Among the Ruins: Post-war Reflections of a Radical Traditionalist*. Rochester: Inner Traditions, 2002.
[3] Evola, 'Four Excerpts', in *Italian Fascism*, Schnapp (ed.), p. 283.
[4] Evola, 'Four Excerpts', in *Italian Fascism*, Schnapp (ed.), p. 284.

1~ Because Mussolini was not extreme enough.

OCCULT TRADITIONS

To Christianity's race of slaves and children of God, will be opposed a race of
liberated and liberating beings who interpret God as a supreme power that
one may freely obey or do battle against in a manly fashion with one's head
held high, immune to the taint of feelings, vacillations and prayers. To feelings
of dependence and lack will be opposed a feeling of sufficiency; to the will to
equality, the will of hierarchy and aristocracy.[5]

Evola understood the spiritual aspects of sexuality as being the remedy for modern
Western civilisation.[1] This led him to become extremely involved with the study of
Tantra and magic. He wrote several major works, such as *The Yoga of Power* and *The
Metaphysics of Sex*, which examined the spiritual essence and application of the primal
forces of spiritual sexuality. He saw in the transgressive rituals of Tantra and the power
of magic the most violent paths needed to combat the most extreme and violent period
in European history characterised by a decline in virility, a sense of displacement and
degeneration, violent upheavals, abrupt transformations, and the final collapse of
civilisation.[2] He believed that in the Eastern traditions of Tantra and Western sexual
magic he had discovered the spiritual vision of liberation and freedom from the modern
world and the weapons needed to destroy the emasculated modern West. The occult
mechanisms of spiritual sexuality had now become paths of martial strength and war
in Evola's ideas.

Many of his ideas were echoed in the rise of Italian fascism, which he saw as a possible
vehicle for his own active ideals concerning liberation from the decay of the modern
world, and during the 1920s he became a supporter of the Fascist Party.[6] In 1930 Evola
was very influential in the founding of an esoteric fraternity known as Scuola Mistica
del Fascismo. The formation of this fraternity was under the patronage of Arnaldo
Mussolini and Evola saw it as a possible vehicle for the materialisation of his ideas, and
one that would take on the spiritual leadership of fascism corresponding to sacrifice
for a higher ideal.[7] Evola saw Mussolini's Fascist Party as possessing no cultural or
spiritual foundation, and was passionate about infusing it with a spiritual element in
order to make it suitable for his liberating imperial ideals that might recover the values
of the *Übermensch*, which according to Evola characterised the imperial grandeur of
pre-Christian Europe.

A common ground that Evola shared with Mussolini and other Italian intellectuals
concerning one of the major crises of the modern world that was responsible to a great

[5]Evola, 'Four Excerpts', in *Italian Fascism*, Schnapp (ed.), p. 290.
[6]Despite what many would like to believe, Evola never officially joined the Fascist Party as he was openly
critical of Mussolini at times. However, in 1939 Evola applied to join the Fascist Party so he could enlist in
the war but it was rejected due his critiques of the Fascist Party in various journals.
[7]Hansen, 'Julius Evola's Political Endeavours', in *Men Among the Ruins: Post-war Reflections of a Radical
Traditionalist*, Evola, p. 46.

1-This is wildly overbroad.
2-This is not what Yoga of Power says. Evola does not postulate a merely individual liberation such liberation is impossible.

extent for the prevailing degeneration was the abuse of the sexual drive. Mussolini and other fascist intellectuals were concerned with the growth and virility of the Italian nation that was affected by the increasing infertility and late marriages, and wanted to stimulate the expansion of the Italian people for economic growth, war, and colonial expansion. Evola, although aware of the national validity of these concerns, was more inclined to treat this phenomenon as a dominant feature of the age of Kali Yuga that the modern world was experiencing,

> Today… men instead of being in control of sex are controlled by it and wander about like drunkards… without seeing the guiding principle acting behind their quest for pleasure… It is no wonder that superior races are dying out before the ineluctable logic of individualism, which especially in the so-called contemporary 'higher classes' has caused people to lose all desire to procreate.[8]

The only remedy, as presented by Evola, which could cure the modern world of this rampant pursuit of sexual pleasure as an end in itself would be a return to sacred sexuality, spiritual virility, and the metaphysical essence of solar 'manliness'.

Some of his major publications in these areas of esoteric research coincided with his first significant publication on political matters during the late 1920s, indicating that he did hope for combining his esoteric inclinations with his counterrevolutionary ideas. However, it was his active participation and theoretical interest in magic, alchemy, sexual metaphysics, Hermeticism, and the Eastern traditions of Tantra and yoga, which provided him with the framework for his ideals. In the late 1920s, Evola along with other Italian esotericists, such as Arturo Reghini, Giulio Parese, Ercole Quadrelli, and others, formed the Gruppo di UR.[9] The name of the group, as Renato del Ponte indicated, comes from, "the phonetic value u-r, present in both Chaldaic and the Runic. In the first case it signifies 'fire' and in the second 'bull'… and also 'Aries'; it is probably also a reference to the German prefix 'ur', meaning something primordial or ancient."[10]

The Gruppo di UR published collections of papers written by members of the group, all of whom wrote under pseudonyms.[11] The aim of the group was to promote a transcendence of the individual self and enhance the higher self with the ability to act magically on the world. As Urban writes,

> Magic, for the UR group, meant essentially 'the ars regia and the initiatic

---

[8]Evola, *Revolt against the Modern World*, p. 169.
[9]It has been noted that Russian-born occultist Maria de Naglowska, who became notorious during the 1930s for her performances of sex magic, was also a member of the Gruppo di Ur, and it is believed that she had a sexual affair with Evola. Evola most likely was involved in her sexual rites.
[10]Del Ponte, 'Preface to Julius Evola and the UR Group', in *Introduction to Magic: Rituals and Practical Techniques for the Magus*, Evola and the UR Group, p. xvi.
[11]Julius Evola's pseudonym was EA.

I-should read decreasing.

science of the Self', that is, the 'regal' and 'heroic' art of knowing one's true inner and divine self-nature. However, according to 'Ea' (i.e. Evola), magic is distinguished from mysticism, spiritualism, and the like precisely because it is a practical and active method – 'an experimental science and technique' – that wields power and exerts real effects on the external world.[12]

The essence of magic according to Evola, ~~which~~ is the result of an initiatic process, has an elitist character and the power to distinguish the 'higher initiated man' from the 'ordinary uninitiated man'. The difference is the natural effect that magic has. For the ordinary uninitiated man, knowledge is restricted to the senses and their finite sphere of operation of accidental character that directly experiences the *phenomena* and then assumes the existence of the *noumenon* within a framework of concepts and relations of an abstract character. However, the higher initiated man undergoes the antithesis of experiencing the abstract in a pragmatic way. Experiencing the sensible is merely one perception of reality that the higher initiated man possesses. Initiation corresponds, transforms, and arranges in a hierarchical fashion levels of perception of absoluteness with the experience of the phenomenal belonging to a certain degree of experience, whereas that of the Absolute is only accessible to the higher initiated man. As far as the measure of 'absoluteness' is concerned, Evola wrote,

> One may say approximately that it is determined by the degree of 'active identification', namely by the degree according to which the Self is implicated and unified in its experience, and according to which its object is transparent to it in terms of a 'meaning'. In correspondence to these degrees, the hierarchy proceeds from 'sign' to 'sign', from 'name' to 'name', until it reaches a state of perfect, superrational, intellectual vision, of full actualization or realization of the object in the Self and the Self in the object. This is a state of power and of absolute evidence… There is an ancient saying according to which one did not join the ancient Mysteries in 'to learn', but rather in order to achieve a sacred state through deep experience.[13]

From the perspective of the initiatic process, 'to know' equates with 'being the known object', a realisation that extends when one's consciousness is transformed by active identification, which is not a mystical and emotive state, but an essential and supra-rational one. The transformation of one's consciousness also parallels the acquisition of power as the consequence of active identification with a cause conferring power over that same cause. According to this active and experiential initiatic principle, knowledge and experience are the same. This process of initiation is what established the differences between human beings and reaffirming the principle of 'each to their

[12]Urban, *Magia Sexualis: Sex, Magic and Liberation in Modern Western Esotericism*, p. 140.
[13]Ea, 'The Nature of Initiatic Knowledge', in *Introduction to Magic: Rituals and Practical Techniques for the Magus*, Evola and the UR Group, p. 27.

own, where one's ideals and freedom are proportional to what one is. This was one of Evola's significant assaults on egalitarian understanding of knowledge that characterised the modern world.

Although Evola did state that the term 'magic' in antiquity had negative connotations, he believed that to limit the term 'magic' only demonstrates a partial understanding of the dynamics and principles of magic. Citing *The Magical World of the Heroes*, written by the Italian Hermetic Scholar Cesare della Riviera, which states that magic is synonymous with the art of rediscovering the Tree of Life at the centre of an earthly paradise. Evola's interpretation of this was that it constituted a rediscovery of the primordial state and a reintegration of power at the centre of being. According to this, Evola understood magic as referring to an application of magic as being extension of the initiatic path and which is also present in everything that ritually displays an active and definitive character. In regards to the magus, Evola wrote, "The figure of the magus retains in a highly visible way the ideal of spiritual virility, which is most essential for the higher type of the initiate or adept. The magus has always called to mind the ideal of a dominating superiority."[14] For Evola, the magus belonged to what he defined as the 'regal tradition', which also represented the ideal of adepthood and primordially belonging to a spiritual race of warriors and heroes exemplifying spiritual virility and dominating superiority.

To be able to scrutinise and understand in a definite fashion the principles and dynamics of the magical domain in Evola's philosophy, it is necessary to conceptualise the politics of power on an esoteric level in a framework of spiritualised gender relations. Power, as presented in the esoteric theory of Evola, differentiates from 'force' and functions on its own as an 'unmoved mover', transcending both rationalism and irrationalism through the realisation of the primordial being. The main axiom that distinguishes magic and the initiatic path is the attraction of the powers of the pure forces of the cosmos seeking out the magus as a centre, who in return affirms this cosmic condition through his own spiritualised virility. According to the tradition of magic advocated by Evola,

> In our tradition, power is feminine and seeks a center: he who knows how to give a center to this power through his own renunciation and hardness created by domination of his soul, by isolation and resistance – power is unfailingly attracted to such a person and obeys him as her own male... Being is the condition of power; an impassibility that does not look at it, is what attracts it. Power eludes desire for power, like a woman shunning the lustful embrace of an impotent lover.[15]

---

[14] Ea, 'The Considerations on Magic and its Powers', in *Introduction to Magic: Rituals and Practical Techniques for the Magus*, Evola and the UR Group, p. 259.
[15] Ea, 'The Considerations on Magic and its Powers', in *Introduction to Magic: Rituals and Practical Techniques for the Magus*, Evola and the UR Group, p. 261-262.

Despite this primal power being the essence for the Self, it is not always pleasant as this power has the ability to destroy the magus if his inner resolution fails, and to even contemplate a rejection of these powers is impossible as they are attached to the centre of the initiate in a natural way, yet also becoming substantially different from the non-initiate as an effect of the powers now endowed within the magus. Just as the magus is inseparable from the powers he has now been endowed with through the initiatic path, the magical act, manifesting from real causality or the power that produces the effect, is also inseparable from it. However, endeavouring to examine these possible magical acts and their effects in relation to the adept who has walked the initiatic path transcends common human measures and motives, as they have the quality of the 'centre' and remain aloof to notions of 'good and evil'.[16] Although there is a strong emphasis on the individual and an elite group of initiates in his esoteric writings, there are indications that he hoped that the occult activities of the Gruppo di UR might have an effect on a grander scale. As del Ponte wrote,

> Evola himself wrote that the aim of the 'chain' of the UR group, aside from 'awakening a higher force that might serve to help the singular work of every individual', was also to act 'on this type of psychic body that begged for creation, and by evocation to connect it with a genuine influence from above'... in order to ultimately exert an effect on the prevailing forces in the general environment.[17]

Evola, discovering during the early period of the Gruppo di UR the transgressive ritual of 'left-handed' Tantra, he came to the realisation that this radical Eastern tradition embodied many of his ideals already expressed in his magical pursuits. Evola had long admired Hindu religion and culture, especially the Hindu social system of the *varnas*, 'castes', which he saw as the genuine embodiment and expression of a 'Traditional' society. Although Evola did inherit from Orientalists quite a distorted understanding of Tantra, he was far well-versed in Tantric philosophy and practice in relation to others[18] who tried to adopt elements of Tantric ideas and rituals into their own esoteric systems, such as Theodore Reuss and Aleister Crowley. But nevertheless, he continued to portray Tantra modified with elements, which he conceived as necessary if Tantra was to conflict with the decaying modern world. After the Second World War, Evola intensified his interest in Tantra with the publication of *The Metaphysics of Sex* and *The Yoga of Power*, believing that he had found the remedy for the decline of the West. For Evola, Tantra embodied an awareness of sexuality in contrast with the promiscuous and

---

[16]In relation to the meaning of this Evola corresponds it to the words of the god Krishna in the *Bhagavad Gita* IV, 6; IX, 8, "In me all the universes are already fulfilled; yet by dominating my nature, I manifest myself among beings and I act."
[17]Del Ponte, 'Preface to Julius Evola and the UR Group', in *Introduction to Magic: Rituals and Practical Techniques for the Magus*, Evola and the UR Group, p. xxxvii.
[18]This was primarily due to his correspondence with Sir John George Woodroffe, also known as Arthur Avalon, who sent Evola copies of his translations of Tantric texts.

purely hedonistic aspects of sex in the West on the one hand, and on the other, Freudian repression. Also, again inspired by Nietzsche, Tantra, in Evola's opinion, stood in opposition to the withdrawal of Christian spirituality and celebrated instead liberation within the world instead of ascetic beliefs for salvation in life after death. The very concept of *shakti*, 'power', inherent within Tantric philosophy and practice, echoed the spiritual virility which he had sought through magic, which was the necessary cure for the dying modern world. In Evola's words,

> We must reawaken to a renewed, spiritualised 'feeling' for the world... a feeling for the as 'power', as the agile and free rhythmic dance of Shiva, as a sacrificial act (Veda). This feeling will breed strong, hard, active, solar, 'Mediterranean' beings; beings made of force and eventually only of force.[19]

However, "Shiva is the Lord, not only of Yoga and the phallus, but also of destruction and the all-consuming fire of time that consumes the universe at the end of the cosmic age."[20] For Evola, Tantra as a system of religious belief and practice transcends both good and evil, and even the *Übermensch*. The *siddha*, the 'perfected individual', transcends the boundaries of the *pashus*, the 'bestial man', and morality itself. The path of the *siddha* is a path of liberation from all mundane human features for,

> The ethics of the Path of the Left Hand and the disciplines lead to the destruction of human limitations (pasha), forms of anomia, or of something 'beyond good and evil', which are so extreme that they make the Western supporters of the theory of the superman look like innocuous amateurs... We are dealing here with a liberty that... has no equivalent in the history of ideas.[21]

This manifestation of the path presented by the possibilities of Tantric expression were suited for Evola to the chaotic, violent, and degenerative modern world as an inherent part of Evola's formula of *Cavalcare la Tigre*, 'Ride the Tiger', where the differentiated individual uses the dark violent sexual powers of the modern age against it. These differentiated individuals that 'Ride the Tiger' are at once generous and cruel, committing acts that might be seen as conventionally immoral, respecting cosmic hierarchy, and with the knowledge and ability to rule. This path for the differentiated individuals, the virile heroes of Evola's ideals, is a path that embraces violence as an act of transgression[22] and a path of worshipping the destructive aspects of Shiva and Kali. Evola compared this also to the worship of Dionysus,

---

[19] Evola, 'Four Excerpts', in *Italian Fascism*, Schnapp (ed.), p. 283.

[20] Urban, *Magia Sexualis: Sex, Magic and Liberation in Modern Western Esotericism*, p. 156.

[21] Evola, *The Yoga of Power: Tantra, Shakti, and the Secret Way*, p. 188.

[22] Evola also sees this echoed in the *Bhagavad Gita* where Arjuna is willing violation of all social taboos by fighting and killing even his own friends to achieve absolute liberation.

> Both the western pre-Orphic worship of Dionysus… and the Eastern worship of Shiva, Kali, Durga and other fearful divinities are characterised by the acknowledgement and glorification of destruction, violation and incitement: they admit expression of a liberating frenzy, very often strictly linked to orgiastic experience in a ritual, sacrificial and transfiguring framework.[23]

The final transmutation of the path will be the manifestation of an individual disciplined, rigid, war-like, and infused with the pure forces of the cosmos and infinity itself, elevated to godhood, and liberated from the inferior elements of humankind and the degenerative modern world.

Evola's search for liberation in a radical sense from the world of modernity, a world in which materialism, corruption, violence, chaos, and decay reign supreme, led him to aspire a return to a virile and heroic 'Traditional' past that could that only be achieved in his eyes by overcoming the bourgeois boundaries, Christian morality, and the fragile human condition. However, for this liberation to become a reality, an exercise of violence is necessary in the form of a heroic battle cry destroying the archons of modernity. Urban in his chapter 'The Yoga of Power: Sex Magic, Tantra, and Fascism in Twentieth-Century Europe' adequately observes that although Evola to an extent identifies an element of ecstasy in the transgression of sex and violence in his transgressive ideals that echo Marquis de Sade's parallelism between destructive violence and sexual pleasure, Evola's ideas were quite different as they did not reflect a sense of carnal pleasure.[24] For one to become a god and soar with the pure forces of the cosmos, he believed that it was necessary to break through and overcome the constraints of the human condition and modernity, which only the violent, powerful, and liberating path of sex magic and Tantra could provide, and then expanding as a declaration of a counterrevolution against the modern world. This path was also expressed with his ideal of 'Ride the Tiger', where the differentiated individual affirms the transcendental will to power found in what Nietzsche conceived as the Dionysian man as the vital force of the pure forces of the cosmos soaring through the modern world bringing destruction and despair to the masses, yet immense power the individual who re-affirms his position amongst the ruins through initiation, liberation, and counterrevolution.

---

[23]Evola, *The Metaphysics of Sex*, p. 109.
[24]Urban, *Magia Sexualis: Sex, Magic and Liberation in Modern Western Esotericism*, p. 159-160.

BIBLIOGRAPHY

Del Ponte, Renato, 'Preface to Julius Evola and the UR Group'. In *Introduction to Magic: Rituals and Practical Techniques for the Magus*, by Julius Evola and the UR Group. Rochester: Inner Traditions, 2001.

Evola, Julius, *The Metaphysics of Sex*. New York: Inner Traditions, 1983.

Evola, Julius, *The Yoga of Power: Tantra, Shakti, and the Secret Way*. Rochester: Inner Traditions, 1992.

Evola, Julius, *Revolt against the Modern World*. Rochester: Inner Traditions, 1995.

Evola, Julius, 'Four Excerpts'. In *Italian Fascism*, edited by Jeffrey T. Schnapp. Lincoln: University of Nebraska Press, 2000.

Evola, Julius and the UR Group, *Introduction to Magic: Rituals and Practical Techniques for the Magus*. Rochester: Inner Traditions, 2001.

Evola, Julius, *Men Among the Ruins: Post-war Reflections of a Radical Traditionalist*. Rochester: Inner Traditions, 2002.

Hansen, H. T., 'Julius Evola's Political Endeavours'. In *Men Among the Ruins: Post-war Reflections of a Radical Traditionalist*, by Julius Evola. Rochester: Inner Traditions, 2002.

Urban, Hugh B., *Magia Sexualis: Sex, Magic and Liberation in Modern Western Esotericism*. California: University of California Press, 2006.

WIZARDS AT WAR
BUDDHISM AND THE OCCULT IN
THAILAND

BY

GWENDOLYN TOYNTON

Magic continues to function to this day, not as a means of altering objective reality, but in dispelling unease and restoring confidence in the individual.

Bronislaw Malinowski, *Magic, Science and Religion and Other Essays*

Today many people tend to perpetuate the belief that magic and the occult are no longer practiced in the modern era, except by small minority groups. This however, is a completely erroneous view, which is unfortunately typical of the 'occidental colonialist' mindset, which still believes that magic is only practiced by primitive peoples or in the distant past. Nothing however, could be further from the truth, where on the periphery of the Western world, magic and occult traditions continue to flourish, and are just as vibrant as they were hundreds of years ago. It is merely a testament to Western hegemony that we dismiss the occult traditions of these people as being inferior to our own stagnant philosophical value systems, safe and secure in the illusion that our way of life is somehow superior to theirs. It is the intention of this paper to examine an occult tradition which is alive and occupying a position of mainstream belief in a country in the present era, to demonstrate that occult traditions are still very much alive today, and continue to prosper within their own cultures and societies. For the purpose of this research, I have chosen the country of Thailand, which is by no means a Third World country, and shall attempt to demonstrate how the belief in magic perpetuates there, whilst exploring its relationship with Buddhism in the region.

In August 2008 Bun Rany, the wife of the Cambodian Prime Minister Hun Sen, led Buddhist monks and soldiers to the site of the historic Hindu temple Preah Vihear to call upon their ancestors to protect the temple. The site of the Preah Vihear temple is located on disputed land, perched atop a cliff on Cambodian soil, but with the most accessible entrance to the site located on the Thai side of the border. This eleventh century temple is sitting on the border between the two countries, but the borderline itself has never been clearly demarcated, because the area is littered with landmines

I- Compade Wendy, Lol.

left over from decades of war. Ownership of the temple was originally awarded to Cambodia, but dispute between the two countries flared up when Preah Vihear was granted United Nations World Heritage status. Desperate to resolve the issue, both sides deployed military forces, but when they were unable to reach a solution to the conflict, Cambodia and Thailand resorted to supernatural means. Fearing that the magical abilities of Cambodia's Buddhist monks would weaken Thailand, residents throughout the province of Si Sa Ket wore yellow to help protect Thailand from Cambodian magic.

Though Buddhism is not often thought of as a religion that practices magic, in such communities as those found in Thailand and Cambodia, there can be no doubt that Buddhism shares common ground with belief systems that are primarily associated with the use of magic. Both countries have a long history of engagement in spiritualist and animistic practices. When Buddhism first arrived in these regions, it came into contact with pre-existent traditions that believed in spirits, both benevolent and malevolent, and a developed system of magic which was to be feared and revered, depending on whether or not it was used for good or ill. For Buddhism to thrive in this environment, it was necessary to develop a complex system of interaction between Buddhism and what has been called the 'spirit religions'. Debate still exists as to whether or not the two systems have become completely integrated or not, although the interaction betwixt the two traditions is often referred to as an example of syncretism. On the subject of interaction between Buddhism and spirit religions in Thailand, the academic B. J. Terwiel states the following,

> When I interviewed the villagers in Central Thailand on the relationship between Buddhist and non-Buddhist aspects of their religion, a variety of reactions were observed. The more sophisticated informants generally stated that the Lord Buddha had never forbidden rituals of ancient origin. Other persons hesitatingly made up their own minds with regard to the orthodoxy of the ritual, but on subsequent occasions contradicted their own judgment. Many were at a loss to classify rituals or beliefs under rubrics such as 'Buddhist' and 'non-Buddhist'.[1]

It would appear from this statement that the boundary between the use of magic by the indigenous traditions of Thailand and the practice of Buddhism is not apparent to many of the inhabitants of Thailand themselves. This is most likely due to the fact that the people of rural Thailand are raised in a society where the two systems are found closely entwined together. The religious traditions of Thailand have always included the belief in spirits and the ability to manipulate them by means of magic. For example, in Thailand preservation of the *khwan*, the 'spirit of life', is considered to be of utmost importance, as is ensuring that *phi*, 'malevolent spirits', do not enter the body. Control

---

[1]Terwiel, *Monks and Magic: An Analysis of Religious Ceremonies in Central Thailand*, p. 3.

of these spirits is greatly emphasized in rural Thai culture, as the service of these spirits can be employed to improve the qualities of day to day existence.

In the lives of ordinary Thai people, more value is placed upon the improvement of their current existence than on transcending the cycle of rebirth, as is advocated by Buddhism. The relationship between the members of the *Sangha*, the 'community of Buddhist monks', and the practitioners of magic in Thailand, combine in a variety of ways the spirit religions that deal with the *laukika*, which concerns aspects of gain in this world, with Buddhism, advocating the importance of salvation and ideas of transcendence, *lokottara*. Thus, in Thailand, magic is utilized to address matters in the mundane world, and religion is adopted to address the sacred. This relationship is complicated even further by the fact that in Thailand almost every adult male will become a member of the *Sangha* at some stage in his life, for in rural areas the taking of vows is considered to be an essential element in preparation for adult life. Given the wide range of magic and animistic beliefs which operate within rural Thailand, these men will carry a variety of beliefs and practices with them into the *Sangha*, not all of which will be compatible with Buddhism. In accordance with this, religious opinions are not questioned during ordination. As a direct result, villagers can be found entering the *Sangha* for a variety of reasons, as is reflected in the following Thai rhyme,

Ordination to fulfill a promise to the Gods,
Ordination to escape poverty,
Ordination to flee from a wife,
Ordination to save money,
Ordination to eat better food than at home,
Ordination to join one's friends at the monastery.[2]

Thai belief does not only consist of beneficial gods and spirits. It also abounds with belief in ferocious spirits of pure malevolence, from whom the villagers seek magical protection. Amongst these classes of malevolent spirits are such beings as the *preed*, a giant, looming shape with a small head that emits a sharp piercing sound as a reflection of its past sins; the *phii krasy*, a type of parasite which inhabits human bodies, feeds on excrement, and is shaped like a human head with entrails protruding from beneath; and the *phi baan*, the ghosts of ancestors that hover around their previous home and watch their descendants with malignant jealously. Whilst it is possible for these sprits to be exorcised, Buddhism chooses to deal with their interfering presence in another way. The correct approach for a Buddhist to cause the sprits to cease meddling in the affairs of their human victims is to preach to them, thus converting the spirits involved to a more benign nature. There are certain canonical texts which serve this purpose of protection, which can also be recited at specific times in order to avert misfortune.

---

[2]Terwiel, *Monks and Magic: An Analysis of Religious Ceremonies in Central Thailand*, p. 20.

These texts are known as the *Phraa Parit*. The source of the magical power of these texts has not yet been clearly identified, but Y. Ishii, author *of Sangha, State & Society: Thai Buddhism in History*, claims that whilst some possessed a magical content from the beginning as modifications of Hindu rites, others such as the *Mangalasutta* originally had no magical connotations.[3]

Indeed, for most people, including some who chant them, the *Phraa Parit* are incomprehensible, being in Pali. Rather, I believe, the magic of the *Phraa Parit* stems from three factors, the social recognition that *Phraa Parit* should be chanted for certain purposes, such as blessing; the existence of an established formula for their chanting; and the sanctity attributed to the character.[4]

The use of *Phraa Parit* is a means by which to ensure protection, as it provides good luck and disperses misfortune whether caused by the presence of spirits or not. As is seen in the above passage, the presence of magic being used by the *Sangha* is not overtly explicit in the *Phraa Parit* and it is interpreted to be so by the lay audience. They do not understand the words the monks recite, but because of the respected state of the *Sangha* in Thailand, the lay community assumes that it must be not only beneficial, but also powerful.

Another type of magic practiced by the Thai *Sangha* is the manufacture of amulets. These amulets are employed for a variety of reasons, including protection from diseases, black magic, and accidents. Of these amulets, the ones portraying the Buddha are the most popular, although some also are made in the likeness of famous monks and King Chulalongkorn, who is also known as Rama V, one of Thailand's most revered kings. The sanctity of the subjects portrayed upon the amulets is a reflection of the beneficial powers they are thought to contain. The Buddha images vary in size, from anywhere between two and eight centimeters, and can be manufactured from wood, metal, ivory or resin, although frequently they are made from a selected combination of these elements, pressed into a mould, and baked.[5] To create a pressed or printed image, *phraaphim*, a monk needs not only a mould, recipe, and the proper ingredients; he also requires an advanced knowledge of spells and sacred script.[6] The inherent sanctity of the amulet is not always thought to be sufficient enough, hence its power needs to be enhanced by means of the correct recitation of spells and texts. The most simple of these sacralisation rites is known as *plugseeg*.[7] At the culmination of *plugseeg* the monk will either blow upon the Buddha image or draw over the amulet with the index finger

---

[3] Ishii, *Sangha, State & Society: Thai Buddhism in History*, p. 21..
[4] Ishii, *Sangha, State & Society: Thai Buddhism in History*, p. 21.
[5] Terwiel, *Monks and Magic: An Analysis of Religious Ceremonies in Central Thailand*, p. 74.
[6] Terwiel, *Monks and Magic: An Analysis of Religious Ceremonies in Central Thailand*, p. 75.
[7] Terwiel, *Monks and Magic: An Analysis of Religious Ceremonies in Central Thailand*, p. 77.

of his right hand.[8] During the manufacture of amulets, the *Sangha* is also invited to perform a consecration rite known as *phutthaphisek*.[9] The use of magic within the *phuttaphisek* is illustrated by the fact that is desirable for at least one of the monks participating in the *phutthaphiseek* to be either advanced in meditative technique or in the Brahmanic rites known as *saiyasat*.[10] These rites are intimately entwined with another type of Thai ritual, namely the ceremony held to consecrate Buddha images, which infuse the representation with the auspicious wisdom and power associated with Prince Siddhartha's victory over the demonic Mara, and the subsequent obtainment of enlightenment by Siddhartha. During this ritual monks chant in Pali or preach in northern Thai several texts, including the *Buddha Abhiseka*, which can be translated as 'consecrating the Buddha image'.[11] This text focuses on the powers of the mind attained by the Buddha that are associated with his enlightenment. Both the consecration of images and amulets draw their impetus from this core idea.

One specific example of a text dealing with the extraordinary supernatural powers of the Buddha that occupies a position of prominence in Thailand is *Bimba's Lament*.[12] By his magical power he created a crystal path in the sky from the eastern boundary of the city of Kapilavastu to its western perimeter. Then, ascending into the air the *Tathagata*, surrounded by many previous Buddha's, walked on the sky bridge he had miraculously created. He also performed other miracles, such as appearing to walk above the heads of the *Sakyans*.

Tattooing is another magical practice that is widespread throughout Thailand. At some stage in their adult life many Thai males will receive a tattoo of some description or another. This is of significance because in the culture of rural Thailand, tattoos are representative of magical power. The magical power of these tattoos stems in part from the tattooist, for whilst both layman and monk may be a tattooist, there is a vast difference in the scope of their work and the designs used. The types of work which may be employed by a monk are restricted. As a monk, he is limited to tattooing the upper parts of the body, for not only would it be seen as sexual misconduct on the part of the monk to tattoo the lower areas, the upper parts of the body represent the higher, more spiritual aspects of humanity, whereas the lower regions represent mankind's more base, animalistic attributes. The tattoos done by the monk are also limited in application. The monk may bestow tattoos that are of a beneficial or protective nature. Other tattoos, such as those which bestow things such as sexual virility, can only be performed by members of the lay community.

---

[8]Terwiel, *Monks and Magic: An Analysis of Religious Ceremonies in Central Thailand*, p. 78.
[9]Ishii, *Sangha, State & Society: Thai Buddhism in History*, p. 23.
[10]Ishii, *Sangha, State & Society: Thai Buddhism in History*, p. 25.
[11]Swearer, 'Consecrating the Buddha', in *Buddhism in Practice*, Lopez (ed.), p. 50.
[12]Bimba was the Buddha's wife, who he left to pursue the life of an ascetic.

Another Thai rite involving magical skills of the members of the *Sangha* is the *Wong Dai Sai*, 'Encircling with Holy Thread'.[13] This is a type of consecration rite designed to protect a place from evil. It is believed that the consecrated place will be protected by the power of the Three Gems and the *Phraa Parit*.[14] During this rite, cotton is affixed to an image of the Buddha, stretched clockwise around the place to be consecrated,[15] and finally wound back to its point of origin at the Buddha image.[16] If the thread should snap at any stage it is considered to be an ill omen. The main doctrinal link between Buddhism and the spirit religions is found in the incidences where magic is employed by the *Sangha* as a transfer of merit. The theory of the transference of merit is based upon the concept that, when a member of the lay community performs a virtuous deed, such as making a donation or feeding a monk, the gods witness the act and empathize with the process. The *Sangha* themselves are referred to as being a *na bun*, a 'field for merit', as is found in the *Sanghnussatibhavana*.

The greater the purity of the monk, the more magical merit he is said to generate. The sanctity of the monk himself is the source of belief in the efficacy of his magical power. The magical power that is generated by the monk is also classed as being superior to that of a layman, but, by its very nature, is more limited in its application. A monk is also deemed to be more superior to a spirit, and, thus, a monk should never be seen to supplicate himself before a spirit. When a member of the *Sangha* addresses a spirit, he never raises his hands in supplication, in contrast to the layman who will raise his hands when requesting favour from a spirit. The superior magical status of a monk stems from his purity, and, the monk must do nothing to compromise his superior position. Part of the magical power which results from the monks' purity is derived from celibacy. A monk should never touch a female, human, or animal, and is forbidden to even receive an object that is directly given to him by a woman.[17] In order to receive an object given by a woman, the monk must first take a piece of cloth and place it upon the floor, upon which the woman will then place the gift on whilst the monk holds the edges of the cloth.[18] The cloth is used as a medium by which to transfer merit since there can be no direct contact between a monk and a woman. The merit flows from the fingers of the monk holding the cloth to the woman who has donated the cloth. The medium of the cloth must be used so as not to deprive the female donor of the merit she would otherwise not receive. One of the reasons for which a monk may not have contact with women are both not only because of the temptation of sexual misconduct, and also because women are believed to be associated with a type of magical power said to be diametrically opposed to that of the monk.[19] This is due to the fact that menstruation is

---

[13]Ishii, *Sangha, State & Society: Thai Buddhism in History*, p. 22.
[14]Ishii, *Sangha, State & Society: Thai Buddhism in History*, p. 22.
[15]As is the way of beneficial magic. Anti-clockwise is considered to be used for evil purposes.
[16]Ishii, *Sangha, State & Society: Thai Buddhism in History*, p. 22.
[17]Terwiel, *Monks and Magic: An Analysis of Religious Ceremonies in Central Thailand*, p. 114.
[18]Terwiel, *Monks and Magic: An Analysis of Religious Ceremonies in Central Thailand*, p. 114.
[19]Terwiel, *Monks and Magic: An Analysis of Religious Ceremonies in Central Thailand*, p. 115.

associated with dangerous magical power, and is classed as being capable of destroying some of the beneficial power of the *Sangha*.[20]

Another aspect of magic in Thailand, which needs to be considered, is the import of magical systems via India. The branch of Buddhism found in Thailand is an older form known as Theravada, and its links to Hinduism are much stronger than those of the later Buddhist schools. For example, in the book *Abhidhamma Chet Khamphi Ruam*, or *A Summary of the Seven Books of Abhidhamma*, there are elements of cosmology, cosmogony, buddhology, ethics, epistemology, and language that are integrated into a yantric and mantric system.[21] This system is very much similar to that found in Indian magic, and it is reasonable to assume that many of the formulas found within are directly based on Hindu mantras. These are broken down into component syllables for recitation by the Buddhist practitioner. The mantra *Namo Buddhaya*, 'Homage to the Buddha', is correlated with the five vowels, symbolizing the five *dhatu*, the 'five elements' of water, earth, fire, air, and aether. Furthermore, in the following passage from the *Seven Books of Abhidhamma*, we also find a formula which contains correlations with the Hindu Tantric yoga techniques, dividing the body into a solar right and lunar left, and creating what appears to be Buddhist *cakra* centres. This integration of the occult, Tantra, and Buddhism is by no means unique, for it is prolific in Tibetan Buddhist texts and practices.

One possible explanation of how this similarity between Thai Buddhist and Hindu occult techniques occurred can be found by examining the magical history of a third South East Asian country, namely Burma. In the late eighteenth and early nineteenth centuries, Burmese kings imported large numbers of Sanskrit texts from India on topics such as medicine, alchemy, incantation, and astrology.[22] In Burma, these Buddhist wizards are practitioners of what is called the *weikza-lam*, the 'path of occult knowledge'. This tradition still exists today in Burma, and the largest of the groups practicing this occult path are based in the city of Pegy and are called the *Manosetopad Gaing*. Like their Thai counterparts, this organization focuses their interest in the occult on the powers attained by the Buddha whilst on the path to enlightenment. They also believe that the relics of the Buddha, which in Burmese is *dat-law* and in Pali *dhatu*, are possessed of a kind of majestic power that he infused in them through the force of his *Samadhi*.[23] The similarity between this branch of magic with that of the Thai people is amply illustrated in the following extract from a magical treatise by the *Manosetopad Gaing*,

A person wishing to practice the path must first suffuse his mind with thoughts

[20] Terwiel, *Monks and Magic: An Analysis of Religious Ceremonies in Central Thailand*, p. 115.
[21] Swearer, 'Consecrating the Buddha', in *Buddhism in Practice*, Lopez (ed.), p. 336-337.
[22] Pranke, 'On becoming a Buddhist Wizard', *Buddhism in Practice*, Lopez (ed.), p. 343.
[23] Pranke, 'On becoming a Buddhist Wizard', *Buddhism in Practice*, Lopez (ed.), p. 345.

of the Three Jewels, and cultivate loving kindness toward the various grades of nats… the nats referred to here include powerful nature spirits dwelling in trees, the earth, and mountains, minor deities who preside over the use of magical incantations and diagrams, and medicine spirits whose domain includes the well-known herbs and minerals of alchemical lore.[24]

From this passage, it is clear that the *Manosetopad Gaing* not only uses Buddhist motifs, such as the Three Jewels, they are also drawing upon a much older tradition of spirit religions and animistic world views. These Buddhist wizards, however, are also drawing upon Hindu texts on supernatural lore, and, if such texts entered the Burmese magico-religious system, then it is entirely possible that influences from India may help to explain what appears to be a mantric and yantric tradition within the Thai *Seven Books of Abhidahamma*.

With their magical prowess and the protection of the *Sangha*, why do the Thai people fear the magic of Cambodians? Cambodia is also a country with a long history of occult practices. For instance in the Khmer book *The Tale of Ancient History* there is a legend of Prince Chey Ahca who led a ghost army against the Siamese.[25] More recently, we also find records of Po Kambo, who, in 1866, protested against French colonial rule and was alleged to know a magical formula that deflected bullets. Even as recently as the 1970s and 1990s, Khmer soldiers utilized magical tattoos in a similar manner to that of their Thai enemies, and used mantras written in Pali and Sanskrit, the holy languages of Buddhism and Hinduism, to protect them in battle.

All of the magic employed by the *Sangha* in Thailand is based on one important concept, the sanctity and purity of the *Sangha* themselves. The forms of magic the *Sangha* use are limited in scope by this fact, for they can use only what is generally referred to as 'white magic', that which benefits another and causes no harm. Use of magic to harm another or for personal gain would result in expulsion from the *Sangha*. Similarly, a monk may not use magic that serves to improve virility of a layman or create love charms, as this could severely impair the powers of the monk which stem from his sexual abstention. A monk may not request the spirit world for aid, for this would compromise the superior status of the monk who is deemed to be beyond the mundane affairs of this world. Whilst the power of the *Sangha* is more limited in application than that of layman, it is also deemed as stronger, for it stems from otherworldly sources, as opposed to the spirits who remain bound to this world. As such, villagers come to the monk knowing that when they treat the monk with a proper attitude of respect, the cosmic forces shall share their merit and transfer it to demonstrate approval. The transfer of merit thus benefits not only the *Sangha*, but the laity as well even providing protection in times of conflict. It is via this transfer of merit and the integration of the spirit religions with

[24]Pranke, 'On becoming a Buddhist Wizard', *Buddhism in Practice*, Lopez (ed.), p. 351.
[25]Siam being an earlier name for Thailand.

OCCULT TRADITIONS

Buddhism that occult traditions still occupy a position of prominence in Thailand, a position so prestigious that even today, when conflict breaks out, these Buddhist wizards go to war.

BIBLIOGRAPHY

Ishii, Y., *Sangha, State & Society: Thai Buddhism in History*. Honolulu: University of Hawaii Press, 1986.

Lopez, Jr. D. S. (ed.), *Buddhism in Practice*. New Jersey: Princeton University Press, 1995.

Pranke, P., 'On becoming a Buddhist Wizard'. In *Buddhism in Practice*, edited D. S. Lopez, Jr. New Jersey: Princeton University Press, 1995.

Swearer, D. K., 'Consecrating the Buddha'. In *Buddhism in Practice*, edited by D. S. Lopez, Jr. New Jersey: Princeton University Press, 1995.

Terwiel, B. J., *Monks and Magic: An Analysis of Religious Ceremonies in Central Thailand*. Surrey: Curzon Press, 1975.

WOMAN WAS THE ALTAR
THE WICCAN GREAT RITE:
SEX, TEA, AND RELIGION

BY

SORITA D'ESTE

Assist me to erect the ancient altar, at which in days past all worshipped, the great altar of all things. For in old times woman was the altar. Thus was the altar made and placed.

The Book of Shadows[1]

Magic, religion, and sex; potent words which, when combined, often evoke strong emotional feelings and reactions in the repressed, religiously indoctrinated, socially inhibited, and close-minded.[2] Even in these times of mass media, which has desensitised Western society in so many ways, just to mention sex magic often causes startling reactions fuelled by misapprehensions. Thus, the idea of the Great Rite, a central mystery in traditions of initiatory Wicca,[3] with its magical and religious overtones reaching their zenith in the act of sexual union, has been at the root of many debates and rumours. Misunderstandings exist not just in secular society, but also within the magical and pagan communities about this ceremony, and quite possibly rightly so.

Today, there are many different traditions of practice which use the term 'Wicca' to describe themselves, and within the context of this paper, I am using the term to refer specifically to the esoteric traditions in which members can trace their initiatory lineage to Gerald Gardner, 'Gardnerian', or Alex and Maxine Sanders, 'Alexandrian', or who otherwise practice an initiatory form of the tradition which closely follows the practices, beliefs, and liturgy taught in the Gardnerian and Alexandrian traditions. Within these traditions there are three initiations, each of which takes place after a period of study and practice, though there are significant differences in how the degrees are bestowed, as well as in regards to the requirements for a candidate to be deemed suitable or ready for advancement to the next degree, due to the decentralised nature of the tradition. The liturgies for each of the three initiations are contained in the *Book of Shadows*, which is a book of rituals and spells, copied by an initiate from their initiator. The origins of the majority of these rituals have been shown[1] to originate in the books of

---

[1] See D'Este, Sorita and Rankine, David, *Wicca Magickal Beginnings: A Study of the Possible Origins of the*

the medieval grimoire tradition, Christian liturgy, and Freemasonry, embellished with generous helpings of the writings of the infamous British occultist Aleister Crowley and that of Charles Leland, an American anthropologist.[1]

For the textual analysis of the Great Rite which follows, I have used public domain versions[2] of the text, based on original manuscript copies of Gerald Gardner's *Book of Shadows*. Of course minor textual differences between the handwritten copies of different initiates will exist, but for the purposes of this paper such differences are not relevant, as we are concerned with the precedents and origins of the rituals, rather than its development in initiatory covens ~~subsequently~~.

Subsequent

By its very nature, the Great Rite is one of the most private ceremonies of the Wiccan tradition, and it is usual for all members of the coven to turn their backs or leave the circle when it is being performed in 'actuality', that is as a sexual consummation, rather than in 'token', that is its symbolic form without sexual consummation.[2] The Great Rite is performed by a High Priestess and High Priest who perform it as part of their elevation to the Third Degree, or who have already attained the Third Degree and who are performing the ceremony for another purpose, such as celebration or consecration. As an act of sexual union, it is performed only between two consenting adults and ordinarily such a couple are sexual partners outside of the context of magical work.[3] Traditionally the rite is designed for use between a man and a woman, rather than two people of the same sex. Arguments for and against the enactment of this rite by two individuals of the same-sex abound, and debate is likely to continue on the subject for some years.[3]

Origins, Symbolism, and Practice

In preparation for the Great Rite, the altar will be set up according to tradition, the magic circle will be cast, and the guardians of the Watchtowers will be evoked to guard and witness proceedings. All participants will be admitted to the circle and all other celebration, worship, or work will be done and completed before the enactment of the Great Rite begins,

> Magus: Ere we proceed with this sublime degree, I must beg purification at thy hands.

The High Priestess then proceeds to perform the purification, which traditionally

---

Rituals and Practices Found in This Modern Tradition of Pagan Witchcraft and Magick. London: Avalonia, 2008.
[2]See http://www.sacred-texts.com/pag/gbos/gbos05.htm.
[3]See http://www.thewellhead.org.uk/GP/Gay2.htm.

1 - precisely.
2 - who is now repressed?
3 - so is this the exact opposite of Tantra.

involves binding the Magus and then tying him to the altar. She then scourges him, a total of forty strokes, admitted in batteries of three, seven, nine, and twenty-one, a sequence and total number given in a number of rites in the *Book of Shadows* with the purpose of attaining purification. When she is done, he is untied and the process is repeated on her by the Magus, after which a Eucharistic feast of wine and cakes are shared between all present.

Gerald Gardner, who is known by some as the 'Father of Wicca', provides the first published account of this method of scourging in his novel *High Magic's Aid*, "Thou first must be purified. Taking the scourge from the Altar, she struck his buttocks, first three, then seven, then nine, then twenty one strokes with the scourge".[4] The use of flagellation for the purpose of purification seems to hark back to the medieval Christian flagellants who used self-inflicted pain to alter consciousness and purify their souls, though there are also recorded examples of where the initiates of a medieval witch coven was allegedly scourged by the Devil during ceremonies. It is, however, not completely clear from the accounts as to what the exact purpose of the scourging in these medieval covens was, other than the possibility that it might have been as punishment for disobedience. In one example from 1678, one Katherine Liddel of Scotland claimed, amongst other things, "that he (the devil) was cold to the touch, and his breath like a damp air, and that he scourged them oft, and was a most wicked and barbarous master."[5] Within the tradition different reasons are given for the relevance of the total number of forty strokes, the most common being that it corresponds to the number of knots on a traditional scourge, for example five knots each on the eight strands of the scourge, eight representing a concept known as the 'eight paths to power' multiplied by five, five being the points of the pentagram.

An interesting precedent for the forty strokes with the scourge can be found in the Bible where St Paul says, "Of the Jews five times received I forty stripes save one."[6] The canonical laws of the time prohibited the use of more than forty strokes and in an effort to avoid any violation of the law by mistake it was common practice to give one stroke less. It was furthermore customary for the person who was being punished to be tied to a low pillar for the duration of the scourging to ensure that they would be forced to lean forward, a practice echoed in Wicca. Cyprian, in his third century work *The Life of Caesarius Arelatensis*, describes this practice. It is then, as an aside to note, that after Solomon, Cyprian was probably the most attributed author of magical grimoires, including the black book *Clavis Inferni*, or *Keys to Hell*, which provides instructions for the control of the demon princes of the four cardinal directions.

Clearly, however, the use of bondage and flagellation also allows for parallels with

[4]Gardner, *High Magic's Aid*, p. 183.
[5]Linton, *Witch Stories*, p. 140.
[6]Corinthians 11: 24-25.

1 - Mortification, and bondage, will move.

erotic BDSM to be drawn, with the roles of dominance and submission being interchangeable. It has been suggested that the use of this technique could be credited to a sadomasochistic preference held by Gerald Gardner for its use to raise magical power. This popular notion can in part be supported by the fact that the use of the scourge, flagellation, bondage, and sexual energies are central to many of the rituals presented in Gardner's *Book of Shadows*. It is also ironic that these practices, which are so central to the initiatory tradition taught by Gardner, have been whitewashed out of the public image of the initiatory traditions, and are nearly non-existent in the exoteric traditions. In fact, adherents to pop-culture Wiccan traditions are often surprised and appalled by the idea of any form of ritual nudity, bondage, or scourging, being unaware of its importance in the traditional rites. Then the rite continues,

Magus: Now I must reveal to you a great Mystery.

The High Priestess assumes what is known as the 'Osiris Position', standing naked with her scourge and ritual wand, her arms crossed over her chest. The Magus kisses her on the lips. The Magus now declares the body of the High Priestess, who in this rite is the representative of the Goddess, as being the altar for the ritual,

Magus: Assist me to erect the Ancient Altar, at which in days past all worshipped, the Great Altar of all things. For in the old times a woman was the Altar. Thus was the altar made and placed.

The High Priestess now lies down in the centre of the circle in the pentagram position.[7] If there is a coven present, an assistant may cover her with a veil.[2]

There are some noteworthy parallels here between the practices in Wicca and those found in the Preliminary Mass of Gold, the first initiation ritual into the Brotherhood of the Golden Arrow,[8] a mystical sex magic order founded by Maria de Naglowska in 1931 in Paris. In the Preliminary Mass of Gold the Priestess lies down in a west-east orientation, the Priestess blesses the wine, which is held by a male and the cup is placed on her genitalia, all of which are echoed in the rites taught by Gerald Gardner two decades later. The Brotherhood of the Golden Arrow was a mystical Gnostic sex magic order, who amongst other things, celebrated the mysteries of both the masculine and feminine divine in their rituals, primarily as Lucifer and Satan as the masculine, and the Mother and Sophia as the feminine. Their focus on Lucifer and Satan, as well as explicit sex magic practices, gave rise to the popular suggestion that they were a Satanic order.

Contemporary to the public emergence of Wicca, this idea of woman as the altar is

---

[7] Her arms and legs being outstretched in a west-east orientation.
[8] North, Robert, *The Grimoire of Maria de Naglowska*. USA: New Flesh Palladium, 2010.

1 - Both the ancient traditional!.
2 - Why?

prominently found in the writings of Dion Fortune's novel *The Sea Priestess*, where the hero Wilfred Maxwell has a soliloquy about his fiancé Molly saying,

> When the body of a woman is made an altar for the worship of the Goddess who is all beauty and magnetic life, and the man pours himself out in worship and sacrifice, keeping back no part of the price but giving his very self for love, seeing in his mate the priestess serving with him in the worship - then the Goddess enters the temple.[9]

Fortune was likely to have been inspired by earlier esoteric works in her writing and the same sources may have also influenced the flow of ideas which culminated in the Great Rite. One such influential text, *La Sorcière*, written by the French historian Jules Michelet in 1862, argued that witchcraft had been the original religion of Europe. Michelet, on describing the preparations undertaken by the witch, declared, "With equal solemnity she purifies her person. Henceforth she is the living altar of the shrine."[10] Michelet presented a model of a nature and fertility cult, which was led by priestesses and had managed to survive and flourish underground during the Middle Ages as a sanctuary for oppressed women. Michelet's work laid the groundwork for later writers and anthropologists, such as Charles Godfrey Leland and Margaret Murray, both of whose work would be highly influential on the emergence of Wicca. In addition to emphasising the character of the witch as a positive figure, Michelet also cited the idea of the naked body of the witch as the altar, writing that, "At the Witches' Sabbath woman fulfils every office. She is priest, and altar, and consecrated host."[11]

In doing so, Michelet may in turn have been drawing on accounts from the witch trials and the famous case of *La Voisin*, a major French scandal of the seventeenth century. In 1679, one of King Louis XIV's mistresses, Madame de Mountespan, enlisted the aid of Catherine Monvoisin, known as *La Voisin*, an infamous sorceress and poisoner. Both the women played the part of altar for black masses performed by Abbé Guiborg, a renegade Catholic priest. Noteworthy in the descriptions of these events are that, "as often as the priest was to kiss the altar, he kissed the body,"[12] and "at the end of the Mass, the priest went into the woman."[13] A side note of interest here is that the women were described as holding black candles in their hands during the ceremony and that the chalice would be placed upon their naked bellies, a practiced echoed in the Great Rite when consecrations are performed, and it is interesting to consider these similarities in the light of constant denial on the part of Wicca that it has any associations with Satanism.

---

[9]Fortune, *The Sea Priestess*, p. 220.
[10]Michelet, *Sorceress: A Study in Middle Age Superstition*, p. 123.
[11]Michelet, *Sorceress: A Study in Middle Age Superstition*, p. 99.
[12]Cavendish, *The Satanic Mass*, p. 373.
[13]Cavendish, *The Satanic Mass*, p. 373.

1- Witchcraft is a debase ment of one or more traditional European religions'
2- This is incorrect.
3 - Was Louis XIV involved?

Magus: And the sacred place was the point within the centre of the circle, as we of old times have been taught, that the point within the centre is the origin of all things. Therefore should we adore it [The Magus kisses the High Priestess on her pubic area].

Here the reference to "the point within the centre of the circle" is most likely a reference to the Sun, the symbol of which is a circle with a dot in the centre. This is then also a symbolic reference to the phallus of the male, who as the channel for the god of the tradition also represents the Sun, which will join in an act of sexual union with the Priestess in the centre of the circle, their union being the 'origin of all things', as it is through sexual union that new life is created.

Therefore, whom we adore, we also invoke, by the power of the lifted lance. [Invokes], O circle of stars [kiss], whereof our Father is but the younger brother [kiss], Marvel beyond imagination, soul of infinite space, before whom time is ashamed, the mind bewildered and understanding dark, not unto thee may we attain unless thine image be of love [kiss].

This section of the liturgy is drawn directly from the Gnostic Mass by Aleister Crowley, where the original text reads,

Thee therefore whom we adore we also invoke, by the power of the lifted lance.[14]

O circle of stars whereof our Father is but the younger brother, marvel beyond imagination, soul of infinite space, before whom Time is ashamed, the mind bewildered, and the understanding dark, not unto Thee may we attain, unless Thine image be Love.[15]

Crowley wrote the Gnostic Mass, which is also known as *Liber XV*, whilst travelling in Moscow and would later write about it in his autobiography saying that,

I wished therefore to construct a ritual through which people might enter into ecstasy as they have always done under the influence of appropriate ritual. In recent years, there has been an increasing failure to attain this object, because the established cults shock their intellectual convictions and outrage their common sense. Thus their minds criticize their enthusiasm; they are unable to consummate the union of their individual souls with the universal soul as a bridegroom would be to consummate his marriage if his love were constantly

---

[14]Crowley, *Magick*, p. 587.
[15]Crowley, *Magick*, p. 588.

reminded that its assumptions were intellectually absurd.[16]

Much of the symbolism of the Gnostic Mass is sexual, and although it is not stated, a note on the Gnostic Mass by Crowley implies that the priest and priestess engage in sex magic after the rite is over and the congregation departed.[17] Crowley wrote, "Certain secret formulae of this Mass are taught to the Priest in his Ordination,"[18] which fits with his emphasis on the 9° heterosexual union of the Ordo Templi Orientis, also referred to as the O.T.O., and again parallels the practice in Wicca where the coven usually leaves the circle if there is to be sexual consummation.

Therefore, by seed and root, and stem and bud and leaf and flower and fruit do we invoke thee.

This was also in part inspired by Crowley's Gnostic Mass, which contains the phrase, "By seed and root and stem and bud and leaf and flower and fruit do we invoke Thee."[19] Crowley, in turn, took his inspiration in writing this piece from the poem *Song of Proserpine*, by the early nineteenth century poet Percy Bysshe Shelley,

Sacred Goddess, Mother Earth,
Thou from whose immortal bosom
Gods and men and beasts have birth,
Leaf and blade, and bud and blossom,
Breathe thine influence most divine
On thine own child, Proserpine.[20]

Magus: O, Queen of space, O dew of light, O continuous one of the Heavens [kiss]. Let it be ever thus, that men speak not of Thee as one, but as none, and let them not speak of thee at all, since thou art continuous, for thou art the point within the circle [kiss], which we adore [kiss], the fount of life without which we would not be [kiss].

Some of the wording here is again drawn from Aleister Crowley, this time from his channelled text the *Book of the Law*, where it relates to the ancient Egyptian stellar goddess Nuit, "O Nuit, continuous one of heaven, let it be ever thus, that men speak not of Thee as one but as none; and let them not speak of Thee at all, since Thou art continuous!"[21] The Magus now performs an eightfold kiss, which marks eight points

[16]Crowley, *The Confessions of Aleister Crowley: An Autohagiography*, p. 714.
[17]As noted by Kenneth Grant in Crowley, Aleister, *Magick in Theory and Practice*. London: Routledge, 1986, p. 436
[18]Crowley, *Magick*, p. 597.
[19]Crowley, *Magick*, p. 588.
[20]Percy Blythe Shelley, *Song of Proserpine*, 1820.
[21]Crowley, 'Chapter I', in *Liber AL vel Legis sub figura CCXX*.

which when joined together produces the symbol used to represent the Third Degree in Wicca, being that of an upright pentagram with a triangle on top of it on the body of the High Priestess, with the five points of the pentagram being the feet, knees, and genitalia, and that of the triangle, the breasts and lips. This is the same pattern followed during the fivefold kiss which is usually performed by the Magus on the High Priestess whilst she stands or sits on the altar in preparation for the ceremony of Drawing Down the Moon, in which she becomes a vessel for the divine and for initiations.

Superimposing this symbol formed by the kisses on the Qabalistic Tree of Life provides us with one of the many layers of symbolism found in the Great Rite. The points of the upward pointing triangle correspond to the Supernal Triad on the Tree of Life, comprised of the *sephiroth* of Kether at the top, Chokmah at the bottom right, and Binah at the bottom left. These *sephiroth* correspond to the pure divine source with Kether, meaning 'Crown', Chokmah, 'Wisdom', as the masculine divine, and Binah, 'Understanding', as the feminine divine. The five points of the pentagram correspond to more of the *sephiroth*, these being Daath, 'Knowledge', at the top; Chesed, 'Mercy', at the upper right; Netzach, 'Victory', at the lower right; Hod, 'Splendour', at the lower left; and Geburah, 'Strength', at the upper left.

These *sephiroth* have planetary attributions, but it is their elemental attributions which are particularly relevant here. Chesed corresponds to water, Netzach to earth, Hod to air, and Geburah to fire, providing a complete balanced group of the four elements. Daath, which is a pseudo-*sephira* and has some of the properties of a *sephira*, equates to spirit and also occupies the position of gateway on the Tree of Life between the Supernal Triad and the seven lower *sephiroth*, which represent increasingly tangible levels of divine manifestation. The three *sephiroth* that are left out of this sequence are particularly significant in Wicca, being Tiphereth, 'Beauty', which is solar; Yesod, 'Foundation', which is lunar; and Malkuth, 'Kingdom', which represents the kingdom of the four elements, or in other words the Earth. However, it could be argued that the Great Rite represents the union of the polarity of female and male, which in Wicca is equated to the Moon and Sun, and the act of union is one of manifestation equating to Malkuth. Thus, the missing *sephiroth* could be seen not as missing, but rather as the participants and the act of the Great Rite itself.

Following the symbol being marked by kisses, the ceremony continues,

> Magus: And in this way truly are erected the Holy Twin Pillars Boaz and Joachim [kisses breasts]. In beauty and strength were they erected, to the wonder and glory of all men.

This line is heavy with Qabalistic symbolism and could have been inspired by the work of any of the contemporary traditions and writers at the end of the nineteenth

1 – Oh my god. Not this crap.

and beginning of the twentieth century. Occult authors, such as Lévi, Papus, Mathers, and Fortune, all wrote about the Qabalah, and used a great deal of Qabalistic imagery in their work. However, it is most likely that the inspiration came once again from Aleister Crowley and his Gnostic Mass. In this rite, the Priestess is seated naked on the altar, between the Black and White pillars. Boaz and Jachim are the two pillars in the porch of the Temple of Solomon, which are equated to the black and white pillars of the Tree of Life. These are the Black Pillar of Severity and the Goddess, and White Pillar of Mercy and the God of the Tree of Life. The Black Pillar of Severity is on the left and the White Pillar of Mercy is on the right. The Middle Pillar of Balance represents the gateway to the temple, the entranceway to the mysteries. This symbolism is also clearly expressed in the High Priestess tarot card in the Rider Waite deck. This deck, which was first published in 1910, was illustrated by the magical artist Pamela Colman-Smith. In this trump card, the High Priestess is seated on an altar between the two pillars, with the black pillar on the viewer's left and the white pillar on the viewer's right. The pillars are marked with the letters 'B' and 'J' respectively, representing Boaz and Jachim.

Qabalistic symbolism permeates Wiccan liturgy, practice, and beliefs, though, often, practitioners today seem to be totally unaware of its omnipotent presence in their workings. It is, for example, the symbolism of the Black and White Pillars as representing feminine and masculine that determines the placing of the symbols or statues of the Wiccan deities on the altar, with the Goddess on the left and the God being placed on the right. The unnamed Middle Pillar of Balance between the Black and White Pillars corresponds to the centre line of a person, with the *sephiroth* equating to the crown, Kether, and pure divinity; the heart, Tiphereth, and the Sun; the genitalia, Yesod, and the Moon; and the feet, Malkuth, as the four elements.

Another significant reference, which can be seen in part of the ritual text, is to the Ethical Triad, which are the three *sephira* of Chesed, Geburah, and Tiphereth in the middle of the Tree of Life. The words 'Beauty', 'Strength', and 'Glory' refer to the *sephiroth* which comprise this Triad. The name of the *sephira* of Tiphereth means 'Beauty', Geburah means 'Strength', and the alternative name commonly used for Chesed is Gedulah, which means 'Glory'. This is not the upward pointing triangle of the Third Degree symbol, but rather it is the downward pointing triangle of manifestation of divine power reflecting the divine union of the Supernal Triad comprised of Kether, Chokmah, which crowns the White Pillar, and Binah which crowns the Black Pillar.

At this point in the rite, any members of the coven who are present will leave the circle if the rite is to be consummated in sexual intercourse. The Magus then continues,

> O Secrets of secrets that art hidden in the being of all lives. Not thee do we adore, for that which adoreth is also thou. Thou art that and That am I [kiss].

Again this line of the liturgy is taken from Crowley's Gnostic Mass, where the original reads, "O secret of secrets that art hidden in the being of all that lives, not Thee do we adore, for that which adoreth is also Thou. Thou art That, and That am I."[22] This statement affirms the presence of the divine within the Magus and the High Priestess, expressing a view which is echoed in other rites in the *Book of Shadows*, such as the Charge of the Goddess,

> I am the flame that burns in every man, and in the core of every star [kiss]. I am Life and the giver of Life, yet therefore is the knowledge of me the Knowledge of Death [kiss]. I am alone, the Lord within ourselves whose name is Mystery of Mysteries [kiss].

The rite continues with these words, again taken from the work of Aleister Crowley, where the original text refers to Hadit, the male principle in the context of the original text. Here then the Magus is essentially declaring his own divinity by identifying himself with Hadit. The original text reads, "I am the flame that burns in every heart of man, and in the core of every star. I am life and the giver of life, yet therefore is the knowledge of me the knowledge of death...[23] I am alone: there is no god where I am."[24] The eighteenth century Masonic tract *The Grand Mystery Lodge Laid Open*, described the five points of fellowship, where bodies should touch during the ritual embrace, as "foot to foot, knee to knee, breast to breast, hand to back, cheek to cheek."[25] This is clearly the origin of the use of this term in the Great Rite, though it is not identical. Here we should however clarify that the five points of fellowship from a Masonic viewpoint are defined as part of the work undertaken by a Mason. In Masonry, as in Wicca, the five points of fellowship are represented by the symbol of the pentagram. For the Mason, this may also represent the five wounds of Christ when he was crucified at Golgotha.

The reference of "lance to grail" is undoubtedly taking into consideration the sheer quantity of material borrowed from it, a reference to the use of a lance and cup in the Gnostic Mass. However, it can also be interpreted as being a reference to the lance and grail of Arthurian legend, perhaps in an effort to imply Celtic mysteries and myths on which many, including Gardner, were keen to associate themselves with. In doing so, the emphasis is then superficially moved to the sexual symbolism of the union of the lance and grail, but becomes an issue for Wiccans who feel anger towards the Church and Christianity, as the symbolism of the lance and grail is in reality a reference to the blood of Christ, with its origins in the legend where Joseph of Arimathea used the grail to collect Christ's blood after his side was pierced by the lance when he was

---

[22] Crowley, *Magick*, p. 588.
[23] Crowley, 'Chapter II', in *Liber AL vel Legis sub figura CCXX*.
[24] Crowley, 'Chapter II', in *Liber AL vel Legis sub figura CCXX*.
[25] *The Grand Mystery Laid Open*, 1726. NP.

hanging on the cross, and is therefore a symbol of the blood and flesh of the man-god of Christianity in this context.

Another point worth noting here is that, in one of the early Books of Shadows texts written by Gerald Gardner, the text instead reads "genitalia to genitalia"[26] and it would seem therefore that the use of "lance to grail" was a conscious decision on the part of Gardner or one of his colleagues in the early stages of the Gardnerian movement. This might have been an effort to include those who did not wish to, or for some reason could not, consummate the rite in actuality, and who preferred celebrating it in a symbolic form instead. Alternatively, it might have been that at this stage there was a need to try and whitewash the practices in an effort to separate it from the other similar sex magic practices that were considered Satanic, which is just as likely when you take into consideration the level of media interaction which was sought by Gerald Gardner and some other early Gardnerians of the period who were trying to, and had some success in doing so, promote the idea that Wicca was a survival of a nature loving pagan religion, rather than the forgotten child of magical practices steeped in Judaic-Christian symbolism, or worse, that of traditions considered to be Satanic!

The ritual union is then enacted by the Magus and High Priestess in the circle, who conclude the rite by declaring in unison,

> Magus and High Priestess: Encourage our hearts, Let thy Light crystallize itself in our blood, fulfilling us of Resurrection, for there is no part of us that is not of the Gods.

Not surprisingly, even this last part of the ritual text is taken from Crowley's Gnostic Mass, where the original reads, "Make open the path of creation and of intelligence between us and our minds. Enlighten our understanding. Encourage our hearts. Let Thy light crystallize itself in our blood, fulfilling us of Resurrection."[27]

The Great Rite and Image Problems

Although Wiccans often try to present a clean-cut image of Wicca to the public and to other traditions within the wider magical community, it contains numerous practices which present causes for concern. Firstly, by its nature as a mystery tradition, the practices, beliefs, and rituals of a coven are considered oath-bound and private. The tradition also employs the use of both flagellation and bondage as part of its rituals, blindfolds are used during initiation rites, and rituals are often performed skyclad.

---

[26]See Farrar, Janet and Farrar, Stuart, *The Witches Way: Principles, Rituals and Beliefs of Modern Witchcraft* Washington: Phoenix Publishing, 1984.
[27]Crowley, *Magick*, p. 589.

These things alone, before we enter into the realms of ritualised sex, are enough for comparisons to be made with BDSM and other fetish practices, with their leanings towards dominance and control.

The use of flagellation and bondage hints at something dangerous and forbidden, the idea of men and women dancing around skyclad unashamed of their nudity, combined with ideas of horned gods and magic, awakens a primal fear of losing control and being helpless within the minds of those who have been conditioned to the modern world, whilst also being visually stimulating and exciting. The combination of fear and titillation in turn transforms into feelings of guilt and self-loathing, which provides the fuel for the attention given by the media for these aspects of the practices of Wicca. This has fuelled many misapprehensions through the media portrayals of Wicca, and understandably so. After all, there can't be many parents who would feel comfortable with the idea that their teenagers are running around naked in the woods with other naked men and women, worshipping phallic gods with horns, and moon goddesses who are unashamedly sensual, with the knowledge that they will also be blindfolded, tied up, and scourged! No amount of reassurance that this is a 'religion' is likely to put their minds at ease.

So then it is only natural that initiates of the tradition, especially those who are keen on gaining a positive image of Wicca in the media and a wider acceptance of it as a religion within the wider community, have sought to exorcise the idea of sex magic from the public image of the tradition, and instead focusing on the symbolic ideas of union, as well as drawing comparisons with the historical *Hieros Gamos*, 'Sacred Marriage', and also with Tantra, which they consider to be more acceptable to the general public from whom they seek acceptance.

The Great Rite and the *Hieros Gamos*

The Great Rite is often described as *Hieros Gamos*, the sacred marriage of the Priestess and Priest, the Goddess and the God, and Wiccans take the view that this rite has its origins in sacred marriage rites, which they believed took place all over the ancient world. Controversially however, whilst there are some scholars who argue that the *Hieros Gamos* was a widespread phenomenon, others argue that the evidence for this claim is lacking and that it might not have existed at all, or that if it did it was a very rare and unique practice.[2] The oldest and best known historical example of the *Hieros Gamos* is that celebrating the goddess Inanna in ancient Sumer. The second millennium B.C.E. text called *The Joy of Sumer*,[3] describes a ritualised union between the queen, who acts as the priestess representing the goddess Inanna, and the king as representative of the shepherd god Dumuzi. In it the people first prepare the bridal bed with sweet-smelling cedar oil, arranging rushes, and spreading a sheet over the bed. We

1 - Only the repressed oppose weirdness, LOL.
2 - Ιεροσ Γαμοσ is a mythical concept, not a rite.
3 - Which from the date must be a version.

are then told that the queen, that is Inanna, bathes herself with soap in preparation for Dumuzi, the king, who then joins her thus,

> The king goes with lifted head to the holy loins,
> Dumuzi goes with lifted head to the holy loins of Inanna.
> He lies down beside her on the bed.
> Tenderly he caresses her, murmuring words of love:
> O my holy jewel! O my wondrous Inanna!
>
> After he enters her holy vulva, causing the queen to rejoice,
> After he enters her holy vulva, causing Inanna to rejoice,
> Inanna holds him to her and murmurs:
> O Dumuzi, you are truly my love.[28]

The people then make offerings, which include food and the burning of juniper resin as incense after which they perform rites. At this point the union of Inanna and Dumuzi culminates, as the narrative continues,

> The king embraces his beloved bride.
> Dumuzi embraces Inanna.
> Inanna, seated on the holy throne, shines like daylight.
> The king, like the sun, shines radiantly by her side.
> He arranges abundance, lushness, and plenty before her.
> He assembles the people of Sumer.[29]

The festivities and rites conclude with feasting and the honouring of Inanna as the 'First Daughter of the Moon', 'Lady of the Evening'[30] and the 'Joy of Sumer',[31] showing the emphasis placed here not only on the actual union between the priestess and king, but also the emphasis placed on honouring the goddess as being the bestower of joy and plenty through the feast. Some of the descriptions given of Inanna in this text are also later echoed in the descriptions given to other goddesses, including that of the Shekinah in Jewish mysticism, who is also implicated in acts of sacred sex in medieval Kabbalistic texts and commentaries.

---

[28]Kramer and Wolkstein, *The Joy of Sumer, in Inanna Queen of Heaven and Earth: Her Stories and Hymns from Sumer*, p. 108.
[29]Kramer and Wolkstein, *The Joy of Sumer, in Inanna Queen of Heaven and Earth: Her Stories and Hymns from Sumer*, p. 108.
[30]Kramer and Wolkstein, *The Joy of Sumer, in Inanna Queen of Heaven and Earth: Her Stories and Hymns from Sumer*, p. 108.
[31]Kramer and Wolkstein, *The Joy of Sumer, in Inanna Queen of Heaven and Earth: Her Stories and Hymns from Sumer*, p. 108.

Whilst, superficially, there are parallels between the sacred marriage of Inanna and Dumuzi and the Great Rite, the rituals have little in common other than the idea that the man embodies the god and the female the goddess, and that they then join in an act of sexual union. It is however possible to see how this ancient practice could have been a source of inspiration for some of the symbolism found in the Great Rite. There is also a difference in purpose, as the Great Rite is used for different purposes and is not celebrating the mysteries or mythic cycle of particular historical deities, whereas the sacred marriage is part of an established mythic cycle and cosmology.

There has been a move in recent years by initiates and scholars towards making comparisons between the Great Rite and the Tantric *Pancamakara* Rite, also known as the 'Rite of the Five M's'. These comparisons can only be ascribed to a lack of knowledge, understanding, and appreciation of the Western Esoteric Tradition and its layers of symbolism which has been distilled from the mystical practices of many thousands of years. Even this paper only touches upon some of those layers contained within the Great Rite, so many more can be revealed by looking more deeply at the origins and through gnosis gained in practice. The *Pancamakara* Rite comparison, whilst allowing a student to learn more about the practices of an unrelated tradition, simply does not bear any relation to the practice or liturgy of the Great Rite. It is a complex and devotional process, with numerous steps, sexual consummation being one of the last ones in a very long process, which involves the memorisation of long lists of gods, goddesses, spiritual beings, myths, and cosmologies, as well as practical workings, meditations, and so on. The two rituals are so different that any attempt at a meaningful comparison can only become frustrated and will not be valid.

The Great Rite, the Qabalah, and the Emergence of Western Sex Magic

As it has already been illustrated, the Great Rite is replete with Qabalistic symbolism, and, to further understand why this is so, it is necessary to examine ideas of sexual union as a form of spiritual practice in the Kabbalah, as the origin of the Qabalah. The sixteenth century Kabbalist, Rabbi Moses Cordovero, 1522-1570 C.E., who systemised the Kabbalah into the root of what it is now, wrote about the Shekinah and sexual union. His teachings are extremely clear, and perhaps surprisingly graphic in their instructions to husband and wife considering the period they date from. In a commentary on the *Zohar* he wrote, "Their desire, both his and hers, was to unite Shekinah. He focused on Tiphereth, and his wife on Malkuth. His union was to join Shekinah; she focused correspondingly on being Shekinah and uniting with her husband, Tiphereth."[32] Cordovero may have drawn inspiration from the fifteenth century writings of Ephraim Ben Gerson, who, in his homily to a groom, gave very

---

[32]Azulai, *Or ha-Hayyim,* seventeenth century C.E.

clear instructions for the magical process to be enacted during the sexual act,

> Thus do Kabbalists know that thoughts originate in the rational soul, which emanates from the supreme. And thought has the power to strip off and rise and reach its source, and when reaching its source it attains communication with the supernal light from which it came, and both become one. When thought once again stretches down from on high, all becomes one line in the imagination, and the supernal light comes down through the power of thought that draws it down, and the Shekinah is found down below. The clear light then spreads to the thinker's location. So did early priests reach communion with the supremes through thought in order to draw down the supreme light, and all beings would thus grow and multiply and be blessed in accordance with the power of thought.[33]

If we look particularly at the alchemical imagery from the sixteenth and seventeenth century of the union of the king and queen, we can see a strong case for a symbolic precursor of the Great Rite. In these images the empowered man and woman, or the king and queen, are united sexually in a sacred vessel, such as a sepulchre, The Rosary of the Philosophers, *La Bugia*, or flask, *Anatomia Auri*, which can be seen as representing the otherworldly space of the magic circle as a place of divine union.

Although there are many earlier precedents of the *Hieros Gamos* and sacred sex, the Great Rite in Wicca is most likely to draw its practice from the Thelemic magical orders of the early twentieth century, like the Ordo Templi Orientis, Great Brotherhood of God, and Fraternitas Saturni, which all used sex magic as part of their practices. By the 1930s, although an act of sexual magic might have seemed socially shocking, on an esoteric level there were several magical orders which performed sex magic in Europe and America, including the Czech Universalia, the French Fraternity of the Golden Arrow, and the Thelemic orders mentioned previously.

The late nineteenth and early twentieth century saw a number of pioneers employing the use of sex for magic and union with the divine manifested through the sexual partner, whose work would influence those who followed, and who are only now starting to receive the recognition their work deserves. Foremost amongst these were the American sex magician Pascal Randolph, 1825-1875, and the American sexual mystic Ira Craddock, 1857-1902. Not only did Randolph travel considerably, meeting a number of prominent European occultists, such as Eliphas Lévi, Hargrave Jennings, Kenneth Mackenzie. and Edward Bulwer-Lytton, but he also founded the Hermetic Brotherhood of Luxor. This magical order included sex magic teachings and was the inspiration for its inclusion in the Ordo Templi Orientis. Indeed, Randolph's words in

---

[33]Gershon, *Homilies*, fifteenth century C.E.

his last public speech would see expression through the Thelemic teachings of Aleister Crowley,[34] with Randolph declaring the 'omnipotence of will'. Randolph's writings covered a range of esoteric topics, including sex magic, with one of his best known works being publicised as *Magia Sexualis*. This work was nearly lost, as at one point only a French copy of this work existed, which was translated by the Russian sexual mystic Maria de Naglowska, founder of the Brotherhood of the Golden Arrow and herself a keen advocate of sexual magical practices. Maria de Naglowska's practices veered towards BDSM and were within a Luciferian and Satanic framework, peculiarly in keeping with her being based in Paris[35] during the 1930s when she created the order and its rites and taught them to the surrealist and symbolist artists who lived there.

Craddock wrote on a number of key themes, including the importance of sustaining sexual pleasure and the retention of semen, advising men that if they did ejaculate, that,

> When he takes his thoughts away from the bodily sensation just before the last thrill comes which precedes ejaculation, to fix them, not upon something on the bodily plane, but to lift his thoughts to that which he considers the very highest and grandest power in all the universe, call it by what name he will- -First Cause, Unconscious Energy, Primordial Substance, Jehovah, Brahma, Allah, God, the Ultimate Force, the Divine.[36]

Aleister Crowley wrote a review of some of Craddock's work in his *Equinox* Vol 3 No 1, saying of her 'sexual' writings,

> I am very far from agreeing with all that this most talented woman sets forth in her paper, but she certainly obtained initiated knowledge of extraordinary depth. She seems to have had access to certain most concealed sanctuaries.... She has put down statements in plain English which are positively staggering. This book is of incalculable value to every student of occult matters. No Magick library is complete without it.[37]

The Great Rite contains many layers of symbolism, but there is no doubt that based on the evidence, it is a child of Crowley's Gnostic Mass, and as such one of the Great Beast 666's hidden legacies. Whilst it is difficult for many Wiccans, especially those who have come to the tradition from a feminist and Goddess-spirituality perspective, to accept and acknowledge the influence Crowley had on this and other rituals within the tradition, others are finding deeper meaning in the texts by studying the source

---

[34] Who was interestingly born in the same year of 1875.
[35] Just over two hundred and fifty years after Catherine *La Voisin* and her Satanic sexual rites.
[36] Chapell, *Sexual Outlaw, Erotic Mystic: The Essential Ida Craddock*, pp. 186-187.
[37] Crowley, *The Equinox*, Volume 3 No. 1, p. 280.

texts from which they have been borrowed, combined with practice. The Great Rite will probably remain the most controversial and easily misunderstood rites of Wicca, but maybe that is part of its mystery and appeal.

This paper only touches on the first layers of symbolism and history of this rite, and there is a great deal more to unveil. For now, however, it seems appropriate to end with a quote from Pascal Randolph, whose work undoubtedly influenced many who would follow, including the magical orders previously mentioned, even though he is rarely credited. In writing on sexual magic Randolph said,

> The union of the man with the woman must be innocent. Lust for pleasure must not be the main purpose. Transcending carnal pleasure, aim at the union of the spirits, if you want your prayer to be exhausted in ecstasy. If you conform to these principles, the sexual act will become a source of spiritual and material force for you and a fountainhead of wisdom, happiness and peace. In magic, you search for that which is called the fortune of spirit.[38]

---

[38]Randolph, *Magia Sexualis*, p. 45.

BIBLIOGRAPHY

Cavendish, Richard, *The Satanic Mass*. London: Pan Books Ltd., 1977.

Chappell, Vere, *Sexual Outlaw, Erotic Mystic: The Essential Ira Craddock*. Maine: Red Wheel/Weiser, 2010.

Crowley, Aleister, *Liber AL vel Legis sub figura CCXX*. London: O.T.O., 1938.

Crowley, Aleister, *The Equinox*, Volume 3 No. 1. Maine: Red Wheel/Weiser, 1971.

Crowley, Aleister, *The Confessions of Aleister Crowley: An Autohagiography*. London: Arkana, 1989.

Crowley, Aleister, *Magick*. Maine: Red Wheel/Weiser, 2000.

D'Este, Sorita and Rankine, David, *Wicca Magickal Beginnings*. London: Avalonia, 2008.

D'Este, Sorita and Rankine, David, *Practical Elemental Magick*. London: Avalonia, 2009.

D'Este, Sorita and Rankine, David, *The Cosmic Shekinah*. London: Avalonia, 2011.

Farrar, Janet and Farrar, Stuart, *The Witches Way: Principles, Rituals and Beliefs of Modern Witchcraft*. Washington: Phoenix Publishing, 1984.

Farrar, Janet and Farrar, Stewart, *A Witches Bible Complete*. New York: Magickal Childe Inc., 1991.

Fortune, Dion, *The Sea Priestess*. Maine: Red Wheel/Weiser, 2003.

Fries, Jan, *Kali Kaula: A Manual of Tantric Magick*. London: Avalonia, 2010.

Gardner, Gerald, *High Magic's Aid*. London: Michael Houghton, 1949.

Kramer, Samuel Noah and Wolkstein, Diane, *The Joy of Sumer, in Inanna Queen of Heaven and Earth: Her Stories and Hymns from Sumer*. London: Harper Perennial, 1984.

Linton, Lynn, *Witch Stories*. Montana: Kessinger Publishing, 2003.

Michelet, Jules, *Sorceress: A Study in Middle Age Superstition*. Charleston: Forgotten Books, 2010.

North, Robert, *The Grimoire of Maria de Naglowska*. USA: New Flesh Palladium, 2010.

Randolph, Pascal B., *Magia Sexualis*. Rome: Ediz Mediterranee, 1987.

Rhodes, H. T. F., *The Satanic Mass*. New York: Citadel Press, 1955.

Skinner, Stephen and Rankine, David, *The Veritable Key of Solomon*. Singapore: Golden Hoard Press, 2008.

Wolkstein, Diane and Kramer, Samuel Noah, *Inanna Queen of Heaven and Earth: Her Stories and Hymns from Sumer*. London: Harper Perennial, 1984.

TREADING THE SPIRAL MAZE
CHANGING CONSCIOUSNESS
IN WICCAN RITUAL

BY

MELISSA HARRINGTON

Awake, my soul! Not only passive praise
Thou owest! Not alone these swelling tears,
Mute thanks and secret ecstasy. Awake,
Voice of sweet song! Awake, my heart, awake!
Green vales and icy cliffs, all join my hymn.

Samuel Taylor Coleridge, *Hymn in the Vale of Chamouni*

The occult traditions teach ritual as a means to facilitate transformative spiritual experiences. This philosophy and praxis can be traced through Hermetic texts, such as the *Corpus Hermeticum*, and beyond to ancient Greek and Egyptian philosophy. Prototypes of the ritual practice of modern day witches are clearly described in the enduring grimoire traditions[1] and practitioners employ similar techniques to those described in Cornelius Agrippa's *De Occulta Philosophia*, completed in 1510 and first published in London in 1651. This paper describes Wicca's use of simple magical ritual to create a sacred space, or *temenos*, in which practitioners facilitate a change in consciousness. This use of ritual creates a mental and physical space that enables the practitioner to undergo a psycho-spiritual journey from mundane consciousness to magico-religious trance, and back again, with profound and prolonged effects, which remain congruent and manageable for adherents living and working in wider society.

Magic is often described as causing change in consciousness. The change in consciousness achieved in magical ritual resonates with practitioners at a deep experiential level. I suggest that this is achieved by creating powerful liminal experiences in initiation that are reinforced by regular liminoid experiences within the magical circle of such focused intensity that spiritual transformation occurs at will. Anthropologists of religion have long discussed the idea of liminality in ritual. The term 'liminality', which Arnold van

---

[1] See D'Este, Sorita and Rankine, David, *Wicca Magickal Beginnings: A Study of the Possible Origins of the Rituals and Practices found in this Modern Tradition of Pagan Witchcraft and Magick.* London: Avalonia, 2008.

Gennep first used in 1909, can be understood as a conscious or unconscious subjective state of being on the threshold between two different existential planes. Van Gennep identified a threefold structure in rites of passage in small scale societies that included pre-liminal rites of separation, liminal rites of transition, and post-liminal rites of incorporation. He suggested that this was a universal pattern for most ritual passages, and indeed modern Wiccan initiations can be seen to follow this pattern. Victor Turner continued this work by expanding it to create theories that apply to wider society. He argued that there are few instances of truly transformative liminal ritual in large scale society, but there are liminoid experiences, and if these affect the spatial and temporal realms together the experience can be intense.

Witchcraft has always been a liminal activity. The witch in history was both human and monster, seductive fey and vindictive hag, the woman next door who could kill or cure with a glance. Country folk were warned to avoid twilight, the Devil's Hour, and witching will forever be associated with midnight, the time between the hours of two days. Contemporary Wiccan festivals celebrate the turning of the Wheel of Life, and thus take place at times of seasonal and celestial change. Esbats work with the phases of the moon, marking its changes and integrating ancient beliefs into the spiritual power of attuning to the ebbs and flows of the celestial tides. The Wiccan circle is described as a place 'between the worlds', between the worlds of men and the domains of the outer spaces. Wicca teaches how to get to traverse these realms and return energized, empowered, and spiritually satisfied.

In the following paragraphs, I have created a simple model of the magic circle as a sacred space that is reinforced physically, psychically, mentally, and spiritually at each meeting. The space that is created maybe temporary in the physical world, but acts as a series of pathways to deeper states that become etched into the witch's psyche and are a means to reach deep communion with godhead, before returning smoothly to normal consciousness. Long term experience of the spiritual states that are achieved in the circle can lead to practitioners being able to access these states at will, for they are taught how to open out into divine consciousness, and how to withdraw and close that connection down. In doing so, witches retain and are able to willfully access the memory and viscerally felt emotions of these states, but return to function fully in the mundane realm. Hugely transformative liminal rites, such as initiations, can, however, lead to weeks or months of varying degrees of altered states of consciousness, as the initiation is assimilated, and it is the lament of many practitioners that it is not possible to explore the possibilities of deep ritual and meditational immersion further than at a week or two's holiday by undertaking a monastic form of contemporary paganism, if only for a period of one's life.[1]

There is, of course, a long history within ceremonial magic of withdrawal to perform intense rites, such as the Abramelin operation, which, however, requires a manservant and a place set apart from the world, to be maintained for six months. Perhaps, in

1 - Showing they have no fucking clue.

the future, there will be centers or charities that will allow for more avid students of the mysteries to undertake such sojourns in the inner realms, but, until then, such experiences remain mainly a luxury undertaken by people such as the notorious Aleister Crowley, who spent his massive inheritance on a bohemian and magical life, dying poor but leaving one of the most comprehensive accounts of magic written yet.[1] For most, however, magic must be performed at a weekend in a modest home, with work calling on Monday. However, it is this feature of the world affirming status of modern witchcraft that allows practitioners to access transformative realms of consciousness, which are not normally associated with large scale societies, and a level of communion with the divine that permeates their existence, while remaining fully immersed in contemporary Western culture.

Just as Wiccan initiation has some similarities with initiations in traditional small societies, it is no surprise that the ritual form of this new religious movement draws heavily on techniques of magic that have been passed down through the mysteries for centuries. Such magical technology has hundreds of years of tried and tested methodology for creating the mental and psychic space necessary for the transformative spiritual experience that has been sought by practitioners of the mysteries from ancient times and into the present day.

Wiccan ritual is performed within the sacred space of the magical circle. The circle is seen as a symbol of wholeness and continuity, and forms the basis of the sacred geometry of Wicca. This geometry is used in many religious forms where the circle, square, and triangle are the basis of enduring and universal sacred architecture. Legends of King Solomon, treatises of the Freemasons, ecclesiastical architecture, theories of the golden mean,[2] and so on, all utilize the idea of a perfect geometry, and any research into the symbolism of magic circles through the ages will show varying versions of the circle, square, and triangle. However, it is also useful to view the Wiccan circle as a spiral maze, a sacred labyrinth the witches tread in dance, a mental maze into the central states of consciousness of the rite moving through levels of consciousness as they go to and from its center.

The path of the maze can be seen as one that crosses a series of thresholds. These are not exactly the liminal zones of van Gennep's transformatory initiations, but they can be usefully viewed as liminal in the sense of thresholds of consciousness. The circle consists of layers of liminality that lead to the central liminoid space where transformation and communion with the divine occurs. This is generally not discussed in the teachings of Wicca, nor written about in the *Book of Shadows*, but is as much a part of the tradition as the central religious rites of invocation of the gods or celebration of the sacrament of cakes and wine. Just as the initiations show some similarities to initiation rites of other cultures and times, the circle casting and consciousness changing of Wicca bears similarities to the creation of sacred space in many different traditions and cultures.

1 - Whom.
2 - Which does not relate to the square, circle, and only vaguely to the triangle.

This paper outlines Wicca's basic pathways to changing of consciousness, including in it the often forgotten or underestimated aspects of consciousness change that form the outmost layers of liminality, yet integral to the process.

Liminal Change – Mundane Level One – Step One
Debriefing, Acknowledging, and Setting Aside the Mundane

The journey begins as the coven member leaves home or work for the covenstead. The journey is often taken up by learning and revising parts of the ceremony from a script. The covenor will also be carrying seasonal food and drink for the feast, and seasonal foliage or flowers for the circle. On arrival they take tea and coffee, and chat about mundane things like traffic and jobs, which is an essential debriefing of the mundane side of life. All the conscious and immediate impediments to concentration are acknowledged before they are put aside for the preparation of the circle.

Liminal Change – Mundane Level One – Step Two
Preparing for Ritual

The greeting and settling phase moves into the first preparation stage where the covenstead or outdoor site is set up for the rite. Outdoor fires are made up, woodpiles stocked, and altars set up. Indoors the host will have done a lot of work preparing their home for visitors and magic, but there are always things to do, such as polishing candlesticks, arranging flowers, sorting out the altar, the feast, and so on. Hosts will have sorted out mundane issues, such as where guest will be sleeping, providing bedding towels, and so on, but they usually leave the final temple set up to be a group activity in which all can work mentally and physically towards the rite together.

When the space that will become sacred is prepared, step one is usually completed so the mundane cares have slipped away or been put aside as the coven becomes more ready to undertake the rite. The altar and space is set up with flowers, candles, and various pieces of ritual regalia pertaining to the rite that is to be performed. These decorations help transform the space into one of otherworldliness and beauty, and are strong visual cues throughout the rite that correspond to symbolism in the rite itself.

As the physical environment of the ritual is set up the coven moves into step two, the phase during which wine will be opened and the ritual and work for the night will be discussed. People who have not had a chance to shower or bath will do so, so they are purified in body as well as in mind as the circle is cast. Covenors change into their robes, often splitting to spend some time in male and female changing rooms before finally coming together to start the rite. This pre-ritual separation allows time for female group bonding in the form of grooming, applying perfume and putting on ritual jewelry, and for men to undertake their own form of 'male mysteries'.

Once physically and psychically prepared for ritual, many witches feel they are now in their ritual persona, a persona they work with consciously by taking a magical name at initiation that symbolizes strengths they wish to achieve or aspects of divinity they wish to embrace. They may change this name at any time, and although many people do not, others' history of slowly changing magical names provides an indication of how their spiritual journey has evolved in their time in Wicca.

The final mundane activity is the 'talk through', in which all assemble ready for the rite, and talk and rehearse it so that it can flow smoothly without queries or stage directions once it is in process. Wine is served with nibbles that may stave off hunger pangs, adding to the convivial atmosphere from which the coven leaves to start the rite. This talk through varies in the time it takes, as it is the last stage of group preparation for the rite and 'psyching up' for the ceremony itself.

Liminal Change - Magical Level One – Step One
Setting up the Ritual

Having made the first steps from mundane to magical mindset, the coven is now ready to transform the space from mundane to magical space. Whether the rite is to be in the most ancient stone circle or the sitting room of a suburban home, the circle is always consecrated and purified anew for each rite. Each time the circle is cast it reinforces the belief and practice that it stands for.

Attunement

The coven enter and are ready to start. Already they are beginning to change their breathing patterns to allow breath to become slow and steady, each will spend an amount of time 'grounding and centering' before an attunement is said to attune all present. In an inexperienced group this may take some time, but an experienced group will follow almost imperceptible clues and cues and seem to move as one mind.

Purification of Place and People

The circle is swept with a broom. This has many levels of meaning, including symbolizing the brushing away of consciousness of the everyday world and the identification of the participants with the mythology of witchcraft, with the besom being long imagined as the witch's tool for travel to the sabbat. If the circle is held outdoors it has a practical advantage of removing the last few twigs that might be uncomfortable underfoot.

Simple purifications and blessings of salt and water are performed, with words that have changed little over the centuries of the grimoire traditions, although they have been honed and streamlined for modern tastes. Salt represents earth, whilst the water, incense, and candle represent the other elements into which the fifth element of spirit is drawn through consecration. These consecrated substances are thought to have purifying properties and are sprinkled around the circle and on the participants themselves. This consecration moves the covenors further into sacred space, as they feel they are now purified and ready to encounter their gods. In early Gardnerian Wicca, participants were also scourged lightly as a form of purification. Today it is more normal to only scourge initiates undertaking one of the three degrees of initiation. This ritual act of purification by flagellation may hark back to classical times, or to Christian and Eastern ideas of mortification of the body for spiritual enlightenment.

Liminal Change – Magical Level One – Step Two
Casting the Circle

After the place and participants are suitably purified, the sacred space is demarcated by the High Priestess. She carries a consecrated sword and makes an evocative conjuration of the sacred circle. The sacred space is literally carved out, reinforcing the delineation started with the sweeping and the purification. The coven works with the same mental imagery, using the same creative visualization to 'see' and create the circle's bounds. However, as a group process, at times it may fail. Some participants in circles with the anthropologist Tanya Luhrmann, one of the first to study magic academically in Britain,[2] complained that she 'crashed' circles. They felt her uncertainty as a non-believer transmitted to the structure of the circle itself and that she was the broken link in the chain of belief that made it possible to perform the mental magic that must happen before the transcendental magic can occur. One described it to me as "sickening" and stated that she felt "ill for a week afterwards."

I have experienced it once myself when I was helping an inexperienced woman run a simple university meeting. I was holding together a circle with a lot of inexperienced people, when at the end of a successful rite she suddenly declared the circle open and seemed to throw away the carefully constructed protection we had been working to hold together. I and another experienced friend who was helping felt the energy drop instantly and quite horribly, as if we literally had held a large elastic band around the group and then had it broken abruptly letting pure energy out and all manner of mixed energies from the student union into our vulnerable psyches. Since we were in a magical trance state, accessing all the experience we had to hold the circle for people who were not used to it all, the random energies of the student union felt magnified

---

[2]Luhrmann, T. M., *Persuasions of the Witch's Craft: Ritual Magic in Contemporary England.* Oxford: Blackwell, 1989.

and oppressive, and we both instantly had to shut down our own magico-mental space as quickly as we could. When we compared experiences later we found that we had both used closure techniques that mirrored concepts of the chakras, Reiki, Tai Chi, and the New Age aura systems, to shut down and protect ourselves and our psyches by the quickest means possible.[3] It was a mistake neither of us made again, and now our 'open' work is much more diluted, in which neither of us open out as much as we might in a coven of like-minded friends. Leading Wiccan author Viviane Crowe writes extensively on the chakras and Wicca, and I have found that it is not system I tend to use at all, but in this instance the system made instant sense.

Janet and Stewart Farrar's books have formed the template of many Wiccans' early work in creating ritual. They describe the circle as a sphere, a protective bubble that will contain the energy the coven raises and buffers them from the world outside. This bubble is formed by layers of ritual words, gesture, and meaning. These layers are reinforced visually, physically, aurally, and olfactorily by concentration used in performing these ritual gestures, the specific sound of bells, and soft temple music, along with the smell of the incense and the shimmer it brings to the circle. The familiar yet otherworldly beauty of the prepared circle transports Wiccans to another reality, grips their imaginations, and moves them from the mundane to the magical space in which the rites take place.

Liminal Change - Magical Level One – Step Three
Protecting the Circle

Once the sacred space has been defined it is protected. Geometrically the circle is counterpointed by including the cardinal directions, where it becomes a kind of compass and is a 'circle squared'. Each cardinal point is known as a watchtower or a quarter. Watchtower rituals have a very long history and are particularly associated with the Elizabethan magic of John Dee, Queen Elizabeth I's astrologer. Quarters are a more modern appellation that refers to the quartered circle, with each watchtower or quarter corresponding to one of the four elements. The guardians of those elements are summoned. These guardians also have a long history in ceremonial magic and have been depicted under variant names according to tradition, although in Wicca they tend to now be standardized. The High Priest summons the lords of the elements at each cardinal point, asking them to guard the circle and witness the rite. He takes the ceremonial blade and draws an invoking pentagram appropriate to the element force he is summoning at each cardinal point. All members of the coven join in with the appropriate visualizations, working as a team, all using similar mental imagery and

---

[3]Leading Wiccan author Viviane Crowe writes extensively on the chakras and Wicca, and I have found that it is not system I tend to use at all, but in this instance the system made instant sense and I used it on a reflex.

psychic effort to ensure the benevolent presence of the 'mighty ones'. Once the coven is sure each guardian has turned up, attended by the appropriate elemental force, the High Priest says "Hail and welcome!" This is echoed by all, who bow to the summoned presence.

Liminal Change - Magical Level One – Step Four
Raising the Power

Once the elements have been summoned to the sacred circle the 'power is raised', which is done by dancing in a ring and chanting. A commonly used chant is known as the 'Witches Rune' by Doreen Valiente. As the chant continues the witches visualize a cone of power raising from the ground and beginning to whirl around the circle, the chant increases in velocity and in fervor until it peaks, and as the final chorus winds around the temple, stone circle, or wood, the cone of power is flung upwards and settles to veil the circle from the outside world keeping the magical power within, and as some say, to "raise the temple to the stars." Only now are the people and place ready for the invocation of the gods. The cone of power is very much aligned to the triangle of manifestation in ceremonial magic, but in Wicca this is inside the circle rather than outside of it, as it is an aid to the invocation of deity rather than the evocation of spirit. As once described by Petrus Bonus, the medieval Italian alchemist,

> In this conjunction of resurrection, the body becomes wholly spiritual, like the soul herself, and they are made one as water is mixed with water, and henceforth they are not separated for ever, since there is no diversity in them, but unity and identity of all three, that is, spirit, soul and body, without separation forever.[4]

Central Rites of Invoking the Gods

The slow but sure journey from mundane consciousness to magico-religious trance has now been accomplished, and the circle is set and the ritual can proceed. Now and only now can a nominated High Priest and Priestess 'take on' the God and Goddess. This is considered to be one of the most important parts of any rite and one of the most sacred aspects of the Wiccan experience. It is at the heart of the Priest's and Priestess' path of Wicca, in which the gods are embodied physically by members of the coven. This possession by deity is unlike the ecstatic Vodou traditions of the African diaspora. It is facilitated within a ritual framework that owes much to Western ceremonial magical forms, and the deepest form of the possession only lasts throughout the short and dignified ritual drama. It is however believed to have a permeating effect on all

---

[4]Fabricius, *Alchemy: The Medieval Alchemists and Their Royal Art*, p. 198.

participants in the rite.

Each circle is 'built' up to the moment when a male and female initiate stand close to the altar and the Wiccan deity is invoked into them by another initiate, using ritual intention, gesture, and words, backed up by similar intent from the rest of the coven. When entranced they speak for the gods either with a 'charge', a piece of prose that draws on previous experiences of this state, or spontaneously from the depths of the entrancement. The experience felt by the invokee and all other members of the coven at this point is believed to be one of the ineffable mysteries at the heart of Wicca itself. Often the deity invoked is a seasonal aspect of Wiccan divinity, as portrayed by the gods of the elder pantheons. Thus it is an anthropomorphic presentation of the seasonal, stellar, or solar cycle. Integrating the ancient, and some say archetypal symbolism into one's psyche, has a powerful effect on the ritualist who 'carries' the God or Goddess, as well as the ritualists who experience the God or Goddess manifesting in the hermetically sealed psychic space they have created. The transformatory experience lingers on and it is believed to be a major part of the spiritual journey of each initiate.

In certain rites it is customary for each member of the coven to come before the person who is channeling the divine force to receive a blessing, which sometimes is wordless and brief. Witches report a much altered state of consciousness at this point, with invokees often not remembering what they said or for how long anyone communed with them, and are also sometimes seen to have appeared physically changed during the rite. Those who commune with the gods often feel that they receive answers to questions they were looking for, healing, or comfort in times of stress.

The most commonly used charge in Wicca is the Goddess Charge, which was created by Doreen Valiente in the 1950s from earlier versions that drew upon various older sacred and ethnographic sources. It finishes with the Goddess saying, "if that which thou seekest without thee, thou findest not within thee, thou shalt never find it; for I have been with thee from the beginning and am that which is attained at the end of desire." In Wiccan rituals the initiates experience the gods as being both without and within, discrete and greater entities or archetypes, and a part of the greater divine of which we are all a reflection. After ritual upon ritual, where each member of the coven becomes the God or Goddess incarnate and feels the power and liberation of that moment, there is no going back. For Wiccans the gods are always with them, within touching distance, and just a whisper away.

The Central Rite of Sabbat

Sabbat ceremonies begin in sacred space that is built as normal, but the ritual invocations are conducted within mythic psychodramas drawn from various ancient or folkloric sources. They incorporate enactment of Wiccan philosophies regarding the human life cycle from preconception to reincarnation and its place in the cycles of the cosmos. The rites anthropomorphize nature whilst celebrating ancient and universal festivals of seasonal change, hope, harvest, and honoring the dead. Participants are constantly reminded that there is the Wheel of Life that all must pass through. Each sabbat has particular ritual and festivities linked to it. Samhain is the feast for the dead in which the newly departed and the ancestors are honored. It offers connection to the ancestors and an understanding of the flow of the life force though the aeons, as well as a valuable space for allowing unresolved grief and sadness to be felt and actively remembering those we love. Samhain's polar opposite is Beltane, in which the peaking of the life force around the first of May is celebrated with joy for the coming of summer and much merry maypole dancing. Festivals are a time of celebration and feasting, as the dance of Goddess and God take the initiates around the changing seasons. Taking part in such ceremonies is believed to unveil the mysteries in nature as the Wheel of Life turns, with each witch gaining their own ever growing personalized understanding of eternal ineffable truths about life and death in the universe, in which these forces interplay with each other.

The Central Rite of Esbat

Esbats, or full moon circles, are celebrated on the thirteen full moons of the year. They begin as all circles begin and include invocations of the God and Goddess, but they also focus on spellcraft. Effecting change through magic is believed to be possible by working with the gods, the tides of nature, and an understanding of the connections in the interconnected web of the universe. Spells can take many forms and are a type of creative visualization-focused prayer. Wiccans include the use of dancing, chanting, incense, trance, and meditation in their work, and use various tools to help them. Concentration is aided by knotting cords or whirling round in a cord wheel. Incense, herbs, and potions are used ingredients that are linked in the witches' minds to the desired outcome. Talismans codify and draw on energies that are believed to be evocable according to the phases of the celestial bodies. In some ways the accoutrements of magic, such as ceremonial wands, are just props, but they are powerful props since they have been consecrated with intent and are believed to be imbued with the magic that they have performed over the years, as well as being psychologically associated with the forces of the universe that they represent. When the witch begins to dance around the circle using long familiar words or grasps the tools that have been used for magic over the years, they leave behind other layers of rational thought and go with the flow of the rite they are enacting until all is concentrated on that intentional moment and all is left behind, except the moment and the achievement. For that instant nothing else is the focus of thought, word, and deed of everyone in the room, and then the intent is flung out into the ether to take root and manifest. At this point the rite continues.

The Central Rite of Cakes and Wine

At the end of formal ritual and spellcraft, Wiccans always enact a ceremony of cakes and wine. This is at once the peak of the rite and the beginning of its closure. Wicca ritually externalizes the quest for integrated self that is at the heart of much psychology and philosophical thought. In Wiccan ritual the High Priestess carries the sword, which is the male symbol, and the High Priest carries the cup, the female symbol. At the final consecration of the communion wine the High Priest kneels before the High Priestess, salutes her as the Goddess, and in an integrated ritual action by both parties the sword and cup unite. For Wiccans this ritual of cakes and wine is a sacred moment when the masculine and feminine unite as one, but in a ritual setting that emphasizes the yin yang balance of two halves of one whole. At this moment the people enacting the cakes and wine, which is symbolically the Great Rite of union of male and female, release the powers that have been invoked into them and the energies that remain are channeled into the communion cup to be physically shared amongst all participants. After the cup has been consecrated and the food shared, the High Priest asks the High Priestess, "will Goddess join the mortals," and she replies, "let us sit as Witches," at which point the ritual part of the evening is over and all relax.

Liminal Change - Magical Level Two – Step One
Feasting

After cakes and wine it is time to enjoy and celebrate the sacred space that has been created. The work has been done and now it must be grounded. Feasting is a time of fun, frolic, and good food, which often leads to singing and making music, to dancing and to talking about magic, and leading into jokes about the evening or the group. The eating is very much a celebration of all that has been achieved, as well as a celebration of the season's offerings in food and appropriate beverages. It can be great fun and last for a long time with wild dancing or quiet contemplation. Whatever it turns out to be, it is a place of mental and magical decompression, with the participants moving through layers of their psyche, as a diver moves though the depths to the surface and the world of land and air. It is a place to become more aware of the body where people may feel cold and don cloaks, tired or energized, depending on the what rites have been performed and what part they took in the rite. The feast is seen to ground the participants to bring them back to a less ethereal sense of being and the length of time it take varies enormously depending on how the ritual went and how the participants feel. At a certain point the feast will slide from a hallowed fellowship close in feeling to the cakes and wine to a more mundane consciousness when the time arrives to clear things away and return through the spiral maze to whence the circle was entered.

Liminal Change – Magical level Two - Step Two
Closure

After the ritual and the magic, each circle winds down out of the maze, coming back through the maze through complex yet familiar signs, symbols, gestures, and words. It is custom to say a closing prayer where some people choose to put this right at the end of the rite to closely mirror the path by which they entered the spiral maze, but most choose to use one to end the last active part of the rite before winding out of the circle through the watchtowers. This prayer gives thanks to deities, spirits, elemental beings, and all that have been at the rite, followed by a more formal license to depart as used in ceremonial magic, but which in essence performs the same function.

The circle is closed by bidding goodbye to the lords of the elements and devoking the pentagrams that were earlier invoked. Different Wiccan lineages use different forms of the pentagram to summon the watchtowers, but whichever have been used are literally reversed in an act of banishing. Some covens teach the visualization of the reabsorption of energy that was projected from the invoking tool as the devoking pentagram is drawn. The lords of the elements are bid hail and farewell, and the devoker turns to the center and says, "Merry meet and merry part and merry meet again." This is followed by hugs all round before the witches leave the circle. This may be the only physical contact coven members have shared all evening and serves to ground the participants further by bringing them back to a more physical state, as well as emphasizing the social nature of the group.

A final act of ritual significance is the libation of the cakes and wine, some of which is always reserved and dedicated to the gods, returning the divine force back to the earth in an act of sacrifice, prayer, and thanksgiving. This is reverently cast to the ground, returning the essence of the divine to the earth in a final act of sealing and closure, which may be done after the circle has closed.

Liminal Change - Mundane Level Two
Closure

The coven now seeks closure in the mundane realm, normal clothing is put back on, dishes cleared, washing up done followed by coffee, tea, and general chat with the conversation moving from the magical to the mundane, such as lifts home or who is sleeping where if staying the night. The mundane activities of tidying and sorting bring the witches back to normal bodily consciousness, and it is at this point that the circle is truly over. As it started with tea and coffee, it ends with tea and coffee, the elixir of life and panacea in British culture from whence modern Wicca arose. The symbolism of that tea is not to be underestimated, as it is what is offered to any guest and at any moment of repose in general. It is that which underscores the social element of the group and the return to the routines and norms of the mundane, as much as it is a cue to leave the premises and a refreshing drink.

The effects of the magical ritual may not be immediately apparent and participants may take some time to return fully to normal consciousness, as they will see omens or experience synchronicities that relate to the rite. It is normal to encourage the keeping of a diary to record such phenomena and dreams that follow, which can yield rich material when analyzed long after the rite has receded from memory.

Clothing, or the lack of it, plays an important part in the suspension of 'normal' consciousness and creation of an alternative reality. Skyclad is common in Wiccan ritual. Gerald Gardner, the first leading figure in the revival of modern Witchcraft, was a fervent nudist, firmly believing in the health giving properties of sun and air bathing. He was so ardent in this belief that he owned the five acres nudist colony in St. Albans and held his coven meetings there in a cottage in the woods. Nudity is often seen as a daunting proposition prior to initiation, not because of a lack of trust in the coven, but because of a fundamental fear of looking ugly or inadequate. After initiation many Wiccans report a feeling of liberation and fast growing confidence in their bodies. Nudity during the first initiation adds to feelings of nervousness and helplessness, however the rite itself soon takes over the initiate's conscious mind and many often report that they only remember being naked when they prepare to leave the circle. Nudity also increases the intimacy of the group in that one is more likely to trust a group of people with whom one is so intimate. Robes and ritual regalia also help to shift consciousness through otherworldy and iconic imagery. Jewelry may be consecrated, or have certain connections to various lineages of witches.

The maze has appeared throughout time as a symbol of the path that must be negotiated to reach other levels of consciousness and to contact other worlds. Labyrinths feature in myth, legend, folklore, and mandalas in the spiritual traditions of the East. The spiral is a useful symbol to work with when thinking of moving through levels of consciousness, particularly in its symbolism of the return journey where one can exit the maze and return safely to mundane consciousness. It offers a series of doorways that lead to a place of seclusion and safety where we are shut off from the outside world. That outside world then becomes 'other' to the reality of magical consciousness for the duration of the rite. Reaching and leaving other worlds and consciousnesses successfully requires care and guidance from others that have trod the maze before, others who may have been part of setting up whatever particular maze we walk through in the form of ritual, tradition, and initiatory experience. Ancient esoteric systems provide maps for traversing such mazes, albeit in their own forms, with the Kabbalah in particular being favored by Western magicians.

In sociological terms Wicca is a religion that offers a re-sacralized and re-enchanted world view, with a communitas that is world affirming, for example made up of people who walk between the worlds using ancient magical methods to enrich their daily lives. The rites described here are key markers in the re-enchantment and re-sacralization of the religious landscape of the West through contemporary paganism, magic, and related spiritualties. An exploration of academic literature on ritual leads to a complex debate on the meaning of ritual and belief, which often contests the simpler Gennep/Turner/Geertz models. Practitioners tend to simply accept and work with the paradigm that ritual is action based on belief, taking these words at face value, then contesting the results, rather than deconstructing the meaning of the methodology. This would tend to be in psycho-magical discourse, with popular scholarly books emphasizing the psychological, such as Vivianne Crowley's *Wicca* [5], which explains various aspects of magical consciousness in Jungian terms, and Serena Roney Douglas' *Where Science and Magic Meet* [6]. Within academia, pagan scholars, such as Susan Greenwood, have offered a new rapprochement between the academic study of anthropology and the reality and validity of practitioners' experience of magic and the otherworld, which may herald a new paradigm in understanding contemporary ritual.

In practical terms, witches carry their gods within them in the living temples of their hearts, setting up sacred space as when and wherever it is needed. Most of the guidance on building these temples of living devotion is taught within the oral tradition and dies with each mentor, thus creating a religion that is lived in word, breath, body, and blood, transmuting with the spirits of those that live it but never dying away. Practitioners may gather at sacred spaces of the ancestors, such as stone circles, but when they leave they leave nothing tangible apart from a tingle in the atmosphere, the whisper of their words in the wind, and a trace of incense in the air. But results and the markers of these rites remain, for with each rite they are etched ever more deeply into the witches' psyches where a silver trail glimmers lightly, guiding their next journey back through the hidden pathways of the spiral maze to the spiritual treasure at its heart.

[5]Crowley, Vivianne, *Wicca: The Old Religion in the New Age*, London: Aquarian Press, 1989.
[6]Douglas, Serena Roney, *Where Science and Magic Meet, Exploring our Psychic Birthright*. Somerset: Green Magic Publishing, 2010.

BIBLIOGRAPHY

Agrippa, H. C., *Three Books of Occult Philosophy*. London: Chthonios Books, 1986.

Bell, Catherine, *Ritual: Perspectives and Dimensions*. Oxford: Oxford University Press, 2010.

Bonus, Petrus, *Introductio in divinam Chemiae artem*. Rome: Basilea, 1572

Bracelin, Jack L., *Gerald Gardner, Witch*. London: Octogon Press, 1960.

Crowley, Vivianne, *Wicca: The Old Religion in the New Age*. London: Aquarian Press, 1989.

Dee, John in Casaubon, Meric, D. D. (ed.), *A True and Faithful Relation of What Passed for many Yeers Between John Dee... and some spirits...* New York: Magickal Childe Publishing, 1992.

Dee, John, *Quinti Libri Mysteriorum*. British Library, MS Sloane Collection 3188.

D'Este, Sorita and Rankine, David, *Wicca Magickal Beginnings: A Study of the Possible Origins of the Rituals and Practices found in this Modern Tradition of Pagan Witchcraft and Magick*. London: Avalonia, 2008.

Douglas, Serena Roney, *Where Science and Magic Meet, Exploring our Psychic Birthright*. Somerset: Green Magic Publishing, 2010.

Fabricius, Johannes, *Alchemy: The Medieval Alchemists and Their Royal Art*. Texas: Bookman, 1996.

Farrar, Janet, and Farrar, Stewart, *The Witches Way: Principles, Rituals and Beliefs of Modern Witchcraft*. London: Robert Hale, 1984.

Gilchrist, Charles, *Sacred Geometry*. www.charlesgilchrist.com, 2011.

Greenwood, Susan, *The Anthropology of Magic*. London: Berg, 2010.

Harvey, Graham, *Ritual and Religious Belief: A Reader*. London: Equinox Publishing Ltd., 2005.

Hutton, Ronald, *The Triumph of the Moon, A History of Modern Pagan Witchcraft*. Oxford: Oxford University Press, 1999.

Jung, Carl G., *The Red Book, Liber Novus*. Edited by Sonu Shamdasani and Mark Kyburz, and translated by John Peck. New York: W. W. Norton and Co., 2009.

Luhrmann, T. M., *Persuasions of the Witches Craft: Ritual Magic in Contemporary England*. Oxford: Blackwell, 1989.

Partridge, Christopher, *The Re-Enchantment of the West, Vol. 1: Alternative Spiritualities, Sacrililzation, Popular Culture and Occulture*. London: Continuum, 2004.

Starhawk, *The Spiral Dance: A Rebirth of the Ancient Religion of the Great Goddess*. San Francisco: Harper, 1999.

Turner, Victor W., *The Ritual Process: Structure and Anti-Structure*. Chicago: Aldine, 1966

Valiente, Doreen, *An ABC of Witchcraft Past and Present*. London: Robert Hale, 1973.

Valiente, Doreen, *Natural Magic*. London: Robert Hale, 1975.

Valiente, Doreen, *Witchcraft for Tomorrow*. London: Robert Hale, 1978.

Valiente, Doreen, *The Rebirth of Witchcraft*. London: Robert Hale, 1989.

Van Gennep, Arnold, *The Rites of Passage*. Translated by M. B. Vizedom and G. L. Caffee. Chicago: University of Chicago Press, 1960.

Von Worms, Abraham, *The Book of Abramelin: A New Translation*. Edited by Georg Dehn. Lake Worth: Nicholas Hays, 2006.

AKEPHALOS BEING AN ATTEMPTED RESTORATION OF THE RITE OF THE HEADLESS ONE, ACCORDING TO THE STELE OF JEU THE HIEROGLYPHIST

BY

MATTHEW LEVI STEVENS

I summon you, the Headless One, who created earth and heaven, who created night and the day, you who created the light and the darkness.

PGM V. 96-99

Here is an outline of the Rite of the Headless One, based on the text given in the *Stele of Jeu the Hieroglyphist*, with my attempt at a pronunciation guide for each 'barbarous' name and word in the footnotes for English speakers who did not have the benefit of a classical education including ancient Greek.

First write the characters of the names ΑΩΘ ΑΒΡΑΩΘ ΒΑΣΥΜ ΙΣΑΚ ΣΑΒΑΩΘ ΙΑΩ on a strip of clean papyrus. As in this first instance the names are to be written, rather than spoken, and it makes more sense to me that this should be done in the original Greek characters. Having done so, mark either end of the strip with the 'beneficial sign',

Then hold the strip to your forehead, stretched from temple to temple, the names facing outward. Take up position at your altar, or other place of working, and face the north. Visualise the strip as a serpent swallowing its own tail and vibrate the names,

AÔTH ABRAÔTH BASYM ISAK SABAÔTH IAÔ.[1]

As you do so, imagine your mind expanding to the very limits of consciousness, until the Ouroboros encircles the cosmos, the names you have vibrated radiating out through

---

[1] 'Ar-ot' arb-Ra-rot' bar-zoom ee-zark zar-ba-rot' ee-ar-o.

the universe and begin to recite the following, vibrating the names and words of power where indicated,

> I summon you, the Headless One, who created earth and heaven, who created night and the day, you who created the light and the darkness; you are Osoronnophris, whom none has ever seen; you are Iabas; you are Iapos; you have distinguished the just and the unjust; you have made the female and the male; you have revealed the seed and the fruits; you have made men love each other and hate each other.

> I am Moses your prophet to whom you have transmitted your mysteries celebrated by Israel; you have revealed the moist and the dry and all nourishment; hear me!

> I am the messenger of Pharaoh Osoronnophris;[2] this is your true name which has been transmitted to the prophets of Israel. Hear me, ARBATHIAÔ REIBET ATHELEBERSÊTH ARA BLATHA ALBEU EBENPHCHI CHITASGOE IBAÔTH IAÔ;[3] listen to me and turn away this daimon.

> I call upon you, awesome and invisible god with an empty spirit, AROGOGROROBRAÔ SOCHOU MODORIÔ PHALARCHAÔ OOO.[4] Holy Headless One, deliver him,[5] from the daimon which restrains him, ROUBRIAÔ MARI ÔDAM BAABNAÔTH ASS ADÔNAI APHNIAÔ ITHÔLÊTH ABRASAX AÊÔÔY;[6] mighty Headless One, deliver him,[7] from the daimon which restrains him, MABARRAIÔ IOÊL KOTHA ATHORÊBALÔ ABRAÔTH[8] deliver him,[9] AÔTH ABRAÔTH BASYM ISAK SABAÔTH IAÔ.[10]

> He is the lord of the gods; he is the lord of the inhabited world; he is the one whom the winds fear; he is the one who made all things by the command of his voice.

---

[2]The obvious interpretation is that this name is a form of Osiris. One of Crowley's perhaps more credible innovations is that this is a corruption of the Egyptian *asar-un-nefer*, meaning 'myself made perfect'.

[3]ar-R-bar-t'-ee-ar-o Re-ee-bet ar-t'-el-eb-eR-set' ar-Ra blart'ar arl-bew eh-behn-F-khee kht'ars-go-ee ee-bar-ot' ee-ar-o.

[4] ar-Rog-og-Ro-Rob-Rar-o so-khoo mo-do-Rio F-ar-lar-R-khar-o o-o-o.

[5]You are to state the name of the person who this rite is being performed for.

[6]Roob-Ree-ar-o mar-R-ee o-darm bar-arb-nar-ot' arz-ss ar-don-ey ar-F-nee-ar-o eet'o-let' ar-bR-ar-zarks ar-er-o-o-oo.

[7]You are to state the name of the person who this rite is being performed for.

[8]mar-bar-R-rar-ee-o ee-o-el ko-t'ar art'o-R-eeb-ar-lo arb-ra-rot.

[9]You are to state the name of the person who this rite is being performed for.

[10]ar-ot' arb-ra-rot' bar-zoom ee-zark zar-bar-ot' ee-ar-o.

Lord, King, Master, Helper, save the soul IEOU PYR IOU PYR IAÔT IAÊÔ IOOU ABRASAX SABRIAM OO YY AY OO YY ADÔNAIE,[11] immediately, immediately, good messenger of God ANLALA LAI GAIA APA DIACHANNA CHORYN.[12]

I am the headless daimon with my sight in my feet; I am the mighty one who possesses the immortal fire; I am the truth who hates the fact that unjust deeds are done in the world; I am the one who makes the lightning flash and the thunder roll; I am the one whose sweat falls upon the earth as rain so that it can inseminate it; I am the one whose mouth burns completely; I am the one who begets and destroys; I am the Favor of the Aion; my name is a heart encircled by a serpent; come forth and follow.

Upon successful completion of the rite, it is said that the Headless[13] One will appear and subject to you all daimons, "so that every daimon, whether heavenly or aerial or earthly or subterranean or terrestrial or aquatic, might be obedient to you and every spell and scourge which is from God." Here the papyrus adds, just for good measure, "And all daimons will be obedient to you."[14] What more could one want?

This strange and potent rite, with its heady mix of Egyptian, Greek, Jewish, and even Samaritan ideas of God, barbarous names of invocation, and strange words of power, is quite possibly the entry point of a key concept into the Western Magical Tradition, and perhaps constitutes the foundation stone of a whole occult tradition of its own. Its worldly origins are lost in antiquity, coming down to us in an obscure fragment of papyrus that was, perhaps, a last desperate attempt to preserve something of the Old World of the many gods before it was too late and the new world order of the One True God closing the door on magic forever, or at least tried to. Resurfacing as an antiquarian curiosity in Victorian times, it is undoubtedly the adoption of the rite by one of the most notorious enfant terrible of that era, the self-styled 'Great Beast', Aleister Crowley, which has contributed most to its survival into contemporary occultism. However, I would argue that it is also due to his efforts that most readers are only aware of a distorted and heavily embroidered version. It is time to strip away the obfuscations of the last hundred years and try to get to grips with the original in all its potent and puzzling glory.

---

[11]ee-eh-oo poo-R ee-oo poo-R ee-ar-ot' ee-ar-er-o ee-o-o-oo ar-bR-ar-zarks sarb-R-ee-em o-o oo-oo ey o-o ee-ee ar-don-ar-ee-ay.
[12]arn-lar-lar lar-ee g-ay-ar arp-ar d-ay-ar-kharn-nar kho-R-oon.
[13]Somewhere between Goodwin's original and Crowley's adaptation, the Greek *Akephalos*, meaning literally 'Headless', but also perhaps 'without beginning', came to be replaced by the approximation 'Bornless'. This is the name that has stuck ever since, but the present author feels it is more authentic to restore the meaning that, even if it is stranger, can perhaps be considered more authentic.
[14]This version of the Rite of the Headless One is taken from Betz, Hans Dieter (ed.), *The Greek Magical Papyri in Translation, including the Demotic Spells*. Chicago: University of Chicago Press, 1996.

Much of contemporary occultism continues to draw from, and be shaped by, the foundation laid down at the end of the nineteenth century by the Hermetic Order of the Golden Dawn, and then built upon by not only its most infamous student Aleister Crowley. Crowley took the bones of their teachings and used them to shape the conceptual framework of his New Aeon cult of Thelema, and also the rituals of the various Orders he created and re-created to serve it, such as the Argenteum Astrum and the Ordo Templi Orientis, to name but two. This dual influence continues to spread throughout almost all of Western magic, and much of neopaganism in general, but also his peers and progeny, from Dion Fortune to Israel Regardie and Kenneth Grant, and not forgetting that even freewheelers like Austin Osman Spare and Gerald Gardner also had some acquaintance with or background in the likes of the A∴A∴ and O.T.O. So we see this influence crop up again and again, not just among the 'usual suspects', such as the various groups claiming descent from the Golden Dawn or Crowley, but also among less obvious 'heirs', including Chaos magic, the various branches of Wicca, Voudon-Gnostic practitioners, the Church of Satan along with its various copyists, and a Left Hand Path school like the Temple of Set.

One concept that originates from this wellspring, and is indeed symptomatic of just how widespread its influence has been, is the Knowledge and Conversation of the Holy Guardian Angel, which is a series of rites aimed at connecting the practitioner with what may be considered as anything from a Higher Self to literally the intermediary or even embodiment of whatever deity he or she chooses to engage with. Whether it be thought of as the *genius* of the Hermetic Order of the Golden Dawn, the *augoeides* of Iamblichus, the *atman* of Hinduism, the *daimon* of the ancient Greeks, or indeed, either a literal messenger from the divine or the idealised embodiment of all that is highest and best in one's True Self. The seeking of contact with this entity is considered by many to be the central most important operation in magic, which should not only come above and before any other, but of which success or failure is a key determinant as to any further progress.

Aleister Crowley writes in 'Chapter 83' in *Magick Without Tears*, "It should never be forgotten for a single moment that the central and essential work of the Magician is the attainment of the Knowledge and Conversation of the Holy Guardian Angel."[15] And in 'Chapter 21' of his magnum opus *Book 4* he goes as far as to say,

> ...the Single Supreme Ritual is the attainment of the Knowledge and Conversation of the Holy Guardian Angel. It is the raising of the complete man in a vertical straight line... If the magician needs to perform any other operation than this, it is only lawful in so far as it is a necessary preliminary to That One Work.[16]

---

[15]Crowley, *Magick Without Tears*, p.107.
[16]Crowley, *Book 4*, p. 91.

The origin of this idea, of attaining to the Knowledge and Conversation of the Holy Guardian Angel, can be found in the *Book of the Sacred Magic of Abramelin the Mage*, attributed to one Abraham of Worms.[17] This classic grimoire was translated into English by the head of the Golden Dawn, Samuel Liddell MacGregor Mathers, and its system formed a cornerstone of that Order's method. Crowley was most likely introduced to it by either his unofficial mentor within the Order, Alan Bennett, or fellow initiate George Cecil Jones, with whom he would later founded the Argenteum Astrum in a short-lived attempt to create a 'New! Improved!' version of the Golden Dawn. Abramelin presents a long, complicated program of arduous and gruelling devotions, involving six months of repeated celibacy, fasting, all-night prayer vigil, meditations, and rituals of ever-increasing frequency and intensity, requiring the aspirant to take time off from work, marriage, and family life, and also purchase a property just to create the right environment for the working.

Not surprisingly, this has proven to be a major stumbling block, even for independently wealthy men like the young Crowley, but the lure of a direct hotline to God or whatever would reveal to you your True Will and give you power over angels, demons, and elementals, thereby opening up all the powers of magic, was not to be given up in a hurry. When the Abbey of Thelema was created in Cefalù, Sicily in the 1920s with the express intent of being a spiritual college where aspiring adepts could learn how best to discover their True Wills, the question of attaining to the Knowledge and Conversation of the Holy Guardian Angel became a burning one. After a particularly promising student Frank Bennett had experienced a spontaneous Gnostic 'contact', Crowley penned *Liber Samekh*, which was first published as an appendix to his *Magick in Theory and Practice*, with the hope that it would be an express handbook for the process. His source for the ritual he penned was the Rite of The Headless One, which he had already published as the preliminary invocation of his edition of the *Goetia* as far back as 1904. Although the original text of the *Stele of Jeu the Hieroglyphist* has no connection whatsoever with the *Ars Goetia* of the seventeenth century grimoire known as the *Lesser Key of Solomon*, in many people's minds the association has stuck.

The true origins of the *Stele of Jeu the Hieroglyphist*, who wrote it, when, where, and why,, are lost in the mist of antiquity. Little or nothing of any certainty is known, but we can perhaps imagine along certain lines. The *Stele of Jeu the Hieroglyphist*[18] was most likely written by a wandering scribe who was still able to read Egyptian hieroglyphs and who probably eked out a living transcribing texts for a clientele who wanted to be able to access the esoteric wisdom of the Egyptians, but regrettably were without

---

[17]This is just one manifestation of the legend of the Jews as magicians that we will see surface in this tale.
[18]It has been suggested that the author was simply 'a Jew' who knew hieroglyphs. Some connection has been made with the Gnostic *Books of Jeu*. As these are also known as the *Books of IEOU*, a vowel sequence is obviously suggestive of the Greek Hermetica, but perhaps such attributions are misleading. Curiously, the *Books of Jeu* deal with the creation of Aeons by way of 'Knowledge of a Word'.

the ritual framework of temple practice. Like many of the papyri, this was found in a cache of papers sealed in amphorae and stashed against discovery and the elements in a cave. The brothers Ali, who were looking for a stray goat, literally stumbled onto the cache amid pottery fragments, and quickly realised they were on to something. From there the papyrus made its way, via the then unregulated black market in Egyptian antiquities, into the hands of the Swedish consul in Alexandria, a Mr Anastasi, who later sold it to the British Museum in London.

The first translation to appear anywhere was by a Dr William Goodwin, who published in 1852 as *Fragment of a Graeco-Egyptian Work Upon Magic*.[19] Goodwin was fairly scathing in his comments upon the text dismissing the combination of Egyptian, Greek, and Jewish terms as symptomatic of the confusion of the more pagan Gnostics, and the barbarous words of power as being akin to the gibberish of the superstitiously primitive. Despite this, it came to the attention of Mathers and his Golden Dawn, who thought it was just the sort of thing they needed to lend their ritual theatrics a touch of Greco-Egyptian authenticity. One of the central premises of the Rite of the Bornless One is that man can act as God. Goodwin quotes Porphyry in regard to this heresy,

> The magician lies in order to compel the heavenly powers to tell the truth: for when he threatens to shake the heavens, or to reveal the mysteries of Isis, or the secret thing that lies hid at Abydos, or to stop the sacred boat, or to scatter the limbs of Osiris to Typhon, what a height of madness does it imply in the man who thus threatens what he neither understands nor is able to perform.[20]

I see the text as a survival of the Egyptian origins of theurgy. Egyptian priests generally divided their time in office between two particular types of role, the first being *sems-neter*, where they were in the service of the gods performing mostly temple duties and officiating at ceremonies; and the second being *paxer-neter*, where they were literally acting as gods to cast spells, perform divination, and so on. Here, perhaps, is one of the beginnings of the split between what has come to be thought of as all-too-separate categories, with 'religion' in the case of the former, and 'magic' in the case of the latter.

The Rite of the Headless One draws, at the time of writing, on the newly established idea of Moses being the prototype magus who saw God face-to-face and came back with His Word to impart His Law and act in His Authority. In his *Vita Mosis*, Philo of Alexandria, a contemporary of Christ and the Apostles, added to the already accepted notion of Moses as prophet and lawgiver the concept of the 'superior magician' representing *Logos*, 'Word',, and articulating a *Nomos*, 'Law', based on that *Logos*;

[19]Goodwin, William, *Fragment of Graeco-Egyptian Work on Magic, from a papyrus in the British Museum.* Cambridge: Deighton, Macmillan and Co., 1852.
[20]Goodwin, *Fragment of Graeco-Egyptian Work on Magic, from a papyrus in the British Museum*, p. vi.

secondly, that such a magus no longer needed to be transported in ecstasy like the shamans of old to receive intimations of the divine, but can instead be raised up so that he apprehends them through direct personal knowledge, or gnosis.

As such, the Rite of the Headless One may be seen as the seed by which the ultimate blasphemy against the spiritual monopoly of the monotheist religions survived to later re-manifest in our postmodern world, for surely the goal of the magus has always been, rather than simply to know the Will of God and be its instrument or vessel, to act as such in his own right? This too is ultimately the breaking point between the Right Hand Path and the much-maligned Left Hand Path, inasmuch as they can be considered to have any real validity in the modern world, as hopelessly divorced as it is from both nature and any idea of the divine, that the key difference in approach is ultimately whether one seeks to subsume oneself in service of some higher power, whether that be Church, God, Nature, or State, or whether they would continually seek to define, examine, refine, and apply their own individual sovereignty.

Perhaps in the final analysis it is meaningless to ask whether one can ever truly act above whatever notion of God or the gods one has, but maybe it is enough to decide in which direction one's actions and intents are directed, such as whether to serve in another's kingdom or seek to assert one's own. To my mind the fact that the Rite of the Headless One is a survival from a time when such options were still considered, and is not a working whose end result is an ecstatic union with the divine, rather one in which an identification with the divine. Claiming the ability to act as such makes it an ideal tool for those of our times who would truly seek to walk the Path of the Magus, and in so doing speaking the Word that establishes a Law and creates a World. Few are called, fewer will try, and fewest still will succeed!

BIBLIOGRAPHY

Betz, Hans Dieter (ed.), *The Greek Magical Papyri in Translation including the Demotic Spells,* Chicago: University of Chicago Press, 1992.

Crowley, Aleister, *The Goetia.* Boleskine Foyers Inverness: Society for the Propagation of Religious Truth, 1904.

Crowley, Aleister, *Book 4.* London: Wieland and Co., 1913.

Crowley, Aleister, *The Confessions.* London: Mandrake Press, 1929.

Crowley, Aleister, *Magic Without Tears.* New Jersey: Thelema Publishing Co., 1954.

Flowers, Stephen E., *Hermetic Magic: The Postmodern Papyrus of Abaris.* Maine: Red Wheel/Weiser, 1995.

Goodwin, William, *Fragment of Graeco-Egyptian Work on Magic.* Cambridge: Deighton, Macmillan and Co., 1852.

Kaczynski, Richard, *Perdurabo: The Life of Aleister Crowley.* Arizona: New Falcon Publications, 2002.

Regardie, Israel, *Ceremonial Magic: A Guide to the Mechanisms of Ritual.* London: Aquarian Press, 1980.

Webb, Don, *Seven Faces of Darkness.* Texas: Runa-Raven, 1996.

THE HOLY GUARDIAN ANGEL
A GOLDEN THREAD IN THE TAPESTRY OF BEING AND BECOMING

BY

COMPANION ABRAXAS

Every human being is led and guided by the Holy Guardian Angel.
Yet only a few are aware of this.

Paul Foster Case, *Tarot Fundamentals*, Lesson 32

The study of the Holy Guardian Angel is multifaceted and has its image in the hearts and minds of many cultures and arcane histories of humanity. One of these images is found in Plato's Myth of Er, wherein Socrates describes how souls are sent into this world, each with a divine guiding spirit or angel, and how these angels guide each human being through this incarnation. However, the process, as we read, becomes one of self-discovery as those who return in the next incarnation must cross the Plain of Oblivion where the River of Forgetfulness flows. Each soul was required to drink some of the water in varying quantities, and as the new soul drank they forgot everything. So, in regards to the Holy Guardian Angel to whom we are granted as our guide in this incarnation, it becomes a task of reawakening from our forgetfulness as to our true nature. The Angel is not something separate from who and what we are, but is that innate spark of intelligence that gradually unfolds within each personality from one incarnation to the next, until full realization is clarified and we are finally made whole in the bonds of the One Universal Life.

The Holy Guardian Angel is the essence of our true nature, our higher selves perfect and whole in that totality which aligns it to us and us to the One Universal Life, which is the Qabalistic idea known as the Yechidah or the Universal Father-Mother. The Holy Guardian Angel is an archetype to which we can align ourselves in the process of becoming whole as individuated personalities through that which we call Knowledge and Conversation of the Holy Guardian Angel. Through the Holy Guardian Angel one discovers the hidden word of one's calling or vocation, which leads to the development of a personality through a process which Jung called 'individuation'. Through this rectifying process the Holy Guardian Angel guides us through a host of trials and tribulations along our Path of Return, which can be seen as an alchemical process where our seven interior stars or metals are refined and aligned to a cleaner and clearer expression of that 'still small voice' of our Holy Guardian Angel.

A great part of this process of regeneration is facilitated by a 'burning of the dross', as I call it, which at its heart is a psychotherapeutic process of purification. It is imperative to the process of Knowledge and Conversation that we slowly and wisely remove the mental and emotional obscurations that blind us from the Knowledge of our Angel. And in doing so we allow ourselves to listen to that subtle, intuitive communication that has been whispering to us from inception, and in that new found awareness seeking the inner dialogue of true Conversation with our Higher Self. That said, it is on this important note of dross burning that I wish to share an insightful quote from Paul Foster Case regarding the prime importance of this alchemical action,

> Incineration burns to ashes the dross and refuse of the old ways of thinking. It consumes all the residue of our erroneous interpretations of experience. This residue remains in subconsciousness even after putrefaction is complete.

> That is to say, even when we consciously attribute all action to the One Reality and deny the personal origination of anything whatever, latent tendencies remain which must be purged out.

> We ourselves cannot purge them out because self-consciousness cannot penetrate into the depths of subconsciousness. Hence the work of putrefaction must precede that of incineration because in the process of incineration something has to be brought to bear which cannot be done by the alchemist himself. A higher power has to be invoked. This is one reason that all sages are agreed that they owe their success in the Great Work to the Grace of God.

> In the work of incineration, a higher power takes the place of the alchemist. Recognition of this higher power is given in the Rosicrucian vow connected with Key 14: "I will look upon every circumstance of my life as a particular dealing of God with my soul." By "soul" we are to understand the whole psychic nature of man.

> In magical texts this stage of incineration is sometimes called "the knowledge and conversation of the Holy Guardian Angel."

> Incineration, therefore, is the purging and refinement of the desire nature, which, when it is thoroughly cleansed and purified, having passed through the death of its old forms, becomes the Great Medicine. Our own personal consciousness, as we have said, is inadequate for the performance of this part of the work. Yet the work itself proceeds from the level of self-consciousness into

the subconscious field where the actual incineration occurs.[1]

Herein then is the process from which the seven interior metals are fired by the life breath of the Holy Spirit, the Holy Guardian Angel, and made pure in that self-realization that proffers adepthood. This in turn is synonymous with individuation or that state of wholeness and beauty that comes when we are perfectly aligned with our True Will and the vocation or our life.

That said, the process is not for the faint of heart, but solely for those who desire to such a state of wholeness and that they are willing to enter into the regenerative flames with their whole being and face, 'the good, bad, and the ugly'. To do the Great Work of transmuting their interior lights to resonate with that one Light whose source is the One Universal Life. How to engender this process as an act of empowerment and not a lifeless expression of intellectual examination and emotional venting? Here is whispered the anecdote to all life's ills and the prime agent of wholeness and healing... Love. In the words of Paul Foster Case, I share the following wisdom,

Thus the practice of the Great Work calls for a third endeavor, in addition to the invocation of spiritual power from the level of superconsciousness, in addition to the daily and hourly turning of the mind inward toward the Center. This third endeavor is summed up in one word – LOVE.

For we can seek power from above, and make strenuous efforts to reach the Inner Center, and yet miss the one indispensable thing.

We may know intellectually that power comes from the superconscious, and be persuaded that the treasure of treasures is hidden within man himself. Yet if we seek power in order to wield it over others, or hunt for the treasure in order to give us an advantage over our fellows, we shall fail miserably in our quest for the Stone of the Wise.

The true occultist never forgets that he is in this school of life to gain knowledge and understanding of man, and to perfect himself in the art of LOVE. In all alchemical writings, the red stage is said to be the final completion of the Operation of the Sun. That is, knowledge and understanding though necessary, are but preliminary to LOVE, and without LOVE there is no fulfillment.

It is all summed up in the wise counsel of the best of alchemists:

"LOVE your enemies, bless them that curse you, do good to them that

---

[1]Case, *The Great Work*, Lesson 45.

despitefully use you."

Here we speak without any veils of metaphor. Not for the wise occultist is the meaningless, abstract LOVE for humanity that fools prate about.

In the practice we speak of now, the objects are definite and specific. Not those who are "our sort," not those for whom we feel a spontaneous sympathy, but those who "rub us the wrong way," and seem to us to be our natural antagonists, provide us daily and hourly with an inexhaustible supply of raw material for this part of the practice of alchemy.[2]

It is through this practice of Love that we heal that which lies between self and other, which is the error that has separated us from the Call of our Angel, from the word which would unite us with our totality. In the process of engendering love for ourselves, first and foremost, and then to those near and dear, and finally to the whole of humanity, we begin to bridge the ocean to that other shore whose solar radiance is our own reflection in the mirror of awakening. Ultimately, that is what has created and driven us from birth to death, and the 'calling' is one of Love finding our alignment to that principle that can bring us the union we seek in this Great Work. As Shaw writes,

> According to the [Chaldean] Oracles the Demiurge filled each soul with a "deep eros" (eros bathus) to draw it back to the gods. The deep eros of the Oracles, like the innate gnosis or essential desire (ephesis) of the De Mysteriis, was present in the soul but anterior to consciousness. It was the desire that drew the soul down into a mortal body and led it back to its immortal ochema (soul vehicle)...[3] That the soul's embodiment was the ultimate sunthema (receptacle) of its ascent remains an insoluble paradox, but appropriately, for the lover it is a commonplace experience. In the erotic dialectic discussed by Plato in the Symposium (200-202), the separation of the lover from the beloved was the sine qua non of their attraction and unification.[4]

And as is quoted in the *Book of the Law*,

> For I am divided for love's sake, for the chance of union.[5]

Through the practice of Love we develop spiritual eyes which are granted a truer vision of what has separated us from the divine. When these eyes are opened the enemies and adversaries of our life are recognized as friends wearing terrible masks while they show

---

[2]Case, *The Great Work*, Lesson 51.
[3]Shaw, *Theurgy and the Soul: The Neoplatonism of Iamblichus*, p. 124.
[4]Shaw, *Theurgy and the Soul: The Neoplatonism of Iamblichus*, p. 125.
[5]Crowley, *Liber AL vel Legis sub figura CCXX*, I, 29.

us how to engage in this game of life. Through this instruction we learn to transmute the illusory desires of the outer sense impressions and are enabled to remove the edifice of the mistaken assumption that there is a real separation between us and all sentient beings. In time, we discover the truth that everything in the field of manifestation is interrelated. We begin to see our personal existence as part of the whole cycle of being and becoming. We perceive that the events of today are directly connected with the entire past, and just as rightly united with the future.

This knowledge releases us from the bondage of delusion and suffering by unveiling the truth of our relations with the One Universal Life, as well as connecting us to the greater picture of human evolution as a larger process of the Great Work. For those who have arrived at the Gnosis of their Holy Guardian Angel and are in conversation with that intelligence, there is the definitive realization that the process is one of service to those still with obscurations veiling them from self-discovery. As Paul Foster Case informs us,

> It is conscious identification with Universal Spirit. Perfect peace, perfect bliss, perfect knowledge. All this it is, and more than this (Key 21).

> The Administrative Intelligence, which corresponds to the final Tarot Key (21), really means "the serving Intelligence."

> Cosmic consciousness, or the realization of identity with the universal Spirit, finds expression in work for the more complete manifestation of the heavenly order here on earth.

> He who knows the truth must live it. He becomes thenceforth a servant of the ALL. He does this, not as a duty hard to carry out, but as a natural expression of his realization of his true place in the cosmic order (Key 21). For such a person, all selfish preoccupation with personal aims is automatically at an end (Key 16).

> He looks on his personal existence as being a manifestation of that exquisite adjustment which maintains the cosmic equilibrium.

> In his vision, all he does is naught but the manifestation of Karma; and because he has made himself, as a personality, utterly receptive to the influx of the Universal Will, whatever action he engages in is extraordinarily effective (Key 11).[6]

And what aligns us to this Universal Will and that desire to connect it to our lives and

---

[6]Case, *Tarot Interpretations*, Lesson 32.

the Great Work? Upon recapitulation, it would seem that the whole process of life is towards the collective reunion of family whether in Heaven or the recollection of future incarnations of sentient life, which seems to be reflected in the 'day-to-day' dynamic of our own personal lives from births to deaths. The family is the collective core of our relation on planet Earth. Which as the Hermetic saying states, "as above, so below."

So this is not an outlandish association that our Great Work is about the reunion with the Universal Mother-Father as their children and a return to that Edenic place of our origin. In the words of Dorothy in the *Wizard of Oz*, "There's no place like home…" And perhaps on our trek to the Emerald City of Tiphareth, from which that alignment to the Knowledge and Conversation of our Holy Guardian Angel is manifested, we realize that we can find the intelligence, fearlessness, and love to rectify that fear of the wickedness of world into a return to that primal Eden we call home for all of us, completing our journey upon this living Tree of Life.

THE EUCHARISTIC FEAST OF AGATHODAIMON

BY

COMPANION ABRAXAS

Ancient and potent Protector, Agathodaimon, hail! We adore thee and thee we invoke.

Glorious Serpent-god, encircling the Equal Cross, Knouphis-Agathodaimon, hail! We adore thee and thee we invoke.

The Magician, *Crown of the Twelve Rays*

The Tides are when they are most potent and desired. The Magician is to wear the Robe, Pentacle of Quintessence or personal Lamen, and the Ring. The Bomos is to be set in the East of center, so that the communicant standing at center is directly before it. The Bomos is to be draped with the Red Gold Drape and upon it are to be placed the Mystical Tessera, the Lamp, the Bell, the Patella with bread or wafers, and a goblet of red Wine. The Incense is to be frankincense, benzoin, and oil of yellow sandalwood.

The Opening

You are to perform the Setting of the Wards of Power. Standing in the center of the place of working, or as near the center as the arrangement of the chamber will allow, you are to face the East and perform the Calyx. Inhaling, visualize the Tongue of Flame, the Divine Spark at the *Corona Flammae*, above your head. Exhaling and vibrate **EI**. Inhaling and raising your arms in Tau, palms up, you are to know that you are a balanced being ready to receive the divine light. Exhale, strengthening the visualization of the Flame. Inhale and visualize a shaft of Light from the *Corona Flammae* descending to the sphere of the *Instita Splendens*. Exhale and vibrate **'H BASILEIA**. Inhale and bring your left hand to your right shoulder, recognizing the martial forces of your being. Exhale and vibrate **KAI 'H DUNAMIS**. Inhale and bring right hand to left shoulder, recognizing the jovial forces of your being. Exhale and vibrate **KAI 'H DOXA**. Incline your head at bottom of your breath. Inhale and feel the solar center radiate with life-giving light and love. Exhale and vibrate **EIS TOUS AIONAS**.

Advance to the East. Beginning at that point and returning there, move counter clockwise around the place of working with your hand outstretched, tracing the circle. After completing the circle, return to center and face the East. Vibrate, **HE PELEIA KAI HE HUGRA HO OPHIS KAI TO OION.**

While still facing the East, make the gesture Cervus. Vibrate at the first point **ATHANATOS.**

Vibrate at the second point **SELAE GENETES.** Turn to face the North and make the gesture Cervus. Vibrate at the first point **ISCHUROS** and at the second point **KUROS.** Face the West and make the gesture Cervus. At the first point vibrate **ISCHUROS** and at the second **PANKRATES.** Face the South and make the gesture Cervus. Vibrate at the first point **ATHANATOS.** Vibrate at the second point **THEOS.**

Face the East. Assume the Wand posture. Vibrate, **GAIA KAI HO ICHOR TOU OURANOU.** Still facing the East, raise your arms to a Tau and vibrate, **TO THE EAST SOTER. TO THE SOUTH ALASTOR. TO THE WEST ASPHALEIOS. TO THE NORTH AMUNTOR.** Repeat the Calyx.

Perform the Battery of 1.

Energize by the first formula of the *Clavis Rei Primae*, the Rousing of the Citadels.

Next recite the Crown of the Twelve Rays,

> **Ancient and potent Protector, Agathodaimon, hail! We adore thee and thee we invoke.**
>
> **Glorious Serpent-god, encircling the Equal Cross, Knouphis-Agathodaimon, hail! We adore thee and thee we invoke.**
>
> **Abundant goodness bestowing, Agathodaimon, hail! We adore thee and thee we invoke.**
>
> **Terrible invincible God, Knouphis-Agathodaimon, hail! We adore thee and thee we invoke.**
>
> **Holy Shepherd of thy People, Agathodaimon, hail! We adore thee and thee we invoke.**
>
> **Thou Winged Splendor with broad pinions of emerald and gold, Knouphis-Agathodaimon, hail! We adore thee and thee we invoke.**
> **Divine Priest of the Sun, thou white and scintillant, Agathodaimon, hail!**

We adore thee and thee we invoke.

Aid of the Seeker for Truth, Knouphis-Agathodaimon, hail! We adore thee and thee we invoke.

Immortal Guide of the Wise, Agathodaimon, hail! We adore thee and thee we invoke.

Mighty Champion of the Way, Knouphis-Agathodaimon, hail! We adore thee and thee we invoke.

Orient Spirit of Light, Agathodaimon, hail! We adore thee and thee we invoke.

Now and ever blessed, crowned with the Crown of Twelve Rays, Knouphis-Agathodaimon hail! We exalt thee!

The Eucharist

Stand West of the Bomos facing the East. Perform the Battery of 3.

Raise your arms in the Psi Posture. Visualize the *Corona Flammae* as a sphere of intense brilliance. Draw the light of the *Corona Flammae* down into the *Orbis Solis* where it expands into a sphere of rose and gold radiance. Cross your arms over your chest, right over left, and state,

O wise and noble Agathodaimon, I offer these creatures of wine and bread,
May you enlighten my mind and still my heart with your word.
May the radiance of your crown be extended upon me and this feast that it may fulfill the Beauty of this Great Work.

Draw the light down from the *Orbis Solis* into the *Instita Splendens* where it expands into a sphere of white radiance. Draw a charge of rose and gold flame from the *Instita Splendens* and let it pass into the *Orbis Solis*. Assume the ophiomorphic form of Agathodaimon.[1]

Next, extend light upon the Bread and Wine with the Orante formulae saying, **En Deus Est, Deus Est!** Next taking the Bread and elevating it above your head declare, **I, Agathodaimon raising this token of bread shall make of it my flesh.** You are to

---

[1]Serpent form with nacreous white scales. Eyes yellow, with black pupils. Wings as of an eagle, plumage of rich green, feather tips bordered with gold. From the serpent's head dart rays of brilliant golden light.

consume the Bread.

Next taking the goblet of Wine and raising it above your head declare, **I, Agathodaimon raising this token of wine shall make of it my blood.** You are to consume the Wine.

Next proclaim,

> **The Holy One shall arise**
> **And his voice shall cry in the dawn,**
> **Yea, his mighty voice shall cry in the dawn.**
>
> **He shall go forth in his name Knouphis**
> **And his fearsome loveliness shall scourge the worlds.**
>
> **A thousand Aeons shall adore him,**
> **And men shall seek death.**
> **The earth shall tremble,**
> **The voice of the Holy One shall sound in the tempest.**
>
> **The Gnostic shall stand in contemplation.**
> **He shall lift up his hands in adoration.**
> **Above him shall be the Diadem of Light,**
> **And these shall be the words of the Gnostic,**
> **Terror and vastness are about me**
> **But the broad wings of the Serpent enfold me.**
>
> **The fleeing darkness is before me.**
> **But I keep in concealment the glory which is mine**
>
> **And the time is not yet when I shall unveil my face,**
> **Yet I stand in majesty and power and bliss unending!**
>
> **These shall be the words of the Gnostic in adoration of the Holy One.**

At this point you shall pause in silence for a moment allowing the radiance of Agathodaimon to fade into your magical personality.

The Closing

Perform the Battery of 1.

Proclaim,

In the bond of Holy Light, by the coming forth of the Phoenix and by the effulgence of the Morning Star do we call upon you, High Guardians, we who are the continuators of your Work.

O Luminous Ones behold and hear us. Not without our own questing do we seek Gnosis, nor without our own endeavor to achieve the Supreme Good, but that the sowing shall be crowned in the harvest.

For oneness of purpose do we call unto you, for that joy of resolve which is the Wine of the Will, transforming all that was strange to it. For living light and for luminous life do we call unto you, O Hidden High Ones! So Light and Life shall be drawn at last to the radiance of one Star, and that Star shall mount to the unshadowed height.

EN GIRO TORTE SOL CICLOS ET ROTOR IGNE.

The Spiritual Sun has turned the Ages in a Circle and is their Mover with Fire!

So be the Work accomplished
In the Light of the Glorious Star!

Perform the Battery of 3-5-3.

The Rite of the Solar and Lunar Mysteries of the Altar of Eros for the Consecration of the Talismans of Helios and Selene

BY

ΔΑΜΩΝ

And I, breathing magic spells, potent at the solar altars, whose chants and conjurations not even cymbals can silence, I who inhabit the scorching lands below and starry Heavens above, barefoot, my golden robe unfastened, go forth on my roaming way in the deep stillness of the dawning hour to draw down the golden visage of Helios.

The Magos of the Sun, *The Calling of the Magos of the Sun*

And I, breathing magic spells, potent at the lunar altars, whose chants and conjurations not even cymbals can silence, I who inhabit the lunar lands below and starry Heavens above, barefoot, my silver robe unfastened, go forth on my roaming way in the deep stillness of the lunar hour to draw down the silver visage of Selene.

The Maga of the Moon, *The Calling of the Maga of the Moon*

The Calling of the Cosmos

The Magos of the Sun is to come to the solar adorned Temple of Helios on the last hour of the Sun on the day of the Sun clad in his golden robe and bearing whatever else he desires corresponding to the solar rays. He is to be wearing the Talisman of the Sun.[1] Yet around him is darkness outstretching into infinity and this he shall contemplate before any ritual gesture. He is to face the East and recite, **Silence! Silence! For I am a star, wandering about with you and shining forth out of the deep, OXU O XERTHEUTH!**[2] Raising his palms above his head he is to chant **ANOCH**. Placing

---

[1] The Talisman of the Sun is to be constructed from gold on the day and hours of the Sun. Upon it are to be placed signs, symbols, names, epithets, jewels, and whatever other correspondences the Magos desires.
[2] *PGM* IV. 575.

his arms across his chest he is to chant **PHNOUTH**. Drawing his palms down he is to chant **BAINPHOUN**. Burning a solar flame upon the Altar he is to sacrifice with his right hand frankincense whilst chanting **ACHEBUKRÔM** and carving the Sign of Helios. Burning a lunar flame upon the Altar he is to sacrifice myrrh with his left hand and chant **AKTIÔPHIS** whilst carving the Sign of Selene. The Magos is to draw the Moon and the Sun into the Air above him whilst chanting **AIÔÔIAIAÔIÔA**.

The Seven Unveilings of Infinity

He is to remain facing the East and sacrifice frankincense in abundance. There he is to stretch out his right hand to his left and his left hand to his left and chant **A**. He is to face the North putting forward only his right fist and chant **EE**. Facing the West he is to extend both hands in front of him whilst chanting **ÊÊÊ**. Turning to the South he is to place both hands on his stomach and chant **IIII**. Returning to the East he is to touch the ends of his toes, look into the Earth and chant **OOOOO**. He is then to place both hands on his heart, gaze into the Air and chant **UUUUUU**. Placing both hands on his head he is to look up to the Heavens and chant **ÔÔÔÔÔÔÔ**.[3]

The Seven Conjurations of the Cosmos

Facing the East the Magos of the Sun is to chant **A EE ÊÊÊ IIII OOOOO UUUUUU ÔÔÔÔÔÔÔ**. Facing the South **I OO UUU ÔÔÔÔ AAAAA EEEEEE ÊÊÊÊÊÊÊ**. To the West **Ê II OOO UUUU ÔÔÔÔÔ AAAAAA EEEEEEE**. To the North **E ÊÊ III OOOO UUUUU ÔÔÔÔÔÔ AAAAAAA**. Again facing the East and looking into the Earth **O UU ÔÔÔ AAAA EEEEE ÊÊÊÊÊÊ IIIIII**. Looking into the Air the Magos is to chant **U ÔÔ AAA EEEE ÊÊÊÊÊ IIIII OOOOOOO**. And looking up to the Heavens **Ô AA EEE ÊÊÊÊ IIII OOOOO UUUUUUU**.[4]

The Theurgic Creation of the Perfect Body

The Magos of the Sun is to see the Sun extending from the Heavens whilst carving the Invoking Unicursal Hexagram of Helios and chanting **ACHEBUKRÔM**. Gazing into the Air he is to see the Moon, carve the Invoking Unicursal Hexagram of Selene and chant **AKTIÔPHIS**. He is to invoke Earth by carving the Invoking Unicursal Hexagram of Earth and chanting **PERÊPHIA**, charging his Physical Body. He is to invoke Water carving the Invoking Unicursal Hexagram of Water and chanting **IÔÊDES**, charging his Etheric Body. Then Fire by carving the Invoking Unicursal

---

[3]*PGM* XIII. 824-834.
[4]*PGM* XIII. 852-871.

Hexagram of Fire and chanting **APHTHALUA**, charging his Astral Body. Air is to be invoked by carving the Invoking Unicursal Hexagram of Air whilst chanting **IÔIE ÊÔ AUA**, charging his Mental Body. Finally he is to invoke Spirit by carving the Invoking Unicursal Hexagram of Spirit whilst chanting **IÔGARAA**, and then **THÔPULEO DARDU**, charging the Spiritual Body and thus becoming the Perfect Body.

The Calling of the Magos

He is to sacrifice yet more frankincense and recite, **I call upon you, eternal and unbegotten, OGDOAS, who are one, who alone hold together the whole creation of all things, whom none understands, whom the gods worship, whose name not even the gods can utter. Inspire from your exhalation, ruler of the pole, him who is under you**[5] **for I am a Child of Earth and my Race is from the starry Heavens. I call upon you, AIÔN, who are greater than all, the creator of all, you, the self-begotten, who see all and are not seen; for you gave Helios the glory and all the power, Selene the privilege to wax and wane and have fixed courses, yet you took nothing from the earlier born darkness, but apportioned things so that they would be equal; for when you appeared, both order arose and light appeared. All things are subject to you, whose true form none of the gods can see; who can change into all forms. You are invisible, Aion of aions!**[6] **Create a whirlwind of power, quickly! I call on your name, the greatest among gods.**[7] **Open, open, four quarters of the cosmos, for the lord of the inhabited world comes forth. Gods, archangels, angels, decans, daimons, and spirits rejoice, for Aion of aions himself, the only transcendent, invisible, goes through this place. By the name AIA AINRUCHATH, cast up, Earth, for the lord, all things you contain, for he is the storm sender and controller of the Abyss, master of fire.**[8] **I call on your names, the greatest among gods. If I say it complete there will be an earthquake, the Sun will stop and the Moon will be afraid and the rocks and the mountains, the sea, the rivers and every liquid will be petrified and the whole Cosmos will be thrown into confusion. I call on you, IUEUO ÔaEÊ IAÔ AEÊ AI EÊ AÊ IOUÔ EUÊ IEOU AÊÔ EI ÔÊI IAÊ IÔOUÊ AUÊ UÊA IÔ IÔAI IÔAI ÔÊ EE OU IÔ IAÔ, the great name. Become for me lynx, eagle, snake, phoenix, life, power, necessity, images of god, AIÔ IÔY IAÔ ÊIÔ AA OUI AAAA E IU IÔ ÔÊ IAÔ AI AÔÊ OUEÔ AIEÊ IOUE UEIA EIÔ ÊII UU EE ÊÊ ÔAOÊ CHECHAMPSIMM CHANGALAS EÊIOU IÊEA ÔOÊOE ZÔIÔIÊR ÔMURUROMROMOS, the seven auspicious names. Ê II UU ÊÊ OAOÊ.**[9]
Greetings, O lord, you who are the way to receive favour for the universe and

---

[5] *PGM* XIII. 843-848.
[6] *PGM* XIII. 64-71.
[7] *PGM* XIII. 871-872.
[8] *PGM* XIII. 327-334.
[9] *PGM* XIII. 870-888.

for the world in which we dwell. Heaven has become a place of dancing for you, ARSENOPHRÊ; O king of the heavenly gods, ABLANATHANALBA; you who possesses righteousness, AKRAMMACHAMAREI; gracious god, SANKANATHARA; ruler of nature, SATRAPERKMÊPH; origin of the heavenly realm, ATHTHANNOU ATHTHANNOU ASTRAPHAI IASTRAPHAI PAKERTÔTH SABAÔTH ÊRINTASKLIOUTH ÊPHIÔ MARMARAÔ. Let my ability to speak and command not leave me. Let every god, archangel, angel, decan, daimon, and spirit pay attention to me, for I am PERTAÔ MÊCH CHACH MNÊCH SAKMÊPH IAÔOUEÊ ÔÊÔ ÔÊÔ IEOUÔÊIÊIAÊA IÊÔUOEI! Grant to me that which I ask and that which is your will![10]

The Hymn to Helios

Now that the Magos of the Sun has set into motion the gnostic creation of the Cosmos and himself, he is to face the Altar of the Sun and chant **IIIII**. He is to sacrifice frankincense whilst chanting **HÊLIOS** six times and then recite, **Hear golden titan, whose eternal eye with broad survey, illumines all the sky. Self-born, unwearied in diffusing light, and to all eyes the mirror of delight. Lord of the seasons, with thy fiery car and leaping coursers, beaming light from far. With thy right hand the source of morning light, and with thy left the father of the night. Agile and vig'rous, venerable Sun, fiery and bright around the heav'ns you run. Foe to the wicked, but the good man's guide, o'er all his steps propitious you preside. With various founding, golden lyre, 'tis mine to fill the world with harmony divine. Father of ages, guide of prosp'rous deeds, the world's commander, borne by lucid steeds, immortal Zeus, all-searching, bearing light, source of existence, pure and fiery bright bearer of fruit, almighty lord of years, agile and warm, whom ev'ry pow'r reveres. Great eye of nature and the starry skies, doom'd with immortal flames to set and rise dispensing justice, lover of the stream, the world's great despot, and o'er all supreme. Faithful defender, and the eye of right, of steeds the ruler, and of life the light. With founding whip four fiery steeds you guide, when in the car of day you glorious ride. Propitious on these mystic labours shine, and bless thy suppliants with a life divine.**[11]

The Calling of the Magos of the Sun

Sacrificing frankincense he is to recite, **And I, breathing magic spells, potent at the solar altars, whose chants and conjurations not even cymbals can silence, I who inhabit the scorching lands below and starry Heavens above, barefoot, my golden**

robe unfastened, go forth on my roaming way in the deep stillness of this solar hour to draw down the golden visage of Helios. The Magos of the Sun is to look to the Heavens and chant **HÊLIOS** whilst carving the Invoking Heptagram of Helios. Looking into the Air he is to chant **HÊLIOS** whilst carving the Invoking Heptagram of Helios. To the Earth **HÊLIOS** whilst carving the Invoking Heptagram of Helios. To the North **HÊLIOS** whilst carving the Invoking Heptagram of Helios. Turning against the Sun to the South he is to chant **HÊLIOS** and carve the Invoking Heptagram of Helios. Turning with the Sun to the West **HÊLIOS** whilst carving the Invoking Heptagram of Helios. And finally turning with the Sun to the East **HÊLIOS** again carving the Invoking Heptagram of Helios. He is then to sacrifice frankincense and chant **HÊLIOS** six times.[12]

The Conjuration of Helios

The Magos of the Sun is to recite the ritual verses, chant the holy names, see the cosmic signs, and perform the magical gestures, **Borne of the breezes of the wandering winds, golden-haired Helios who willed the flame's untiring light, who drive in lofty turns around the great pole; who create all things yourself which you again reduce to nothing. From you come the elements arranged by your own laws which cause the whole world to rotate through its four yearly turning points.**[13] **I invoke you, the greatest god, eternal lord, world ruler, who are over the world and under the world, mighty ruler of the sea, rising at dawn, shinning from the East for the whole world, setting in the West. Come to me, you who rises from the four winds, for whom Heaven has become the processional way. I call upon your holy and great hidden names which you rejoice to hear; the Earth flourished when you shone forth, and the plants became fruitful when you laughed; the animals begat their young when you permitted. Give glory and honour and favour and fortune and power to me. I invoke you, the greatest in Heaven, ÊI LANCHUCH AKAPÊN BAL MISTHÊN MARTA MATHATH LAILAM MOYSOUTHI SIETHÔ BATHABATHI IATMÔN ALEI IABATH ABÔTH SABAÔTH ADÔNAI, the great god, ORSENOPHRÊ ORGEATÊS TOTHORNATÊSA KRITHI BIÔTHI IADMÔ IATMÔMI METHIÊI LONCHOÔ AKARÊ BAL MINTHRÊ BANE BAINCHCHUCHCH OUPHRI NOTHEOUSI THRAI ARSIOUTH ERÔNERTHER, the shining Helios, giving light throughout the whole world, for you are he who becomes visible each day and sets in the Northwest of Heaven and rises in the Southeast. In the first hour you have the form of a cat; your name is PHARAKOUNÊTH. Give glory and favour to me. In the second hour you have the form of a dog; your name is SOUPHI. Give strength and honour to me. In the third hour you have the form of a serpent;**

---

[12]Towards the Heavens, Air, Earth, North, South, West, and East the Magos is to raise the Talisman of the Sun after carving the Invoking Heptagram of Helios consecrating it in the solar rays.
[13]*PGM* VIII. 73-80.

your name is AMEKRANEBECHEO THÔUTHI. Give honour to me. In the fourth hour you have the form of a scarab; your name is SENTHENIPS. Mightily strengthen me for the work I undertake. In the fifth hour you have the form of a donkey; your name is ENPHANCHOUPH. Give strength and courage and power to me. In the sixth hour you have the form of a lion; your name is BAI SOLBAI, the ruler of time. Give success to me and glorious victory. In the seventh hour you have the form of a goat; your name is OUMESTHÔTH. Give sexual charm to me. In the eighth hour you have the form of a bull; your name is DIATIPHÊ, who becomes visible everywhere. Let all things done by me be accomplished. In the ninth hour you have the form of a falcon; your name is PHÊOUS PHÔOUTH, the lotus emerged from the Abyss. Give success and good luck to me. In the tenth hour you have the form of a baboon; your name is BESBUKI. Give sexual potency to me. In the eleventh hour you have the form of an ibis; your name is MOU ROPH. Protect me and give me luck, from this present day for all time. In the twelfth hour you have the form of a crocodile; your name is AERTHOÊ. Give me power over the Nile. You have set at evening as an old man, who are over the world and under the world, mighty ruler of the sea, hear my voice in this night, in these holy hours, and let all things done by me, be brought to fulfilment. Please, lord KMÊPH LOUTHEOUTH ORPHOICHE ORTILIBECHOUCH IERCHE POUM IPERITAÔ UAI. I conjure Earth and Heaven and light and darkness and you the great god to rejoice with me,[14] you who are set over the East wind and the world, for whom all gods serve as bodyguards at your good hour and on your good day, you who are the Agathos Daimon of the world, the crown of the inhabited world, you who rise from the Abyss, you who each day, rise a young man and set an old man, CHARPENKNOUPHI BRINTANTÊNÔPHRI BRISSKULMAS AROURZORBOROBA MESINTRIPHI NIPTOUMI CHMOUMMAÔPHI. I beg you, lord, do not allow me to be overthrown, to be plotted against, to receive dangerous drugs, to go into exile, to fall upon hard times. Rather, I ask to obtain and receive from your life, health, reputation, wealth, influence, strength, success, charm, favour with all men and all women, victory over all men and all women. Yes, lord, ABLANATHANALBA AKRAMMACHAMAREI PEPHNA PHÔZA PHNEBENNOUNI NAACHTHIP OUNORBA, accomplish the matter which I want, by means of your power.[15] Helios, I adjure you by your great name, BORKÊ PHOIOUR IÔ ZIZIA APARXEOUCH THUTHE LAILAM AAAAA IIII OOOOO IEÔ IEÔ IEÔIEÔ IEÔ IEÔ NAUNAX AI AI AEÔ AEÔ ÊAÔ.[16] Helios, Helios, hear me, Helios, lord, great god, you who maintain all things and who give life and who rule the world, toward whom all things go, from whom they also came, untiring, ÊIE ELÊIE IEÔA ROUBA ANAMAÔ MERMAÔ CHADAMATHA ARDAMATHA PEPHRE

---

[14]*PGM* IV. 1596-1715.
[15]*PGM* XXXVI. 211-230.
[16]*PGM* I. 222-231.

ANAMALZÔ PHÊCHEIDEU ENEDEREU SIMATOI MERMEREÔ
AMALAZIPHIA MERSIPHIA EREME THASTEU PAPIE PHEREDÔNACH
ANAIE GELEÔ AMARA

MATÔR MÔRMARÊSIO NEOUTHÔN ALAÔ AGELAÔ AMAR AMATÔR
MÔRMASI SOUTHÔN ANAMAÔ GALAMARARMA, hear me, lord Helios![17]

The Invocation of Helios

The Magos of the Sun is to sacrifice frankincense and carve the Invoking Heptagram of Helios six times whilst chanting **HÊLIOS** and then the Sign of Helios at the centre of the Heptagram whilst chanting **ACHEBUKROM.** He is to recite, **I have called on your names, signs, forms and sung your hymns, the greatest god, eternal lord, world ruler, who are over the world and under the world, mighty ruler of the sea, rising at dawn, shinning from the East for the whole world, setting in the West. Come to me, HÊLIOS HUPERIÔN TITAN ÊLEKTÔR ELEUTHERIOS SÔTÊR, bring me into union with you!**

The Magos of the Sun is to embrace theurgic union with Helios through conscious meditation and the feeling of the presence of the god, along with his attributes, signs, and effects. He is then to journey into a state of being of gnostic reverie through the unconscious euphony of the holy hymns, names, titles, and epithets of the god without cessation. Upon threshold the Magos of the Sun is to prepare his Perfect Body for the invoked reception of the god and then in mystic fervour become the god himself. He is to remain in silent contemplation as the god of the Sun incarnate until the beckoning of the Maga of the Moon.

The Maga of the Moon is to come to the lunar adorned Temple of Selene on the first hour of the Moon on the day of the Moon clad in her silver robe and bearing whatever else she desires corresponding to the lunar rays. She is to be wearing the Talisman of the Moon.[18] She is to perform the ritual gestures of the Calling of the Cosmos; the Seven Unveilings of Infinity; the Seven Conjurations of the Cosmos; the Theurgic Creation of the Perfect Body; and finally, the Calling of the Maga.

The Hymn to Selene

Now that the Maga of the Moon has set into motion the gnostic creation of the

---

[17] *PGM* VII. 528-539.
[18] The Talisman of the Moon is to be constructed from silver on the day and hours of the Moon. Upon it are to be placed signs, symbols, names, epithets, jewels, and whatever other correspondences the Maga desires.

Cosmos and herself, she is to face the Altar of the Moon chant **AAAAAAAAA**. She is to sacrifice myrrh whilst chanting **SELÊNÊ** nine times and then recite, **Hear, goddess queen, diffusing silver light, bull-horned, and wandering through the gloom of night. With stars surrounded, and with circuit wide night's torch extending, through the heavens you ride: female and male, with silvery rays you shine, and now full-orbed, now tending to decline. Mother of ages, fruit-producing Mene, whose amber orb makes night's reflected noon: lover of horses, splendid queen of night, all-seeing power, bedecked with starry light, lover of vigilance, the foe of strife, in peace rejoicing, and a prudent life: fair lamp of night, its ornament and friend, who givest to nature's works their destined end. Queen of the stars, all-wise Goddess, hail! Decked with a graceful robe and amble veil. Come, blessed Goddess, prudent, starry, bright, come, moony-lamp, with chaste and splendid light, shine on these sacred rites with prosperous rays, and pleased accept thy suppliants' mystic praise.**[19]

The Calling of the Maga of the Moon

The Maga of the Moon is to recite, **And I, breathing magic spells, potent at the lunar altars, whose chants and conjurations not even cymbals can silence, I who inhabit the lunar lands below and starry Heavens above, barefoot, my silver robe unfastened, go forth on my roaming way in the deep stillness of the lunar hour to draw down the silver visage of Selene.** Sacrificing myrrh, she is to look to the Heavens and chant **SELÊNÊ** whilst carving the Invoking Heptagram of Selene. Looking into the Air she is to chant **SELÊNÊ** whilst carving the Invoking Heptagram of Selene. Looking to the Earth she is to chant **SELÊNÊ** whilst carving the Invoking Heptagram of Selene. Turning to the North **SELÊNÊ** and carving the Invoking Heptagram of Selene. Turning against the Sun to the South **SELÊNÊ** whilst carving the Invoking Heptagram of Selene. Turning with the Sun to the West **SELÊNÊ** whilst carving the Invoking Heptagram of Selene. Turning with the Sun to the East she is to chant **SELÊNÊ** whilst carving the Invoking Heptagram of Selene. She is then to sacrifice myrrh and chant **SELÊNÊ** nine times.[20]

The Conjuration of Selene

The Maga of the Moon is to recite the ritual verses, chant the holy names, see the cosmic signs, and perform the magical gestures, **I call upon you who have all forms and many names, double-horned goddess, MÊNÊ, whose form no one knows except him**

---

[19] *Orphic Hymn to Selene.*
[20] Towards the Heavens, Air, Earth, North, South, West, and East the Maga is to raise the Talisman of the Moon after carving the Invoking Heptagram of Selene consecrating it in the lunar rays.

who made the entire world, IAÔ, the one who shaped you into the twenty-eight shapes of the world so that you might complete every figure and distribute breath to every animal and plant, that it might flourish, you who has wax from obscurity into light and wane from light into darkness.[21] Come to me night-shining, triple-sounding, triple-voiced, triple-headed, Selene, triple-pointed, triple-faced, triple-necked, and goddess of the triple ways, who hold untiring flaming fire in the triple baskets, and you who oft frequent the triple way and rule the triple decades with three forms. O goddess, you who rise up an awful sound with triple mouths and from toneless throats you send a dread, sharp cry. Hearing your cry, all worldly things are shaken: the nethergates of and Lethe's holy water and primal Chaos and the shining chasm of Tartarus. At it every immortal and every mortal, the starry mountains, valleys and every tree and roaring rivers, and even the restless sea, the lonely echo, and daimons through the world, shudder at you, O blessed one, when they hear your dread voice. Come here to me, goddess of the night, beast-slayer, come to me with love. And heed my prayers, Selene, who suffer much, who rise and set at night, O triple-headed, triple-named MÊNÊ MAPZOUNÊ, fearful, gracious-minded and Peitho. Come to me, horned-faced, light-bearer, bull-shaped, horse-faced goddess, who howl doglike; come here, she-wolf, and come here now, mistress of night and chthonic realms, holy, black-clad, round whom the star-traversing nature of the world revolves whenever you wax too great, you have established every worldly thing, for you engendered everything on Earth and from the sea and every race in turn of winged birds who seek their nests again. Mother of all, who bore Eros, Aphrodite, lamp-bearer, shining and aglow, Selene, star-coursing, heavenly, torch-bearer, fire-breather, woman four-faced, four-named, four-roads' mistress. Hail , goddess, and attend your epithets, O heavenly one, harbour goddess of the crossroads; O nether one, goddess of depths, eternal, goddess of dark, come to my sacrifices. Fulfill this of which I ask, and as I pray give heed to me, lady, I ask of you.[22] Come, AKTIÔPHIS, mistress, Selene, only ruler, swift fortune of daimons and gods, NEBOUTOSOALÊTH IÔI LOIMOU. And the first companion of your name is silence, the second a popping sound, the third a groaning, the fourth a hissing, the fifth a cry of joy, the sixth moaning, the seventh barking, the eight bellowing, the ninth neighing, the tenth a musical sound, the eleventh a sounding wind, the twelfth a wind-creating sound, the thirteenth a coercive sound, the fourteenth a coercive emanation from perfection. Ox, vulture, bull, beetle, falcon, crab, dog, wolf, serpent, horse, she-goat, asp, goat, he-goat, baboon, cat, lion, leopard, fieldmouse, deer, multiform, virgin, torch, lightning, garland, a herald's wand, child, key. I pray to you, mistress of the whole world, the stable one, the mighty one, APHEIBOÊÔ MINTÊR OCHAÔ PIZEPHUDÔR CHANTHAR CHADÊROZO MOCHTHION EOTNEU PHÊZON AINDÊS LACHABOÔ PITTÔ RIPHTHAMER ZMOMOCHÔLEIE TIÊDRANTEIA

[21] PGM VII. 756-765.
[22] PGM IV. 2522-2566.

OISOZOCHABÊDÔPHRA,[23] hear me mistress Selene!

The Invocation of Selene

The Maga of the Moon is to sacrifice myrrh and carve the Invoking Heptagram of Selene whilst chanting **SELÊNÊ**. At the centre of the Heptagram she is to carve the Sign of Selene whilst chanting **AKTIÔPHIS** and then recite, **I have called on your names, signs, forms and sung your hymns, the greatest goddess, you who have all forms and many names, double-horned goddess, whose form no one knows except him who made the entire world, the one who shaped you into the twenty-eight shapes of the world that it might flourish, you who has wax from obscurity into light and wane from light into darkness. Come to me, SELANAIA MÊNÊ AIGLÊ PASIPHAE, bring me into union with you.**

The Maga of the Moon is to embrace theurgic union with Selene through conscious meditation and the feeling of the presence of the goddess, along with her attributes, signs, and energies. She is then to journey into a state of being of gnostic reverie through the unconscious euphony of the holy hymns, names, titles, and epithets of the goddess without cessation. Upon threshold the Maga of the Moon is to prepare her Perfect Body for the invoked reception of the goddess and then in mystic fervour become the goddess herself. As the goddess of the Moon incarnate she is to beckon the Magos of the Sun by sounding the Bell nine times and then six times. The Magos of the Sun as the god of the Sun incarnate is to answer her call and join the Maga of the Moon as the goddess of the Moon incarnate in her Temple.

The Coalescence of Purifying Water and Consecrating Fire

The Maga is to take the Cup of Water in both hands and raising it above her head she is to proclaim, **And so therefore first that priestess who governs the works of Fire must sprinkle with the lustral waters of the loud resounding sea.** She is to lower the Cup and take it to the East. With the Cup in hand, she is to trace the Greek Cross of Water in the East. Dipping her fingers into the Cup of Water the Maga is to cast the Water three times in the East forming the Triangle of Water. After this she is to perform the same ritual gesture in the South, West, North, into the Earth, the Air, and towards the Heavens. In the East, she is to raise the Cup of Water high and declare, **I form to be coalesced with Water.** The Magos is to take the Censer of Fire in both hands. Raising it above his head he is to proclaim, **And when, after all the phantoms are banished, you shall see that holy formless Fire which darts and flashes at the hidden depths**

---

[23] *PGM* VII. 766-794.

of the Cosmos, hear now the voice of Fire. He is to lower the Censer of Fire and go to the East tracing the Greek Cross of Fire and then casting the smoke of the Censer of Fire three times forming the Triangle of Fire. After this he is to perform the same ritual gestures in the South, West, North, into the Earth, the Air, and towards the Heavens before facing the East. Raising the Censer of Fire high he is to declare, **I form to be coalesced with Fire**.

The Whisperings of the Solar and Lunar Mysteries of the Altar of Eros

The Magos and the Maga as the incarnations of Helios and Selene are to retire to the Altar of Eros and remove each other's robes. The Magos of the Sun is to whisper to his Maga of the Moon, **From you, the Moon, the power of generating and growing greater, of increasing and decreasing. For you are conversant in manifest and occult things, the ecstatic dance for the manner of life, giving growth to itself and others**. The Maga of the Moon is to whisper to her Magos of the Sun, **From you, the Sun, the seductive and scorching flame setting ablaze in ecstasy the holy perfume of frankincense, the shimmering cymbals and ritual drumming of the Cosmos. For you are the formula of IAÔ, I being the Sun immortal, A the echo of the voice of Creation in the beginning, and Ô the echo of the voice of Union in the end.** The Maga is to whisper to her Magos, **And I, Daughter of Selene, shall receive you deep inside my silver womb lost within an abyss of eros and mania undergoing the sensation of life, death, and rebirth through the orgasm of the Sun and Moon, the sacrifice of the Solar and Lunar Mysteries of the Altar of Eros**. The Magos is to whisper to his Maga, **And I, Son of Helios, shall dance within your silver womb blazing with golden rays from the fiery Heavens above to initiate and become with you the orgasm of the Sun and Moon, the sacrifice of the Solar and Lunar Mysteries of the Altar of Eros.**

The Embrace and Consecration of the Solar and Lunar Mysteries of the Altar of Eros

The Magos of the Sun is to beckon his Maga with gestures of erotic impetus to embrace him whilst whispering to her words of fiery passion with his form and essence being the reflection of the glory that he is and that which he embodies. The Maga of the Moon is to entwine herself in his embrace and respond with sensual poetics and erotic gestures with her form and essence being the reflection of the beauty that she is and that which she embodies. They are to arouse each erotically until the orgasmic pulse is soaring from the Earth below and to the Heavens above, and from the Heavens above to the Earth below, setting ablaze their holy desire for each. They are to engage in the Mysteries of the Altar of Eros, with their erotic fires being as ecstatic as possible, their gaze fixed upon each other, and feeling the solar and lunar rays permeating their

Perfect Body. Upon the edge of their orgasm the Magos and the Maga are to ritually concentrate on allowing the orgasmic power to initiate a state of gnostic trance. Before yielding to their orgasm they are to concentrate intensely upon the union of the solar and lunar rays, the Magos receiving the Moon and the Maga receiving the Sun whilst in their state of gnostic trance. They are to remain like this for as long as possible before extracting the fluids from the Mysteries of the Altar of Eros. The Maga of the Moon is to consecrate her Talisman of the Moon with their orgasmic fluids and a sacrifice of myrrh, whilst carving the Invoking Heptagram of the Selene followed by the Sign of Selene nine times. She is to proclaim, **And I Maga of the Moon, Selene incarnate, consecrate this Talisman of the Moon for my Magos of the Sun.** The Maga is then to place the Talisman of the Moon around the neck of her Magos. The Magos of the Sun is to consecrate his Talisman of the Sun with their orgasmic fluids and a sacrifice of frankincense whilst carving the Invoking Heptagram of the Helios followed by the Sign of Helios six times. He is to proclaim, **And I Magos of the Sun, Helios incarnate, consecrate this Talisman of the Sun for my Maga of the Moon.** The Magos is then to place the Talisman of the Sun around the neck of his Maga. The Maga of the Moon is to enter the Temple of Helios, sacrifice frankincense in abundance and perform the Calling of the Maga of the Sun. She is then to proclaim, **For I have received the Sun,** before initiating slowly the divorce of her Perfect Body from the form of Selene. The Magos of the Sun is to remain in the Temple of the Moon, sacrifice myrrh in abundance and perform the Calling of the Magos of the Moon. He is then to proclaim, **For I have received the Moon,** before initiating slowly the divorce of his Perfect Body from the form of Helios.

The Veiling of the Cosmos

The Magos is to retreat to the Temple of Helios. Facing the East he is to recite, **O gods who are in the East** and then chant **ÔAÔÊÔÔEOÊIAÔ**. Facing the South he is to recite, **O gods who are in the South** and then chant **III**. In the North, **O gods who are in the North** and then chant **AAÔ**. Turning against the Sun to the West he is to recite, **O gods who are in the West** and then chant **THÊ**. Moving against the Sun to the South he is to kneel on his right knee. Standing, he is to keep rotating against the Sun until he reaches the East. Looking down to the Earth he is to recite, **O gods who are in the Earth** and chant **THOU**. Looking into the Air he is to see the Moon and recite, **O gods who are in the sub-Lunar realms** and then chant **THÊ**. Looking into the Air he is to see the Water and recite, **O gods who are in the Primeval Waters** and then chant **AATHÔ**. Looking to the Heavens he is to recite, **O gods who are in the Heavens** and then chant **ATHÊROUO**.[24] The Maga is also to perform the Veiling of the Cosmos but in the Temple of the Moon.

---

[24] *PGM* XIII. 641-646.

THE CALLING AND ADORATION OF AION, AND THE SPELL OF THE MYSTIC FLAME

BY

ΔΑΜΩΝ

O you who are the Cosmos, who does extend from Heaven to Earth, and from the Earth that's in the middle of the orb of Cosmos to the ends of the Abyss! O AIÔN, you I call upon, you I adore!

The Magos of Aion, *The Calling and Adoration of Aion*

The Calling of the Cosmos

The Magos of Aion is to face the East before the coming of dawn. He is then to recite, **Silence! Silence! For I am a star, wandering about with you and shining forth out of the deep, OXU O XERTHEUTH!**[1] Raising his palms above his head he is to chant **ANOCH**. Placing his arms across his chest he is to chant **PHNOUTH**. Drawing his palms down he is to chant **BAINPHOUN**. Burning a solar flame upon the Altar he is to sacrifice with his right hand frankincense whilst chanting **ACHEBUKRÔM** and carving the Sign of Helios. Burning a lunar flame upon the Altar he is to sacrifice myrrh with his left hand and chant **AKTIÔPHIS** whilst carving the Sign of Selene. The Magos is to draw the Moon and the Sun into the Air above him whilst chanting **AIÔÔIAIAÔIÔA**.

The Seven Unveilings of Infinity

With the coming of dawn he is to remain facing the East, sacrifice frankincense in abundance, and recite, **Hear me, O Goddess! whose emerging ray leads on the broad refulgence of the day; Blushing Eos, whose celestial light beams on the world with red'ning splendours bright. Angel of Titan, whom with constant round, thy orient beams recall from night profound; Labour of ev'ry kind to lead is thine, of mortal life the minister divine. Mankind in thee eternally delight, and none presumes to shun thy beauteous sight. Soon as thy splendours break the bands of rest, and eyes**

---

[1] *PGM* IV. 575.

unclose with pleasing sleep oppress'd; Men, reptiles, birds, and beasts, with gen'ral voice, and all the nations of the deep, rejoice; For all the culture of our life is thine. Come, blessed pow'r! And to these rites incline; Thy holy light increase, and unconfin'd diffuse its radiance on thy mystic's mind.[2] Then he is to stretch out his right hand to his left and his left hand to his left and chant **A**. He is to face the North putting forward only his right fist and chant **EE**. Facing the West he is to extend both hands in front of him whilst chanting **ÊÊÊ**. Turning to the South he is to place both hands on his stomach and chant **IIII**. Returning to the East he is to touch the ends of his toes, look into the Earth and chant **OOOOO**. He is then to place both hands on his heart, gaze into the Air and chant **UUUUUU**. Placing both hands on his head he is to look up to the Heavens and chant **ÔÔÔÔÔÔÔ**.[3]

The Seven Conjurations of the Cosmos

Facing the East the Magos of Aion is to chant **A EE ÊÊÊ IIII OOOOO UUUUUU ÔÔÔÔÔÔÔ**. Facing the South **I OO UUU ÔÔÔÔ AAAAA EEEEE ÊÊÊÊÊÊ**. To the West **Ê II OOO UUUU ÔÔÔÔÔ AAAAAA EEEEEEE**. To the North **E ÊÊ III OOOO UUUUU ÔÔÔÔÔÔ AAAAAAA**. Again facing the East and looking into the Earth **O UU ÔÔÔ AAAA EEEEE ÊÊÊÊÊÊ IIIIII**. Looking into the Air the Magos is to chant **U ÔÔ AAA EEEE ÊÊÊÊÊ IIIII OOOOOOO**. And looking up to the Heavens **Ô AA EEE ÊÊÊÊ IIIII OOOOOO UUUUUUU**.[4]

The Theurgic Creation of the Perfect Body

The Magos of Aion is to see the Sun extending from the Heavens whilst carving the Invoking Unicursal Hexagram of Helios and chanting **ACHEBUKRÔM**. Gazing into the Air he is to see the Moon, carve the Invoking Unicursal Hexagram of Selene and chant **AKTIÔPHIS**. He is to invoke Earth by carving the Invoking Unicursal Hexagram of Earth and chanting **PERÊPHIA**, charging his Physical Body. He is to invoke Water carving the Invoking Unicursal Hexagram of Water and chanting **IÔÊDES**, charging his Etheric Body. Then Fire by carving the Invoking Unicursal Hexagram of Fire and chanting **APHTHALUA**, *charging his Astral Body. Air is to be invoked by carving* the Invoking Unicursal Hexagram of Air whilst chanting **IÔIE ÊÔ AUA**, charging his Mental Body. Finally he is to invoke Spirit by carving the Invoking Unicursal Hexagram of Spirit whilst chanting **IÔGARAA**, and then **THÔPULEO DARDU**, charging the Spiritual Body and thus becoming the Perfect Body.

---

[2] *Orphic Hymn to Eos.*
[3] *PGM* XIII. 824-834.
[4] *PGM* XIII. 852-871.

The Calling of the Magos

He is to sacrifice yet more frankincense and recite, **I call upon you, eternal and unbegotten, OGDOAS, who are one, who alone hold together the whole creation of all things, whom none understands, whom the gods worship, whose name not even the gods can utter. Inspire from your exhalation, ruler of the pole, him who is under you**[5] **for I am a Child of Earth and my Race is from the starry Heavens. I call upon you, AIÔN, who are greater than all, the creator of all, you, the self-begotten, who see all and are not seen; for you gave Helios the glory and all the power, Selene the privilege to wax and wane and have fixed courses, yet you took nothing from the earlier born darkness, but apportioned things so that they would be equal; for when you appeared, both order arose and light appeared. All things are subject to you, whose true form none of the gods can see; who can change into all forms. You are invisible, Aion of aions!**[6] **Create a whirlwind of power, quickly! I call on your name, the greatest among gods.**[7] **Open, open, four quarters of the cosmos, for the lord of the inhabited world comes forth. Gods, archangels, angels, decans, daimons, and spirits rejoice, for Aion of aions himself, the only transcendent, invisible, goes through this place. By the name AIA AINRUCHATH, cast up, Earth, for the lord, all things you contain, for he is the storm sender and controller of the Abyss, master of fire.**[8] **I call on your names, the greatest among gods. If I say it complete there will be an earthquake, the Sun will stop and the Moon will be afraid and the rocks and the mountains, the sea, the rivers and every liquid will be petrified and the whole Cosmos will be thrown into confusion. I call on you, IUEUO ÔAEÊ IAÔ AEÊ AI EÊ AÊ IOUÔ EUÊ IEOU AÊÔ EI ÔÊI IAÊ IÔOUÊ AUÊ UÊA IÔ IÔAI IÔAI ÔÊ EE OU IÔ IAÔ, the great name. Become for me lynx, eagle, snake, phoenix, life, power, necessity, images of god, AIÔ IÔY IAÔ ÊIÔ AA OUI AAAA E IU IÔ ÔÊ IAÔ AI AÔÊ OUEÔ AIEÊ IOUE UEIA EIÔ ÊII UU EE ÊÊ ÔAOÊ CHECHAMPSIMM CHANGALAS EÊIOU IÊEA ÔOÊOE ZÔIÔIÊR ÔMURUROMROMOS, the seven auspicious names. Ê II UU ÊÊ OAOÊ.**[9]

The Rite of the Hidden Stele

The Magos of Aion is to recite the mystic formulas of the Hidden Stele, **Hail, entire system of aerial spirit, PHOGÔLÔA! Hail, spirit who extends from Heaven to Earth, ERDÊNEU, and who extends from the Earth, which is in the middle chamber of the cosmos, unto the very borders of the Abyss, MEREMÔGGA! Hail**

[5] *PGM* XIII. 843-848.
[6] *PGM* XIII. 64-71.
[7] *PGM* XIII. 871-872.
[8] *PGM* XIII. 327-334.
[9] *PGM* XIII. 870-888.

to you, spirit who comes to me, who possesses me, and who graciously departs
from me according to the will of the god, IÔÊ ZANÔPHIE! Hail, beginning and
end of invariable nature, DÔR ÊSLAOPHÔN! Hail, revolution of untiring service
by heavenly bodies full of inexhaustible service, RÔGUEU ANAMI PELÊGEÔN
ADARA EIÔPH! Hail, radiance of the universe subordinate to the Sun's rays, IEO
UÊÔ IAÊ AI ÊÔU OEI! Hail, orb of the night-illuminating unequally shining
Moon, AIÔ RÊMA RÔDOUPIA! Hail all spirits aerial images, RÔMIDOUÊ
AGANASOU ÔTHAUA! Hail to those to whom the greeting is given with
blessing, to brothers and sisters, to holy men and holy women. O great, greatest
round, incomprehensible figure of the universe, heavenly ENRÔCHESUÊI! For
in Heaven, PELÊTHEU; O one shining with heavenly light, ADAMALÔR; O
luminous one, ALAPIE; O dark-looking one, IEPSERIA; and of Aither, IÔGARAA;
and in the Aither, THÔPULEO DARDU; O fiery one, APHTHALUA; O watery
one, IÔÊDES; O wind-like one, IÔIE ÊÔ AUA; O earthy one, PERÊPHIA; O
moist, fiery and cold spirit! I glorify you, god of gods, the one who brought order
to the universe, AREÔ PIEUA; the one who gathered together the Abyss at the
invisible foundation of its position, PERÔ MUSÊL O PENTÔNAX; the one who
separated Heaven and Earth and covered the Heavens with eternal, golden wings,
RÔDÊRU OYÔA; the one who fixed the Earth on eternal foundations, ALÊIOÔA;
the one who hung up the Aither high above the Earth, AIE ÔÊ IOUA; the one who
scattered the Eir with self-moving breezes, ÔIE OUÔ; the one who put the Water
roundabout, ÔRÊPÊLUA; the one who raises the hurricanes, ÔRISTHAUA; the
one who thunders, THEPHICHUÔNÊL; the one who hurls lightings, OURÊNES;
the one who rains, OSIÔRNI PHEUGALGA; the one who shakes, PERATÔNUL;
the one who produces living creatures, ARÊSIGULÔA. O god of the aions, for you
are great, lord, god, ruler of all, ARCHIZÔ NUON THÊNAR METHÔR PARU
PHÊZÔR THAPSAMYDÔ MAPÔMI CHÊLÔPSA.[10]

The Calling and Adoration of Aion

The Magos is to call upon and adore Aion by sacrificing frankincense and reciting,
O you who are the Cosmos, who does extend from Heaven to Earth, and from
the Earth that's in the middle of the orb of Cosmos to the ends of the Abyss! O
AIÔN, you I call upon, you I adore! O you who does enter into me, who are the
beginning and end of my nature naught can move! O AIÔN, you I call upon,
you I adore! O you who stares upon the stellar dance of the Cosmos, for you the
Heavens rotate! O AIÔN, you I call upon, you I adore! O you who are the liturgy
of nature's elements! O you who are the illumination of the solar rays and the disk
of the night shining Moon that shines unequally! O AIÔN, you I call upon, you
I adore! O you who are the liturgy of nature's elements, eternal spirit all of the

[10]*PGM* IV. 1115-1116.

aithereal statues of the gods! O AIÔN, you I call upon, you I adore! I call upon and adore you, AIÔN, whoever does restore the Cosmos, and who does store the depth away upon its throne of settlement no eye can see, who places Heaven and Earth apart, and who brings them into union. O you who hangs up the Aither in the lofty height, and scatters the Air with your moving blasts, who makes the primeval Waters dance and roar! O you who raises up the whirlwind of the Fire from above, and below you make thunder, lightning, rain, and shakings of the Earth, O god of aions! Mighty you are, lord god, O master of the all! O AIÔN, you I call upon, you I adore! Come to me AIÔN, god amongst gods, in your hieratic pose, your mystic form self-hidden from the eyes of the profane by the sevenfold serpent coiled around your heavenly form with the Zodiac between its coils. For you fix the course of Helios and Chronos. Four are your wings pointing to the Heavens above and the Earth below, for you are the ruler over the four winds and of the four seasons as Helios and Chronos. Your head is the head of a lion when you manifest yourself to me, with a fiery flowing mane; your mouth brandishing devouring teeth and breathing tongues of flame. You bear the fiery torches of initiation. I call upon and adore your beautiful and dreaded visage that only you can manifest to me.

The Magos of Aion is then to journey into a state of being of gnostic reverie through the unconscious euphony of the chanting of **AIÔN** until the visage of Aion is manifested in gnostic vision.

The Magos is to place his hands on his heart and chant **AIÔN** before reciting, **Whatever I say must happen, for I have your name as a unique phylactery in my heart, and no flesh, although moved, will overpower me; no spirit will stand against me, neither daimon nor visitation nor any other of the evil beings of Hades, because of your name, which I have in my soul and invoke. Also be with me always for good, a good god dwelling on a good man, yourself immune to magic, giving me health no magic can harm. ANOCH AIEPHE SAKTIETÊ BIBIOU SPHÊ SPHÊ NOUSI SEÊE SIETHÔ SIETHÔ OUN CHOUNTIAI SEMBI IMENOUAI BAINPHNOUN PHNOUTH TOUCHAR SOUCHAR SABACHAR ANA of the god IEOU ION EON THÔTH OUTHRO THRÔRESE ERIÔPÔ IUÊ AÊ IAÔAI AEÊIOUÔ AEÊIOUÔ ÊOCH MANEBI CHUCHIÔ ALAPAÔ KOL KOL KAATÔN KOLKANTHÔ BALALACH ABLALACH OTHERCHENTHE BOULÔCH BOULÔCH OSERCHNTHE MENTHEI, for I have received the power of the prophets, and of the great god, daimon IAÔ ABLANATHANALBA SIABRATHILAÔ LAMPISTÊR IÊI ÔÔ god. Do it, lord PERTAÔMECH CHACHMÊCH IAÔ OUÊE IAÔ OUÊE IEOU AÊÔ EÊOU IAÔ.**[11] **Come to me, AIÔN!**

---

[11] *PGM* XIII. 795-821.

The Invocation of Fire

The Magos of Aion is to perform the Invocation of Fire to manifest within the Mystic Flame. He is sacrifice perfumes corresponding to Fire and recite, **O ever untam'd Fire, who reign'st on high in Zeus' dominions ruler of the sky; the glorious Sun with dazzling lustre bright, and Moon and stars from thee derive their light; all taming pow'r, aitherial shining fire, whose vivid blasts the heat of life inspire; the world's best element, light-bearing pow'r, with starry radiance shining, splendid flow'r, O hear my suppliant pray'r, and may thy frame be ever innocent, serene, and tame.**[12] The Magos of Aion is to look to the Heavens and chant **APHTHALUA** whilst carving the Invoking Pentagram of Fire. Looking into the Air he is to chant **APHTHALUA** whilst carving the Invoking Pentagram of Fire. To the Earth **APHTHALUA** whilst carving the Invoking Pentagram of Fire. To the North **APHTHALUA** whilst carving the Invoking Pentagram of Fire. Turning against the Sun to the South he is to chant **APHTHALUA** and carve the Invoking Pentagram of Fire. Turning with the Sun to the West **APHTHALUA** whilst carving the Invoking Pentagram of Fire. And finally turning with the Sun to the East **APHTHALUA** again carving the Invoking Pentagram of Fire. He is then to sacrifice more perfumes corresponding to Fire and carve the Invoking Pentagram of Fire over the Mystic Flame five times whilst chanting **APHTHALUA.**

The Invocation of Spirit

The Magos of Aion is then to perform the Invocation of Spirit to manifest within the Mystic Flame. He is to sacrifice perfumes corresponding to Spirit and recite, **O Mighty first-begotten, hear my pray'r, two-fold, egg-born, and wand'ring thro' the air, bull-roarer, glorying in thy golden wings, from whom the race of Gods and mortals springs. Ericapaeus, celebrated pow'r, ineffable, occult, all shining flow'r. From eyes obscure thou wip'st the gloom of night, all-spreading splendour, pure and holy light hence Phanes call'd, the glory of the sky, on waving pinions thro' the world you fly. Priapus, dark-ey'd splendour, thee I sing, genial, all-prudent, ever-blessed king, with joyful aspect on our rights divine and holy sacrifice propitious shine.**[13] The Magos of Aion is to look to the Heavens and chant **IÔGARAA** whilst carving the Invoking Pentagram of Spirit. Looking into the Air he is to chant **IÔGARAA** whilst carving the Invoking Pentagram of Spirit. To the Earth **IÔGARAA** whilst carving the Invoking Pentagram of Spirit. To the North **IÔGARAA** whilst carving the Invoking Pentagram of Spirit. Turning against the Sun to the South he is to chant **IÔGARAA** and carve the Invoking Pentagram of Spirit. Turning with the Sun to the West **IÔGARAA** whilst carving the Invoking Pentagram of Spirit. And finally turning with the Sun to

---

[12] *Orphic Hymn to Fire.*
[13] *Orphic Hymn to Protogonus.*

the East **IÔGARAA** again carving the Invoking Pentagram of Spirit. He is then to sacrifice more perfumes corresponding to Spirit and carve the Invoking Pentagram of Spirit over the Mystic Flame five times whilst chanting **IÔGARAA**.

The Spell of the Mystic Flame

The Magos of Aion is to recite from the Heavens above to the Mystic Flame below, **I call upon you, the mighty living one who shows forth your splendour in the fire, you unseen father of light! Awaken this daimon of the Mystic Flame and come forth into this fire, inspiring it with your holy spirit. This flame shall be your house for this mystic vision of mine, so come forth into this fire and be open for me! Let there be light, your rays shining from Heavens above to the Earth below, come, lord, god of gods, AIÔN, shine forth! I adjure you by the holy names of the cosmic Fire, so that you might abide with me in this same hour until the vision of things I desire appears to me. Give ear to me, hearken to me, for I adjure you by the holy names of the cosmic Fire, so that you might abide with me in this same hour until the vision of things I desire appears to me. I adjure you by the holy names of the cosmic Fire, O fire-walker, PENTITEROUNI, light-maker, SEMESILAM, fire-breather, PSURINPHEU, fire-feeler, IAÔ, light-breather, ÔAI, fire-delighter, ELOURE, beautiful-light, AZAI, Aion, ACHBA, light-master, PEPPER PREPEMPIPI, fire-body, PHOUÊNIOCH, light-giver, AÔI, fire-sower, AREI EIKITA, fire-driver, GALLABALBA, light-forcer, AIÔ, fire-whirler, PURICHIBOOSÊIA, light-mover, SANCHERÔB, thunder-shaker, IÊ ÔÊ IÔÊIÔ, glory-light, BEEGENÊTE, light-increaser, SOUSINEPHIEN, fire-light maintainer, SOUSINEPHI ARENBARAZEI MAPMAPENTEU, star-tamer, ÔIA. Open for me, PROPROPHEGGÊ EMETHEIRE MORIOMOTURÊPHILBA, because on account of the pressing and bitter and inexorable necessity, I invoke the immortal names, living and honoured, which never pass into mortal nature and are not declared in articulate speech by human tongue or mortal speech or mortal sound, ÊEÔ OÊEÔ IÔÔ OÊ ÊEÔ OÊ EÔ IÔÔ OÊÊE ÔÊE ÔOÊ IÊ ÊÔ OÔ OÊ IEÔ OÊ ÔOÊ IEÔ ÔÊ IEEÔ EÊ IÔ OÊ IOÊ ÔÊÔ EOÊ OEÔ ÔIÊ ÔIÊ EÔ OI III ÊOÊ ÔUÊ ÊÔOÊE EÔ ÊIA AÊA EÊA ÊEEÊ EEÊ EEÊ IEÔ ÊEÔ OÊEEOÊ ÊEÔ ÊUÔ OÊ EIÔ ÊÔ ÔÊ OÊ EE OOO UIÔÊ.**[14] You I invoke, mightiest god, lord of the stellar dance, for you the Heavens rotate, you who enlighten all, and as you pour your rays into the world you shall pour yourself into this flame, O god of gods! O Logos who orders the night and the day, who slays the dragon, you, holy one, to whom the East and West give praise to, who are blessed by all gods, angels and daimons. You who has your throne about the height of the Cosmos, appear to me for I have called upon you with the holiest names of the mystic Fire. Enter, appear to me, O lord, for I am the one who has been born to Earth and is now

---

[14]*PGM* IV. 591-615.

born unto Heaven. Enter, appear to me, O lord of mighty names, whom all have in their hearts, who makes the names of gods move! Enter, appear to me, who has the power and strength in fire, whose throne is above the seven poles, enter, and give me answer with your holy voice or vision that I may clearly hear and truthfully about this thing.

When the presence of Aion is manifested within the flame the Magos is to recite, **Hail lord, O god of gods! Hail to your powers ever more, O lord!** There the Magos of Aion is to receive the mystic vision he desires.

The Veiling of the Cosmos

The Magos of Aion is to face the East and recite, **O gods who are in the East** and then chant **ÔAOÊÔÔEOÊIAÔ**. Facing the South he is to recite, **O gods who are in the South** and then chant **III**. In the North, **O gods who are in the North** and then chant **AAÔ**. Turning against the Sun to the West he is to recite, **O gods who are in the West** and then chant **THÊ**. Moving against the Sun to the South he is to kneel on his right knee. Standing, he is to keep rotating against the Sun until he reaches the East. Looking down to the Earth he is to recite, **O gods who are in the Earth** and chant **THOU**. Looking into the Air he is to see the Moon and recite, **O gods who are in the sub-Lunar realms** and then chant **THÊ**. Looking into the Air he is to see the Water and recite, **O gods who are in the Primeval Waters** and then chant **AATHÔ**. Looking to the Heavens he is to recite, **O gods who are in the Heavens** and then chant **ATHÊROUO**.[15]

---

[15] *PGM* XIII. 641-646.

The Hymnic Adoration and Invocation of Thoth

BY

ΔΑΜΩΝ

Thoth, son of Re, Moon, of beautiful rising,
Lord of appearing, light of the gods,
Hail to you, Moon, Thoth,
Bull in Khmun, dweller in Hesret,
Who makes way for the gods!
O Thoth, you I adore, you I invoke!

Who knows the secrets,
Who records their expression,
Who distinguishes one speech from another,
Who is judge of everyone!
O Thoth, you I adore, you I invoke!

Keen-faced in the ship of millions,
Courier of mortals,
Who knows a man by his utterance,
Who makes the deed rise against the doer!
O Thoth, you I adore, you I invoke!

Who contents Re, advises the sole lord,
Who lets him know whatever happens;
At dawn he summons in Heaven,
And forgets not yesterday's report!
O Thoth, you I adore, you I invoke!

Who makes safe the bark of night,
Makes tranquil the bark of day,
With arms outstretched in the bow of the ship!
O Thoth, you I adore, you I invoke!

Pure-faced when he takes the stern rope,
As the day-bark rejoices in the night-bark's joy,
At the feast of crossing the sky!

O Thoth, you I adore, you I invoke!

Who fells the fiend,
The Ennead in the bark of night worship you lord Thoth,
They say to you,
"Hail, son of Re, praised of Re, whom the gods applaud!"
O Thoth, you I adore, you I invoke!

They repeat what your ka wishes,
As you make way for the place of the bark,
As you act against that fiend:
You cut off his head, you break his ba,
You cast his corpse in the fire,
You are the god who slaughters him!
O Thoth, you I adore, you I invoke!

Nothing is done without your knowing,
Great one, son of a great one,
Who came from her limbs,
Champion of Harakhti, wise friend in On,
Who makes the place of gods,
Who knows the secrets, expounds their words!
O Thoth, you I adore, you I invoke!

I give praise to you, Thoth,
Straight plummet in the scales,
Who repulses evil,
Who accepts him who learns not on crime!
O Thoth, you I adore, you I invoke!

The vizier who settles cases,
Who changes turmoil to peace;
The scribe of ma'at who keeps the book,
Who punishes crime, who accepts the submissive!
O Thoth, you I adore, you I invoke!

Wise among the Ennead,
Who relates what was forgotten!
O Thoth, you I adore, you I invoke!

Counsellor to him who errs,
Who remembers the fleeting moment,
Who reports the hour of night,

Whose words endure forever,
Who records them in the list,
Who knows those in it whose words endure forever!
O Thoth, you I adore, you I invoke!

Thoth, son of Re, Moon,
You who distinguished the tongue of every foreign land,
You who recalls all that has been forgotten,
You who balances the scales,
Scribe of the gods, lord of the books,
Counter of the stars, lord of magic!
O Thoth, you I adore, you I invoke!

Hail to you ibis-headed one,
Who knows all secrets,
Great is your word.
A royal offering to you,
Thoth, lord of writing, lord of Khmun,
Who determines ma'at,
Who embarks Re in the bark of night.
May you hear your suppliant's adoring and invoking praise!
O Thoth, you I adore, you I invoke!

For you are the righteous one towards the courtiers,
If a wrong is told your tongue is skilled to set it right.
You are the recorder of royal laws,
Who gives directions to the courtiers,
Wise in speech,
There is nothing you ignore.
You are the adviser to the gods,
Who teaches mortals their course,
Without forgetting your charge.
You are the one who reports to the lord of the two lands,
Who speaks of whatever was forgotten,
Who does not ignore the words of the lord.
For you are a just one of god when being on Earth,
You satisfy ma'at every day.
You have shunned wrongdoing,
Never have you done evil since birth; Indeed you are a gentle one,
One wise, one calm, who listens to ma'at.
May you always be in the crew of the neshmet-bark,
At its feast in the region of Peqer.

You are the herald of the council,
Who does not ignore the plans of his majesty!
O Thoth, you I adore, you I invoke!

For you are Thoth,
Son of Re, iah-Djehuty, the Moon god,
Sheps, lord of Khemennu,
Asten, Khenti, Mehi, Hab, and A'an.
You are the one who distinguished the tongue of every foreign land,
Who recalls all that has been forgotten,
Who balances the scales,
Scribe of the gods,
Lord of the books,
Counter of the stars,
Lord of magic.
For you are he who is like the ibis,
Who knows all secrets,
Great is your word!
O Thoth, you I adore, you I invoke!

CPSIA information can be obtained at www.ICGtesting.com
Printed in the USA
LVOW101346030712

288728LV00015B/23/P